British Spas from 1815 to the Present

A Social History

British Spas from 1815 to the Present

A Social History

PHYLLIS HEMBRY

Edited and Completed by
LEONARD W. COWIE
and EVELYN E. COWIE

The Athlone Press
London

First published 1997 by
THE ATHLONE PRESS
1 Park Drive, London NW11 7SG

© L. W. Cowie and E. E. Cowie, 1997

British Library Cataloguing in Publication Data
*A catalogue record for this book is available
from the British Library*

ISBN 0 485 11502 6

Library of Congress Cataloguing in Publication Data
Hembry, Phyllis M. (Phyllis May)
  British spas from 1815 to the present : a social
history/Phyllis Hembry
    p. cm.
  Continues: The English spa, 1560–1815.
  Includes bibliographical references and indexes.
  ISBN 0 485 11502 6 (alk. paper)
1. Health resorts—Great Britain—History. 2. Great
Britain—Social life and customs—19th century.
3. Great Britain—Social life and customs—20th
century. I. Title.
DA665.H37   1997
613′.122′094109034—dc20   96–43104
                                                      CIP

Typeset by
RefineCatch Limited, Bungay, Suffolk

Printed and bound in Great Britain by
Bookcraft (Bath) Ltd

Contents

CONTENTS

Phyllis Hembry – A Memoir

Dr. Phyllis Hembry was not a cloistered scholar. After a successful early career in the civil service, she decided to concentrate on an academic career, pursuing her interest in history, especially local history. This new commitment involved serious research and a readiness to share her knowledge and expertise and to serve the study of history in any way she usefully could. A scholarly publication, *The Bishops of Bath and Wells 1540–1640*, appeared in 1967. She became a member of the Historical Association, serving on its Council, and was, for a time, Honorary Secretary to the Local History Committee. For several years she was Chairman of the Cheltenham and Gloucester Branch of the Association and later was also active in the West Wiltshire Branch and the Wiltshire Record Society. She edited the *Calendar of Bradford-on-Avon Settlement Examinations and Removal Orders 1725–1798*, which was published in 1990. The distinction of her scholarship was recognized when she was elected a Fellow of the Royal Historical Society.

Her research, as well as her other commitments, was carried out alongside a dedicated career in teaching. When she retired from her last teaching post as Head of the History Department at Cheltenham Ladies' College, she had time to concentrate on research. This made possible the completion of *The English Spa 1560–1815* and encouraged her work for the next volume. Sadly she died in 1992 with the subject still unfinished. It was her wish that her papers should be made available for research and, if possible, to be prepared for publication. This has been made possible through the care and concern of Joyce Hayward, a friend and colleague, to whom the papers were entrusted.

Joan Lewin

List of Illustrations

Acknowledgements

For permission to reproduce illustrations we wish to thank the following:

Robert Hale Ltd (Plate 1. The Pump Room, Tenby Wells, 1839, from The Spas of England by Peter J. Neville Havins), High Peak Borough Council (Plate 3. Vichy Douche, Thermal Baths, Buxton, from Historic Buxton and its Spa Era), Mrs Isabel Ide (Plate 5. from The Celebrated Melksham Spa), The Leamington Society for the map on page 15, and Bath and North East Somerset Council for the map on page 64.

Preface

In the Preface to her *The English Spa 1650–1815*, published in 1990, Phyllis Hembry wrote: 'The present volume traces the evolution of the spas to 1815, and I hope to cover the subject to 1914 in a sequel.' By the time of her death, she had collected a considerable amount of material for this second volume and written several drafts of her proposed chapters.

Our first task has been to put these into a final shape and make any necessary additions to form the first nine chapters of this book. She had organized its plan on the same lines as for her previous volume, and we have sought to follow her intentions.

She included in her notes a few references to Scottish, Welsh and Irish spas, which we have expanded to form another chapter to the book. Since there has recently been an increased interest in the spas and new writings upon their medical and environmental importance, we have also extended the book to the present time. Neither of these two chapters are in such detail as she gave to the subject. The Conclusion is based on her reflections on her researches, but includes as well a discussion of present-day attitudes towards the latest history of the spas.

L.W.C.
E.E.C.

1

The Spas in 1815:
The Earlier Legacy and
New Competition

By 1815 taking the cure was a well-established custom. The English habit of going to a domestic spa to drink health-giving mineral waters or to bathe in them had been reinforced during the wars against France ending that year, when the Continent was closed to English travellers. The attraction of the spas to many visitors was, however, the enjoyment of their social life rather than the search for health. From about 1750, aided by the increasing network of improved roads and more regular and commercialized transport services organized from recognized urban coaching centres, the more mobile leisured upper and middle classes were ready to endure long, uncomfortable journeys in the pursuit of health and entertainment. Altogether from about 1560, when Bath in Somerset and Buxton in Derbyshire attracted these water-seekers, about 175 of these spa centres were operating, though not all at once. By 1815 the more recently operating larger urban spas – Cheltenham, Harrogate, Leamington, Malvern and Matlock – had more than one spa centre, unlike the older ones – Bath, Buxton, Scarborough and Tunbridge Wells – where mineral water facilities were mostly concentrated on one site. But most English spas were small, rural places, promoted by a local landlord aided by a physician or apothecary. Here the pump-room and baths and sometimes dressing or waiting rooms were usually housed in one building. The only neighbouring structures might be lodging houses or an inn.[1]

By 1815 many minor spas, ceasing to attract long-distant, better-off customers, had fallen into disuse, serving only humble locals, who believed the mineral-water springs could cure simple ailments such as sores. Such now-neglected spas were Astrop in Oxfordshire, Wellingborough in Northamptonshire and Richmond in Surrey, where the wells were closed. These had attracted royalists and been centres of political intrigue. Others out of use were at Barnet, Northaw and Wanstead in Hertfordshire, Horwood near Wincanton and Glastonbury, both in Somerset. But as some spas faded from existence, the general profitability of such small social centres and the opening of new coaching routes encouraged fresh entrepreneurs to risk capital in founding a spa. By 1815 there were probably some 40 viable spa centres. Others, formerly in much repute and much frequented, such as Epsom, Cobham (Claremont), Streatham, Dulwich and King's Newham, were little used.[2]

The urban spas were an aspect of the general urban renaissance. Bath, now doubled from its sixteenth-century size with a new town outside its walls, still held primacy of space and was the wonder of Europe; its social life was second only to the capital's. Visitors were offered a spacious pump-room, two assembly rooms, a theatre, several libraries and reading rooms, coffee houses, many shops and extensive lodging accommodation. But already Cheltenham and Leamington Spa, both expanding rapidly with new towns adjacent to the old settlements, were the fashionable spas and a distinct challenge to Bath. They had acquired a spa's apparatus, several drinking or bath centres, assembly rooms, libraries, a theatre, hotels and lodging houses and pleasure gardens. Harrogate dominated the north; although slow in expansion it had drinking wells, a pump-room, assembly room and theatre. Of Bath's earlier rivals, Buxton had been revived in the 1780s by the development of a new spa town, Lower Buxton adjoining the old Upper Buxton, through heavy investment by the Duke of Devonshire, but Tunbridge Wells had succumbed to relative stagnation.

Significant also was the growing number of medium-sized settlements where rural villages were becoming urban resorts, like Clifton developing around the Bristol Hotwells, Ilkley, Malvern and Matlock. The architecture of many of these spas was strongly influenced by the Palladian style of the age.

In Tudor and Stuart times the use of mineral waters had religious and political overtones which attracted government attention, but these had yielded to a new secular approach with strong medical support.[3]

Royal and noble support was no longer as important as in Stuart times, but was not despised. After Queen Anne's second visit to Bath in 1703 and George II's possible visit to Sydenham Wells, George III's stay at Cheltenham in 1788 was the only spa sojourn of a reigning monarch in the eighteenth century. But princes and princesses came and were welcome as helping to consolidate a fashionable habit, which attracted not only the nobility and gentry but also wider social classes – the clergy and other professional men, artists, men of letters, merchants and traders, holidaying farmers and entertainers besides the sick poor. The

2

unemployed and vagrants hoped to gain from the better-off either in service or dishonestly. Women came with male visitors or alone; the new spa society unprecedently enabled men and women to mix socially and publicly more equally, even in mixed bathing, only coffee houses usually remaining restricted to men. Mingling of the sexes, often on a visit of a fortnight or more, was novel and encouraged a new polite society where social control evolved through a new routine of accepted behaviour often guided by a master of ceremonies. The modes and manners adopted at spas set a wide pattern for social behaviour in upper- and middle-class society.

This vast leisure market gave new opportunities for capital investment, drawing off the profits of agriculture, commerce and, increasingly in the north, industry. The better security of property rights after the Revolution of 1688 encouraged a more positive attitude to investment in spas – the provision or improvement of unprecedented water-taking and bathing facilities, lodgings for visitors and pleasures and diversions. Drinking wells were paved and walled around and sometimes canopied, and, where demand warranted it, pump-rooms, ranging from primitive sheds to fully equipped long-rooms, were provided to shelter the drinkers. Bath-houses were erected over cold baths, and the sites of baths and wells were often landscaped with bushes, trees and walks, and fenced around. In the larger spas, assembly rooms were built as leisure centres, and seven spa towns – Bath, Buxton, Cheltenham, Harrogate, Leamington, Scarborough and Tunbridge Wells – had a purpose-built theatre before 1815. Originally, primitive barn-like buildings were adapted for the players, but now theatres reached new standards of comfort and convenience, though they usually opened two or three times weekly for the summer season only. Coffee houses were an important amenity in the older spas: by 1815 Bath had three, Tunbridge Wells two (one for men and exceptionally, one for women) and Harrogate one. Here while taking tea or coffee one could also read the newspapers at leisure, but soon separate lending libraries and reading rooms competed with coffee houses as news and gossip centres.

Spas were important centres of communication about matters political and social. Libraries, with their manifold functions, became focal points for new kinds of social life at the spas. Lending libraries were much in demand by visitors with time to spare, especially in wet weather, and their stocks of books were often sufficient to warrant the compilation of a catalogue. Libraries often acted as registries for furnished accommodation and domestic servants, both much in demand during the season. Libraries sold tickets for local entertainments, balls, assemblies, concerts and theatres, collected relief funds after special

3

appeals, displayed visitors' books of new arrivals and facilitated the exchange of gossip. Another form of investment, pioneered by Bath, was the pleasure garden laid out on the model of Ranelagh or Vauxhall.

By the early nineteenth century amenity standards were rising. The old cold baths and douches were spurned now that coal was available for furnaces to heat water; hot, warm, tepid and vapour baths appeared, and cold baths were mere adjuncts of these. Contemporaries thought the new bath complexes, compared with the old, were 'enormously expensive'. The Manor Baths built at Askern in Yorkshire in 1814 cost £1,000.

Where a municipality owned the site of a spring, as at Bath, Scarborough, Northampton and Beverley in East Yorkshire, they kept control of their valuable property, and like the Merchant Venturers of Bristol, who owned the Hotwell Spring, leased it or the rights of admission to it to tenants. Otherwise it was often a local landowner who established a spa, like several Dukes of Devonshire at Buxton. Local gentry and small landowners commonly owned the small spas and accounted for some three-quarters of spa promotions. The next most active promoters were small groups of medical men who either started a spa alone or in partnership with landowners. These developments were part of the contemporary retail revolution and general commercialization of leisure.[4]

But landowners and other proprietors were careful in founding spas. They considered their possible financial return from fees paid by visitors for drinking or bathing, the sale of sweetmeats and refreshments and charges for entertainment. An economically sound venture was also important to their retainers and others employed in attending on or lodging the visitors. So the concept of the seasonal subscription was born, a financial device never before used on such a scale, by which the consumer paid for goods and services not at the point of consumption but in advance, for a period of a month or more or the entire season. And so a new economic feature of social life became common – the subscription society. Subscription could be used to anticipate revenue and underwrite the cost of new ventures with comparatively little risk to the entrepreneur. Once the customer paid the initial payment, his attendance at the original place or function was almost assured, and from this capture of the consumer other incidental expenditure could ensue. Subscription was a sure way to commercialize leisure, which was applied not only to the use of drinking wells and baths but to all manner of projects, such as admission to assembly rooms, balls, concerts and pleasure gardens. Subscriptions were also raised by coffee houses, newsrooms, libraries and bands of musicians who performed during the drinking sessions at the wells and at evening social functions.

The private investor expected a profit, as when Lord Aylesford in

1813 opened his well at Leamington to drinkers at 2s. 6d. weekly, but the sick and poor were considered. Bath admitted the needy into the baths at 6d. a time, and its Mineral Water Hospital provided free attention. Buxton had its Bath Charity Fund dating from the sixteenth century and set aside a well and a charity bath for the poor. Leamington Spa had a similar fund from 1806, Willowbridge in Staffordshire offered the poor special terms, and the minor spa of Somersham in Huntingdonshire admitted the poor free from 5 a.m.to 7 a.m.[5] Other rural spas may have helped the poor since parish authorities often paid the sick to take the waters.

Payment by subscription was an economic device used not only for both pleasure and health facilities, but also for places of worship. The influx of visitors to spas for a prolonged spell meant the overcrowding of places of worship in season. At the larger spas the ancient parish church, if it existed, was inadequate for the extended congregations. A way of meeting this situation, especially in spas and other fashionable areas, was to establish proprietory chapels built by subscriptions and maintained by pew rents. These were often, as in Cheltenham, evangelical in worship.

Investment in spas was encouraged by the popularity of travel among the leisured classes, who undertook tours of Britain, often lasting weeks or months, to inspect stately homes, ancient ruins, picturesque scenery, ecclesiastical buildings and even industrial sites.[6] Another incentive to spa founders was the contemporary improvement in transport, not only to the urban spas, but also many minor local spas, previously not readily accessible. These had already benefited from the network of better roads now used by regular commercial coach and wagon services. Almost as important was the provision within urban spas of ways of taking visitors to baths, pump-rooms, assemblies and other places of entertainment. Bath, Cheltenham and Scarborough provided carriages and sedan chairs, the operators of which, limited in number, were under strict control as to their uniforms, stands and charges.

Difficulties faced those undertaking the sometimes vast building enterprises needed to provide the pump-rooms, centres of amusement, stables, mews and coach-houses, as well as the terraces, squares and crescents for lodging accommodation. One of these was the problem of bringing building material to the sites. At first this had to be by road, but during the eighteenth century the construction of canals was a great advantage, and in the next century the railways were to be a still greater benefit. Legal hindrance in the shape of property rights was another difficulty, as at Bath where both the corporation and larger private investors had to buy out many small men. During the eighteenth century, Enclosure Acts, eliminating rights in the common fields to release land for building, were a necessary prelude to expansion at several spa towns. Cheltenham obtained its Enclosure Act as late as 1801 and needed a further act to cover another area in 1833. Also in the eighteenth century, several urban spas faced a local social problem, when the corporation was moribund or the parochial system was inadequate, and adopted the device of an Improvement Commission. Later Buxton, Harrogate, Leamington and Malvern had to follow suit.

By 1815 other social problems were facing several spa towns, particularly Bath. Settled residents were beginning to move into them, many of them leisured people of private means attracted by the economical living conditions, pleasant surroundings and many amenities of the well-developed social life. This brought changes to the old mixed, public communal life with transient support for tradesmen, hotel-keepers and entertainers. And throughout the country some of the older rural spas, by-passed by new coach routes, did not attract such residents, but at the same time were finding it difficult to retain visitors with their primitive, now-scorned cold baths.

A threat to many spas came from the newly emergent seaside resorts. By 1815 a nascent seaside industry was already established, and in this 'dipping age', as a contemporary called it, a rash of sea-bathing places marked the English coastline. The physical features of the spas were often copied by private estates in the seaside resorts in the form of planned architectural units of assembly rooms, crescents, squares, terraces, sheltered promenades and pavements raised above the level of the muddied roads, together with massive investment in hotels and inns, boarding and lodging houses. Another hallmark of the seaside places was their similar pattern of social organization under a master of ceremonies, with assemblies, concerts, clubs, societies, theatres and libraries.

A guide of 1806 to watering-places listed 34 sea-bathing locations of which four – Brighton, Scarborough, Southampton and Bridlington – had already acquired custom as spas, so there were 30 English seaside rivals to the spa resorts and three – Aberystwyth, Swansea and Tenby – in Wales. Thirteen provided bath-houses with rooms for hot and cold baths fed by tidal waters, but bathing in the sea was now becoming fashionable, especially from the newly introduced bathing machines, which were possessed by 25 resorts, Scarborough leading with 40. As sea-bathing was found to be pleasurable and believed to be medically valuable, these places offered a serious challenge to the spas.[7]

Since the age of aristocratic patronage was now generally beginning to decline, both spas and seaside resorts were increasingly having to rely upon other visitors. They mostly catered for the wider market of the middle ranks of society. The leisured élite who wished still to enjoy distinctly aristocratic and even royal surroundings made their way to the many Continental spas now that peace had come to Europe in 1815.

It has been calculated that there was a sixteen-fold increase in the English exodus to the Continent after 1815, and it continued to grow during the following years.[8] Continental spas usually had the advantage over the more mundane English spas of a beautiful location in mountainous scenery with bracing, health-giving air, large parks, casinos – gambling was a great attraction – and a glittering society. There the socially ambitious could see and be seen, the rich seeking the company of aristocrats who in turn sought that of kings. These fashionable Continental spas joined the domestic seaside resorts to provide the unassailable competition facing the British spas during the years after 1815.

2

Leamington Spa

The exile of Napoleon to Elba was celebrated in Leamington in August 1814. A subscription list was started by the principal inhabitants, and the money raised was distributed in sums ranging from 5s. to 15s. per cottage and 2s.6d. to each agricultural labourer. The poor organized their own fête, a tea-drinking at the Bowling Green Hotel, 'where hilarity, happiness and concord seemed to be the order of the day. Some of the gentry in the village distributed cakes to the children liberally, and a fiddler played country tunes to the younger females, who tripped gaily on the enamalled green.' Afterwards participants were invited to the theatre.[1]

By this time Leamington in Warwickshire and Cheltenham in Gloucestershire, only 44 miles apart, were two fashionable spas that, despite competition from seaside resorts and Continental spas, were attracting a marked increase of custom. They had now replaced Bath and Tunbridge Wells in providing the standard by which lesser spas were measured. For example, the small Wiltshire spa at Melksham founded in 1816 hoped to 'vie in every desirable convenience with Cheltenham and Leamington'.[2] Leamington was still officially 'the village of Leamington Priors', but commercial and medical interests now claimed it was a 'town' and called it 'Leamington Spa'.[3] Discoveries of fresh springs had brought it from a single 'briny puddle' to challenge Cheltenham. Indeed, it was said that whenever Cheltenham unearthed a new source of waters, Leamington 'to keep pace with its rival . . . , never failed to discover soon afterwards an equal number of springs'.

By 1816 they had a nearly equal number of 'spa centres.' Leamington had seven – the Old Well; Abbott's Baths (1784); Wise's Baths (1790); Robbin's Baths (1806); Read's Baths (1810); the Royal Pump Room (1810); Smart's Baths (1816) – and Cheltenham eight, while Bath City had only one (not including its peripheral spas) and Malvern two. But unlike Cheltenham, a market-town with brewing and cloth industries before becoming a spa, Leamington had no economic base except as an agricultural settlement, and its mushroom growth questioned the recent argument that resort towns developed most rapidly where the original settlement had already acquired some urban amenities, such as inns, markets, transport links, shops and coffee houses.[4]

Leamington's rise was still more spectacular than Cheltenham's. In the 1780s Leamington Priors was but a small village consisting of a manor house, church, poorhouse, smithy, mill and a few thatched cottages by the River Leam; but by 1815 the fashionable 'old town' had the Assembly Rooms, the Bedford and Regent Hotels and about 22 houses on the west side of Lower Union Parade and two dozen in Cross Street, while the 'new town' north of the river had the Baths and Pump Room, the Apollo Rooms, the theatre, several inns and boarding houses and an increasing number of new dwellings.

Though the village had mineral springs exploited by physicians from the early eighteenth century, its way to prosperity began in 1784 when William Abbotts, who owned the Black Dog Inn, erected a new mineral-water drinking well, which attracted local people and later others; but the aristocracy and gentry really established its fame. Prominent among them was John Russell, sixth Duke of Bedford, apparently persuaded by his relations, the Warwick bankers of Russell and Tomes, to invest in it profits from his Bloomsbury estate. He had an interest in the Bedford Hotel, opened in 1811, and recommended friends and relations to take the waters in Leamington. Their fashionable patronage during the following years was largely responsible for the expansion which the town had achieved by 1815.

Yet it seemed then that its development had halted. As it was virtually an enlarged village spa with a population of about 1,000, it was particularly difficult for it to meet the national economic depression following the war against France. Important spas now needed the resources of a considerable town. Only such spas could have pump-rooms, assembly rooms, theatres, libraries, museums and other requirements as well as considerable accommodation for visitors. Moreover spa customers were more discriminating and demanded different types of baths – hot, warm and cold – and they wanted pumps and baths with elaborate fitments and carpets. They expected also the daily social round now customary in spas – early morning bathing and drinking of the waters, followed by an airing on the parades; then riding and driving, tea-drinking and card-playing; and an evening ball at least once a week.

Increasing rivalry between the spas produced proliferating guides and other literature. The different virtues of the mineral waters at each spa were widely written about and debated, all claiming distinct therapeutic qualities. Leamington asserted, 'The list of diseases finding relief here is a long one', and claimed that its saline, sulphureous and chalybeate springs were especially advantageous in cases of 'dyspepsia or indigestion, sluggish liver and affections of the digestive apparatus generally'.

It gained a particular advantage in 1811 when Lord Middleton based his hounds there, and by the next year other packs hunting locally, as the *Warwick Advertiser* reported, were Lord Foley's, Lord Vernon's, Sir Thomas Mostyn's and the Quorn. This made it a hunting centre with a winter season supplementing the normal summer season beginning in late April and ending with the Warwick September races. This became possible early in the century with the construction of the Warwick to Napton branch of the Warwick to Birmingham Canal, by which abundant coal for winter warmth could be brought from the Midland collieries.

Publicity by town guides could not save Leamington from the post-war recession. Bertie Greatheed, a local farmer, who sold much of his 65 acres north of the river for the initial building of the new town, noted in June 1816 'the unexampled distress of the times' and 'a miserable scarcity of money'. He was surprised that on Midsummer Day all his tenants managed to pay their usual rents to him at the Bedford Hotel. Visitors were few that year; and two of the baths in the old town got into difficulties. In that year also the Postmaster received only about £200 for letters compared with £300 the year before.[5] Greatheed decided that agricultural land would be an enhanced investment; he bought 85 acres out at Hill Wootton in 1816.

The spa could no longer rely on the wealthiest classes for its endowment and development. Several Warwickshire businessmen had already sought to gain wider support for Leamington. A vital need was a better organized social life. A guide book said that visiting noblemen and gentlemen 'of great distinction' acted as stewards at balls, assemblies and other functions, but a Master of Ceremonies, as at Bath and Cheltenham, should take charge.[6] One of the businessmen, Joseph Brookhouse, tried in vain to find an experienced candidate as able as the social guides of the other spas, probably because the remuneration offered was inadequate for ambitious men; but by March 1814 he found 'a person at Bath' with 'very agreeable manners'. He was James Heaviside, who came in April 'to see the place' and accepted the post.[7]

It was hoped that he could assure Leamington's future as a major spa, but he did not like the post. The hotel-keepers and proprietors of the assembly rooms had, as in the northern spas, established themselves in strong control of the social life; and, also as in the north, guests in the chief establishments elected 'presidents' from among senior visitors to manage some social obligations, such as collections for the Leamington Spa Charity.[8] So Heaviside's influence was limited, and when a junior vacancy at the Lower Room in Bath occurred in the autumn of 1815, he quickly applied, urging his Leamington experience as a qualification. He gained this post and held it with that at Leamington for at least two years, for he boldly claimed a benefit poll at Leamington in mid–August 1817, but the dual mandate was not easy.[9] In 1817 he succeeded to the senior post at Bath in the Upper Rooms, but its regulations did not allow him to hold both posts as their winter seasons clashed, so in February 1818 he reluctantly resigned from Leamington.

There was an immediate contested election for his successor. Two retired army officers came forward as candidates, Captain Isaac Buxton and Captain Charles Stevenson, and Greatheed was canvassed by both. Buxton, however, had inadequate support from the subscribers to the rooms, who had the right of election, and he withdrew to Leicester, declaring that he would apply again at the next vacancy, but nothing more was heard of him. Stevenson was elected unanimously and took office that season, holding it until 1822. He was followed by several successors until the 1840s when private parties were replacing public assemblies, and the post lapsed.

Despite the current uncertainty, the search for mineral springs suitable for commercial exploitation continued. When a new spring was discovered to the south beyond the Ranelagh Gardens, there was talk between 1816 and 1824 of establishing a grand spa there, and there were plans for a splendid suite of baths and a pump-room, but the site was too far from the new town. In April 1816, however, a chalybeate spring was unearthed on the west side of Clemens Street in line with those already feeding two of the baths. Benjamin Smart, a Quaker, whose father owned the Rock Mills, Milverton, was the proprietor of this spring, and, despite opposition from the owners of the existing baths, he persisted in developing it. In August 1816 he opened his Imperial Sulphureous Medicinal Font and Ladies' Marble Baths. It had five baths, four of which were marble, and the entrance formed a pump-room to which the nobility and gentry were freely admitted; and the premises included also an assembly room and a library. But these also were too far from the new town and did not last many years.

The resurgence of the town's economy began about 1818. During the 1820s businesses were set up by both townspeople and others from London, Birmingham and Oxford as well as those experienced in the resort trade in Bath and Cheltenham, especially dressmakers and milliners. As in other spa towns, entrepreneurs moved into the town, hired rooms for the season or even a few weeks and then departed; but others

11

set up permanent businesses. Among these, John Vallaton, who had fashionable shops in Bath, Cheltenham and London, opened an establishment in 30 Clemens Street; James Clare at 8 Park Street came from London with muslins, chintzes and dresses, as did Stone and Company, mercers, and Page the haircutter from Woodman's in Piccadilly. There was also a wine and spirits vault beneath the Assembly Rooms. Other establishments included a hatter, a carriage-maker and a toyshop, which sold also the birch rods that were considered an essential part of the furniture of contemporary nurseries and schoolrooms.

In addition, the town became an important education centre, especially for girls. There were schools for 'young ladies' kept by the Misses Walker and the Misses Smith at 6 and 14 Upper Union Street, by Mrs Barnett in Charlotte Place and by Mrs Worcester in Assembly Place. Their pupils were denied the social pleasures of the spa town. They were kept steadily at their lessons, receiving especially instruction in such fashionable accomplishments as drawing and music, and subjected to strict moral supervision and discipline, which was enforced by 'personal chastisement', perhaps making the schoolmistresses valuable customers of the toyshop.

By now John Bisset, a wealthy Scotsman, was well established in the town. He took his wife and daughter to try the waters of Leamington in 1811 and, attracted by the possibilities of providing entertainment for visitors, returned the next spring. He leased the Apollo Rooms in Clemens Street, where he opened a picture gallery and newsroom which became a social centre in the town. He claimed to be supported by 400 noblemen and others and went on to bring to Leamington his Museum of Curiosities, which he set up under his wife's care in a house being built in the new town. Visitors could view his exhibits there, which included the coronation gloves of Elizabeth I and Mary, Queen of Scots, for a subscription of a guinea a season, 5s. a month or 3s. a week. In 1815 he published *A Descriptive Guide to Leamington*, and in 1828 *The Origin, Rise and Progress of Leamington Spa*. He returned from a visit to London in 1819 with many pictures, which he housed in his new Paragon Picture Gallery in the Royal Parade, at the same time selling his Apollo Rooms and museum and library. He built several houses in the old town, including one for himself – Belle Vue Place in Ranelagh Street in 1817, which he built as an investment – but by then the old town was no longer fashionable, and seven years later it was still unoccupied. In 1832, then 72 years old, he sold his paintings and retired from business. He died later that year, esteemed as a benefactor to the town.[10]

Also attracted by Leamington and able both to contribute to its life and profit from it was Dr Henry Jephson, who joined a practice there in 1818, but in 1827 became an MD at Glasgow University and went to

Cheltenham, only to return to Leamington in response to a petition from its people. He developed a flourishing practice at 7 York Terrace and, although mindful of the needy, his professional income was said to be £20,000, the largest in the world. As early as 1831 he was able to have built for himself a 'princely, splendid' mansion with 14 bedrooms at 78 Warwick Street, Beech Lawn, giving during its construction a Christmas dinner to 140 tradesmen and workmen at the Star and Garter Inn.

Jephson was an outstanding example among doctors who became wealthy by promoting spas. Like his contemporary, Dr Gully at Malvern, he actively upheld the medical value of mineral waters, regularly supervising his patients at the Pump Room. He invested profitably in the Warwick and Leamington Brewery of 1832 and the New Leamington Gas Company of 1834. He was Chairman of the Leamington and Warwick Banking Company of 1827 and in 1845 was on the provisional committee to promote the Warwickshire and London Railway. Having bought a farm near Leamington that year, he was hailed as a landed proprietor by the *Leamington Courier*; and by 1873 he owned 432 acres and also large interests in insurance. His health broke down under the strain of all this activity, and in 1848, at the age of 50, he became blind, retired and took little part in affairs, except as a governor of nearly every blind asylum in England and a life governor of 43 such institutions.[11]

Hoteliers also were important in the town's development. One was Thomas Rackstraw, who came from Oxford and in 1816 took over the New Hotel in Clemens Street, enlarging it and renaming it the Blenheim Hotel. It was advertised extensively from 1818, and in 1822 the Duke of Marlborough stayed there. Until Rackstraw's death in 1829, it was among the leading hotels in the old town. Another prominent hotelier was John Russell, who took over the Bath Hotel in Bath Street in 1820, making it an important coaching centre, able to hold its own with the rival Royal Hotel (established in 1814) in the High Street. The Bath Hotel accommodated the post and mail coaches, and 20 coaches left it each morning by 1829, including the Liverpool Rocket, the Cheltenham Pilot and the Crown Prince (to Birmingham and London).

Russell contributed more to the town's life. By now its inhabitants realized that the old parish authorities could not meet all the needs of the combined old and new towns. In 1825 they obtained from Parliament 'An Act for Pavement of Flagging, Lighting, Watching, Cleansing, Regulating and Improving the Town of Leamington Priors'. A new electorate of the principal residents and tradesmen chose 28 Commissioners to implement the Act and spend a rate levied by the parish vestry. At an early meeting they purchased a strait waistcoat 'for the use of the parish' and ordered the setting up of the town stocks.

The Commissioners also appointed a Treasurer, Scavenger,

Surveyor, Constables and Watchmen. They chose Russell as Surveyor with particular responsibility for the maintenance and repair of the roads and overseeing the layout of new ones. Easing the flow of traffic was vital, and in 1839 he was commended for raising the carriage road in Royal Parade to the level of the foot pavement and converting the steep hill to the canal bridge on the Tachbrook Road into a gentler ascent. New roads were staked out north of the Leam from the bridge, and a new bridge replaced the old dangerous one over the Avon at Emscote. He supervised the marking of streets and putting numbers on house-doors, and had the pavements flagged with stone. In addition, he ensured that the occupiers of houses and buildings swept the pavements and sides and backs of these before 9 a.m. each Tuesday and Saturday. He retired in 1831 with great honour, recognized as an 'active and intelligent officer' whom Leamington was 'fortunate' in having to secure the construction of its roads so much admired by visitors.

Among Russell's achievements was the building of a 'neat market place' under an arcade with shops near the Bath Hotel. Better market facilities were needed by the growing town, and besides fresh country produce and coal conveyed by the canal, the market sold fish brought by coach from London. During the season, furniture was often auctioned there, which helped tenants taking unfurnished houses for the season to equip their homes. In 1841 this market was enlarged with an ornamental Grecian entrance and called the Prince's Market.[12]

The two most notable signs of Leamington's economic recovery were the building of the Regent Hotel and the Parthenon Assembly Rooms. The Regent Hotel was built in 1819 opposite the Upper Rooms by John Williams, previously manager of the Bedford Hotel. With a small garden on the north side, it was a massive building of three storeys and a garret above. It originally had its main entrance, surmounted by the royal arms, on the south side; the entrance on the Parade was added in 1849. The dining-room held 120 and the adjoining public room 200. Along the grand staircase and corridors, it was claimed, hung many valuable paintings by Gainsborough, Lely, Kneller and Lawrence.

Leamington now had two hotels fit for royalty. When the Prince Regent came to the town in September 1819 he visited the Royal Hotel and the chief sights – the libraries, the new Pump Room and Baths – and inspected William's New Hotel, which he allowed to be renamed the Regent Hotel. It became the town's premier hotel. The Duke of Wellington and his sister, the Marchioness of Wellesley, stayed there in April 1827, and the Duchess of Kent and Princess Victoria went there in 1830. When Williams retired in 1834, John Russell at a farewell dinner in the hotel commended him for the erection of 'that spendid monument' over which he had presided so successfully.

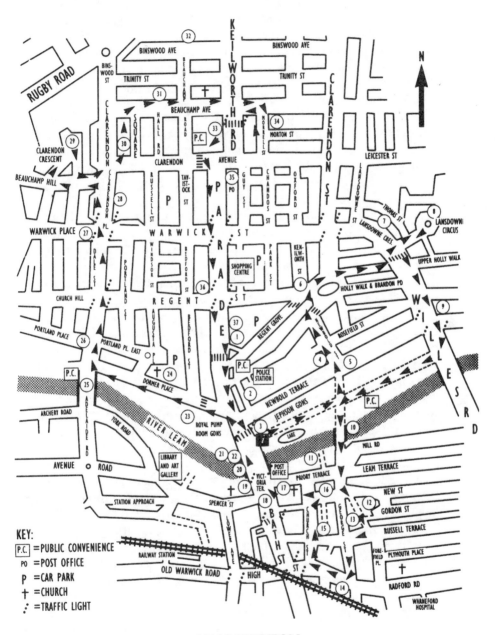

KEY:
P.C. = PUBLIC CONVENIENCE
PO = POST OFFICE
P = CAR PARK
† = CHURCH
∴ = TRAFFIC LIGHT

LEAMINGTON

The Parthenon Assembly Rooms, immediately opposite the Bowling Green Inn, were the biggest venture of Robert William Elliston, an actor and lessee of Drury Lane, who established an economic 'empire' in Leamington. The building, opened in 1821, was more magnificent than any other in old Leamington. The central block had a colonnaded front at the first floor level and a five-arched arcade on the ground floor. The ballroom on the upper floor was 62 feet by 31 feet and 20 feet high. The lower floor had a tea-room, a reading room and a library with 12,000 volumes, which was dubbed the County Library of Research. Behind the reading room was a charming promenade and garden in the manner of some contemporary Cheltenham library gardens. Subscriptions for the season's balls were 15s. for ladies and a guinea for gentlemen; and the town ball, previously held at the Bowling Green Inn, was transferred there.

As in other spa towns, the theatre did not flourish and had a difficult time. A theatre had been founded in 1813 by John Simms, and his company performed in it two or three nights a week. Elliston took it over in 1817, and during the next few years William Macready, Charles and Edmund Kean and Jenny Lind appeared there, but it lacked support and faced continual financial difficulties.[13]

Elliston's other holdings in Leamington included the Ranelagh Pleasure Gardens Exotic Nursery, comprising 10 acres of flower and fruit gardens east of Brunswick Street. Established in 1811, they were in an indifferent state until John Cullis took them over in 1814. In three years he tastefully laid them out with gravel walks, and a stand was built where a military band played in the evenings. In September 1819 he commemorated the Prince Regent's visit with a grand fête, for which James Bisset wrote an additional verse for the National Anthem. By 1824 there were hot-houses, conservatories and greenhouses as well as extensive shrubberies and walks where in season subscribers could promenade to view the peach and nectarine trees and grape vines while listening to the music. There were gala nights and special firework displays as at Bath and the Montpellier Gardens at Cheltenham.[14]

Elliston interspersed his acting in London with visits to his 'favourite Leamington' to supervise his businesses, but in addition to his losses on the theatre the Parthenon had cost him £25,000, and competition with the Upper Rooms reduced his profits. He went bankrupt in 1827 and died in 1831. His son Henry, after advertising the theatre for sale as an auction-room, public room or shop, closed it in 1833, and the town lacked a theatre for the next 15 years.[15] He had to sell the Parthenon also, but persisted in trying to promote entertainment in the town, finally taking over the Parthenon again in 1838 and reopening it as the Royal Music Hall.[16]

As in other spa towns, increasing population required not only opportunities for pleasure but also for religious worship. Many of the spa's early promoters were Dissenters, whose first place of worship was the Congregational Chapel built in 1816 in Clemens Street.[17] At the same time the old Parish Church of All Saints could not contain the ever-larger congregations. By November 1812, John Wise, the Rector, had bespoken stone from Greatheed's quarry, and in 1816 a new transept on the south side was complete. Soon afterwards a dignified spire was added to the old square tower. More alterations in 1825 provided altogether 568 seats, 290 of them free. Still space did not meet the demand, and a second service had to be provided for visitors, paid for by subscription. Further extensions were made in 1830, 1832 and 1834 until at last a large enough church was obtained in 1867 when it was almost entirely rebuilt.

A foreign visitor's description of Leamington in 1826 showed its development during the first 10 years of peace. It was,he wrote,

'a rich and elegant town, containing 10 or 12 palace-like inns, four large bath-houses with colonnades and gardens, several libraries, with which are connected card, billiard, concert and ballrooms (one for 600 persons), and a host of private houses, which are almost entirely occupied by visitors and spring out of the earth like mushrooms.'[18]

It grew from about 2,000 to 6,000 in the 1820s and more than doubled in size in the 1830s.

Leamington had become an entrenched hunting town. The Warwickshire Hunt Ball of 1822 was the social event of the year, taking precedence over the Leamington Dress Ball, and it was claimed that the word 'season' had become a meaningless term in the town, which would soon be the favourite winter residence of both vale-tudinarians and votaries of pleasure. The recently married Duke and Duchess of St Albans were visitors in July 1827, and the Duke resolved to make Leamington his winter abode to join the Warwickshire Hunt. The Duchess reputedly said,

Well your Grace, if you can find amusement in the field for the day, I will endeavour to provide for the evening, and we will see if we cannot make Leamington as pleasant in winter as it is gay in summer.

The *Leamington Spa Courier* in 1828 reported that no other watering-place in the kingdom had greater attractions for hunting gentlemen. The huge stone hotels were likened to hunting-lodges, and the hunting fraternity had their own exclusive societies, the best-known being the select Oyster Club. Dr A.B. Granville, the leading authority on spas in the middle of the century, and a visitor to them, agreed in *The Spas of England and Pricipal Sea-Bathing Places* (1841) that Leamington's progress was due to hunting as much as to water-drinking. Within a radius of 25 miles there were at least 140 covers for the North Warwickshire, the Drake's, the Atherstone and the Pytchley hounds. The disadvantage, however, was that the adjacent countryside, although flat and suited for hunting, was also dull without anything of the romantic and pictuesque, which visitors to other spas enjoyed in day excursions. In the later years of the century the *Leamington Spa Courier* still published the hunting tally of the season; but in 1858 it reported no high scores in Leicestershire, Northamptonshire or Warwickshire. For example, Warwickshire had 'bagged' only 84 foxes in 123 days hunting.

The development of the 'new town' north of the river, which several early nineteenth-century speculators in Leamington decided to lay out as the focus of the fashionable winter season, proceeded slowly and uncertainly because, like the Ellistons, they had difficulty in raising enough capital for their ventures. 'Every road leading into Leamington', wrote Granville, 'has been seized upon and flanked with buildings,' and he thus summed up the situation:

> The multitude of houses of every description – this launching out of builders and shop and hotel keepers into thoughtless specula- tions has been attended by incessant changes in the ownership of property followed by bankruptcy. Many begin with a magnificent shop one season, who are compelled to close it before the next. A bold and high-spirited hotel keeper, who has struggled through several seasons, has taken his place at last in the Gazette; while some other less fortunate speculators in brick and mortar, having come to the wrong end of their purse, have been glad to make over their responsibilities for whatever they could get to some successor, equally bold in the undertaking and destined probably to be equally unsuccessful in the end.

Consequently the shift of the social and commercial life from south to north was gradual. The new town was laid out in a generous pattern with broad avenues for the movement of horse-drawn traffic, but the horses and vehicles were at first kept in the old town. Both the main coaching hotels, the Bath and the Royal, were there. Even by 1829 four of the hunting and livery stables were in the lower town, and only one, the Bedford Mews, was north of the Leam. This balance had changed by 1850, when the number had quadrupled to 22 mews and stables, of which 16 were now in the new town.

Improvements undertaken by the Commissioners made possible the town's continued expansion during that period. Under them Leamington pioneered gas street-lighting so necessary for evening entertainments and activities. The Leamington Gas Works was established in 1819 in a building near the canal; and a plan of it in 1823 exists. These works lighted the streets of the old town, and four years later the Warwick Gas Company gained a contract to illuminate the new town. A minor crisis arose in August 1828 on the eve of a charity ball in the Pump Room when the lighting failed, especially in the back streets, but a hasty message to both the Leamington and Warwick works restored the gas pressure and brilliant illumination to the town.[19] Gas was introduced into the Parish Church in August 1830, and 19 lamps replaced the former glimmering oil wicks.[20]

In the first six months of 1829 gas lighting cost the Commissioners £193 11s 3d. to the Leamington company and £236 16s 8d. to the Warwick company. In 1834, when the town had 223 gas lamps, it wished to secure a uniform system of lighting as the Warwick company charged 15s. per thousand feet for its gas, while the Leamington company charged only 12s. The Leamington Priors New Gas and Coke Company, in which residents bought shares, was formed to purchase the right to supply gas to the whole town. It erected a new, extended gas works costing £40,000 in 1838, and by 1850 was supplying 412 public lights.[21]

Rapid urbanization brought public order problems. Offences noted in 1828 included breaking and entry at the Angel Inn, stealing pictures worth £60 from James Bisset's shop and warehouse in Ranelagh Terrace, damaging trees and fences in Holly Walk and, in 1830, stealing apricots and pears from a garden and orchard in Bath Street.[22] After several attempted solutions, including the voluntary enlistment of respectable citizens as nightwatchmen, the Parish Officers and Commissioners hired able-bodied men of good character as uniformed beadles to patrol the streets and remove all vagrants, beggars and disorderly persons, and especially to prevent annoyance to congregations going to or leaving church. By 1848 thirteen such men under a Superintendent were employed in the winter and ten in the summer at an annual cost of £966 7s 9d.[23]

In 1829 Thomas Oldham, the Scavenger, was made responsible for cleaning the streets at £50 a year using three horse-drawn watering-carts engaged by the Commissioners. He was also the lessee of the water-mill and from 1832 employed it to raise water into a tank from which to fill these carts, and under contract from the Commissioners he laid the first water-pipes for domestic use in the old town. The next year these pipes were extended into the new town, and a service reservoir was made. Then came fire–plugs, stand pipes for street-watering and service pipes laid into many houses which had hitherto relied on wells and pumps.[24]

Local travel had changed greatly since about 1812 when James Bisset found the village's only public transport was a hired sedan, bath–chair or donkey. Bye-laws issued by the Commissioners in 1829 showed the multiplication of traffic. These required a licence for each hackney coach, car, bath–chair, pony–chaise or carriage to stand or ply for hire, as also for each porter, basket-man, barrow-man and barrow-woman. Stands were fixed for hackney coaches, bath and sedan chairs and fly-carriages; the number was limited, and fares were controlled. To keep the streets clear of obstructions, wagons and carts could only stop there to load and unload. Wheelbarrows and handbarrows had to bear their owner's full name, and horses, carriages or carts could not be cleaned in public highways. A necessary rule for this hunting spa forbade the exercising of horses in built-up roads, and employers were obliged to prevent their servants doing this.[25]

By now Leamington possessed the essential elements of a spa, and the next 20 years or so saw steady major development when most of the celebrated streets were built. The situation of the housing market was changing. Investment in hotels and lodging houses produced only a fluctuating income, even with an assured winter season. More building of new dwellings for the increasing number of permanent residents was now undertaken. Apart from confidence brought by more effective local government after 1825, three other events made this expansion possible – the change of ownership of both the Willes and Wise estates, and Bertie Greatheed's further capital for more investment through his substantial inheritance in 1824 from the estate of his uncle, the last Duke of Ancaster, in 1809.

When Edward Willes succeeded in 1820 to the ownership of the estate north of the Leam at Newbold Comyn, he determined to build there. After a tree-lined road was driven through his land from Holly Walk, he engaged T.C. Bannister, a Warwick architect and surveyor, and Samuel Beazley, a London architect, to develop Quarry Fields, a site of 23 acres beyond the present Cross Street and behind the Parade. The plan adopted was for villas around a circus with streets divided into a simple grid pattern and a church. From 1824 most of the land was taken quickly by four local speculators in large blocks at about £800 an acre.

The second promotion by Willes was on about 100 acres in the Beauchamp Wood area north of the new town, to be reached by extending Union Parade through some of Greatheed's land. They both encouraged middle-class settlement there by joint planning of streets to improve access to the town from Warwick through Milverton. Another

London architect, Peter Frederick Robinson, a pupil of Henry Holland, was employed; he suggested grandiose schemes, but eventually the estate was also laid out on the grid system. It was intersected with wide avenues – South Parade (later Clarendon Avenue), Beauchamp Terrace (Beauchamp Avenue), and Binswood Terrace (Binswood Avenue). Robinson planned for 300 first-class houses, but there was little demand for these. By 1829, when building began around Clarendon Square and then Clarendon Crescent, there were only five such houses on the estate, 72 by 1837, and only 108 by 1851, and a score of working-class houses had infiltrated the area. The support of Robert Downes, the vicar of the parish, for the estate was gained by building the Episcopal Chapel (later Christ Church) on land given by Welles, with a road in front forming a splendid vista.

The third and most ambitious project of Willes was to develop his land east of the town, totalling 369 acres north and south of the Leam. He commissioned John Nash, the Prince Regent's architect, to draw up in 1827 an ambitious scheme for the area. This was similar to the Calverley development at Tunbridge Wells, then being undertaken by Decimus Burton, who had worked with Nash. There was, however, neither the capital nor the necessary building capacity for its accomplishment, but the impressive Newbold Terrace and some nearby villas are a remnant of the idea.

In 1836 Willes leased the Newbold Meadows, bordering the Leam, for 2,000 years at an annual rent of £30 to trustees so as to secure the permanence of the gardens as a promenade for visitors and townsfolk. So Leamington secured adequate gardens, then considered an essential feature of resort towns. To honour Jephson for the benefits he had brought the town by attracting to it the opulent and sick, these gardens were taken over and called Jephson Gardens as his memorial, and a statue of him by Peter Hollins was erected on a pedestal in a circular stone temple. No other physician's contribution to a spa town has been so lavishly recognized. By contrast, the generosity of the Willes family in virtually donating land for one of the most valuable amenities of the town was not fully acknowledged until 1873 when an obelisk was raised to the memory of Edward Willes. He was outlived by Jephson, who died in 1878 and was buried at Old Milverton.

The other large local landowner was Matthew Wise, who lived in the manor house during the first part of the nineteenth century and owned many gardens, closes and orchards in the town, but released little land for building. His death in 1816 and the building of Shrubland Hall by Matthew Wise II enabled Matthew Wise III, who succeeded him on his death in 1825, to abandon the old manor house and gardens, and these included in a planned development of 99 acres immediately west of the old town. Two local builders, James Hill and William Peace, bought the manor house and 45 acres of land for £23,000 and by 1838 had built Eastnor Terrace, a row of 13 fine houses.

Further expansion of the town took place during this period, notably Lansdowne Crescent and Lansdowne Circus, which were designed by William Thomas, who subsequently at the age of 43, with a wife and 10 children, emigrated to Canada and then designed St Michael's Cathedral and Lawrence Hall in Toronto. Faced with stucco, the Crescent is graced by a deliberately fretted iron verandah, and the equally effective circus is a ring of paired houses, which also have fine ironwork.

If current plans had not failed and particularly Nash's design of 1827 had been realized, something of the classical style in Leam Terrace and Russell Terrace south of the river suggest that Leamington might have been enriched with more of a Palladian legacy to equal Bath, Cheltenham and Tunbridge Wells. Lansdowne Crescent and Newbold Terrace can, indeed, compare with those streets and crescents, but the town's renown rests upon its Gothic and Tudor style villas,which became the vogue in the 1830s; and the common gabled stucco villa is typical of the town's contribution to the urban scene.

During this period of expansion no success was achieved in forming a spa centre or mounting such large homogeneous developments in squares, circuses or terraces as at Bath, Cheltenham or Clifton, which would have given expression to the achievements of leading architects. The town's prosperity depended mainly on the patronage of a leisured middle class, and in 1846 they occupied more than a third of its 2,752 houses. Leamington was described in 1828 as a place of unexampled rise and celebrity, the best paved and lighted in the kingdom, but also 'comparatively cheap, offering the pleasures of retirement'; and a Board of Health inspector reported in 1851 that the town had neither trade nor manufacture nor an agricultural market to support its economy, but depended on being clean, commodious and healthy in a superlative degree and having good housing.[26]

There was also considerable investment in hotels and inns. By 1824 there were eight leading establishments, including the oldest – the Bowling Green Inn in Church Street. The Royal, Crown, Bath, Blenheim and Castle were in the old town, only the Regent and Bedford being in the new town. Those in the old town sought to maintain their predominance..By 1830 the Royal, Blenheim, Castle and three lesser hotels, the Gloucester, Shakespeare and Union, were rebuilt or entirely renovated, while the Bowling Green was made in 1828 into the Fountain Commercial Inn with 14 bedrooms, five sitting-rooms and stabling and coach-houses; but its former name, so important in the town's history, was not relinquished.[27]

The most remarkable hotel enterprise was undertaken by Michael Thomas Copps, who came from Cheltenham in 1814, took over the Balcony Boarding House and built on its site in 1826 the Royal Hotel, designed by Robinson whom Willes had employed. Its foundation stone was laid by his daughter, Miss Maria Copps, 'supported by several of her young female friends and many other persons of the highest respectability in the town or neighbourhood'. With 100 bedrooms and a dining-room for 150 guests, the three-storeyed edifice was built in a classical style faced with Roman cement in imitation of stone. The main portico was supported by four Doric pillars, the pediment was sur-mounted by the royal arms, and the two rings were embellished with Corinthian pillars.

Besides rivalling Russell's Bath hotel, Copps – an Irishman himself – attracted many visitors from Ireland and allowed a priest the use of a room to say a Roman Catholic mass. The hotel had a flourishing mail and general coach office, which enabled it to rival the Bath Hotel. Copps also kept post-horses at the Gaydon Inn on the Leamington to Banbury road.

By now Leamington had overtaken Cheltenham as a fashionable spa. 'Countless people go there and nowhere else', and they were the social élite, as Granville observed:

At Leamington, unquestionably, no dross of society or even ambigu-ous characters will be found among those who assemble at the Pump Room for their health and the waters. The place is yet too choice and costly to admit of any of the very tip-top of Society. Accordingly one recognized the very moment one entered the Mall, the pale faces of some fair damsels, the hurried and puffing steps of a portly Lady Gertrude, the halting gait of a certain Right Honourable and the saffronised looks of a haughty perambulator, persons of importance in society, members of distinguished and aristocratic families or wealth commoners.

Granville considered also that Leamington had a dozen of the best hotels in England. He stayed at the Royal, although it and its rival, the Regent, were expensive. Like hotels in the northern spas both, with John Gomm's Bedford, operated a service then called *table d'hôte*, pro-viding everything, except sleeping, in public rooms, while the smaller, more fashionable and expensive hotels – the Imperial, Clarendon and Lansdowne (all in Lansdowne Place and opened in the 1830s) had private rooms. The Royal charged three guineas weekly for board with the use of public rooms, but the all-in cost was nearer six guineas; The Bedford's basic charge was £2 16s. Granville alleged that Leamington's hotels were too dear – a first floor suite in the most fashionable hotels might cost eight to ten guineas, and two rooms were seldom to be had for two to three guineas. Outraged local opinion denied this, saying that two rooms in a decent area could be had for 12s. weekly, and even the best rooms cost only £1 or £1 10s. Competition kept prices low, and the return on capital was only 2½ per cent.[28]

The effect of this competition was seen in the fate of several hotels. The Gloucester went bankrupt in 1831, while the Crown's successive owners failed in 1827, 1829, 1831 and 1843.[29] The Royal declined from 1836 through competition from the Regent, whose superior environment attracted visitors. It closed in 1840, and the next year its contents were dispersed in a 29 days' sale. Copps, after an unsuccessful attempt to open Victoria House in Lansdowne Crescent as Copp's Family Hotel, retired to Guernsey, where he died in 1849. The Royal remained empty until its demolition in 1847 to make way for the railway.[29]

Inns and taverns, however, increased from nine in 1829 to 49 in 1846, which included some attached to hotels like the Bedford Tap or those which had ceased to be hotels like the Bowling Green Inn. A considerable work force served the visitors. In 1841 servants were 19 per cent of the population, 373 being in the building industry, and 553 were ostlers, coachmen, valets and other personal servants.[30]

Besides the hotels, commercial undertakings became increasingly concentrated in the new town. Tradesmen began to desert Bath Street and Clemens Street, like Charles and John Elston, music sellers and teachers, who left Bath Street for Regent Street in 1831. By 1830 there were 245 registered professional and tradespeople in the new town and only 201 in the lower. In Regent Street (previously Cross Street) tradesmen occupied 56 of the 86 premises by 1846. The new town acquired a market place in 1838 in a court off Warwick Street. Though grandiosely called Covent Garden (suggesting Russell associations), in 1850 it was a mere unpaved shed without a water supply and adequate drainage.[31]

The contemporary explanation for this migration was that the lower town was damp in winter and less sheltered from the winds. All the prestigious building was in the new town. The closure of the Royal Hotel reduced the old town's coaching trade; and the Ranelagh Gardens were 'a very small momento' of the past, having been ousted by the Jephson Gardens. Patronage went to the new town, leaving the old town deserted and undignified. Gone were the days of grandeur when Charlotte Street received the nobles, Clemens Street the gentry and Bath Street the professionals.[32]

Commercialized entertainment also appeared. A permanent military band, installed by public subscription in 1834, played in the Ranelagh and later the Newbold or Jephson Gardens and in those by the Royal Pump Room in Mall Walk. Archery was introduced in 1829, and the Newbold Archery Ground was opened in 1834; and a tennis court with club facilities was erected in Lower Bedford Street in 1846. Most important were the libraries and newsrooms, which set out to be social centres, as at Cheltenham, Margate and Brighton, by holding concerts and balls. This led to intense competition among these, with bankruptcies and changing ownerships. By 1829, however, the number had stabilized at four, and these still existed in 1843 – the County Library in the High Street, Bettinson's in Upper Union Parade, the Royal Library attached to the Assembly Rooms, and Merridew's in Bath Street. Three others had also appeared – Beck's Lending Library and Printing Establishment in Regent Street, Skettle's Library in Warwick Street and Dew's Theological Library in Victoria Terrace.[33]

Between 1821 and 1831 Leamington's population rose from 2,183 to 6,209 and the number of houses from 481 to 1,193. This was at the time of the expansion of the winter season, which had gradually extended into December with January to March a relatively quiet time, but the first local newspaper, the *Leamington Spa Courier*, established in 1828, published lists of arrivals throughout the year, while the *Warwick Advertiser* had printed none between January and April. The public winter balls, hitherto only monthly, were now more frequent; and the local press and guide-books spoke of Leamington as a place of winter residence. By 1840 the weekly lists of winter visitors were still about half the length of those of the summer peak, but a decade later they rivalled or exceeded them.[34]

The humble village had astonishingly become a leading wateringplace with titled and stylish upper-class visitors and rivalling Bath, Brighton and Cheltenham. Formerly a spa for the sick, it was now an all-the-year-round resort for the wealthy and a winter residence for the hunting fraternity. In fact, by 1838 the aristocratic, military and naval visitors preferred the winter season to the summer and formed a uniformly higher proportion of those coming in winter than in summer. Distinguished users of the well included Princess Augusta in 1822; others followed as visitors, though the bath lists ceased to show many aristocrats. Leamington's importance was shown when the young Princess Victoria and the Duchess of Kent on their way to Malvern made a detour to spend the night of 4 August 1830 at the Regent Hotel, which was illuminated and decorated with evergreens.[35]

The baths' continued prosperity enabled their owners to improve them. In 1832 Matthew Wise III rebuilt his baths as a single-storeyed, classical-style building with two Doric columns fronting the pedimented entrance in the idiom of contemporary pump-rooms; it was demolished in 1850. In 1836 John Goold took over Abbott's original building and replaced it by a more elaborate structure, also in the Grecian style, designed by Joseph Plevins, the Birmingham builder. To meet more sophisticated standards, it had eight baths for hot and cold bathing, a large plunge-bath, a douche bath, a Turkish bath and 'the Seville hot air baths, given solely under the skilled supervision of the manager or matron'. The walls of the bathing-rooms were hung with linen, and the floors were carpeted. It was closed and demolished in 1867.[36]

After the bankruptcy of the Robbins Spring, William Buckle and son, builders, bought it in 1838, pulled down the baths and houses and erected the spacious and elegant Victoria Terrace with a colonade facing the Leam and the new baths, renamed the Victoria Baths, which had a large pump-room with a superb, expensive fountain. There were nine baths, four supplied with a douche, warm portable baths and a crane for lowering invalids into the water. Pleasure grounds with seats were laid out on the adjoining south bank. Though intended to outstrip all rival establishments, the Victoria Baths suffered from proximity to the Royal Pump Room which attracted the most drinkers through the strength of its saline chalybeate, the size of its pump-room and its pleasure ground and music. By 1850 Fairweather's Fumigating Baths were started in Clemens Street; and the enterprising John Oldham, who had begun the waterworks, also established open-air walled swimming-baths of fresh water adjoining his old mill, which was equipped with small dressing-rooms.[37]

Granville, when he visited Leamington, was surprised by its insistence on wearing the 'Leamington Witches' Cap' under the showers. Though unknown elsewhere, the town's shops sold it, and the Pump Room itself supplied the required pointed headgear.

The social calendar assumed a more serious tone with lectures on scientific subjects given spasmodically from 1838 in the Upper Assembly Rooms. In 1848 the Royal Leamington Literary and Scientific Institution was founded to sponsor lectures 'on various topics of intellectual interest' and in 1854 erected its Public Hall in Windsor Street with a large reading room for its 300 members. It was opened to the ringing of the parish church bells and a concert given to a crowded audience.

Henry Elliston's conversion of the Lower Rooms into the Royal Music Hall in 1839 to provide dramatic summer entertainment proved difficult in 1841–42, but avoided closure. In 1849 an attempt was made to give the town a proper theatre again. Mercer H. Simpson adapted a disused Congregational chapel at 14 Clemens Street for this purpose, giving it a covered portico of four square pillars and an entablature.

Contemporary accounts emphasized its comfort and elegance and decoration in white, gold and light blue with rich crimson drapery; and the dominating drawing-room was fitted with chairs, damask cushions, pier glasses and pedestal lamps; but this glory could not save it from failure in 1866. The town lacked a large, purpose-built theatre until 1881.[38]

While from 1820 to 1840 the chief building was of hotels and other secular establishments, by the mid-century the churches were the most important. While All Saints' Church was rebuilding, the ancient parish was divided, and new churches were built. The Episcopal Chapel in Clarendon Avenue became Christ Church in 1840; St Mary's in St Mary's Road was built in 1839 and Holy Trinity in Beauchamp Square in 1847. In addition Roman Catholics had a chapel in George Street (1828), Baptists in Warwick Street (1833) and Congregationalists in Spencer Street (1836) and Holly Walk (1849). The religious census of 1851 recorded some 7,604 seats in all the places of worship, which sufficed for 48.4 per cent of the population, but on that Sunday morning and evening attendances were 4,147 and 4,088. The total number of seats was apportioned as Anglicans 4,330 (57 per cent), Nonconformists 2,774 (36 per cent) and Roman Catholics (7 per cent).[39]

The town's expansion led to a substantial number of professional men settling there besides tradesmen. In 1846 there were 11 estate agents (compared with one in 1826 and six surveyors, two architects and six auctioneers. The medical profession was well represented with 10 physicians and 13 surgeons, together with 16 chemists and druggists benefiting from a local practice by which prescriptions were sent directly to them and not left to the patients' decision. The quality trades included five silversmiths, five artists and eight wine-merchants.

In the labour force in 1841 were 148 cobblers, 231 dressmakers and milliners and 145 laundry workers. There were 12 builders employing 373 workers including 42 bricklayers, 121 carpenters and joiners and 41 plasterers. The Irish influx was shown by the formation of Leamington Irish Labourers' Conjunction Union in 1845 with 117 members, representing 31 per cent of the building force. Leamington, like Cheltenham, relied upon outside labour. The 1851 Census showed that 37 of the 76 heads of artisan households in two streets came from Warwickshire villages, mostly south of the town, and only six were born in Leamington. Other counties contributed 26, and Ireland and Scotland two each. Those engaged in agriculture declined from 10.4 per cent of the population in 1801 to 0.3 per cent in 1841.[40]

While in Bath and Cheltenham domestic servants were 33.7 per cent and 37.4 per cent of the population, they were fewer in Leamington, but they steadily grew. There were 787 and 299 male and female servants in 1831 and 1,889 and 553 in 1851, an increase from 17.5 per cent of the population to 19 per cent. Fashionable Clarendon Square in 1851 had 43 houses and 40 families in residence; most had at least one male servant and all had female servants, with an average of 3.4 servants, not including such possible non-residents as grooms, gardeners and daily women. Exceptional was No. 42, the largest house, where Lady Louisa Ramsay resided with three daughters and three male and nine female servants, but her husband was absent. In lower middle-class Portland Street, only four houses had a male servant, 19 one female servant and the rest, except one with none, two or three.

In 1830 a Mrs Leeson founded an agency which, as in other spa towns, met visitors' domestic needs, Her register office at Grafton House in Gloucester Street served both employers and servants and also dealt with furnished and unfurnished houses and lodgings. The ladies of Leamington had, again as elsewhere, founded in 1842 the Servants' Home and Register in Park Street with a superintendent responsible to the management committee for providing lodging and protection as well as religious instruction and advice to young girls coming to the town to seek posts with unknown employers. In that year it found employment for 326 of its registered girls, but 319 were unemployed or unemployable.[41]

Ever more workless and sick poor came hopefully to the town. In the last two months of 1823 the parish committee had 14 applications for relief but 46 in 1824, 55 in 1825, 66 in 1826 and 60 in 1827. Of this total of 241, 40 were refused or referred elsewhere; the rest had payments or relief in kind such as coal, clothes or shoes. As 108 had single payments, casual relief for a mobile population seemed to be mostly needed. There already was a poorhouse in Parish Field on the road to Southam, but its old buildings were inadequate for the greater number of paupers. In 1829 a vestry meeting of all the £5 ratepayers agreed to replace it. A new three-storeyed building was erected adjoining the Royal Parade in the High Street on land granted by the Earl of Aylesford and Matthew Wise at a peppercorn rent for 999 years, part of it to be set aside for a new town hall. Of the six candidates for the post of overseer of it, John Ballinger offered to take it for £60 a year, but it predictably went at a salary of £100 to the Earl's nominee, possibly the son of his former servant now in charge of the Old Well. This would explain the overseer's office being in Church Walk. Paupers had to go there for their weekly allowance between 11.0 a.m. and 1.0 p.m. or else lose it. And in 1831 beadles were appointed to keep vagrants off the roads.[42]

The poverty of the 1830s coincided with the considerable settlement in the town of professional men who were ready to assist the needy. In 1830 a Fund for Supplying the Poor was established with the vicar, Robert Downes, as chairman, and it immediately spent its balance in hand of £66 8s 2d. on distributing coal. The next year the vicar and John Russell, the banker, helped to found a Benevolent Society; it hired premises and opened a subscription list, augmented by church collections, which by 1842 enabled £500 to be spent annually on food, clothing and medicine for the sick and needy. And 1831 saw also, with Matthew Wise III as President and John Russell as Treasurer, the revival of the Leamington Spa Charity founded in 1806 to enable the sick poor to have the free use of the waters.[43]

John Russell became also Treasurer of the General Hospital and Dispensary established in Regent Street in 1816, which decided in 1831 to build a new hospital. It bought an acre of land for £600 from the Earl of Aylesford, and Dr Warneford, Rector of Bourton-on-the-Hill gave over £3,000 for the project. The central block of the three-storeyed, classical-style Warneford Hospital (as it was soon called) was finished in 1834, and two wards were added in 1838. The measure of the hospital's need was shown in 1842–43 when it had 402 patients and supplied 2,153 free baths.[44]

Dr John Craig, who became Vicar of Leamington in 1839, not only began the rebuilding of the church, but also encouraged the charitable work made yet more necessary by the economic depression of the 1840s which badly affected the town. He reorganized the Benevolent Society so that the relief was given through the church schools to the children's parents. In 1841 a Coal Club was instituted, by which the poor bought coal by twopenny subscriptions, which, together with church collections, brought it over £500 in 1842. In 1840 the Magdalene Asylum (later the Female Penitentiary) was founded in Wise Street for the prostitutes inevitably attracted to the fringes of Leamington society; it admitted 18 girls in just over two years. By 1840 the Charitable Repository at 13 Upper Parade assisted the sale of articles made by ladies in reduced circumstances; from 1840 the nondenominational Dorcas Society distributed clothing, blankets and sheets from the Mill Street Chapel; and District Visitors assisted the poor through the Relief Fund.[45]

The parish council, through restrained by low rating assessments, spent £1,391 18s 11½d. in 1834 on poor relief, £397 7s 6½d. being on weekly relief to paupers, £152 19s 11d. on casual relief to them, £3 11s 3d. on other casual relief, £129 7s. on running the new poorhouse and £23 8s 4d. on removing paupers unable to claim settlement there. In July the parish was owed money on account of 27 bastardy orders, but only two of the fathers were in town; 12 of the mothers were still there, the others, except one, being in Warwickshire. In the face of the cost of illegitimacy to the parish, some suggested the appointment of more voluntary overseers instead of employing the assistant overseer, John. A.

29

Squires, at a salary of £100, but others held that a requirement to perform public office would deter tradesmen settling in the town.[46]

Voluntary aid by charitable societies, churches and chapels was less controversial and was needed by the many destitute poor who particularly suffered in the winter. The Anti-Mendicity Society formed in 1841 relieved hundreds of the homeless beggars continually invading the town, saving both adults and children being sent as vagrants to Warwick Gaol, helping in its first year 5,356 mendicants including 738 children. From the winter of 1840 a Soup and Bread Committee (later called the Labourers' Fund) for the next 35 years found work for the seasonally unemployed in beautifying the public gardens and making new paths. In January 1841 they constructed a walk along the Leam's north bank in return for half-rate wages and soup for their families. That month Dr Jephson headed the subscription list with £21 and every following winter supplied 750 families with 120 tons of coal. Matthew Wise, whom the town's growth had also benefited, gave a loaf of bread and three pounds of beef to each of 94 families every New Year's Day.[47]

Social deprivation spread beyond the back streets as prices fell through a glut of building land in the 1830s, aggravated by the economic depression and the failure of the Leamingtion Bank in 1837, which ruined nearly all builders and speculators. By 1841, a total of 250 houses remained unfinished, and the building boom halted for 20 years. Grand designs ceased, and the town increasingly consisted of middle-class detached villas with large gardens and straggling settlements encouraged by lower rates in outlying areas without paving and street-lighting.[48]

The Improvement Act of 1825 was amended to allow the commissioners to raise a police force and to add tenants of property assessed for the poor rate at £80 to the £60 qualification for a commissioner, so admitting those renting expensive property for short periods. The radicals were dissatisfied, but a third Act of 1847 merely included further powers to provide public baths, wash-houses and also public clocks to regulate the labouring people's daily life. There were some 130 commissioners from whom a business committee of 21 was elected. After the Public Health Act of 1848 Leamington's boundary problems with the village of Milverton to the north-west led to a petition for a government inquiry from 38 commissioners, 13 physicians, 100 tradesmen and others.

The government report of 1850 revealed problems like Cheltenham's. Among the most numerous middle-class houses were slum enclaves, which it condemned. The worst area was a large tract of buildings south of the Leam, chiefly along Bath and Brunswick Streets. William's and John's Courts in Satchwell Street had 16 houses containing 85 people, but each had only one bedroom, and between the two courts was a large open cesspool. Parts of the new town had some of the worst alleys, including those opening from Tavistock and Russell Streets, which were long, narrow, unpaved. improperly drained and damp. Privies were often shared: Page's Buildings had one for 20 people. Swain's Buildings, with weekly house rents of 2s. 6d., had privies under the floor, an inadequate water supply and a badly paved yard. Most streets in the new town had sewers, but many in the old town had none. Most of the water came from wells and pumps, but the poor had no water-butts for storage. Oldham's waterworks supplied 170 better-class houses from seven miles of pipes into 19 streets in the old town and 29 in the new. Cellars flooded, especially when the Leam over-flowed, as recently when the water covered the Jephson Gardens, went along Dormer Place and inundated houses in the valley. The town had 34 slaughter-houses, and some 800 houses had pigsties. A local board of health was suggested to include the town and the contiguous parishes of Milverton and Lillington. Fear of higher rates brought opposition from the two parishes, the Earl of Warwick and the London and North Western Railway which now had a station at Milverton. This brought further inquiries in 1851 and 1857, though the Board of Health was established in 1852 with 15 members and one elected by the Milverton Main Sewerage District.[49]

The railway came as a branch line of the London and Birmingham Railway to a point in Milverton halfway between Leamington and War-wick. Landowners with estates north of the town, including Lords Clarendon and Aylesford and C.P. Percy objected to this as late as 1841. Despite this and the competition for other lines in the area, Parliament approved it in July 1842. The cost of the line with Kenilworth and Milverton stations rose from an estimate of £130,000 to £175,000, perhaps through compensating landowners. It was opened on 9 December 1844 with six daily trains in each directiion between Milverton and Coventry, a number soon reduced to five, although it had 2,500 passengers in the first week, and by mid-May the average weekly receipts at Milverton exceeded £700. These were mostly first-class passengers paying 2s. from Milverton to Coventry, only the first train to Coventry and the last from Milverton having the 9d. third-class passengers. The enterprising William Bosworth's Shakespeare Coach took passengers between Milverton and Stratford-on-Avon, but the proprietors of the Warwick and Birmingham, Warwick and Napton and Oxford Canals protested that the railway threatened their goods traffic in coal, grain and cattle and their profitable passenger service; and, indeed, George Nelson advertised coal at Kenilworth Railway Station at 5s. a ton cheaper than when purchased in Leamington and Warwick.[50]

Plans were soon made to bring the railway to the centre of the town. The Warwickshire and London Railway Company was floated in 1845 to establish communication between Warwick, Leamington, London and Birmingham with an improved line to Cheltenham and the west. The Earl of Warwick, William Congreve Russell and the ubiquitous Dr Jephson joined the directors of the London and Birmingham Railway as promoters. As the London and North Western Railway, it took over the London and Birmingham Railway, and the line was lengthened to a station in Avenue Road which was replaced in 1860 by the present Adelaide Road Station. Then the line to Rugby was ruthlessly extended through the centre of the town, destroying the Royal Hotel and Curtis's Baths to allow it to cross Clemens Street by a tubular bridge and was opened on 1 March 1851. Meanwhile the impressive Eastnor Terrace of 13 houses was also demolished to make way for the Great Western Railway's more direct line to London with a station in Westbourne Terrace, which was opened in 1852. There were now two ponderous bridges crossing the junction of High Street and Bath Street.[51]

The railway reached Leamington at a critical time when its social life, as in other spa towns during the 1840s, was challenged by the counter-attractions of the seaside resorts and Continental spas, and might well have become defunct. In 1842–43 the ephemeral *Leamington Looker-On* deplored the state of the town. The theatre and Royal Music Hall in the Lower Rooms were in difficulty, there were no summer balls in 1841 except during race week, the libraries had abandoned musical promenades, and many lodgings were unlet. The mounting number of visitors in the 1820s and early 1830s had slowed down and was almost static from 1842 to 1847. Leamington had reached the state common to all spa towns when the maintenance of social exclusiveness could only be safeguarded by abandoning public life for domestic entertainment. In vain did Major Hopkins, the Master of Ceremonies, announce in December 1844 the dates of all future balls and ask people to refrain from giving private parties.[52]

But, as the health inspector had remarked, the establishment of a railway station in or near a large town usually led to the extension of public building there. So at 'leafy Leamington' the advent of the railway assisted in the next decade the revival of the old spa with its villas set in spacious gardens amidst maturing trees, for it had been brought within easy commuting distance for the professional and business men of Birmingham and the adjacent industrial midlands, while the journey from London took just over four hours instead of 10 or 11 by stage coach.[53]

3

Cheltenham

Henry Skillicorne, a Bristol merchant captain, married in 1738 a wife who owned the spring discovered earlier in the century at Cheltenham, and developed it as a well with a pump; it was subsequently called the Old Well. It remained, however, a fair-sized market town in competition with neighbouring Prestbury until George III, suffering from severe abdominal spasms, came to drink the waters there in 1788 and made it fashionable as a summer resort. By the end of the century its mile-long High Street was well-paved and lined with inns, and it possessed assembly rooms and a theatre. Its development led to a dwindling supply of water from the Old Well and the establishment of fresh spa centres.

In 1815 these were King's Well (1788), Barrett's Spa (1801), Sherborne Well (1808), Vittoria House (1804), Cambray Spa (1807), New (Alstone) Spa, Montpellier Baths (1809). Although not as great as that of Leamington, its increasingly dangerous rival, its growth was rapid. Its population rose from 3,076 in 1801 to 8,325 in 1811 and 12,388 in 1821, while the number of visitors was estimated at about 2,000 in 1802, 4,000 in 1809, 5,000 in 1815, 15,000 in 1825.[1]

The first marked extension to the town was the Colonnade, erected south-west of the High Street as a prime shopping area in 1791 and extended to form the fashionable Promenade. It linked the old to the new town, where in 1809 Henry Thompson, a London banker, bought some 400 acres of pasture to build the Montpellier Baths. Simultaneously there was much building in the old town north of the High Street. Cheltenham was the fastest expanding wartime spa, and for a time more fashionable than Bath.

In May 1816, when her health began to fail, Jane Austen was induced to spend three weeks at Cheltenham by Mrs James Austen, her sister-in-law, who believed that its waters were better than Bath's. Jane wrote to her sister, Cassandra, 'How much is Cheltenham to be pre-ferred in May,' and revealed that 'the Duchess of Orleans drinks at my pump'. She came home saying that she had enjoyed staying at the white town and walking under the Promenade's leafy trees, but her niece, Caroline, thought her no better.

Eighteenth-century Cheltenham's high patronage continued. Royal visitors included the Dukes of Gloucester and Cambridge besides French, Russian and Danish princes. Among notables were Sir Walter Scott, Marshall Blucher and Jenny Lind. Less welcome was William Cobbett, who in 1821 called the town 'a nasty, ill-looking place, half-clown and half-cockney'; and returning in 1826 he styled it 'a place to which East India plunderers, West India floggers, English tax-gorgers, together with gluttonous drinkers and debauchees of all descriptions, female and male, resort.'[2]

Some visitors were different. Many filled the intervals between drink-ing waters by patronizing the growing number of subscription libraries – seven in 1815 and nine in 1830. Weekly subscription charges increased from 2s. 6d. and 3s. 6d. to 9s. and 10s. in the 1830s.[3] They were described as social centres, 'more adapted for *looking* than *learning*'.[4] They were, as in other spa towns, places of both national and local gossip, supplying London daily newspapers in attached reading rooms. They had subscription books for visitors and residents to support balls, concerts, card-parties, music lessons, benefit occasions for masters of ceremonies and many charitable objects, especially relief funds for local mishaps.

Best known was G.A. Williams's warehouse and library at 104 High Street, some of whose subscription books remain, showing that sub-scriptions ranged from 2s. 6d. weekly to a guinea annually. There were in 1815 slightly over 40 subscribers a month, but double that from June to August. The next year he moved to a handsome corner building, 393 High Street, and opened Williams's British and Foreign Library with a bookshop and reading room. His numbers from June to October that year were 358 and 735 in 1817, the highest monthly figure being 214 in September. Seven years later the total for the five summer months was 1,232, including 92 in January and 97 in December, compared with the average for the best summer months of 89 and 84 in 1815 and 1816. As well as running musical evenings through the week, Williams acted as an estate agent and in 1825 produced *A New Guide to Cheltenham*.

Musicians performed daily at the spa centres. James Haldon, a clari-net player, led those at the Old Well and also played at the Assembly Rooms and elsewhere, and was much in demand for quadrilles and private balls. When he died in 1829 every Cheltenham musician attended his funeral on 8 June, and musical performances ceased for the afternoon.[5] Some 50 noblemen and gentry inaugurated with a dinner the Harmonic Society at the Regent Concert Room.[6] Several businesses served the musicians' needs, including by 1825 Hale and Binfield's Musical Library and Repository next to Plough Inn and Cooper's Harp and Pianoforte Repository and Finlayson's Music Room, both in the High Street.[7]

Various organizations and institutions were formed – a Museum of Natural and Artificial Curiosities (1819) in Montpellier Walk; the Gloucester and Cheltenham Gentleman's Club (1825) with an annual subscription of £3 3s., meeting at the Assembly Rooms; and the Horticultural Society (1831), meeting first at the Sherborne Spa and later holding exhibitions at other spas. Dr Jenner, the vaccination pioneer, formed a Literary and Scientific Institution, which was supported by many physicians including Dr H.C. Boisragon, physician-extraordinary to George IV; in 1835 it erected a handsome classical building on the west side of the Promenade for its lectures and experiments.[8]

In 1814 a dozen esteemed gentlemen, supported by a subscription of £350, met to secure race meetings for Cheltenham like the older spa towns. A donation of £1,000 from the occupant of Berkeley Castle, Colonel William FitzHardinge Berkeley, the fifth Earl of Berkeley's illegitimate son, enabled the first meeting to be held in August 1818 on a course by Cleeve Hill. The hotels were overcrowded, and Punch and Judy shows, candy-sellers, entertainment shows and travelling minstrels flocked there; and a further meeting in October planned the erection of a grandstand. By 1819 the races were 'securely established', and Cheltenham boasted that they made it superior to other wateringplaces. Racegoers were contemporarily estimated to number between 15,000 and 20,000, and they stimulated social life by encouraging gambling, balls and plays. But this flat-racing's popularity declined and was replaced by steeplechasing, with races held annually from 1844 and still today at Prestbury Park.[9]

By 1815 the town entered on the period of massive building immediately following the Napoleonic War. On 29 July 1816 the new Assembly Rooms, built at 'almost incalculable cost', were opened by the hero of the hour, the Duke of Wellington, and his Duchess at a special dress ball attended by 1,400 people. And 1818 saw the completion of the Sherborne Pump Room, later renamed the Imperial Spa.

Pearson Thompson, on inheriting his father's land in 1824, developed it as the Montpellier and Lansdown Estates. His architect between 1824 and 1830 was John Papworth (later John Buonarotti), who adopted the popular Greek revival architectural style, using local materials – lime and cream-coloured freestone from the Leckhampton

Hill quarries, sand from the subsoil and blue lias clay for making bricks which were stuccoed over.

As part of his plans, Thompson wished to enlarge the Montpellier Baths. Papworth's device was to make it a Rotunda by adding a dome on the model of the Italian Villa La Rotonda at Vicenza. This was new in spa architecture, though the Ivanhoe Baths at Ashby-de-la-Zouch, designed by a local architect, Robert Chaplin, had one in 1822, as had the charming but transient Dorton Spa in Buckinghamshire. He succeeded in placing the copper dome above the existing colonade without dwarfing it. He designed also the interior fittings of the circular promenade room beneath the dome with four fireplaces and mirrors above them. This was finished in 1826; a conservatory with rare plants was added in 1829; and the formal Montpellier Gardens in front with winding paths leading through trees and shrubs were opened in 1830. Here visitors could walk or linger talking together away from the noise of the streets.[10]

The Montpellier Spa became the town's fashionable centre, at least during the summer months, to the disadvantage of both the Assembly Rooms and the shady, pleasant Sherborne Pump Room, which had in mid-June 1825 only a sprinkling of company though the musicians played charmingly.[11] On 20 July 1825 its first evening promenade or soirée musicale was attended by some 1,800 nobility and gentry, when elegant gothic-style gas lamps illuminated the Long Walk and magnificent chandeliers the Pump Room.[12] The next year subscription balls, called summer promenade balls, began. Ladies could attend these in promenade costume, but gentlemen still had to wear full dress. Some regretted this laxity, as being like some Continental watering-places, but it was generally popular. The newly recruited Montpellier Band played at these functions, at first in a Chinese pagoda, but later at the end of the Firework Walk and sometimes in the Rotunda. By 1834 they wore a uniform of a blue overcoat with a crimson sash and blue cloth cap with a silver band and tassel.[13]

The standard seasonal charge for promenades and balls was £1 11s 6d. for a family, £1 1s. for a couple and 15s. for an individual, but there were other subscriptions, like a guinea annually for a private key to the pleasure and nursery gardens, which included the extensive lawns, conservatories and three fountains worked by a steam-engine, the largest projecting a jet of water 30 feet high. There were also incidental events, such as concerts, illuminated fétes and galas, the annual charity ball in aid of the Cheltenham Dispensary and Casualty Hospital, and stunts like the ascent in 1837 and 1838 of the Vauxhall Nassau Balloon, so-called because of its record flight of 480 miles from Vauxhall Gardens to the Duchy of Nassau in 1836.

The social life of both the Assembly Rooms and the Rotunda was managed by a committee of public amusements, elected annually first by the company but later by the leading gentlemen residents, though at least by 1829 the summer and winter balls each had their sub-committee. In 1820 Charles Henry Marshall came from Bath to preside as Master of Ceremonies at the Rotunda in the summer and the Assembly Rooms in the winter, and as at Bath he was given a benefit ball at each place. He pleased even the most fastidious and in 1829 was complimented on his courtesy and punctuality. He went in 1837 to be the Master at St Leonards-on-Sea.[14]

To counter Montpellier Spa's luring of custom from the old town, Samuel Bettinson, who had a library in the High Street, developed a similar entertainment. On 29 June 1825 he gave a musical promenade and on 19 July a Grand Concert in his splendidly lighted library and gardens with a firework display and a pianist and lady singer.[15] On the other hand, Charles Duffield and Thomas Henry Weller, who had a Literary Saloon in the High Street, secured the contract from Thompson to promote the evening promenades at the Montpellier Spa.

The other challenge to the older attractions came from Joseph Pitt, of whom it was said in 1812,

> Pitt used to hold gentlemen's horses for a penny, when, appearing a sharp lad, an attorney at Cirencester took a fancy to him and bred him up in his own business. He soon scraped together a little money by his practice in the law and by degrees entered into speculation.

He became a Member of Parliament in 1812 for Cricklade, where he owned half the town's houses, but he was most active in Cheltenham. In 1800 he bought from the Earl of Essex over 100 acres of pasture north of the town, which in 1823 he decided to make the 'new town' of Pittville 'rivalling its parent Cheltenham both in extent and importance'. It was to have 600 houses with a pump-room surrounded by pleasure gardens.

The Pump Room, opened in 1820, was designed by John Forbes and is one of the most imposing in the country, at the end of the Grand Walk which rises by gentle ascent from the lake. Modelled, like the Sherborne Pump Room, on the Temple of Illisus, the entire front and two sides are occupied by a colonnade ornamented at the two corners and above by colossal figures of Aesculapius, Hygeia and Hippocrates and, like the Rotunda, is surmounted by a dome.

Pitt wished the Pump Room to be managed for an annual rent by a lessee drawing his income from selling the waters, charging admission to the gardens and organizing public events. Henry Seymour, formerly

Master of Ceremonies of the Assembly Rooms at Teignmouth, was the first lessee. He interspersed its regular daily activities with special events and attractions. During the season from May to September, patrons took the waters each morning, and throughout the day 'promenaded' in the walks, rides and pleasure grounds. A band played in the mornings and again most afternoons. Subscriptions varied from 5s. for an individual to use the walks for a month, to two guineas for a family to take the waters during the season. Non-subscribers were admitted for 1s. In 1830–40 two or three separately charged special events were held each year at such times as the monarch's birthday or the beginning of the races, usually comprising either a public breakfast followed by a ball or an evening gala fête with a concert and firework display.

Meanwhile the Regent Baths in Regent Street were opened in 1825 to compete with the Montpellier Baths; and in that year also Thomas Billings bought 80 acres of land between the New Baths and Painswick Road for the Park Estate. In the centre of the town, Clarence Parade, Clarence Street and the Clarence Hotel were built, being named after the Duchess of Clarence, who visited in 1827 the principal spas, the Assembly Rooms and Fauconberg House where George III had stayed.[16]

The town's growing population made the old parish church inadequate, especially as since 1794 its pews had become private property. Pitt's plans included a church 'on the elevated ground beyond the spa', but he did not achieve this. His purchase of land brought him the advowson of the parish church which in 1816 he sold to the Simeon Trustees, founded by the Evangelical leader, Charles Simeon, to secure and administer church patronage in accordance with his principles. He announced, 'Cheltenham, where there are 10,000 souls besides 10,000 visitors or nearly so, is mine. It was to be sold for £3,000, and I instantly secured it.'[17]

The Simeon Trustees said they would at once build a proprietory chapel for which capital was raised by selling sittings. Lord Shelborne lent £4,000 and bought 97 of the 137 private pews.[18] Holy Trinity Chapel, designed by G.A. Underwood, an assistant at Sir John Soane's office, was completed in 1823 at the top of Portland Street, then amid fields but adjoining the planned Pittville Estate.[19]

The next two proprietory chapels were designed by Papworth. St John's was built in 1827 at the northern end of Berkeley Street for the fashionable, elegant eastern area along the Upper High Street or London Road. St James's came three years later in the expanding Montpellier district. Thompson was on its building committee, and so was James Fisher, who gave the site on the north-east corner of Suffolk Square, which he was promoting. Ten years later its congregation was described as the most affluent and fashionable in Cheltenham.[20] The pews at both these chapels were secured by paying 1s. at the door.

The three new chapels had a total of about 3,700 seats, but only about 900 free bench-seats in the side aisles. In 1826 Francis Close became Vicar of Cheltenham and erected a free church, St Paul's, for the artisan classes of the Lower High Street area on a field given by Pitt for a nominal £20 and now on St Paul's Road. Forbes designed it in the same classical style as the Pittville Pump Room. Of its 1,600 sittings, 1,230 were free and were all pews and not benches.[21]

Cheltenham's growth also affected transport. By 1825 it had a network of 56 coach services to all major English towns; many went from the new Royal Hotel in the High Street, the leading coaching inn with the Plough and the George. Five coaches left daily for London and three for Malvern, while the Columbia coach ran to the Regent Hotel, Leamington, thrice weekly, so that passengers could spend the day there and return to Cheltenham at night.[22] Rivalry was intense, and in 1825 Haines, Dore and Company started the new independent Alert coach to Bath offering cheaper fares.[23]

Between February and June 1821 Sir Charles Dance pioneered a four-trips-a-day service between Cheltenham and Gloucester with three steam carriages invented by Sir Goldsworthy Gurney. Passengers travelled in omnibus trailers seating 16, accomplishing the nine-mile journey in 50 minutes. The vehicles stank of oiled iron, needed constant stoking with coke and often broke down, but vibrated less than stage-coaches and went up hills better. Moreover, the fares were half those of the coaches, and coke cost 9s. a day compared with 45s. for the horses needed by a daily coach service. But the venture ended when large stones were strewn across the road to a depth of 18 inches, allegedly by coach proprietors, and the Cheltenham Road Bill authorized a heavy toll on steam carriages.[24]

Some residents had their own coaches and horses. Mews were built behind terrace houses as at the Crescent, and there were the Suffolk Mews, St Philip's Mews and the Montpellier Mews with its grand stone arched entry. Building land for detached villas had space for at least one coach-house and stables, like Pulteney Villa in Winchcombe Street. Lake House, an elegant mansion, had two coach-houses and stables to match.[25]

Others relied on livery stables. Newman and Langridge opened the Belvedere Livery Stables in 1818 at the top of Winchcombe Street, and Jones and Ballinger in 1819 took over Robert Ballinger's long-established stables in the High Street.[26] When John Smith acquired Smith's Boarding House in 1814 he engaged a new male cook 'of acknowledged abilities' and supplied customers with horses and provided an elegant barouche and two fashionable chariots with liveried drivers to take them riding. And in 1818 J.D. Kelly, the promoter of the new Assembly Rooms and supporter of the introduction of gas lighting in Cheltenham that year, set up a riding school adjoining the Montpellier Rides.[27]

In 1818 the Town Commissioners controlled street traffic with a regulating bye-law. Sedan-chairs and fly-carriages occupied fixed stands 60 yards apart; donkeys and donkey carts only left their stands after customers' orders; and all fares were fixed. The coming of hackney carriages in 1827 brought complaints that drivers disturbed private houses on the nights of routs and balls and endangered pedestrians. After much opposition, the commissioners eventually issued new bye-laws which included controlling fares for all transport by time and distance which was reckoned from the town's Centre Stone. Other regulations, such as prohibiting butchers or bakers carrying baskets on footpaths, were declared absurd, and justices refused to convict offenders.[28]

In 1808 the commissioners had established a new market in the High Street and leased the market tolls from Lord Sherborne, the lord of the manor, but time made it inadequate. After a new Improvement Act in 1821 they relinquished their rights in the market to him for £500 compensation. He built a larger market opposite the old one, reached by a covered flagway called the Arcade, now Bennington Street, with a range of shops, including Porter's bookshop, on the right and an unroofed space on the left, and it gave on to a spacious square with the market house, 84 by 42 feet, where poultry and eggs were sold. Butchers' shops occupied three sides of the square and greengrocers' stalls the other. This obviated the old street market's inconveniences, and its commerce was hidden behind a Gothic-Oriental screen with three arches which dignified the town's main street, as an illustration of 1850 showed.[29]

Shops slowly spread outwards from the High Street. By 1825 the new Arcade was a shopping centre together with the Promenade Villas where in 1818 Pooley and Smith's drapery store (renamed the Cavendish House in 1839) opened with a staff of eight.[30] There were also some shopkeepers in Well Walk – Mrs Langdon, a milliner and dressmaker, at Norfolk House by 1818 and John Waterfall, a cook and confectioner, at No. 2 in 1824.[31]

The spa engaged hundreds of workers, not only in building and allied trades, but also coachmen, ostlers, carriers, porters, shop assistants, clerks and many domestic servants. In addition, many workers in Cheltenham were engaged in the malting industry and in spinning for the clothiers of Stroud. Its reputation as a fairly lenient poor regime also attracted rural workers to the town. An examination of 653 settlements for 1815–26 shows that 377 came from less than 25 miles; 85 from 25 to 50 miles, the rest from further, a few from Ireland, while the origins of the remainder are uncertain.[32] Many migrants crowded into lodging houses in the lower High Street, and even employed artisans found housing difficult. Most existing building was for upper and middle class visitors, and most terrace houses cost from £1,000 to £3,000. By 1818 the Vestry knew that there were few houses for artisans; but a profitable market existed for 'neat and unadorned dwellings' at about £400.[33]

Domestic servants usually received board and lodging, but their annual wages varied from about £3 to £12 in 1815. A coachman got 14 guineas in 1821, a cook might get 12 guineas, but an ostler had only his board and tips. Later wages seem to have risen through competition for good servants. In 1844 James Agg-Gardner paid John Seller, a footman, £20 with £12 for clothes and 1s. 6d. a week for tea and sugar, and another footman £36 without allowances. Robert Marsh, his coachman, had £25, £15 for clothes and £3 for hats and knee-blacking balls, presumably for his gaiters.[34] Serving women had four to eight guineas.

Some wages fluctuated seasonally – the porter of the Plough Inn in 1822 engaged an assistant for board and lodging and 12s. weekly to be halved in the winter. Servants might settle their employers' bills and receive commission from shopkeepers, who were warned against the practice, and might sell the household 'wash' (mainly vegetable refuse) to pig-keepers, a trade which was reckoned in 1849 to be worth about £2,600 a year from some 1,500 houses and to bring many cooks or housekeepers from 6d. to 1s. a week.[35]

The Michaelmas mop-fairs had traditionally recruited servants for the year, but these were at the end of the Cheltenham season, and since employers now paid monthly or quarterly wages with warning of dismissal, they wanted better ways of selection and training. By 1815 the School of Industry for Girls in the High Street was attempting this, and in 1818 Charles Hayward, a fruiterer and grocer in Chester Walk, opened the Intelligence Office for Servants where they could register for posts.[36] Temporary employment of servants caused problems for visitors, who complained of dishonest servants applying to them with forged references or unmerited 'characters' from previous employers.[37]

Other complaints were about law-breaking and disorder in the town; and from 1815 to 1821 the commissioners tried to police the streets. For four years two high constables and several nightwatchmen were appointed. Then the Improvement Act of 1821 led to the establishment of a permanent watch committee and the division of the town into eight districts, each having a nightwatchman with uniform and equipment provided by the commissioners. Four years later the districts were increased to 12, each with four constables under an experienced commander from London. Finally, when Sir Robert Peel established the Metropolitan Police in 1829, the Cheltenham Commissioners established a similar force in 1831.[38]

Further complaints were made about the roads, especially those on the new estates. Corpus Christi College, Oxford, the owner of most of the property in Devonshire Street and Wilson Street, refused to improve them.[39] A visitor in 1824 asserted that he had not seen a single sweeper on the drives and footways. The hot summer of 1825 led to complaints about the dusty streets, though a William Edmonds was paid to water them twice daily. Leamington readily publicized Cheltenham's uncomfortable, sand-driven streets and condemned the roads to Evesham and Painswick as particularly dangerous.[40] The Improvement Act of 1821 empowered the commissioners to control plans for new buildings and alterations to old ones and to require proprietors to pave and stone new roads when three-quarters of the houses were built, which they compelled them to do in 1828. They could also widen existing roads, and Joseph Pitt managed to get £3,000 from them towards enlarging Portland Passage (later Pittville Street) linking the old town with his projected new spa.[41]

The roads were also badly lit. Some householders put up oil lamps outside on iron posts, and the commissioners put up others along some streets, but these were lit only in the autumn and winter. The proprietors of the new Assembly Rooms secured an Act in 1819 for the formation of a gas company in Cheltenham. The gasworks (which had a tower with a clock face five feet in diameter illuminated at night for the poor inhabitants around the Lower High Street) required over 30 tons of iron pipes, a gasometer and a large quantity of Stourbridge bricks when they were erected in the Tewkesbury Road on a site later called Gas Green.[42] The High Street was first illuminated and Montpellier Parade next, but little beyond there until the mid- century. By 1852 there were 786 public gas lamps and others on private estates.[43]

Water supply was another problem. It 1815 it still depended on wells sunk in sand beds into which sewers often ran, while the springs from the surrounding hills were unused. More water was needed for domestic use, street-watering and fire risks, which were said to be greater in a town with visitors less careful with property than residents. The preamble of an Act in 1825 authorizing a Cheltenham Water Works Company stated it was needed because the town 'has of late years become very populous and is greatly increased in houses and buildings and is likely to increase'. The company constructed a reservoir at Hewletts to tap the springs and piped water to its customers. Five years later it claimed to supply most of the new houses, though the commissioners tried to avoid buying its water by sinking their own wells near the York Hotel and at Sandford and Westhall.[44] In 1841 the town still had two well-sinkers.[45] Sewerage, except for a few ancient drains controlled by the commissioners, depended on open brooks, ditches and private drains until 1833 when another Act produced the Cheltenham Sewers Company, which by 1849 had laid 5,892 yards of sewers linked to 73 houses in 19 streets.[46]

For the growing town, the opening of the Pittville Pump Room in 1830 was a gala event. Visitors came from all over the kingdom, especially from adjoining shires, and from an early hour crowds thronged the streets making for its entrance. There was a marquee holding 500 on the north front and tables everywhere to seat 1,100 for a *déjeuner*.

People greeted this as a sign that the town was now the kingdom's leading watering-place, condemning dismissively its two most fashionable rivals – 'only as a residence . . . Bath is ever mentioned nowadays', despite its prior establishment and continuous fame; and Brighton's reputation depended entirely on past royal patronage. But, despite this seeming height of success, Cheltenham faced grave difficulties. Already there were signs that the days of the Regency spa were passing away.

Fewer people came to take the waters. They went increasingly to English seaside resorts or shared the liking for foreign travel to Continental spas. Those that came adopted the practice of private entertaining which undermined the the Pump Room's social life. And the decline was hastened by Francis Close's extraordinary influence during his 36 years at the parish church. His evangelical principles strongly affected local life. In December 1839, for instance, he founded the Cheltenham Society for the Prevention of the Desecration of the Sabbath, who soon secured the closing of most of the shops previously open on Sundays. 'The power of the Church', wrote W.E. Adams, a local journalist,

> was probably never more remarkably demonstrated anywhere than it was in Cheltenham during many years of the middle of the nineteenth century. As a matter of fact, the history of the town for all that period was the history of a single churchman.[47]

Cheltenham was now at the transitional stage of Tunbridge Wells in the 1740s and Bath in the 1820s, becoming a residential and educational town in which many people valued the churches and schools more than the spa centres. Royal and aristocratic visitors no longer came, and the middle-class inhabitants lacked the old Regency exuberance. Moreover, the town gained newcomers from retired Indian army officers and colonial administrators whom the climate suited. Granville was told that it had many 'spinsters and old maids . . . , widows and half-pay yellows from the Indus and the Ganges, together with lots of Methodists and teetotallers'.

Pittville was in difficulty by 1830, which was perhaps why neither Joseph Pitt nor his son attended the festive opening of the Pump Room. The estate was expected to cost £7,000, but he was said to have already paid £30,000.[48] Its plan of 1826 shows two central gardens with roads and terraces on each side interspersed with villas and two squares named after the Dukes of Clarence and Wellington, and beyond this a garden with the lake and Pump Room in the background. The year before, however, land speculation caused a local financial crisis and interrupted the work, which was never completed. He could not compete with the more fashionable further side of the town.[49] Of the planned 600 houses, only 100 had been built, and not until 1853 were there 505.

Nevertheless Pitt insisted that the estate was to be built as an entity like the Pultney Estate at Bath. All houses had to adhere to approved designs (Neo-Gothic and Tudor Gothic, brick behind stucco fronts and adorned with classical columns) and cost at least £700. Building plots were sold either to people wanting to build their own houses or to builders who bought on mortgage from him. The residential style of the houses befitted the changing times, having two or three storeys and a basement. Householders paid an annual rent of one to ten guineas to maintain pleasure grounds, carriage drives, footpaths and sewers, and each had a key to the railed-in lawns. As in Montpellier Gardens, the gardens were reserved to the owners, who could only admit servants if in charge of their children.[50]

Pitt claimed to have spent £40,000 on Pittville, but when he died in 1842 it was reported to be £500,000. He owed about £150,000, mostly to business associates, and his estate was worth less than £13,000. Among his creditors was his second son, Joseph Pitt the Younger, who became the owner of the Pittville Pump Room.[51]

Pittville was not a lucrative investment, though Henry Seymour continued various attractions such as galas, fêtes and the Pittville Horticultural Association to rival that at the Rotunda. In May 1839 a Grand Temperance Festival was organized with a tea-party in the Pump Room. All, it was said, shared in the pleasure except 'a few votaries of Bacchus' who went to an inn in the High Street. The event was symptomatic of the town's more sober outlook.[52] Pittville was usually little patronized. The Revd F.E. Witts in 1833 found that 'but a few individuals were in the splendid Pump Room'.[53]

The financial crisis of 1825 also struck Pearson Thompson. Few builders bought plots in his Lansdown Estate. In 1830 he leased his entire Montpellier-Lansdown property to two wealthy local architect brothers, Robert and Charles Jearrad, who promptly dismissed Papworth, but to his anger retained his plans without payment and used them, though abandoning his plan for a circular plot like the Circus at Bath and replacing it by the large unusually convex Lansdown Crescent. They did not attempt to make it a spa centre; the houses were designed as both wealthy permanent residences and seasonal lodgings.[54]

The Jearrads also took over in 1834 the Sherborne Spa, which had been bought in 1825 by Colonel Berkeley and Robert Morris, the banker, who renamed it the Imperial Spa and tried to compete with the new spas. They installed a fine new organ and introduced musical promenade concerts and later archery. The local press in 1830 spoke of their 'indefatigable exertions', but these did not succeed, and they were criticized for allowing rubbish to collect on the east side of the bridge over the Chelt leading from the Promenade. The Spa was closed in in 1837, and the Pump Room was demolished and re-erected on vacant ground at the west end of the Promenade where it stood until 1937 when it was demolished and replaced by an ABC cinema.[55]

On the former site of the Sherborne Spa, Robert Jearrad built (as a contemporary said 'this luxurious and straggling resort of fashion) the Queen's Hotel, to an observer 'a very fine building on an immense scale' and to another an 'enormous pile'.[56] Outstanding in the spa towns and among the largest in the country, it was an imposing building in a classical style with a grand portico entrance, more dominating than anything yet created in Cheltenham and inspired by one of the Temples of Jupiter in Rome. The cost was £40,000 exclusive of furnishings, and it comprised a spacious coffee room, billiard rooms, 70 best bedrooms, 30 servants' rooms, 16 elegant sitting-rooms and three suites of apartments. Yet it had an uncertain start: in June 1841 it employed 27 indoor servants and four in the stable, but only 45 guests were in residence.[57]

The proprietors of the Old Well also made 'considerable improvements' in 1829. The rear of the Pump Room was converted into a spacious front, a new carriageway enabled visitors to drive up to the well, and footpaths were laid with flowering shrubs and luxuriant evergreens. Two pairs of gates with wrought-iron gateposts which were erected, topped with a ball surmounted by a pigeon commemorating the origin of the Old Well, probably belong to this time. Merrett's map of 1834 shows one pair on the west of the Old Well Lane (Montpellier Street) and the other where St George's Road now runs. Two of these historic gates exist in a country road at the Crippets.[58]

In the 1829 season, special events besides concerts and balls were held. During the Cheltenham Gold Cup Races in July the Old Well Walk was lighted with gas through a specially laid pipe; in August a gala night was claimed to attract 1,100 fashionable dancers under the variegated lamps, who watched a large fire balloon let off; but in September a 'very excellent picnic lunch' was drenched by a downpour. In the following years, however, support declined, and by August 1838, when the centenary of the spa's foundation was celebrated with a public breakfast in the morning, the planting of a commemorative oak in the afternoon and a well-attended evening fête, its days were numbered.[59]

In 1837 its site was part of the property bought from William Nash Skillicorne, the great-grandson of the original founder of the Cheltenham Spa, by the newly formed Bayshill Estate Company in which Henry Norwood Trye of Leckhampton Court was prominent. Before the sale, Skillicorne engaged Arthur Parker, a London architect and house agent, to plan an ambitious estate there. It was to form a rough triangle with the Old Well Walk as its base and a Royal Circus (imitating Bath and reminiscent of Papworth's circular plot) as its apex and having a circular observatory with a rotunda.[60] Work began with building classical-style residences 'of a superior grade' in ranges of crescents, parades, squares and detached villas. But the company had insufficent resources; it abandoned the plan of 1837 including the Royal Circus and by 1848 was bankrupt with 110 unsold lots of building land.[61]

The last attempt to establish another independent estate had more success than the others. This was the Park, an area of 100 acres laid out in 1833 by its owner, Thomas Billings, as a central park enclosed by an oval tree-lined carriage drive; and in May 1837 the Gloucestershire Zoological, Botanical and Horticultural Society was formed with a share capital of £10,000 to form gardens in the Park. Its chairman was Trye, now recalled by nearby Trye's Road. By the autumn the grand promenade was under construction, the northern boundary wall built and an entrance lodge, designed by Samuel Whitfield Daukes, a Gloucester builder and architect, finished. This again was a subscription venture with the usual entrance fees – £1 1s. for an individual, £1 11s 6d. for two of the same family and £2 2s. for a family group.

The gardens were designedly opened on 28 June 1838, Queen Victoria's coronation day, with the now conventional floral and horticultural exhibition and fireworks; but by then the Company was in financial difficulties. Daukes bought it out in 1839 and made the gardens into a pleasure park with flower-beds round a lake and grounds for cricket and archery. The houses, still in Cheltenham's neo-Greek style, were probably mostly finished by then.[62]

By now it was increasingly realized that Cheltenham's future lay with its residents. There was a demand to maintain the public amusements to attract strangers, who would like society there and decide to remain. 'The staple commodity of Cheltenham is pleasure,' it was urged in 1839, and unless promoters of estates, owners of property, tradesmen and others sustained its public amusements, the beautiful town would sink as rapidly as it rose, and grass would soon grow in the streets.[63] The maintenance of the winter season was considered important to encourage a more settled population and compete with Bath, Brighton and Leamington. So from November 1837 the Rotunda, famed for its summer promenades, initiated winter afternoon promenades with the band playing from 2.30 to 4.30 'after the fashion of the Pump Room, Bath'. It and adjoining rooms were kept closed with fires to make them warm and comfortable.[64] At the Assembly Rooms the winter balls began in late November, but were fortnightly now, not weekly, in the hope of a better attendance and avoiding conflict with private parties. But these efforts made a loss; and in 1838 the Easter Monday balls in the Assembly Rooms were so thinly attended that they were abandoned the next month.

The town also faced competition from two other West Midland spas – Leamington and Malvern. Coaches linked Cheltenham with both these rivals; Leamington publicized Cheltenham's disadvantages, asserting that no boring could provide it with enough mineral water; and Malvern property was advertised in the Cheltenham press.[64] Cheltenham knew too about the growing threat from seaside resorts and foreign spas. The *Cheltenham Journal* observed how the town's promoters 'strain every nerve to merit approbation . . . while foreigners should have their pockets filled for the price of a song'.[65] The Duke and Duchess of Beaufort, whose Badminton seat was near Cheltenham, visited Wiesbaden and other German spas in 1839.[66] And the increasing provision of municipal baths assisted the decline of mineral-water bathing. Bathing, said the *Cheltenham Journal* in 1830, had become the prevailing luxury, and many towns now had warm and tepid baths.[67]

By 1841 Cheltenham's expansion was clearly slower. The number of houses built in the Cheltenham Union in 1801–21 was 1,701, which almost trebled in 1821–41 to 4,954, but while 119 were built in 1821, 297 in 1824, 653 in 1825 and 774 in 1826, it was only 159 in 1841, when there were at least 647 empty houses,and many districts built none. Like Bath earlier, Cheltenham was now overbuilt.[68]

Meanwhile Francis Close's influence was increasing. It was epitomized by his struggle with Colonel Berkeley in which the new evangelical morality opposed Whig and post-Regency liberality. Close began by attacking the Cheltenham Races and their on-course amusements. In 1827 he preached a sermon 'On the Evil Consequences of Attending the Racecourse', which was printed as a tract and sold many editions. He did not secure the end of the Races, but the associated fair was strictly purged. In May 1839 the Theatre Royal was burnt down. Like other theatres in spa towns, it had faced difficulties, but Berkeley supported it, brought professional players there and sometimes acted himself. Close prevented the opening of a new regular theatre while he was in the town.[69]

Not that his efforts in the 'Close Borough' were entirely negative.[70] Besides St Paul's, he established four new churches in the town. The first and largest was Christ Church, designed by the Jearrads and consecrated in 1840 for the Lansdown and Bayhill Estates and the poor of Alstone parish. With 2,075 seats, 485 of them free, it was financed by 160 proprietory shares at £105 each, together with subscriptions and donations at a total cost of £18,111 15s 7d.[71] St Philip's, consecrated in 1844 on a site in Leckhampton given by Trye, served the Park Estate. St Peter's, designed by Daukes in neo-Norman style and consecrated in 1849, had 1,050 seats, including 700 free, and cost £4,651 in the area south of the Tewkesbury Road which was so poor that respectable people feared to live there, and for several years the Sunday morning congregation was sparse.[72] Lastly, St Luke's, consecrated in 1854, served the fashionable Sandford district, which had a poor area also. It cost £5,397, raised only by public offerings, and seated 1,040. Half the seats were free, but pew rents for the rest paid the curate.[73]

Close appointed the incumbents to these churches, so strengthening evangelicalism in the town. *The Illustrated Cheltenham Guide* of 1845 stated, 'Theology has now become so necessary as part of polite education,' and a Scottish visitor wrote in 1837, 'The Sabbath is better kept in Cheltenham than anywhere else in Britain.' The religious census of 1851 reported that the town was better provided with churches than most British places.[74] Shortly before his death, Simeon visited Cheltenham in 1836 and commented, 'Truly at Cheltenham I had almost a heaven upon earth.'[75] However, the *Cheltenham Journal* in 1829 thought, 'The godly odour of religious sanctity has made a sad inroad upon our former propensities.'[76]

Close aimed also to provide education for all classes in Cheltenham. For the education of the poor, he did not want the church schools of the National Society, but between 1827 and 1848 founded six infant schools administered by a committee under his chairmanship. They gave children an elementary education with evangelical religious instruction – 'We teach them the necessity of being "born again", that they may become God's dear children by adoption and grace and walk in newness of life.'[77] He sought support from spa attenders, examining the children publicly in the Montpellier Rotunda as described by the *Cheltenham Journal* in June 1829:

The company were numerous and highly respectable, and the children, about 150 in number, performed their evolutions in such a way as to give general satisfaction. After they had marched round to their various lessons at their lesson posts and had sung a few tunes, they were marched into a temporary gallery erected for the purpose and having been . . . examined as to their knowledge of the Scriptures by our worthy incumbent, Mr.Close, they were marched into the adjacent grounds, the master playing the clarinet at the head of them, to which they kept step and sang in admirable time and tune.'[78]

To acquire suitable teachers, Close founded in 1849 two training colleges – St Paul's for men and St Mary's for women. These provided for his schools and then gained a national reputation, attracting evangelical students from elsewhere and giving the town fresh transitory inhabitants, young men and women who studied there and did their teaching practice in its schools and in nearby villages.

Close's greatest contribution to Cheltenham's reputation as an educational centre was the establishment of the two schools for the town's new classes. Cheltenham College, founded in 1841 with a majority of day-boys, declared in its charter that 'only gentlemen' could be shareholders, but stated 'no retail trader being under any circumstances considered' so that professional and business classes were included. The school was immediately successful, appealing to those classes because the evangelical teaching placed more emphasis on Divinity than on the Classics and taught modern subjects, which were desirable now that entry into the army and civil service was by public competition.[79]

Cheltenham Ladies' College, founded in 1853 to give a 'first-rate education to the daughters and young children of noblemen and gentlemen', was in all senses to be the school to replace the old spa life. It also had a liberal curriculum, which was even more unusual in a girls' school. The subjects taught were 'Holy Scripture and the Liturgy of the Church of England, the Principles of Grammar, the elements of Latin, Arithmetic, Calesthenic Exercises, Drawing, French, Geography, History, Music and Needlework.' For German, Italian and Dancing there was an extra fee.[80]

Close also revived two existing schools. The first was the tiny old Charity School which he moved in 1847 from the loft of the north porch of the parish church to new buildings in Devonshire Street, where its numbers rose to 150 in three years. The second was the Grammar School, maintained by Corpus Christi College, Oxford, from the chantry revenues of the parish church given to it for that purpose by Richard Pate, a wealthy Elizabethan tobacco-grower. Despite a great increase in its endowment, its building in the High Street was now decayed, it had only 34 pupils, and the master's salary was inadequate. Pressure on the fellows of the College secured the school's removal to new buildings in

1852 with a revised constitution. Four years later it too had 150 pupils and as long a waiting list.[81]

Preaching in 1841, Close said, 'The Bible is conservative, the Prayer Book conservative, and it is impossible for a minister to open his mouth without being conservative.'[82] And his and the clergy's political influence aggravated local political dissension.[83] The commissioners could not provide adequate public services. Gloucester had to send extra engines for serious fires.[84] Sewage from the Pittville Estate discharged into Wyman's Brook and from the Park Estate into Hatherley Brook.[85] The commissioners needed more money, especially as much new property in the estates was not assessed for rates. A new Improvement Bill sought in the spirit of the Municipal Corporations Act to give wealthier ratepayers some administrative power through elected commissioners, but it was defeated by an alliance of Liberals and Radicals with Joseph Pitt and Thomas Billings.[86] The Reform Act of 1832 made Cheltenham a parliamentary borough with one member, the first being Colonel Berkeley's brother, Craven Fitzhardinge Berkeley; but this Liberal victory did not satisfy the Radicals, who in 1834 founded their *Free Press* and a Mechanics Institute in Albion Street for political discussions;[87] and by 1840 the tradesmen's assistants, some 120 in number, had an evening-room with a library.[88] In 1839 the Chartists held a meeting in the Riding School in Regent Street and demonstrated in the parish church, to Close's indignation. Such local unrest harmed Cheltenham's appeal to visitors.

Education and a residential population slowly affected Cheltenham. As late as 1849 the Board of Health Inspector observed, 'There are no manufactures, and the great mass of the inhabitants depend upon the influx of visitors for their employment and support.'[89] Even the long-based brewing industry employed only 55 men (including five journeymen) and 18 malsters. It was still a consumer society living on the provision of quality market goods and services, a social centre in a rural setting. The Census of 1841 showed it had a workforce of 13,184 (including assistants, journeymen and apprentices) forming 38.39 per cent of a total population of 34,338.

Cheltenham's fringes were still agricultural. Farming and allied occupations (six cattle-dealers, five horse-dealers, 13 millers and others) composed 3.5 per cent of the workforce. The 71 farmers and 352 agricultural labourers were mainly in rural communities among the small craftsmen and labourers of Charlton Kings and around the hamlets of Westhall and Benhall, Arle with Arle Court, Alstone with its mill and the Cold Bath Cottages, a reminder of the now defunct Alestone Spa. Many gardeners in Alstone worked for the Jessop brothers living in James Villa and Jessop Lodge.

The 4,931 servants formed most of the workforce, though it included 273 gardeners, many of whom were engaged in market gardening and not private service. Many households had one male to two, three or four female servants; there were 3,565 female and 900 male servants. Including gardeners, there were 460 others of specified occupations, among them 95 charwomen, 41 housekeepers, 26 grooms and 19 cooks. About 769 households had living-in servants and only six had nine servants or more, the largest being in Charlton Kings – Moorend House with 12 and Charlton Park with 10. A minority, 23 households, had seven or more; 21 (mostly on the Lansdown Estate and in the Promenade and Imperial Square) had six; 22.8 per cent had four or five, mostly four; and 71.8 per cent had two or three.[90]

Next came the shopkeepers, traders and distributors of goods at 11.8 per cent. Of the 1,558 traders, 662 were in the food trade, the largest groups being 139 bakers, 132 butchers and 107 grocers. Luxury trades included 24 confectioners and 22 wine and porter merchants. There were 15 fishmongers, 34 greengrocers and 15 tea-dealers. The 390 laundresses were scattered throughout the town but especially in the outlying districts of Charlton Kings and the Tewkesbury Road where there was space to dry washing. Of the other traders, the 43 chemists and druggists were the largest group with 38 coal merchants next. There were 45 hawkers and 2 hucksters, together with 44 migrant commercial travellers. Transport directly employed 233 servants or about 8 per cent of the labour force, some probably being private servants. They included 52 coachmen, 32 chairmen, 26 grooms, four fly-proprietors, 16 flymen and six wheelchairmen. There were also 31 wheelwrights and 91 blacksmiths (who partly served agriculture), besides 18 hauliers and 10 wagoners.

Clothes and fashions (except boots and shoes) was the third largest group at 9.9 per cent, comprising 57 bonnet-makers, 499 dressmakers, 299 tailors and 118 milliners. In Imperial Mews, Alexander Shirer, a mercer and draper with seven female and twelve male assistants and three female servants, had already established the firm later called Shirer and Haddon; and Clement Freebody, silk merchant, managed Cavendish House with two female and seven male assistants, an apprentice and a male and female servant.[91]

Small craftsmen at 9.7 per cent came fourth. There were still a significant number of curriers, saddlers and coopers, but also tinsmiths and 22 jewellers, six of them Jews in Pittville Street. Many small craftsmen lived in Bath Street, but the wealthier, generally with two or three servants, were in Painswick Lawn, Painswick Terrace, Andover Street and Andover Terrace. Sam Martin, jeweller and silversmith, the name of whose shop endures, was in business with his father and brother in Imperial Mews.

Building and construction workers at 9.33 per cent were fifth comprising 357 carpenters, 173 plasterers, 147 painters, 79 builders (including journeymen), 108 bricklayers and 35 brickmakers. Many lived in the Lower High Street, while Samuel Olney lived in Hewlett Street. Sixth at 8.6 per cent were 841 labourers, 112 porters, 95 charwomen, 46 washerwomen and 19 sweeps. On the town's edge along the Tewkesbury Road were 200 or 300 unskilled labourers, others in Stanhope Street and Swindon Street and many Irish in Milsom Street. Journeymen lived at both ends of the town, including Queen Street and Fairview Place.

Professional men comprised 5.5 per cent including, besides accountants, attorneys, bankers, brokers and nurses, 19 physicians and 37 surgeons; Imperial Square had seven physicians and five surgeons. The 95 retired army and 36 navy officers were forerunners of others to come. On the eve of Cheltenham College's foundation, there were 167 teachers, including professors of music and languages, and 23 schools, such as Alstone Villa, Painswick Lawn House and Newfount House. All but one had boarders, and they averaged 11 pupils each; the largest, Bayshill House, had 32.

Entertainment and hospitality comprised 3.4 per cent, which included those engaged in transport. There were seven hotel-keepers, 31 innkeepers and 49 publicans; 28 musicians; and six letter-bearers. Ninth in order at 5 per cent were local and public officials, including the chief constable and 11 police officers, the collectors of taxes, excise and tolls, the parish clerk, the town crier and the sexton. In the year after the introduction of penny postage, the Post Office at 127 High Street employed 22 postmen.[92]

Perhaps nothing did more than the railway to end Cheltenham's era as a seasonal spa. When the Great Western Railway Company planned in 1835 a line from London to Bristol, a local company, the Great Western Union, was formed to construct, in conjunction with the Birmingham and Gloucester Railway Company, a line from Cheltenham by way of Gloucester, Stonehouse, Stroud and Kemble to join the Great Western line at Swindon. Close opposed the idea of the railway – 'the bubbling, hissing, roaring, bellowing monster coming within a few yards of our Parish Church and interrupting our devotions'.[93] And the decision in 1839 to build the station at Lansdown caused controversy. A petition with 600 signatures declared it was to benefit the Lansdown Estate, where a new town would arise, while the High Street and nearby streets would decline into rows of decaying and tenantless houses.[94]

Nevertheless, the station was built there; and in July 1839 the first locomotive was drawn to it along the High Street on a specially prepared lorry drawn by 12 horses. The first passenger train left the station on 23 June 1840 and reached Bromsgrove in an hour and 40 minutes.

Five trains initially ran daily to Birmingham; the first class fare was 11s. 6d., second class 8s. and third class 5s. Close succeeded in banning Sunday trains, and until the Railway Act of 1846 enforced the running of some passenger trains by all lines on Sundays, Cheltenham was the only town in the country to have trains solely on weekdays.

The railway affected the coaches at once. By late July 1840 only one still ran between Cheltenham and Birmingham. The Royal Coach Office reduced fares to Leamington, Bristol and Bath and ran omnibuses, calling also at the Lamb, to Lansdown Station for 6d. each person without luggage and 1s. with luggage.[95]

The local railway company, however, made heavy losses and was finally taken over by the Great Western Railway, which was building a line to Cheltenham with a station at St James's Square on a part of Jessop's Gardens. By a working agreement with the Cheltenham and Gloucester Railway, it connected this with the line to Lansdown Station at a point near the High Street in 1847, and as the Swindon route to Gloucester had been completed in 1845, Cheltenham was now connected by rail with Birmingham, Bristol and London.[96]

The growing railway network with its cheap fares meant that Cheltenham was affected by the new mass travel undertaken by the middle and working classes. Within a few years all the coaches had disappeared from its streets, and the inn yards were quiet, although some private carriages and phaetons were maintained. The George, so long the centre of the flourishing coaching trade, went out of business and was taken over as an auction house by Messrs Engall and Sanders. The railway brought visitors to Cheltenham, but took more instead to the growing seaside resorts whose rapid development they brought about.

4

Bath

William Charles Macready recalled Bath as he knew it when he acted at its Theatre Royal in 1814 and 1815:

> Each day a little after noon the Pump Room ... was literally crammed full with its throng of idlers .... At about three o'clock the pavement of Milsom Street would be so crowded with gaily-dressed people and the drive so blocked with carriages that it was difficult to get along .... The Lower Crescent was a Sunday promenade between morning and afternoon service, presenting the same confluence of visitors.[1]

Another visitor was Fanny Burney (Madame D'Arblay), who in 1815 retired to Bath for the rest of her life. Her impression did not give so prosperous a picture. She wrote in her diary on 29 November 1815, 'This place, with regard to superfine visitors, fills slowly, and the season is expected, not only to be late, but thin of company, from the many families that are rambling abroad.'[2]

During the wars against France, Bath had gained as a residential place from its inland situation away from possible hostile attack. It was now one of the kingdom's 12 largest towns with a population of 38,000 in 1811. But its economy still depended almost entirely on its recreational attractions. When peace came in 1815, the Corporation, Improvement Commissioners and local businessmen hoped for prosperity, but declining receipts from the baths showed the competition it was meeting from the newer spas, notably Leamington and Cheltenham, besides the revival of foreign travel.

In 1815 the Lower Rooms, under Francis John Guynette, Master of Ceremonies since 1811, attracted some 350 patrons to a ball in February

54

and 400 in March. They were significantly called 'residents and visitors', the residents being placed first; and the dancing, formerly ending
at 11 p.m., now lasted until 1 a.m. and was followed by an elegant
banquet. Yet the tenant, J.T. Finegan, made a loss, and the subscribers
held a benefit ball in May to help him and recognize his 'general meri-
torious conduct'. Since Guynette was partly blamed for the situation, it
was conducted by James Heaviside, who had been Master of Ceremonies at Leamington for a season. His dignified and polished manners
added to the evening's pleasure, but he then returned to Leamington,
and another ball was held in Race Week without him.[3]

In October Finegan announced his winter programme of 24 balls
costing £1 5s. for three nights, though he lacked a Master of Ceremonies. Later that month the subscribers unanimously chose Heaviside,
who was surprisingly allowed to retain his Leamington post as well. A
committee of eight was set up to manage the balls, and the rooms were
renamed the Kingston Assembly Rooms. Heaviside presided at the first
ball on 21 November, but now his performance was criticized, and in
December a subscribers' meeting resolved to place the Rooms 'under
express and determinate laws'.[4]

Finegan now tried to make the Rooms provide for both the old
active, past pleasures and the new intellectual, sedentary recreations
of the middle-class residents. These included a series of philosophical
experiments by a Mr Jonas, who had performed at Brighton, Cheltenham and elsewhere.[5] Early in January 1816 Heaviside advertised a
dress ball every Tuesday at the Rooms, but the next week the proprietors revealed that the trusted and lauded Finegan had defaulted
with a considerable sum of money. One member of the Ball Com-
mitte, the Revd James Haviland, resigned, but the others resolved to
maintain its activities, even at much personal loss. Yet for the next
half year the only events in the Rooms were Heaviside's two benefit
balls in February and April and six concerts by the Harmonic
Society.

That autumn a new tenant was found, William Mills, who lavishly
fitted up reading and card rooms for the season beginning on 1 October
when he planned to hold 30 balls, but success eluded him. The Rooms
were now let and only occasional balls held. Intrigues accompanied
financial failure. Haviland led attempts to dismiss Heaviside, who managed, however, to move to the Upper Rooms in 1817. He was succeeded
by Captain C.H. Marshall, who was popular in the town, but went to
Cheltenham in 1820.[6]

His successor, Lewis P. Madden, had a short period of office. It ended
abruptly on the night of 21 December 1820. The lessee of the Rooms,
an oil-merchant, had stored 4,000 gallons of lamp-oil in the cellars,

which caught fire, consuming the entire premises in such a huge blaze that, from the end of the North Parade, 'the surrounding hills seemed tinged with red', and the whole city appeared to be 'involved in one common destruction'.[7] The Rooms were not rebuilt, and Madden became Master of Ceremonies at Tunbridge Wells.

During these years also, the former glory of the Upper Rooms was fading equally rapidly. When Heaviside became Master of Ceremonies there, he had to relinquish his post at Leamington. He failed to arrest their decline, but his efforts were appreciated. When he retired in 1835, he received 'adequate compensation', and in 1837 his portrait by Thomas Shaw of Grosvenor Buildings was hung in the Octagon Room of the Upper Rooms to join those of Nash and other previous Masters of Ceremony. It was declared to be 'a very pleasing likeness' of a gentleman who had served Bath 'without one instance of reproach or censure from the Ball Committee and so deserved this mark of respect and distinction'.[8]

The site of the destroyed Kingston Assembly Rooms belonged to Lord Manvers, who replaced them by a building which he leased to the Royal Literary and Scientific Institution, founded in 1825 for local men of letters, antiquarians an empiricists, which typified the sober, serious organizations now being formed in the town. Another, established a year later, was the Anacreontic Society for the literary-minded, which was supported by two local minor Romantic poets, William Lisle Bowles and Thomas Moore.

Powerfully rivalling the Assembly Rooms were the Sydney Gardens, established by James Gale, a haberdasher, in 1795 and styled the 'Vauxhall of Bath'. Its delights included groves, pleasant vistas, serpentine walks, waterfalls, pavilions, two elegant cast-iron bridges and a sham castle; and the Kennet and Avon Canal was cut through it in 1810. It was essentially a summer pleasure ground, but sometimes it was open until Christmas. Subscribers paid 4s. a month or 10s. a season for admission. Its activities, which continued during the war and later, included public breakfasts, illuminations, promenades and music for which subscribers paid 7s. 6d. a head or 5s. each member of a family. On the four or five gala nights, which attracted 3,000 to 4,000 people, 5,000 lamps were lit. There were also special events such as the public breakfast under the patronage of Countess Manvers to honour Princess Charlotte's marriage on 2 May 1816.[9]

Sydney House, built to provide a suite of public rooms for the Gardens, was by now a lodging house. In 1820 it was advertised as having 'apartments replete with every accommodation as a Family Hotel'. And its south-east corner basement was a tavern for coachmen and chairmen, who were excluded from the Gardens.[10] During this period's craze for hydropathy, the Sydney Hotel (as it was then called) was for several seasons a water-cure establishment.[11]

For the summer season of 1825 the Gardens were replanted and the ride was macadamized, the cascade was removed and an elegant theatre erected which, together with the Hermit's Cot, the water-mill and cosmoramas, was painted by an eminent artist. The Gardens were popular as a pleasure resort until the mid-nineteenth century, when attendance fell badly except at the occasional balloon ascent.

Another sign of changing times came in 1830 when 10 acres of newly formed 'pleasure grounds' were completed and, with the Duchess of Kent's permission – she was then in Bath with her daughter – named the 'Royal Victoria Park'. This, unlike the Sydney Gardens, did not imitate the London pleasure gardens such as Ranelagh and Vauxhall. The grounds were entirely open to the air and without organized entertainments, which were less popular. William Winstone of Gloucestershire wrote from Bath in January 1815 recognizing this, 'Bath still continues to be less abundant in company, particularly of the superior orders, than this advance of season usually promises and the public amusements much neglected.'[12]

Even the sedan-chairs, so important in Nash's time, had all vanished from Bath's streets by the late 1830s to be replaced by hackney carriages and bath-chairs, suited for the larger number of elderly gentlefolk in the town. The Mayor and magistrates sanctioned 50 hackney carriages on the streets, their drivers in blue frock coats and black-glazed hats with each carriage's number painted in white on the front of the hat.[13]

These changes brought a fall in the revenues from the pump-rooms and baths, causing the Corporation continual concern. In 1816 it reduced from £840 to £630 the rent paid by the widowed pumper, Mary Needes, on account of this 'considerable diminution', and allowed her to exhibit pictures and works of art in the Pump Room, but she had to permit a person to drink a single glass of water free of charge. By July next year she again pleaded losses and had half her rent repaid. In September 1818 the next pumper, Mrs Russell, failed in a similar attempt for a half year's reduction of rent;[14] but the same request by her successor, Mrs. Barnes in September 1820 was taken seriously. A committee was set up to examine her letters and accounts, and she recived £100 compensation because of her 'ill success at the pumps', but she was still in arrears by February 1821. Her rent was reduced to £500, but she had to pay the arrears.[15]

A crisis occurred in 1823. In June Sarah Lansdown, a widow, became the pumper at a rent of £500, but by August was in arrears. The committee considered leasing the pumps by auction, but eventually decided to place them under the management of the Mayor, two others and all the physicians on the Corporation. A new scale was fixed at 5s. weekly for each person drinking the water or £2 2s. a year, and no fees or gratuities were to be paid to the pumpers employed by the Corporation. Mrs Lansdown was excused all arrears if she at once quitted the pumps.[16]

The Corporation's direct control of the pumps brought only a brief revival. The Cross Bath Pump Room Subscription Book from the beginning of the new arrangement on 30 September 1823 to the end of December 1829 survives (see Appendix 2) and shows only 29 drinkers during the last four months of 1823, but 59 for the same period in 1824.[17] The total number of drinkers in 1824 was 132, which fell to 105 in 1825 including only 36 in the autumn season from September to December; but 1826 produced 189 visits, of which 36 were in February alone, the highest single monthly figure in the book.[18] In August additional dressing-rooms at the Queen's Bath were planned, costing £200; but trade at the Cross Bath then steadily declined to 148 visits in 1827, 138 in 1828 and 106 in 1829. The period's figures confirm that the busiest time for each year was October to December and February to April; there was normally a drop in May, and the slackest time was June to August.[19]

As part of its general programme of improvements in 1829 the Corporation ordered in March the repairing and painting of the Pump Room, but in April was dismayed when the committee reported how expensive this would be and ordered it to consider leasing all the premises; but it decided on continued corporation management and stricter control of the baths' attendants, with dismissal for seeking gratuities, and all proceeds of the public and private baths were to go to the corporation. Three superannuated attendants were granted a life pension of 7s. a week.[20] Prices for bathing were further reduced; private baths now cost the same as the Kingston Baths fom 1810 – 2s. 6d. instead of 3s., and a £1 subscription paid for 10 baths. Two children under 12 of the same family sharing a bath counted as one person. The Park and Montpellier Gardens in Cheltenham at this time had similar family terms when more of the respectable middle classes were coming to spas in family groups.[21]

The Corporation planned also to extend and improve the baths to make them more attractive. Decimus Burton, the architect currently engaged in the Calverley development at Tunbridge Wells, was approached, and suggested reconstructing the Hot Bath with a new reservoir and adding a tepid swimming-bath. This plan, for which he was paid £84 was accepted and executed by George P. Manners, the town architect, in 1830. The old Tepid Swimming Bath, as it was called, was of classic design: the bath was contained in a lofty hall with eight large dressing-rooms and fireplaces along one side. It was all demolished in 1922–23.[22]

Also in 1830 improvements were made to the bar and font in the Great Pump Room for which, together with work at the markets and some debts, the Corporation borrowed £6,000 in July. And the next year it sanctioned the purchase of a new steam-engine for the Hot Bath such as three years earlier Lockwood in Yorkshire had installed to pump the water to its baths.[23]

The baths committee still lurched from crisis to crisis. In September 1829 it again considered leasing the baths, but only the Pump Room was let, and the Corporation still managed the baths. In December yet another remedy was adopted to meet the Cross Bath Pump Room's serious excess of expenses over receipts. All drinking there was discontinued, and water was pumped instead to the Hemming Pump Room where it was drunk at the bar. The Cross Bath Room was to be used for reclining, as were other baths yet to be built.[24]

In addition there were for about 10 years from 1825, attempts to preserve the life of the lower town where, it was said, some invalids preferred to take lodgings, especially in the summer. In May 1825 a meeting of householders in North and South Parades, Pierrepont Street and Duke Street discussed the laying-out of the ground still called the Bowling Green.[25] That year saw also the construction of the Corridor, a covered street of 20 shops, adorned with gold lion-heads, wreaths and a music gallery, to link the two parts of the old city with a direct passage between the market place and Union Street. Two 'ruinous and unsightly houses' in front of the Guildhall were removed to make way for this street, advertised as similar to London's Burlington Arcade and Cheltenham's Arcade of 1823. By May 1825 the terms for its shops were announced, and some were taken by September, but the gates were kept closed until 12 October when the street was opened as 'as popular resort and a fashionable lounge'.[26]

Also in 1825 the Corporation appointed a 'committee for improvements to the Abbey' as its precincts were congested with buildings, some erected against the church walls with dangerous chimneys in the buttresses which caused a threatening fire that October. Property was acquired for demolition by not renewing leases and by buying 'miserable buildings' often at considerable expense.[27] Lord Manvers owned buildings on the south side of the church and only agreed to their removal after a meeting with the Mayor and Town Clerk in July 1834, and the Corporation removed an accumulation of earth there.[28]

Both the Corporation and property owners had a vested interest in resurrecting the lower town's life, and both supported the erection of two bridges to ease the flow of traffic. The growing Bathwick development, reached only from the lower town by a circuitous route or an inconvenient ferry, was linked to the populous Walcoat district by the Bathwick New Bridge in 1827; Lord Darlington met much of the cost as it served his extensive property in Bathwick New Town. On the opening day the Oxford mail and a huge retinue of carriages passed over it.[29] Since about 1816 there had been pressure for a similar connection between the Parades, which suffered from decline and neglect, and Bathwick. After property owners in St James's parish presented a memorial to Lord Manvers urging better communication between the Parades and High Street in one direction and to Bathwick in the other, a committee of proprietors and shareholders promoted the North Parade Bridge, which opened on 9 November 1836, the 'grand finish', as it was described, to the improvements in the lower part of the town.[30]

There were further clearances in the 1820s – in Kingsmead Square, along the Widcombe Side of Old Bridge, 'the wretched pile called Atwood's Passage' off Horse Street and the east and west side of Walcot Street.[31] Residential houses, sometimes set back from the road, were commonly erected in these places, but there was some accommodation for visitors, such as the Lamb Inn in Stall Street, newly erected in 1825 with 37 bedrooms and stabling and coach-houses.[32]

The revival of the lower town encouraged the cultural organizations there. The Royal Literary and Scientific Institution, enjoying a moderate rent for 25 years from Lord Manvers, was well supported, though its membership subscription was as high as 10 guineas.[33] Other organizations were the Mechanics Institute started in 1825 in 20 Westgate Street, which had a reading room with a 'fairly good' collection of books and in 1841 moved to the Orange Grove under the new name of the Athenaeum; and the Horticultural and Floral Society of 1834 to which the Corporation granted £20.[34]

To add to the town's prestige, the Guildhall was refurbished. In 1826 the council room had a new set of tables and chairs; and in 1829, together with the banqueting chamber and other rooms on the same floor and the staircase, it was restored and painted. The chandeliers were renewed in the banqueting chamber, which received a Brussels carpet, curtains and some new furniture; and the council room had new curtains, and the large folding screens were restored.

These improvements formed the background to the visits of two princesses to the town. In August 1827 the Duchess of Clarence, the wife of the future King William IV, came there after her enthusiatic reception at Cheltenham. She was given a cold collation at the Guildhall; and when she became Queen in 1830 she was sent a loyal address, but she never came there again. And when the Duchess of Kent came with her ten-year-old daughter, Princess Victoria, in October 1830, they were similarly entertained by the Mayor, but the only time Queen Victoria came to the town was in 1899 when her train passed through without stopping on the way to Bristol.[35] It failed to gain renewed royal patronage.

The Royal Victoria Park of 1830, laid out south and west of the Royal Crescent, was the reminder of her sole visit. The Orange Grove in the lower town with its gravelled walks and fixed benches was too limited an area to meet the prevalent demand for walks and rides, so, in the hope of rivalling the contemporary Pittville Park in Cheltenham and attracting summer as well as winter visitors, these 46 acres of the new town were now landscaped into a park, which replaced the old, neglected subscription walk and was planted with 25,000 forest trees, evergreens and shrubs. A drive 2,000 yards long was formed together with gravel walks of greater extent. This development employed 200 labourers whose wages cost £2,614.[36]

Though the rate of increase of Bath's population was slower from 1821, it grew from 33,196 (including Walcot, Bathwick, Lyncombe and Widcombe) in 1801 to 53,209 in 1841, that is by 37.6 per cent. Such expansion prompted an enormous programme of church building as in contemporary Cheltenham. In 1820–25 eleven churches were built or largely rebuilt for Bath and its overspill population at Weston, not including St Mary's, Raby Place, at Bathwick, completed in 1820, nor the Thomas Street Chapel of 1830.[37]

Despite Bath's spa trade uncertainties, these years also saw various small initiatives in resort facilities. A Mr Blackwin, in an interesting, belated and unsuccessful attempt to mount a periphery spa at Larkhill, erected his Bladud Spa in 1835. It comprised a dwelling-house and pump-room 28 feet by 18 feet with two bathing and dressing rooms, adjoining two cottages and an archery ground in the village of Lower Swainswick where a mineral spring had been discovered on land which he leased from St John's Hospital. He offered furnished lodgings at his house and claimed to have over 400 subscribers and the support of Lord James O'Brien, Lady Jarvis and George Norman, lately Mayor of Bath, as well as 30 eminent medical men. He did a trade in bottled water also, but the 'hazardous and expensive' venture had failed by 1840. Nearer to the city, a Mr Mills in 1824 ran the Argyle Rooms in Argyle Buildings on a subscription basis and had a billiard room.[38] As in Cheltenham, novelties were promoted to attract custom and supplement the traditional round of concerts, theatres, balls, fêtes, processions and races. These included, besides hot-air balloon ascents and puppet displays, visits by Wombwell's Menagery in 1838, Madame Tussaud's Waxworks in 1832 and Batty's Royal Circus in 1837.

Bath was 'deserted by fashion' it was said by 1832, and that summer the cholera epidemic struck it and other towns. The disease appeared first in Bristol in June, and on 28 July Bath had its first case. Guards were placed to prevent vagrants entering the city, and a timber shed on the Upper Bristol Road and a large warehouse in Avon Street became hospitals. Eventually by 17 October the Bath Board of Health declared the city clear of infection, but after 74 cases and 49 deaths. A smallpox epidemic came in 1837, when Bath had 151 deaths, a number exceeded only by Liverpool. Another cholera outbreak in 1848–49 was worse, but brought Cheltenham only 27 deaths.[39]

These epidemics were probably a cause of Bath's decline as a spa, but there were others. Formerly the health and holiday resort of eighteenth-century aristocrats, it now attracted the affluent consumer society of retired people and the professional classes ministering to them. The *Bath Journal* could still in November 1837 call the opening perform-ance of the 'celebrated' Pump Room band on the 6th of that month the 'signal for the return of the resident gentry from summer excursions and for the influx of summer visitors from all quarters', but again residents came first.[40] Mid-nineteenth century Bath had much to offer permanent inhabitants – it was cheap and desirable. Many growing Victorian towns were being built of brick, but Bath's substantial houses were of local pleasant, creamy freestone in terraces or individual villas with gardens and were serviced now by several nurseries established on the Lyncombe and Widcombe slopes. Rents were reputed to be moder-ate, coal was abundant from the Mendip collieries and was supplied in 1839 by 18 coal dealers and merchants. Shops were well stocked with necessaries and luxuries.[41] Bath's social and economic life was increas-ingly dominated by its residents; visitors went to the newer spas, like Leamington and Cheltenham, growing seaside resorts or Continental watering-places. Milsom Street, gradually infiltrated by shops, lost all its lodging houses by 1842, and the heart of the Bathwick Estate – Argyle Buildings, Henrietta Street, Laura Place and Pulteney Street – with 77 lodging houses in 1811, now had only 21. Bath could offer 533 registered lodging houses, not including boarding houses, in 1811, but by 1839 only 45 were available, a dramatic illustration of the city's changing economy. More visitors went to the healthier outskirts; the wider area of Bath and its vicinity, including Monkton Combe, Tiving-ton and Claverton, had 226 lodging houses in 1842 and seven boarding houses. There were then three hotels – York House kept by John Emeney; St James's in St James's Street kept by William Brett; and the Claverton Hotel at Dundas Aqueduct. One of the most reputable board-ing houses was Hayward's in South Parade, charging in 1840 £2 10s. in the winter and £3 in the summer, only a private sitting-room being extra. Though this was an advance on the fixed rate of 10s. 6d. in 1800, Bath was famed for being cheap.[42]

Maps of Bath in 1825, 1840 and 1852 show remarkably few changes. Some plans devised by 1825 seem to have been abandoned, suggesting that the apparent revival of the late 1820s brought no large building projects. Bath was already built to capacity. By 1825 even much of the Dolemeads, at the terminus of the Kennet and Avon Canal, were covered with terraces, but the Cleveland Estate, west of Great Annandale Road, had still much empty land in 1840, although Great Pulteney Street and adjacent streets and some of Bathwick Hill were completed by 1825. The projected layout of Francis Street and Francis Square between the river and the north side of Great Pulteney Street was abandoned and by 1840 laid out as Bathwick Park, though there was some infilling with Henrietta Villas by 1852. Like the Cleveland Estate, Lord Manvers had planned further building by 1811, which involved laying out the whole of Ham Gardens as Kingston Square with adjoining streets and mews, but this seemed too ambitious and was shelved, though some houses were built in Philip Street by 1811.[43] and, much, later streets with prosaic names like Railway Road and Railway Place appeared there. Along the London Road by 1840 building stretched to the Grosvenor Suspension Bridge and the boundary with Swainswick and westwards from Bath along the Upper Bristol Road to Locksbrook Place. Southwards Widcombe's lower slopes had some houses, but the Widcombe Nurseries occupied much space. Holloway had some building, including Paradise Row, by 1840, but more infilling came after the railway. In the Green Park area beyond Kingsmead Terrace, there was much more open space, though Green Park Buildings, Green Park Place and Norfolk Crescent were built.[44]

For two decades from 1831, the custom of the rich minority (merely 14 per cent of Bath's adult male population) still essentially, as in the eighteenth century, supported many tradesmen and independent craftsmen, often supplying specialist and luxury services, besides artisans, servants and labourers. As well as meeting the needs of residents and spa visitors, Bath was still a regional retail service centre, and with a wide range of services run by many small producers, much social mobility occurred in and between the lower and middle classes. The slight capital needed to start a business tempted many to seek independence, and there was little distinction between masters and journeymen. A clear-starcher could begin with £47, a baker or pastrycook with £50. A large resident proletariat accounted for the intermittent unrest. Of 8,556 men over the age of 20 in 1831, 7,360 were mostly artisans, master craftsmen, shop assistants, retailers and urban labourers, only 1,196 being classified as 'capitalists, bankers and other educated men'; but the

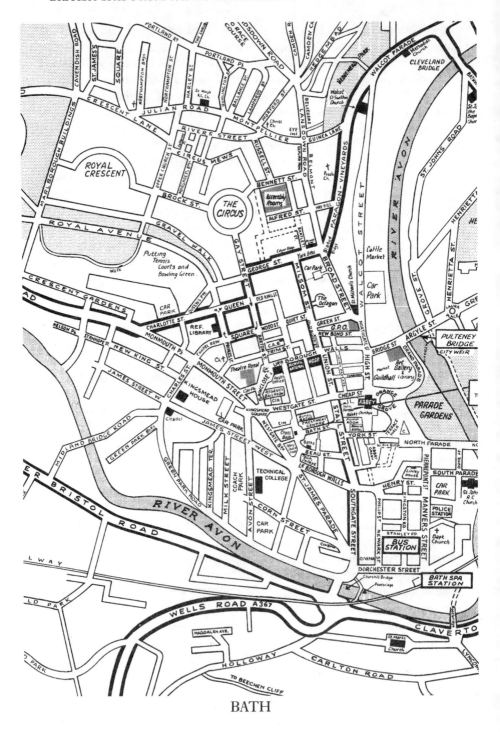

BATH

artisans included many skilled men serving Bath's quality market. A twelfth of Somerset's male population lived in Bath, but half the painters, a third of the pastrycooks and two-fifths of the coachmen. Many craftsmen were concentrated in St James's parish, which had about a quarter of the town's tailors and nearly as many of its carpenters.[45]

Though the rich formed a minority of the total working population of the four parishes in 1831, as many of 37 per cent of it were in domestic service as housekeepers, gardeners, charwomen, grooms, cooks, stewards and footmen, and there were 5,108 male and female servants, mostly living and lodging in Walcot. The next two biggest groups were in the clothing trades 11.5 per cent) maintaining Bath's tradition of sartorial elegance with 695 dressmakers, 491 tailors, 241 milliners and many others, and 11 per cent in small crafts including goldsmiths, umbrella-makers, clockmakers and saddlers. Shopkeepers and traders formed 9 per cent, building and constructional workers 7.7 per cent, professional services 5.9 per cent and entertainment and hospitality, including many innkeepers, 4 per cent. Smaller groups were those in menial services, such as washerwomen and sweeps, and town officials, including policemen, tax-collectors, lamplighters and mayor's officers. The largest single industry was Bath's fashion trade – millinery and dressmaking – employing at least a thousand women including out-workers. The large boot and shoe industry declined; trade directories listed 108 such craftsmen in 108, but 77 in 1839. This was partly due to industrial trouble, but also from 1824 to the introduction of a workshop organization employing 30 men by Messrs Phipps of Margaret Buildings.[46]

Despite the growth of workshop organization and economic diversification, only 1.4 per cent of Bath's population by 1841 were trained workers in major industry, though this excludes Lyncombe and Widcombe where 965 males were employed in manufacturing woollen cloth. The industrial concerns initiated were a flax factory (1802), two soap factories (1830s), a steam-operated factory in Westgate Buildings (1828) with 20 workmen by 1837, and George Stothert's iron foundry in Horse Street (1815).[47]

As in several other spa towns, Bath's changing economy was marked by a growth in the number of schools. In 1839 there were 78 schools, 29 of them boarding-schools,[48] though comparable evidence from Cheltenham which had 23 identifiable small private schools at this time, suggests that some were very small. In fact, Bath was not to have enough to become a school town. Its diversification made it otherwise.

As these developments occurred, Bath's spa function declined. Charles Dickens caricatured it in *Pickwick Papers* (1836–37). During his visit there, Mr Pickwick did not bathe, but took the waters following the traditional routine, having his drink in the morning, joining the afternoon promenade, patronizing the bath-chairs and going in the evening to the theatre and reading-rooms. The Master of Ceremonies assured him that the ball nights at the Assembly Rooms were 'rendered bewitching by music, beauty, elegance, fashion, etiquette and – and above all – by the absence of tradespeople'. But, though Bath was full, and 'the company and the sixpences for tea poured in, in shoals', the company consisted of 'a vast number of queer old ladies and decrepit old gentlemen', several 'match-making mammas', 'various knots of silly young men' and 'divers unmarried ladies past their grand climacteric'.

This is doubtless exaggerated, but the decay was certain. In March 1837 the Pump Room had to be saved with funds raised by a special concert. Declining support for the theatre made it so unprofitable that in December 1839, after decorations and repairs costing £600, the managers advertised it to be let complete with its scenery, library and costumes. A 'spirited attempt' by Sir G. Smart and Mr Loder to revive the subscription concerts in 1822 succeeded temporarily, but in 1837 Loder failed to promote a further series, though he received much praise for his efforts to presrve the town's prosperity.[49] Bath Races were reduced from four to three a year, and the Corporation decided to abandon its vain attempt to manage the Baths and Pump Room profitably and to relinquish control. In June 1840 it invited a lease from 29 September, admitting that 'the waters have, of later years, been strangely neglected.' 'Whims of fashion' were blamed for this situation:

> Bath has not escaped the inevitable fate of every place of fashionable attraction. In common with Cheltenham, Brighton, Leamington and many minor places of resort, it could not *wholly* counteract the inherant love of change of most of the opulent classes.[50]

Granville made three visits to Bath, finding it 'a magnificent city'. A fine sight was its Crescent, lit by large gas lights at night, and not even London's Regents Park could compare with the Victoria Park. Great Pulteney Street was among the most striking in Europe and the new road to Warminster, newly reconstructed, as fine a drive of many miles out of any English city.[51] But he was shocked by some of its sights in 1839 and thought that Bath, once the 'King of the Spas', had fallen sadly. The Upper Rooms, 'dark, dirty and comfortless', were neglected; the Cross Bath was rarely open for public use; the seven new baths attached to the Hot Baths, on which the Corporation had lavished large sums with judgement and discrimination, should have been too few in number, but were underused despite their moderate charges. He compared the situation unfavourably with Baden-Baden where 20 to 30 private baths in each of its six or more hotels were insufficient. The great Pump Room, a 'barren and unfurnished apartment', was unworthy of Bath, and its famed band had become 'the mere semblance of an orchestra', giving a meagre performance which attracted only a score or two of idlers,many of them of the lowest order.[52]

Granville believed that the decline in reputation of Bath's waters and the number of users was largely due to the medical profession. Formerly physicians, content to advise a visitor for a fee on his arrival and departure, attended the Pump Room every morning to meet them, but now they greedily demanded a fee for every visit and rarely attended the Room. Bath was a victim of its own success – its unnatural growth had attracted, Granville said with some exaggeration, over 60,000 inhabitants who crowded the place, and strangers were reluctant to penetrate its turmoil and disorder to seek out the baths and springs, which were concentrated in the most crowded and busy part. Other deterrents to coming there were the mistake of allowing water to be bottled, so that thousands of people drank in their homes water which had lost its virtue in transit, and the turmoil of electioneering over the 'most preposterous of offices', that of Master of Ceremonies. Granville might have added that the publication of his book, *The Spas of Germany*, in 1837, which he admitted had sent thousands abroad to Baden-Baden, Wiesbaden, Ems and other spas, had contributed not a little to Bath's decline, as did the comparative cheapness of the German spas.[53]

Other reasons for its apparent decline in popularity as a spa included particularly competition from the new English spa towns in the Midlands, Cheltenham, Leamington and Malvern in the first half of the nineteenth century, and growing seaside resorts like Margate, Bognor and Southend. Again, there was the constant danger from political and social instability; and in 1830, during disturbances among the agricultural labourers, it was hoped that this would not damage the tourist trade.[54]

As an unreformed borough, Bath experienced the trauma of both parliamentary and municipal reform in the 1830s. After the Lords rejected the second Reform Bill on 7 October 1831, 20,000 people gathered before the Sydney Hotel to hear speeches in favour of reform. And when Captain Wilkins of the Bath Troop of Yeomanry Cavalry, who was a Twerton mill-owner, tried to muster his men to go to Bristol to help quell the serious riots there, a hostile crowd besieged him in the White Hart Hotel. About 300 constables were sworn in to clear the streets, and three ringleaders were subsequently transported. On 15 August 1832 the Political Union, formed to promote the Reform Bill, went in procession to Sydney Gardens with banners proclaiming 'Grey and Reform' –

'Althorpe and Reform – 'We Will Maintain our Rights' – 'We Will be Free.'[55]

When 2,835 of Bath's citizens were enfranchised in 1832, the vote was for the moderate General Palmer and the Radical John Roebuck, though the immediate years showed an uneasy balance between Radical and Tory. The Municipal Corporations Act of 1835 likewise led to an expulsion of the old order; only six of the 42 councillors had held office before. The Radicals then gained a majority, but the Tories were back in 1848, and improvements went on by compromise.[56]

When Chartist meetings were held in May and again in July 1839, the authorities once more feared disturbances, and eight army troops and nearly 1,000 police, special constables and Chelsea pensioners were called out, unnecessarily as it proved. There was plenty of evidence of distress in Bath. In 1832 John Skinner, Rector of Camerton, met a beggar woman in his parish, an 'inhabitant of that wretched place, Avon Street in Bath', who had come into the country to sell matches. And by 1848 Bath had nearly 1,000 pauper children and over 2,000 pauper adults.[57]

The settlement of half-pay and retired officers and elderly spinsters in Bath, together with the disintegration of its social life into private dinner parties and balls, clubs and societies, some of an intellectual nature, also undermined the gaiety of the old communal life. The inns were never the pivot of its social life, as in the the northern spas, and in any event it lacked a good hotel. Except for the York House, the principal hotel, its hotels were old inns, adapted and improved over the years; and good though the best – like the White Hart – were, they could not take suitably both long- and short-stay visitors. Many visitors came in family groups and took rooms in the hotels for the season or a term of weeks. Bath, it was said, had no first-class hotel like other watering-places, and it did lack a purpose-built hotel to equal the Regent (1819) and Clarendon (1820) at Leamington or the grandiose Queen's Hotel (1837) at Cheltenham. Even the York House Hotel under Reilly's management was neglected and filled with 'dirt and drones', and Henry Seymour's Pultney Hotel was merely a superior lodging house, while the Sydney Hotel seems to have lost its reputation by 1839. Contemporaries agreed that fewer people now came to Bath because of the exodus to the Continent during the summer; and it had few inducements to summer residence because its baths, instead of being in the country surrounded by gardens and shady avenues like Cheltenham and Leamington, were in the centre of the town, and invalids had to reside at some distance from them.[58]

Transport was another of Bath's problems at this time. Its coach-trade was extensive and highly organized, though it had now only six posting-houses compared with ten in 1791. These were still headed by the York House Hotel and included the Pultney Hotel in Great Pultney Street. William Lane, trading as Lane and Company, alone sent coaches to 39 destinations.[59] Nevertheless, it was increasingly felt that Bath's means of communication with the rest of the country were not now adequate.

From 1810 Bath was linked to the Thames by the Kennet and Avon Canal. The canal company decided in 1833 to introduce the fast passenger-carrying boats which William Houston was successfully using on the Glasgow and Paisley Canal. It bought one to test and temporarily used it for a passenger and parcels service between Bath and Bradford-on-Avon, where it was called the Scotch boat. It maintained a speed of of 9–12 miles an hour and made the trip in 1½ hours. Passengers could have first or second class cabins and were entertained, at any rate sometimes, by a string band.[60]

This, however, was but a brief success at the beginning of the railway age. In 1837 it was proposed to link Bath and Weymouth by rail, perhaps in an effort to share the resort trade, but the idea was abandoned when it was argued that the whole of the traffic between the two resorts then hardly supported one stagecoach.[61]

Nevertheless, that year did see the beginning of Bath's inclusion within the country's main railway system. When the first plans for this were made public, William Lane immediately announced that, through circumstances beyond his control, he had to remove the royal mail and most of his coaches from the York House Hotel to the recently much improved old and central White Lion Hotel in the High Street.[62] The real reason for the move was to bring the mail-office nearer the railway station then under construction (with a suitably ordered classical front in the local stone) south of the town. And when the line from London and Maidenhead was opened 1838, he had already set up his 'Great Western Railway Coach Office' in the White Lion and for three years profitably arranged for coaches from Bath to meet the trains at Maidenhead.

The railway company wanted to bring a line to Bath, and by August 1840 over 1,000 men worked day and night, even on Sundays, on the track. The first section, 12 miles from Bath to Bristol, was opened on 31 August with the huge crowds and ceremonies now usual for such events, beginning with a splendid breakfast for the directors at the White Lion; and on that day alone 20 trips were run each way giving the public a chance to enjoy this new form of transport.[63]

It was hoped that the railway had come in time to save Bath as a spa town. It encouraged a spirit of revival, and entrepreneurs were again urged to invest in spa enterprises. In November 1840 Messrs Green and

H. Simms became lessees of the baths and pump-rooms, and a reception given by them at the Grand Pump Room to inaugurate the event reminded people of the palmy days of their elegant city when the fame of its mineral waters and splendour of its fashionable amusements had attracted England's choicest nobility and most opulent gentry. Under the new management, as Granville found, the Grand Pump Room was renovated, and promenade concerts were reintroduced.[64] Mr Davidge leased the the theatre in 1840 and made a 'spirited attempt' to restore support for drama in Bath, but in 1845 he was replaced by Mrs Macready, who also conducted the Bristol theatre,and so the same company, as in the past, could perform at both places.[65] When Reilly died, the York House was possessed by John Emeney, who beautified and restored it to make it once more celebrated as Bath's premier hotel.[66] The seasons of 1840–41 were better than for some years, and Granville suggested certain improvemnts to make the situation still better. Among these were the introduction of reclining baths and sudatories and a summer as well as the autumn and winter seasons to make investment worthwhile for entrepreneurs and persuade visitors to stay long enough to enable the curative properties of the waters to take effect. He thought that, if this were done, then Bath, possessing all the necessary resources and offering waters even more effective than those of Baden-Baden, would regain its position as the 'King of the English Spas'.

5

Minor Spas

The post-1815 minor spas, especially those of the 1830s and 1840s, differed from the earlier rather amateurish ones usually established by a single owner. Competition among the spa promoters increased, even among spas within towns such as Cheltenham and Leamington. As knowledge of the modern facilities of Continental spas spread, a range of baths of different orders, better equipment, more comfort and convenience had to be provided at greater expense. Only groups of financiers, industrialists or landed magnates could now themselves raise the necessary capital, such as the Earl of Lonsdale's attempt to develop Shap in Westmorland, the Earl of Thanet's promotion of Skipton in Yorkshire and the Marquess of Hastings' ability (through a fortune based on coal) to abandon his early Moira Spa and establish the Ivanhoe Baths and their environs at Ashby-de-la-Zouch. Other promoters of new spas made a commercial approach by adopting schemes of co-operative investment and planned undertakings and raising the necessary capital by syndicates.

There was a more general awareness of the proximity of a flourishing spa's enhancement of property. Thomas Deacon wrote of the new Willoughby Spa in Warwickshire in 1822:

Land will advance in value perhaps a hundredfold, as in other similar instances – at Bath, Leamington, Harrogate, etc., which, from the medical qualities of their respective waters, first attracted the notice of the immediate residents and surrounding villages, then the medical world, then builders and speculators and lastly noblemen and gentry of the county, who are ever ready to step forward to promote the interest and wellbeing of society and to lend their powerful sanction to the infant establishment; thus it is that places of great and fashionable resort have become, from insignificant villages or the residences of a few poor cottagers, populous and flourishing towns.[1]

Syndicates were formed for promotions at Bishopton in Warwickshire, Melksham in Wiltshire, Thetford in Norfolk, Thorp Arch, Lockwood and Dinsdale in Yorkshire, among others. Syndicates also carried out rescue operations at Gloucester in 1815 after the financial collapse of Sir James Jelf, the banker, the previous year, and at Woodhall Spa in Lincolnshire in 1886 where the original developers, looking for coal, found water containing 'free iodine'. Syndicates became more common as the primitive house containing a pump-room and cold bath was no longer sufficient. Cold baths alone, following growing coal production and improved transport, were not attractive. Hot or at least warm baths, as well as cold, were needed in all spa establishments and sometimes plunge and vapour baths. Besides the cost of coal, capital was needed to construct furnaces, erect pumps and even at Lockwood in 1827 a steam-engine for pumping new water.[2] Although the earliest hot baths at small spas were at Bungay in 1837 and the Hyde Spa at Prestbury 1751, it was not until the 1790s that they appeared at Boston in Lincolnshire and Wigan in Lancashire, then Sapcote in Leicestershire (1806), Melksham (1816), Holbeck on the outskirts of Leeds (before 1817) and Dinsdale (1824). Thereafter both warm baths and cold were normal.

The public baths and wash-houses movement to combat the dirt, disease and smoke of industrialization affected the spas. The old female well-dippers passed into history, and a higher standard of cleaning and other services was expected. A pioneer here was Norwich, which by 1789 had hot, tepid and cold public baths, as distinct from mineral-water baths with dressing-rooms warmed by fires in the winter.[3] Leeds by 1820 had such baths and others artificially prepared to possess the properties and temperature of Matlock and Buxton waters. Exeter and Sunderland had baths by the next year, and Liverpool, Manchester, Wakefield and York also within 20 years. Such initiatives were before the first Baths and Wash Houses Act of 1846 empowering boroughs and parishes to provide baths and wash-houses and to borrow money for this purpose.[4]

The new and improved spas had a purpose-built house, often of some architectural interest, erected over the local spring, which was now seldom left as a detached well head. The spa-house, usually of neo-Gothic or Palladian style, was a square, rectagonal, hexagonal or octagonal shaped building, containing a pump-room, two or three more rooms, each with a bath of different temperature, and a suite of rooms for changing, refreshment or merely sitting between bouts of drinking the waters. The more pretentious spas often had a large room known as the assembly room; and the bleak northern spas, like Hovingham and Croft in Yorkshire, often had a verandah on one side where drinkers could sit protected from the weather.

The railways at first did little to attract more people to spas or determine their location. Until the 1850s most spas still depended primarily on coach services. It was argued for Willoughby Spa in 1822 that 24 daily coaches passed through that village on the London to Holyhead Road.[5] But it was said in 1841 that trade in Gilsland Spa in Cumberland had declined during the last two years, and it was hoped that the Newcastle and Carlisle Railway would increase visitors; this was one of the most beautiful train rides in England, but passengers had to change at Rosehill Station to complete the journey by charabanc. It was confidently predicted at Shap in Westmorland that the completion of the railway between Lancaster and Carlisle would bring more trade there.[6] Railways only exceptionally aided the formation of new spas, as at Braceborough in Lincolnshire, Purton in Wiltshire and Shelfanger in Norfolk, but they obviously affected the date and place of further expansion by established spas, notably at Buxton where development was retarded until the railway came belatedly in 1863.

Spa promotions reached their height during the first half of the nineteenth century and were considerably more than in the previous century. In the decade 1800–09 those datable rose to 14, followed by 11 in 1810–19 and the same number in 1820–29. The period 1830–39 with 30 and also many improvement schemes was the peak of minor spa activity. These years, however, seem to have been a time of over-expansion since, despite 11 spa foundations in the next decade 1840–49, there were only two in 1850–1859. The total for the half-century, 1800–50 was 74, including 7 undated ones, with 43 improvement schemes: that is, 117 further spa investments, not including undated ventures or other large financial involvement in the major spas.[7]

Many small spas were served by railways in that they already had railway stations of their own or within a few miles, either when the spa was founded or soon afterwards. At Ilkeston in Derbyshire, where the staple industry, frame-knitting, underwent an economic crisis early in the century, a mineral spring was conveniently found in 1829 in the land of the Duke of Rutland, whose family, the Manners, had already promoted the Bakewell spa. As the Ilkeston spa developed, the Erewash branch of the Midland Railway passed through the parish and deposited visitors at the small station at the bottom of Bath Street, and the Railway and Commercial Hotel was built adjoining the baths and garden, facing the railway station.[8] Not only the railway but also the growing manufacture of hosiery and lace helped to create prosperity, and Ilkeston's circumstances were typical of several other contemporary spas which were adjuncts of industrial towns. At Hinckley in Leicestershire, also a hosiery centre, where there were three known mineral springs, a fourth was founded in 1847, and baths were opened there in 1849.[9]

Lockwood Spa was another such industrial town on the fringe of the cloth-manufacturing centre of Huddersfield, where a stupendous railway viaduct of 36 arches, resting on lofty stone piers, crossed the River Holne. A company took the initiative in promoting Lockwood, using an old sulphur well from which water was pumped by a steam-engine. It erected baths, claimed to be elegant and commodious, which were opened on 1 June 1847 and consisted of a swimming-bath and separate cold, tepid, warm, vapour and shower baths, set in pleasure gardens and managed by an experienced keeper. These new industrial spas resorted more widely to publicity than before, which was aided by the proliferation of local newspapers. The spas placed advertisements in the summer, beginning in April and ending in late September; there were seldom winter notices. The attractions of Lockwood's setting in romantic, sheltered country, as well as its medical virtues, were advertised in the *Leeds Intelligencer*. The company also publicized its 'commodious inn', the new Bath Hotel, erected near the baths with good stables and a coach-house, and stated its terms in detail. The members of the syndicate operating the Lockwood Spa were not named, but one may have been James Taylor, a local surgeon, who, even before the baths were opened, anticipated some profit by letting a mansion house he owned there. He advertised it in April 1827 as being a short distance from the baths and having four spacious lodging rooms with a dressing-room on each of the second and third floors, two good stables and a large coach-house, all in good repair.

The new spa prospered, and Lockwood rapidly expanded. The foundation of a new chapel to accommodate 900 people was laid in September 1828, and by 1834, when Joseph Whalley had charge of the baths which attracted 10,000 visitors a year, a church had also been built. Some visitors from June 1829 came by the new Harewood Coach, travelling between Huddersfield and Lockwood. By 1849 John Elam had laid out pleasure gardens next to the baths. Lockwood's population grew by over 1,000 in 1841–51, and in 1855 the baths were still its chief attraction. Sometime later Huddersfield Corporation took them over.[10]

Lockwood was rivalled by nearby Slaithwaite with a sulphur spring also within five miles of Huddersfield. Baths were opened there in 1825, two years earlier than Lockwood. It was an industrial spa promoted by Richard Varley of the cotton-spinning firm of Scholes and Varley, who claimed the patronage of the lord of the manor, the Earl of Dartmouth. Since the firm had apparently collapsed that year, perhaps through the bankruptcy of Thomas Varley, a cloth manufacturer of Stanningley in the parish of Calverley, the Varley enterprise seemed to be seeking another investment. Once more an elegant building containing various baths was built with a large newsroom and a bowling green. By the next year two wings were added to the main building with more baths for ladies and gentlemen; and in June, before the start of the next season, Richard Varley entertained his friends and neighbours with refreshments and music in its great room. In June 1829 he celebrated the fifth anniversary of the spa's opening by entertaining some 200 subscribers and their families with tea and a cold collation, and again there had been 'considerable improvement'. Two years later the season began with only 120 guests, but the spa,it was said, promoted the prosperity of the place. Spa proprietors had commonly by now adopted such public relations exercises.

Mid-century Slaithwaite had the Dartmouth Arms and four other inns patronized during the spring and summer by the neighbouring gentry and most respectable trading families, for whom by 1855 a 'Buxton bath' was added and the pleasure grounds were enlarged. Like other northern spas, its season was limited to the long, light days. Later the Varleys passed the property over to the Slaithwaite Spa and Hydropathic Company, which built a second covered swimming-bath in 1902 and a hall on the site of the old one. Two years later the local authority took it over, but it was neglected and the local natural beauty destroyed by atmospheric conditions and the erection of a sewerage works nearby. The Spa Hall was for long a cinema, but then was badly damaged by fire. Varley's vision drained the rates; it was closed in 1938 and eventually demolished. Only Varley Road remains to recall a project which, like most minor spas except a few adopted by twentieth-century renovaters, ended ignominiously.[11]

Another spa venture to tap industrial wealth was at Birley in the Derbyshire parish of Beighton on the Midland Railway some four miles from Sheffield. This was another syndicate effort. Charles Herbert, second Earl Manvers, who had the undeveloped Orston Spa on his Nottinghamshire estate and earlier tried to revive his Kingston Rooms at Bath, assembled for Birley a committee of four, including Thomas Staniforth, the largest manufacturer of sickles, reaping-hooks and scythes in the country, and empowered them in 1843 to build a large establishment with seven baths in this sylvan glen, which previously had a single bath with an established reputation for cures. This was opened on 1 May, walks were tastefully laid out around, and the Spa Lodging House was entrusted to the resident managers of the Baths, George Eadon and his wife, who also served tea, coffee and other refreshments. The Eadons, chosen from 50 applicants for the post, kept the baths open from 7 a.m. to 7 p.m. It was claimed 14 years later that many more cures had been effected since the new baths opened; and an omnibus ran twice daily (except on Sunday) to and from the Commercial Inn, Sheffield.[12]

Another northern spa, Croft on the Yorkshire–Durham border, was known at least from 1668, and as early as 1713 its water was sold in London for 1s. a flask. This came from the Old Spa, a spa-house with a cold plunging-bath which had large flag stones and five steps down to it in a field about a quarter a mile fron the centre of the village, which still attracted sufficient visitors to warrant building accommodation for them. Sir William Chaytor of Croft Hall, the last lord of the manor, erected the Spa Hotel in 1808, presumably with his profits from the Thornley colliery; and a new lodging house and a new bath-house were built before 1822. In August 1820 a grateful patient wrote *Croft Spaw*, a lengthy lyric which ran to three editions in two years and contained these lines:

> A splendid terrace here, too, shines,
> Where elegance with use combines; –
> A handsome range of buildings neat,
> Where strangers oft with strangers meet;
> Bland friendship opes her glowing fires; –
> Aid adds to aid, as each requires,
> And promptly fill's are wants, desires.
> The spacious Inn, – a hotel now nam'd,
> For hospitality is fam'd.
> In it the travellers find a home, –
> Spaw visitants ne'er farther roam.'

Sir William exploited the popularity of spas to develop the New Well discovered in August 1827 south of the village. He erected a long, rectangular, single-storeyed building with five baths, two being private with their own dressing-rooms, and a sunken cold sulphur plunge-bath with steps leading down to it and a boiler house and large wooden reservoir behind. All was finished by 1829. The Spa Hotel, originally a posting-inn, was enlarged with an imposing facade. Besides its many apartments, it had a grand ballroom, billiard room and newsroom for subscribers.

Croft Spa's success was more secure when the London and North-Eastern Railway went through the village, and Croft had its own station in 1851, renamed Croft Spa station in 1896.[13] The Old Spa (or the Sweet Well as it was called) was closed when the new venture started, but people still came for its waters, some from afar, so it was reopened and lodging houses built near it. Its site is now Old Spa Farm or Simpson's Farm. So popular was it that another hotel, the Comet, was prepared for visitors, and the elegant Croft Hall, which in 1841 had become a girls' boarding school, was in 1859 let as a lodging house. Croft still seemed a fashionable resort in the 1890s, as the new station name implied, and under Arthur Riseborough's management the mineral baths were used as late as 1905. The visitors then supported, besides the Spa and Comet Hotels, 17 people who let apartments, and a cab owner. A local man, G.Y. Fletcher, recalled in 1969 coaches and phaetons lining up to deposit passengers at the spa. Then its popularity waned. The Spa House was a confectionary shop for a while and was later made into a tennis club house, but by 1967 was unoccupied and soon afterwards demolished. The Baths remained open until 1958, when the proprietress died. Until 1979, when they were taken down, the spa entrance on the main road south was indicated by two stone pillars marked 'The Spa', recalling the original purpose of the leafy drive leading to the Spa House.[14]

The railway played an important part also in the fortunes of Gilsland Spa in the Vale of Irthing in Cumberland (though the village of Gilsland is in Northumberland). The development of the spa was begun about 1812 by Major Mounsey, the local landowner, when an additional chalybeate spring was discovered near a sulphuretted spring rising into a medieval holy well, which attracted visitors in the eighteenth century and became known as Wardrew Spa. The Shaws Hotel, with hot and cold baths using the sulphuretted water, a library, music and billiard rooms and an assembly room, probably existed by then and was joined by 1815 by the Orchard House and Wardrew House, all three hotels being like the Harrogate hotels, but not so expensive. Mounsey improved the inns and walks and in 1815 built a summer cottage for himself near the Shaws Hotel. Dr W.R. Clanny wrote a treatise of the Gilsland waters in 1815; but when Granville went there about 1840 trade had declined, the spa was little frequented, and he particularly criticized the the lack of medical attention. There was no doctor, surgeon or chemist within miles, though as many as 100 people might be there together. The baths and bathing-rooms were ordinary, low unattractive cottages. Neither Mounsey nor his tenant considered improving Shaws, now the Spa Hotel, because the apartments were small, the district gloomy and the season short as snow often lay on the ground until mid-March. Unlike some contemporary spas, such as Dinsdale, it lacked accommodation for the upper classes. Its custom came mainly from the middle and lower classes, and a 'large number of common people' came from the neighbourhood. Where 'visitors are everything and everybody else nothing', what Granville called this

77

'primitive and village-like' spa, in a narrow vale among rough heath-land, fared badly.[15]

Granville thought it could be revived by the railway, and this proved to be so. The station at Rosehill, on the Newcastle to Carlisle line, was opened in 1838, and a charabanc took visitors from there to Gilsland.[16] Enough visitors came for George Gill Mounsey of Carlisle to erect and partly endow in 1854 St Mary Magdalene's Church there, and when the Spa Hotel was burnt down in 1859, he rebuilt it large enough for 200 visitors. By 1868 the hotel was a convalescent home, but the spa still claimed to be 'much frequented in the summer', and the chalybeate waters were available until the 1920s.[17]

Askern in the West Riding of Yorkshire was another minor spa which survived a decline of wealthier visitors. In the late eighteenth century the Osbaldeston family, lords of the manor, exploited its several sulphur springs beneath the deep waters of Lake Askern by erecting at the water's edge a bath-house, a 'neat stone building', which led to it being in the 1820s an elegant watering-place with three large inns – the Park, Swan and Crown – four bathing establishments with the usual variety of baths and handsome lodging and boarding houses. In 1815 the bath-house was replaced by the larger Manor Sulphur Baths costing £1,000. By then the spa was of sufficient standing for its visitors' lists to appear in the press, though an analysis of the place of residence of 47 visitors listed in the *York Courant* of 24 May 1831 showed that they all came from Yorkshire, except one each from Derby and London, suggesting that its appeal was local.[18]

Askern had a fairly long life as a spa. It was helped by the new turnpike road of 1834 from Doncaster to Selby and northwards, which went through the village, and by the Lancashire and Yorkshire Railway's small station there on the branch line to Knottingley, which linked with the Doncaster branch. In the 1870s it was 'much frequented', and in 1894 two large lodging houses were joined up to form a 'palatial' hydropathic hotel. In 1906 the spa's popularity led the Harwich Express to stop there, but as it was placed in competition with Harrogate to the north and Buxton to the south, it could never be more than a minor spa. Its end came in 1911 when coal, discovered on the hillside, made Askern a mining village. No spa buildings now survive by Lake Askern, though some houses in the High Street belong to its period.[19]

Two examples of syndicate spas were at Melksham in Wiltshire and Thetford in Norfolk. At Melksham an eighteenth-century shaft sunk for coal revealed a chalybeate spring, and another was found in 1814. Encouraged by the existence of the turnpike road to Devizes, the Melksham Spa Company was founded in 1815 by several 'respectable gentlemen', all of whom had profited from the now declining woollen industry. The buildings erected included six large three-storeyed, semi-detached lodging houses forming a crescent (still existing on the north side of the Spa Road), a pump-room and hot and cold private baths. A plan for a similar crescent on the north side never materialized. Simultaneously an Act was obtained to improve 'the pleasing town of Melksham' by paving and improving its footways and cleansing, watching and lighting the streets.[20] T. Ward, a printer, published a guide to the spa, and J.C. Nosworthy, a chemist, traded in bottled water with retail outlets in Bath, Bristol and Salisbury. And, unique among minor spas, some social life was attemped in the summer of 1818. Charles H. Marshall, the Master of the Kingston Rooms at Bath, was brought to organize six balls on alternate Thursdays and concerts with vocal and instrumental performers from Bath.[21] But all this was in vain. Within ten years the spa steadily failed, and there was only one dividend paid on an outlay of £10,000. Granville considered it was too near Bath, 'the great Leviathan'; and John Britton wrote in 1845, 'Fashion, that fickle goddess, has not given them the fiat of her approval.' By then the spa was finished. The pump-room and all the houses were private residences.[22]

Thetford was a prosperous parliamentary borough and a market town on the borders of Norfolk and Suffolk. Although an inland place on the Little Ouse, recently improved river navigation allowed imports of coal and exports of corn, wool and agricultural products. It had four large breweries, an iron foundry and a paper mill and was centrally placed at several road junctions, including the main road from Bury St Edmunds to King's Lynn and that from Norwich to Newmarket and Cambridge; coaches ran to London thrice weekly and to Norwich on alternate days. Improvements had been made – a new bridge and the paving of the principal streets. Many of the adjuncts of a successful commercial and social life were present. The shops, it was claimed, vied with those of London, and there were several inns, the chief being the Bell and the White Hart, besides cheap lodgings with private families in the summer. There was a bank, a circulating library and small theatre open during the Lent assizes. Assemblies in the Guildhall attracted the nobility and gentry, 34 of whom had seats within 10 miles of the town.

All that Thetford lacked to be fashionable was a viable spa. A chalybeate spring, found there in 1746 was not developed; but in 1818 J.B. Faux, the Mayor, paid for laying out a gravelled promenade, the Spring Walk, from the Nun's Bridge to the spring in a field near the mill. Frederick Accum, a chemist of Soho in London, published in 1819 *A Guide to the Chalybeate Spring of Thetford* dedicated to Faux, and the Mineral Spring Company was formed through the initiative of Messrs Munn of the paper mill, who sought to organize a mineral-water trade with 60 agents in East Anglia. The spa venture was patronized by the area's dominant figure, George Henry, fourth Duke of Grafton, Lord-Lieutenant of Suffolk and Recorder of Thetford, one of whose family habitually sat for the borough. On 13 September 1819 he laid the cornerstone of a new plain brick pump-room and baths, which was celebrated by a sumptuous dinner for some 115 people in the decorated Guildhall. No doubt he secured the royal visit of William Frederick, sixth Duke of Gloucester, who on 18 October rode out on horseback to the spring-head to inspect the progress of the spa building. He was interested in spas and frequently visited Cheltenham and other watering-places; he thought Thetford's water was a stronger chalybeate than Tunbridge's.[23]

The *Suffolk Chronicle*, a constant supporter of the new spa, advertised a public dinner in the Pump Room to open the summer season at 4 p.m. on 3 June 1820 with tickets at 14s. each and a cheaper ball at 9 p.m. on 6 June with admission at 5s. each, tea and coffee included. In 1821 a new coach service by a more circuitous route to London through Halesworth, Yoxford, Saxmundham and Aldeburgh was inaugurated. This spa's charms were also celebrated in verse, this time by George Bloomfield, a local man born at nearby Honington in 1757. His poem, *Thetford Chalybeate Spa*, showed a detailed knowledge of the place:

> Up the rich meadow carpeted with grass,
> Oft have I strayed to view the charming scene;
> Embosom'd here, with nature's beauties crown'd,
> The baths refreshing and the springs are found,
> For some with gen'rous zeal have foremost stood,
> And rooms erected for the public good;
> With care advanc'd, the plan in various ways.
> And fairly won the meed of public praise.
> Hither the great and noble have repair'd,
> Their approbation cordially declar'd.
> A prince benevolent of Brunswick's line,
> Encourag'd and commended the design.
> And this shall be our boast as time rolls on,
> Illustrious Grafton laid the cornerstone.

The venture seemed so favourable that the lord of the manor, Sir Thomas Buxton of nearby Shadwell Court, where there was a spring at St Chad's Well once frequented by pilgrims, hopefully found another on his land at Thetford, which he claimed was equal to Malvern water. But the Thetford spa was ephemeral. The removal of the assizes to Norwich in 1833 may have affected it, for the theatre, flourishing during the assize week, was now nearly deserted. In 1838 the bath was filled up and presumably closed. The brick Spa House over the well is now a private dwelling with an added upper storey.[24]

Nearly contemporary with the Thetford enterprise was Gloucester's attempt, following the discovery of a new spring in 1814 adjoining what is now the county cricket ground, to emulate Cheltenham's success by founding another spa to replace the Old Spa at Eagle House, which was probably moribund by 1789. The story well illustrates the need for adequate capital for such ambitious projects. The investor was Sir James Jelf, a local banker and mayor of the city, who tried to develop the spring which was in his grounds. The first announcement, in the *Gloucester Journal* of 5 September 1814, attracted 300 supporters in a week. By early October, with notable patrons including the Duke of Norfolk, Lord Somerset and Sir William Guise, he had erected a pump and a temporary room. Parker's Row, now Brunswick Road, was widened as a handsome approach, and the foundations of the permanent pump-room, 40 feet by 20 feet with hot and cold vapour baths, proceeded, though marred on 27 December by the drowning of a navvy and his son by flood water while working in a tunnel at the pump-room. The new pump-room was a single-storeyed, four-bay building with a canopy, having carved acorn vases at the corner and two reclining lions over the doorway. It was opened on 1 May 1815 to military music by the band of the South Gloucestershire Militia. Thousands came to drink the water on the first day. There were now three known springs in the locality, each of which had its own spout in the pump-room.[25]

The spa itself succeeded, but in 1815 it faced disaster through the bankruptcy of the proprietor's firm, Evans and Jelf. In June plans were made to rescue the spa, including an unsuccessful effort to raise funds on a trustee basis to support Jelf and his family. Public opinion favoured the spa's continuation as an asset to the city, and subscribers were urged to pay under five-year covenants. The next month, the newly erected pump-room, dwelling-house, warm and cold baths, other adjoining buildings, walks and plantations and 14 acres of pasture land were auctioned. Some of the land was offered in eight separate lots for building in the hope that the spa area would be developed as a desirable residential district. It was stated that plentiful brick earth and the transport of building materials by the nearby Gloucester and Berkeley Canal would present an unequalled opportunity for a large, advantageous investment. The whole property was sold for £9,500, John Philpotts buying the immediate spa area for £7,500. By September some 'spirited individuals' were said to have bought the spa for rapid improvement. A new well was sunk to meet immediate demand, and walks were laid out. It was planned to develop the entire district with hotels and houses, while the spa's normal activities were maintained, such as a special public breakfast in June 1817 to honour the King's birthday.

A single owner could not do this. In 1816 a joint-stock company with 26 shares was formed to administer the spa, and over 30 lots of building ground in the immediate vicinity were sold, mainly for lodging houses for visitors and one boarding house. Like Cheltenham in its early days as a spa town, Gloucester lacked suitable lodgings. William Winstone of Quedgeley House on the southern outskirts of Gloucester, writing to his daughter in Devon in June 1817, graphically described the situation:

> The town of Gloucester, which has always been criticised for its dormant state, has at last caught the mania for improvement and fashionable innovation. They are now building to a wonderful extent in all parts of the town, and rumour is that many strangers are waiting patiently for accommodation. The spa was opened some weeks ago with a breakfast fully attended.

He went on to describe the large boarding house and adjacent lodgings being erected and the crowds of donkey carts and phaetons wending towards the 'water drinking asylum' which was of the best taste and reputation. But his rural quiet was threatened – 'You must not . . . be surprised when next you visit Quedgeley if you find us settled inhabitants of a public place instead of our present nest of retirement.'

By 1820 the lodging shortage was largely over. The Revd F.E. Witts, Rector of Upper Slaughter, visiting Gloucester in August, looked around the fresh buildings, including the commodious boarding house with its spacious billiard room; and on another visit in January 1823 he saw Christ Church being built in brick and stucco classical style 'for the accommodation of the inhabitants of the new town, which within these years has arised round the saline springs and forms a genteel suburb to the city'.[26] By 1829 the planned residential area of the new town around Spa Road seemed more like contemporary Cheltenham and Leamington than the old city of Gloucester. Handsome villas, many of neoclassical design, stood in Beaufort Buildings, Montpellier Place, Spa Villas and Brunswick Square and included Ribston Hall, a spacious, elegant mansion erected by John Philpotts, and also Sherborne House and Somerset House (the Judge's Lodgings), both with fine classical facades.

By the 1820s, however, Cheltenham had quickly overtaken Gloucester as a social centre. In 1829 a Mr Wathen rented the spa, which attracted moderate custom until the mid-century when Gloucester's increasing industrialization brought rival opportunities for local investors, and Dr John Baron's departure in 1851 deprived it of a prominent medical promoter. From then it steadily declined. In 1860 the proprietors gave its property to the city, which joined with the Board of Health to establish a public bath around it, but neglected the pump-room. The original baths were removed in 1900, and the demolition of the pump-room in 1960 ended the spa's history. It had, it was said, provided undisturbed quiet for the philosophic mind, but could not compete with Cheltenham's gay varieties of fashionable and polished life.[27]

In Bishopton Spa in Warwickshire also individual effort failed and gave way to a syndicate, which again tried to develop a rural settlement into a middle-class residential area. As Gloucester sought to rival Cheltenham, so Bishopton wished to be another Leamington. Its curate, the Revd Joseph Greene, in the mid-eighteenth century erected primitive buildings over a spring there, but although 'much visited' in 1800, the then owner, William Atkins, who had erected a new building on the site by 1831, could not finance it adequately. He was bought out in 1834 by four Stratford gentlemen – John Bryanston Freer, Deputy-Lieutenant of Warwickshire from 1833 and Mayor of Stratford in 1844 and 1858–60, and concerned with the Stratford-on-Avon Railway and the Stourbridge and Kidderminster Banking Company; William Oakes Hunt, with his brother long-established, prosperous solicitors in the town and clerks to several turnpike trusts, the bridge commmissioners and the canal company; Edmund Derby Ford, manager of the Stourbridge and Kidderminster Banking Company in 1838–57; and William Burman, described as a chemist, druggist, grocer, tea-dealer and maltster and Mayor of Stratford in 1819 and 1833. They all had commercial reasons to develop the spa as an appendage of Stratford. Transport was improving, and from the 1820s the literary pilgrimage to Shakespeare's town was becoming more popular.

The new company demolished Atkins's building and erected a modern pump-room, baths and hotel. It sought publicity by inducing John Daniel, Professor of Chemistry at King's College, London, to write a favourable analysis of the water and fixed the opening in 1837 on Princess Victoria's eighteenth birthday and named it the Victoria Spa with the approval of her mother, the Duchess of Kent. The small pump-room, now a charming private house, was a two-storeyed building with a central projecting double entrance surrounded by a neo-Gothic single-storeyed, semicircular verandah. Adjoining it was the triple-bayed Queen's Hotel in matching architectural style, now divided into two residences, Spa Lodge and Bruce Lodge. The *Warwick Advertiser* reported that the season started with scenes of great gaiety and enthusiasm and was marked by the usual ode.

The promoters now devised an extensive building-scheme to make

Bishopton a middle-class residential area. Freer bought a farm in 1822 and in 1841 the large estate of Bishopton Manor for £9,900; and in 1841 Ford and Blunt bought a farm south of the spa in conjunction with John Rich, another leading landowner. They built a new road, Victoria Terrace, to reduce the distance to Stratford by half a mile, and paid for much of the building of the new St Peter's Church. They wished to sell building plots at inflated prices instead of building houses themselves. This over-ambitious scheme soon failed. Lack of capital forced Freer to raise mortgages – £1,500 on his Church Street house in 1836 and £5,000 on his Bishopton estate in 1844. None of the new building plots advertised in 1844 was sold; but Ralph Potts, a wealthy retired East India merchant, bought land to surround his residence, Linden House, with an estate, not for building plots. By 1855 the developers had sold the entire farm intended for the first phase of building and abandoned their original scheme. Only four houses stood where a fashionable suburb had been planned.

Granville complimented the spa in 1841, saying that nothing at Leamington could compare with it – its equipment was of the best, reaching even luxury standards in the ladies' apartments, where fine fur-lined slippers were provided. Hunt showed him round the Spa, obviously displaying its advantages, but it lacked initial appeal and did not prosper. In January 1841 the baths were let out, and the next year Hunt deserted the company. Soon afterwards the hotel was closed and made into villas advertised as suiting visitors to the spa. By 1854 the spa was pronounced a failure, and financial difficulties in 1863 led Freer to sell his Bishopton property, the venture's origin. Robert Bearman, in his study of the spa, stated that it failed because its buildings were small by contemporary standards and the architecture mediocre, but its pump-room was no smaller than those at longer-lasting Croft, Lockwood and Dinsdale. Bishopton had as short an existence as most contemporary spas. Its pump-room was designed by an otherwise unknown architect, a Mr. Hamilton of Stratford-on-Avon, but the hotel was planned by Samuel Whitfield Daukes (or Dawkes), who bought the Park Estate in Cheltenham as a speculation and built St Peter's Church and St Paul's College and undertook other commissions in Gloucestershire, Sussex and Middlesex. Minor spas' promoters did not usually employ well-known architects, yet some of these small spas lasted longer than Bishopton. In fact it failed, like another Warwickshire project, Willoughby Lodge, in the late 1820s, through Leamington's nearness and success, which dwarfed both nascent spas. As the author of a guide to Willoughby wrote in 1828, Leamington's rapid growth within a few years aroused wonder and admiration, though it was in living memory inferior to Willoughby in fame and population.[28]

In 1861 Charles Ford bought Bishopton House and tried to revive the spa. He bought also the buildings which Freer could not sell and his other Bishopton property in 1862 and was reputed to have spent £3,000 in refurbishing them, which the *Stratford Herald* reported with cautious optimism were officially reopened in 1868. Ford succeeded no more than Freer, and when he died in 1877 George Wells, his son-in-law, inherited the property and tried to auction it. Though described as 'a very profitable investment' at £15,000, it was withdrawn at £2,000. The day of the minor spas was clearly over by the last quarter of the century.

Bishopton Spa failed also because, though near to Stratford, it was comparatively isolated. Thomas Ashwin, who bought out Hunt in 1842, tried unsuccessfully to remedy this by sponsoring a special 'Victoria Spa Coach' to link with the railway at Birmingham, which did not reach Stratford until 1859. But, above all, the promoters lacked nerve, capital and experience in property development. Freer was finally forced to raise enough money by mortgaging all his property.[29]

Wealthy landowners still were better able to raise capital then the industrial and mercantile classes. Death duties did not affect them until 1894. As in the eighteenth century, landowners, the nobility and gentry predominated as spa promoters. Of 36 minor spas which can be dated as having been founded between 1800 and 1860, and where there is evidence of ownership, 29 were established by individual landowners of whom seven were noblemen. Commercial syndicates accounted for seven spas, and the others were two bankers, a cotton-spinner, a mill-owner, a clergyman and two doctors.

A nobleman still investing in spas was John Henry, fifth Duke of Rutland, who exploited a spring, found at the north end of Ilkeston in Derbyshire by building the so-called Old Bath in 1829–30 at a cost of over £1,000. This was enlarged in 1832 and improved in 1845. He was a generous lord of the manor at Ilkeston, which was rapidly expanding in the 1840s; he gave land for a cricket ground and to enlarge the market place. Helped by the coming of the railway, Ilkeston became a notable watering-place by the 1860s.

The Duke was also lord of the manor of another Derbyshire spa town, Bakewell, where an ancestor had in 1697 built the Bath House in Bath Street, which was a stone plunge-bath, 33 by 16 feet, to top a chalybeate spring, which by the late eighteenth century had become a dwelling-house. When Arkwright's cotton-mill (employing some 300 people) brought prosperity to Bakewell, the Duke decided to revive the spa profitably. In the 1830s he built a public promenade called Bath Gardens and a second bath-house with warm and shower baths. Since cold and tepid baths were not now popular, the old bath was probably now neglected because its water remained at 60 degrees Fahrenheit,

85

while that of the new baths could be heated artificially to any temperature. By 1846 there was a subscription newsroom, and nearby was the
Rutland Arms Hotel, managed by William Greaves, who also had
charge of the Old Bath Hotel at Matlock. With an excellent reputation
for comfort and good food and wines, it was acclaimed as 'one of the
best-conducted inns in the kingdom'. With respectable inns and several
lodging houses, Bakewell by the mid-nineteenth century was 'in an
improving state'. The Duke's interest in two spas may well have challenged the Duke of Devonshire's monopolistic hold at Buxton.[30]

Other noblemen were interested in spas. Earl Fitzwilliam in about
1825 sought to revive the New Malton Spa of 1669 in the North Riding
of Yorkshire by adorning it with a handsome pagoda over the well. This
was followed in 1814 by a superior hotel in the adjoining grounds, a
theatre and an assembly room, but only local visitors came.[31]

The prospering mining industry encouraged noble sponsors for two
more spas. The Lambtons, later Earls of Durham, enriched by Durham
coal, continued the development of Dinsdale Spa, opposite the contemporary Croft Spa on the other side of the River Tees. Soon after the
initial construction of the cold bath in 1797, a warm bath and a suite of
dressing-rooms were added, which attracted people from a wider area.
Robert Surtees, the historian of Durham, staying there in 1804–05,
produced a jingle about it, one verse of which ran:

> Of Buxton to tell,
> Compared with this well,
> I hold would be nonsense completely;
> No water is sure
> To perform such a cure,
> And none ever tasted so sweetly.

Doctors, especially John Peacock of Darlington, supported the Spa,
which was so successful that in 1824 a new set of baths, both warm and
cold, was built with other improvements. It transformed the sleepy
village of Middleton-One-Row; three-fourths of it was rebuilt and the
inn enlarged in 1818–28. After the opening of the Stockton and Darlington Railway in 1825, passengers were taken from the Fighting Cocks
Station a mile and a half in a horse-drawn vehicle to the spa, and
Dinsdale had the advantage of being the first English spa to be served by
a nearby railway station.

Accommodation was now inadequate for the influx of visitors, and
Lord Durham (later the first Earl of Durham), whose father, William
Lambton, had discovered the original spring 40 years earlier, built the
large Spa Hotel in a commanding position at the top of the high river

bank above the baths which were below on the brink of the river. Costing £30,000, it was conceived on a grand scale with 70 well-furnished apartments, domestic offices, stables and other amenities. At other spas, only the York Hotel at Bath, the Clarendon and Regent Hotels at Leamington and the Old Hall Hotel at Buxton could vie with it in size, but the need for at least one large hotel in a would-be spa town was being accepted. John Hillier, the manager, opened it with the customary flourishing advertising in the *Yorkshire Gazette* in May 1829, and the *York Courant* gave a list of about 100 arrivals at the Hotel and Middleton-One-Row in June of that and subsequent years. The last week of August produced many visitors for whom there was a weekly ball attended by the local gentry. Although the brick hotel was called 'magnificent . . . resembling a nobleman's country mansion', most visitors still stayed at Middleton-One-Row, either in the central Devonport Hotel or the crescent-like row of one-storey brick lodging houses. Beyond Lord Durham's initial investment in the 1820s, Dinsdale failed to grow.[32]

Granville found its pump-room plain, 'like a servants' hall', and its situation 'lonely and retired'. The only provision for visitors was the Spa Hotel's billiard room (where students from Durham knocked balls about and opulent Cleveland farmers and graziers puffed at their tobacco pipes), a circulating library in a grocer's shop, a bazaar and the local omnibus connecting with the station. The hotel, resulting from over-ambitious planning, closed after a few years, though the building still exists. Yet Dinsdale, having a population of only 169 in 1834, remained a fashionable resort until the century's end, 'growing in popularity' but not expanding physically. No doubt the opening of Dinsdale Station in 1887 helped to prolong its life. It depended presumably on its attractive scenery and being the centre of three hunts – the Lambton, Hurworth and Cleveland.[33] Hunting was by now, as at Cheltenham and Leamington, becoming an expected diversion at a spa.

The other noble coal magnate was Francis, second Earl of Moira and created Marquis of Hastings in 1816, who inherited the Hastings estates in Leicestershire and initiated the Moira Spa on the outskirts of Ashby-de-la-Zouch. A soldier of distinction, he had powers and talents fitting him alike for the camp and Cabinet, and held high office in Scotland, India and Malta, which affected his health and caused his death in 1826. While abroad, his Leicestershire estates were managed by a remarkable native of Ashby, Edward Mammett (1807–60), blind from the age of seven and yet a learned scientist, accomplished musician and successful businessman, who filled many public posts. With the Hastings wealth, his energy and vision transformed Ashby in the 1820s into a fashionable watering-place with a population rising from 3,937 in 1821 to 5,208 in 1841. Unlike Dinsdale, which had excessive spa investment with economic support only from hill-farming, Ashby, a flourishing market town and hosiery manufacturing centre boosted by the wealth of coal-mining, had a broad-based economy.

Soon after the building of the Moira Baths and Hotel in 1805, accommodation was inadequate, despite more building, and Hastings and Mammatt boldly decided to move the spa to Ashby. Probably the collieries and blackened atmosphere deterred the leisured classes from Moira. The Earl and his agent took extraordinary steps to transfer the mineral water to Ashby. At Moira it was conducted by numerous channels into an underground reservoir at a depth of 1,000 feet. An account of 1852 revealed how 'methods were devised' to take it in tanks by rail in five minutes to Ashby, where it was transferred to another underground reservoir capable of providing 2,000 baths. From there it was pumped into an elevated cistern and so, as required, into the new elegant, classical Ivanhoe Baths designed by Robert Chaplin, who practised as an architect and surveyor in Ashby in about 1820–50. The frontage of the baths, completed in 1822, was a colonnade 150 feet long, the architrave supported by 32 massive Doric columns, and a broad central flight of steps led through a spacious portico. Each wing of the building contained six baths, with a separate dressing-room for each customer, and a swimming-bath with shower and douche applications. The centre of the building was surmounted by a dome which lit an exquisitely finished pump-room ornamented in the Grecian style, and on either side were card-rooms. In front of the pump-room the jet of an ornamental fountain rose from an elegant vase and fell into a circular basin. Adjoining the pleasure grounds of the baths, the Royal Hastings Hotel, also designed by Chaplin in the same Doric style, was erected in 1826 by shareholders of £500 each who were later bought out by the Marquis of Hastings. Visitors stayed also at the Queen's Head, White Hart and other inns. A theatre was built in 1828 by Mr Bennett, the manager of the Worcester Company, with boxes, a pit and gallery, which, as at other spa towns, opened only for the summer season when the Worcester players performed. By 1846, however, its attendances were declining, though the increasing population and visitors had required the building of a new church, Holy Trinity, in 1838.

Ashby rapidly expanded in the quarter-century after the opening of the baths. A local guide in 1852, which Mammett helped to compile, emphasized that Ashby was *not* a manufacturing place, though it made hosiery and earthenware, but 'a genteel and respectable town', The main street was improved and modernized by removing the ancient market cross, rebuilding many houses and repaving and flagging the causeways. New streets appeared – Ivanhoe Terrace, Rawdon Terrace, Prior Park Houses and Shrubbery Terrace. Ivanhoe Terrace had lodging houses for visitors to the baths let at £60 a year, but the offensive stench from a nearby brook affected their value. By 1846 John Mammett, probably Edward Mammett's son, lived in the manor house as steward of the manor and land agent to Hastings. He assured the Board of Health inspector, who toured the town with him in 1849, that the Hastings family had spent liberally to improve and make it prosperous; but the cultivated Lord Hastings failed in his wish to create with his wealth another late Regency spa, like Cheltenham or Leamington, centrally in the Midlands, though even by 1861 many invalids and visitors came in the summer to the 22 hotels. Pevsner wrote in 1960 that the Ivanhoe complex was 'something Ashby can and should be proud of', but it was demolished two years later.[34]

Besides the Earl of Manvers at Birley, other noblemen to promote spas were the Earl of Lonsdale at Shap in Westmorland and the Earl of Thanet at Skipton in Yorkshire. In the later eighteenth century a sulphur spring at Shap attracted many people, though there was only a bleakly situated, rough stone bath in a miserable hovel like a peat-cote, called the Wells or Bathing House. By 1820 the cold bath was supplemented by a rusty iron pot-boiler, heated with turf, gorse and heather, and a bath tank formed of an old hogshead. This was in the charge of John and Mary Brown, living about a quarter of a mile away in the Old House, which was about 200 years old and bleak, dingy and sooty. The so-called New House, about 50 years old, adjoined this and was equally comfortless.

The second Earl of Lonsdale of nearby Lowther Castle changed these primitive conditions after inheriting the Lowther estates in 1807. His vast annual income of £80,000–£100,000 was matched by great expenses: he had three other residences and kept 50 horses for hunting. By diverting some of his wealth to create a Shap spa, he transformed the scene. In 1828 he resolved to replace the one small house near the well with a suitable hotel. When the Shap Wells Hotel was finished in 1834, it was optimistically said that Shap would be a fashionable resort. This again was a hotel on a grand scale – a large quadrangular building of two storeys which, like Dinsdale, could sleep 70 people; and Dinsdale and Shap have marked similarities. Both were promoted by wealthy earls in remote situations and in the same latitude (as were two of the four most northerly spas) and were developed at the same time, suggesting competition between their noble promoters.

Granville stayed at the Shap Wells Hotel in 1840, having a double-bedded room facing south, which he said would not have disgraced a first-class London hotel. He thought the new bath-house with hot and cold baths, by then erected a few yards from the hotel near the Old Well, was good enough for the generality, but not for the better class then staying in the hotel. The pump over the original well was later joined in a marble socket, the top of which formed a basin around it, an ornament brought from Italy by one of the Lowther family. Granville was appalled by the difficult access to the spa and urged the erection of a lodge or shelter at the crossroads where the road to Shap branched off the Great North Road. He alleged that visitors using the public coaches, the North Briton and the Invincible which in 1834 left Shap for Liverpool and Manchester at 9.30 every morning and for Carlisle at 5.30 every evening, had to walk three and a half miles, carrying their luggage. His criticisms were apparently heeded. By 1844 there was a shelter at the crossroads, a conveyance took visitors the remaining distance to the hotel, and porters were ready to carry their luggage.

It was hoped that the completion of the line from Lancaster to Carlisle would benefit Shap, and indeed this and the continuing support of the Earls of Lonsdale enabled the spa, among the most taxing and northerly in England, to flourish for several decades. Trains from the north and south arrived at Shap Station between three and four every afternoon and were met by the Spa Wells Hotel's omnibus. The hotel enjoyed a pleasing familiarity; the same visitors came annually, some for 40 years. Lonsdale money enlarged the hotel twice. One account said this was in 1850 and again (with the addition of a third storey) in 1890, but a guide of 1888 spoke of changes 'within the last few years'. A gazeteer of 1900 said 'the wells are becoming a place of fashionable resort. The hotel, now enlarged amd modernized, is still there.[35]

The third nobleman interested in spas was Henry Tufton, seventh Earl of Thanet (1775–1849), who in 1832 succeeded to Skipton Castle with an income of £13,000 from the estates. About the same time, Dr Thomas Dodgson of Water Street, the only physician among four surgeons in Skipton, became interested in the town's sulphur spring used by townspeople to cure sore eyes. Its ownership was disputed, but the Earl's agents now declared it belonged to his lordship, who gave Dodgson a free lease of it. The Doctor erected a small stone Spa House containing a pump-room and 'some neat baths'; but unlike Dindale, Ashby-de-la-Zouch and Shap it lacked the continuity and stability provided by the considerable wealth and local influence of a noble owner. The Earl of Thanet's death deprived it of such patronage; it declined and had collapsed by 1866 when Dodgson died in poverty aged 74. The Spa House survives, but is now a private residence called the Toll House.[36]

The activities of 14 minor landed proprietors investing in spas at this time show that only the wealthiest could afford such speculation. These included Thomas Wilson, whose father had profited from the lead mines on Alston Moor in Cumberland, and Jonathan Richardson, a Quaker banker of Newcastle in the Irish bacon trade. Together they bought in 1828 Shotley Hall in County Durham with its estate of 3,100 acres to develop a spa there. Richardson rediscovered the ancient Holy Well on his share of the land, which he surrounded with trellis work topped with a conical roof. Besides offering building sites for sale, he built two cottages – one a pump-room and the other having two bathrooms lined with mahogany-edged white tiles. He also erected some stone lodging and dwelling houses and shops with Cumberland slates, making a pleasing group near the village of Shotley Bridge. A handsome new Spa Hotel was being built when Granville was there in 1840, and Richardson had grandiose plans, apparently unrealized, for more shops and cottages and that typical spa feature, a crescent of impressive houses, on the upland. He laid out planted landscaping and carriage drives and promenades. The increasing number of visitors made the old church inadequate. Richardson lent his own large villa for Sunday services until a new church was built in 1850 on a site given by Wilson, who also gave £250 towards its cost. By then a well-known landscape painter, Thomas Richardson (1784–48), had publicized the little resort in his *Sketches of Shotley Bridge Spa on the Derwent*; but (though mentioned in 1910 it declined by the mid-century through a lack of economical lodgings for invalids and the proximity of ironworks.[37]

Dorton in Buckinghamshire and Hovingham in Yorkshire both show local landowners developing spas in search of greater profits for their estates. At Dorton a most grandiose functional spa building was attempted in an area without any other spa. The proprietor, Charles Spencer Ricketts, set aside 12 acres in a park with a panoramic view of nine counties and engaged a surgeon at nearby Brill, Thomas Knight, to write the inevitable pamphlet, *The History of the Dorton Chalybeate*, in 1833. The extensive and ornamental single-storeyed building was at the spring below Brill Hill. It was a handsome structure in a Grecian style with a colonnade at each end and a semicircular portico of eight Corinthian columns flanked by two large sashed windows. Topped by an elliptical dome, it contained the pump-room, eight baths, a reading room, billiard room and two ballrooms. Architectually it resembled the contemporary style of Cheltenham, Leamington and Ashby-de-la-Zouch, and its lavish layout was unique among minor spas. The surrounding grounds were laid out in parterres with wide paths enclosed by balustrades, interrupted by pedestals surmounted by stone vases containing plants and evergreens. Knight claimed that the spa, remarkable for the high iron content of its water, was visited by hundreds weekly and often daily, but it lasted only some 30 years. By 1832 it was little patronized, though several substantial lodging houses and shops had been built in Brill. People now preferred the larger and more fashionable spas with their greater range of diversions.[38]

In the North Riding of Yorkshire, Sir William Worsley, created a baronet in 1838, inherited Hovingham Hall and its estates in 1830. An inventive man, whose ideas included tunnels under the Thames, he was a spendthrift who impoverished his estates in a vain attempt to enter Parliament. He wished to turn Hovingham, where a sulphuretted spring was discovered in 1829, from a 'sad-looking village' with a 'miserable wooden hut in which were two baths' (to quote Granville) into a minor Harrogate. Supported by three local doctors, he produced plans for an ambitious spa in March 1835. These plans, which survive, were only partly realized as his ideas exceeded his means, though the total of the 'considerable expense' involved is unknown. They provided for an inn, which became the existing handsome, solid Worsley Arms, and a spa estate largely unbuilt. The carriage road's entrance to the spa was to be opposite the bridge over the stream by the village green and guarded by two double-storeyed lodges with frontages of two Tuscan columns. These lodges never materialized, nor did the public baths, intended as the next building on the left, and the terrace of six lodging houses on the right. The double villa next approached by the road may also not have been built, though one of the many advertisements, a circular of 1 June 1836 addressed to the medical profession, described a desirable family house lately fitted with every convenience to be let to a medical gentleman with some capital. Only the the keeper's house, with a pump-room, cold bath and two dressing-rooms, was built, but facing east, not north as on the plan. Both the plan and a contemporary print show that this Spa House, now delightfully restored, had two gables and dormer windows with a verandah along the length of the front and the north side. The station on the Thirsk and Malton branch of the North-Eastern Railway was then called Hovingham Spa. The spa still attracted many visitors in the summer of 1859, and even 50 years later Mr and Mrs J.E. Richardson could keep a boarding house and manage a farm there.[39]

In southern England, Weymouth, besides its continuing seaside popularity, had from the 1790s two small spas – Radipole (chalybeate), some two miles north of the town, and Nottington (sulphur), a mile further out. By 1822 Nottington had a trade in bottled water, perhaps on a minor scale, and the the Act of 1824 for the new Cerne Abbas turnpike road led its owner, Thomas Shore, a corn and flour merchant with premises on Weymouth Quay and mills at Nottington, to plan further developments. He chose Robert Vining of 68 St Thomas Street, Weymouth, who had partaken in the building of the Esplanade and of a so-called Crescent in Weymouth in 1819[40] to build an octagonal house, commonly called the Round House, containing marble vapour, warm, cold and shower baths, and a pump-room. Local legend ascribed its shape to Shore wishing to eat with his seven sons at an octagonal table in the dining-room; but the idea may come from the Wellington Spa at Spa in Belgium, and in 1859 another was erected at Purton in Wiltshire.[41]

The Nottington Spa's foundation stone was laid with great ceremony on Good Friday, 9 April 1830, after divine service in Broadway Church, at which the incumbent, Mr Dade, preached. A procession, accompanied by the Upway band of music, then went through the village to the spa in the following order:

Operative Masons and Artificers.
The Artist and Builder bearing a Drawing and Design of the
    Octagon Spa and a perfect Model of the same.
The Conveyance holding the Contract for the due performance and
    punctual execution of the work.
Non-Resident, Mercantile and other visiting friends from London,
    Weymouth, etc. two by two.
Mr. Shaw, the Proprietor, supported on his right and left by
    Members of his Family, followed by a long train of respectable
    persons, male and female.'

When the stone was laid, George Shaw spoke for his father, who was overcome by the event. The procession then retired to the Shaw residence where over 100 had a substantial and sumptuous dinner interspersed with speeches. The servants and domestics also were generously feasted. The next day was devoted to a lively dance lasting with 'great spirit' until an early hour on Easter Day. In the local newspaper's next issue, Mr Dade wrote that his sermon on Good Friday had no connection with the subsequent celebrations, which he had not known about.

One of the Shore family, John Shore, was a director of the Guardian Fire and Life Assurance Company, whose Dorchester agent was C.B. Henning, one of whose family owned the spring on his manor of Radipole, where in 1830 he built a Gothic pump-room, a bath-house embowered in trees and the Spa Hotel, producing a doggerel rhyme:

> When Dorsetshire has two Mineral Springs,
> The Demon Disease shall take to his wings,
> And the folk of both country and town
> To drink them shall come down,
> And everyone shall say
> That his sickness has passed away,

And the churchyard no more shall be fed
For there'll be neither sick nor dead.

Until 1832 Weymouth's social life flourished, and doubtless so also did that of its two dependent spas; even Bath feared its rivalry. A rumour held that the town was so full that every lodging house was engaged, which the *Dorset County Chronicle* asserted was maliciously false, claiming that rooms were always available through increased building and departures balancing arrivals. Nottington Spa, considered very important to Weymouth with its hot and cold baths, pump-room and comfortably furnished bedrooms and sitting-rooms, together with a new adjacent group of lodging houses for invalids, was taken over by Charles Jestry, Mayor of Weymouth, in April 1831. The local press gave it generous publicity, perhaps donated by Thomas Shore, whose humanity in allowing the poor a free course of waters was much praised. The distance from Weymouth was said to be a delightful morning's ride, and parties daily visited the now fashionable spa open from 6 a.m. to 8 p.m. On 25 April 1832 Thomas Shore celebrated his son George's majority with a lively birthday party at which the toasts included 'To the success of Nottington Spa.'

That summer cholera came to the west country. Weymouth claimed immunity, but was ringed by outbreaks. Local spas must have suffered, and the epidemic may have finished Radipole Spa, though it is not known when its pump-room and gardens disappeared. Nottington tried to save itself. In late September 1832 a 3d. pamphlet upheld its medical properties, and the press continued to claim that it was the daily resort of all classes. The initiation in 1833 of a new coach route direct from Weymouth to Cheltenham by Dorchester, Blandford and Shaftesbury and not Bath may have been designed to attract spa-minded visitors from Gloucestershire as it went through Nottington, and the spa was advertised in the *Cheltenham Journal* in June 1839. Thomas Cooke, then the spa's proprietor, had a boarding house with private sitting-rooms and a coach-house with stables attached. By 1848, when John Furmidge was its proprietor, it was still in high repute; but a gazetteer of 1900 stated, 'Its use as a medicinal spring has ceased.' The Spa House is now a protected private house with the spring and old pump still in the cellar.[42]

Burnham-on-Sea in Somerset is another seaside resort which sought to be a spa also, though not like Weymouth with annexed inland spas. Recent agricultural improvement had taken place at Burnham, a village on the sandy, seaward belt where the Parret estuary joins the Bristol Channel, and in the early nineteenth century its curate, the Revd David Davies, planned to promote its prosperity with a spa. Studying its geological strata convinced him that mineral waters like Cheltenham's might lie beneath the village, and he financed his project uniquely. The many ships passing Burnham up the Parret to the busy coastal port of Bridgwater negotiated dangerous shoals at the river mouth. In 1801 he replaced the old lighthouse by a new one and was empowered by an Act of Parliament to levy tolls on passing ships. In 1815 he leased it to Trinity House, to whom he sold it in 1829. From this he financed two wells (sulphureous and saline chalybeate), said to resemble Cheltenham's waters, and originated Daviesville Spa, a simple Regency-style development west of the church, which was protected from the sea in 1836 by a massive esplanade 200 yards long. By then a bath-house, now called Stewart House, had been built, containing hot and cold seawater baths and also hot baths fed by the sulphureous spring. Dwelling-houses, described in 1844 as handsome lodging houses, were built, on the north side of the carriage road, giving access to the rear of the bath-house near the sulphureous spring and the pump-room where books and a London newspaper were available. The proprietor or manager of the baths at least from 1836 to 1844 was William John(s), and Robert Wakeman ran the nearby Clarence Hotel, reopened in 1836. Whitburn's livery stables kept a fly and a bath-chair for visitors. Much of this information was given in a pamphlet published in 1836 by Dr George Henning, formerly a physician at the Taunton and Somerset County Hospital. Visitors were now turned away through lack of houses; quite cheap local building materials existed, but the sandy roads of the adjacent parish of Berrow impeded development. Burnham's future was as a seaside resort, though a directory of 1874–75 suggested that the spa then functioned.[43]

Cheltenham's influence may have produced the spa at Hockley in Essex on a turning off the London – Chelmsford – Ipswich turnpike road at Shenfield. The elderly Mr and Mrs Clay moved there after many years in Cheltenham which Mrs Clay, who was asthmatic, found relaxing and weakening, though the water relieved her complaint. They rented a cottage, where in about 1838 a well dug for their use was found to have healing properties, and their home was promptly renamed Hockley Spa Lodge. Granville, who went there, stated that, to succeed, the well or spa house should be enlarged with a pump-room and a series of four bathrooms, and accommodation must be provided for visitors. The 'tolerably good-looking inn' would serve for the present if it were given a more impressive front and some internal improvement, but a first-class hotel was needed and detached cottages ought to be erected on the upper crest of the common to face the view of the river and the distant sea. Another observer suggested 'a few pretty villas', which local gentry would build, and expected a July season for Hockley for invalids who would go to Southend in August and September for sea-bathing. The advice was heeded. In 1842 Spa Road was built with a pump-room, having baths designed by James Lockyer in the Grecian style of Regency Cheltenham. Dr Henry Lave, the Essex antiquary, thought it big enough for Bath, but it was modest compared with other pump-rooms. Cross-shaped in plan, it had a central hall with four annexes, tall arched windows, Tuscan pilasters and a heavy pediment. A little later the two-storeyed Spa Hotel was built at the junction of Spa Road and the main road, but it was not the first-class hotel as at Dinsdale or Shap, which Granville wanted. William Nathaniel Summersall managed the Spa Hotel and also the Pump Room in 1848 and established a trade in Hockley mineral water with London. He still had the hotel 15 years later, but the Pump Room was a Baptist Chapel. At least by 1880 the spa was abandoned as unsuccessful; the Pump Room became a billiard room and in 1947 a clothing factory.[44]

Tenbury Wells in Shropshire was, like Hockley, founded too late. The attempt of Septimus Holmes Godson, the lord of the manor, to create a second Leamington at Tenbury, after a saline spring was found in the grounds of the Crow Inn, was belated and under-capitalized. In 1839 a well was sunk, as reported in the *Bath and Cheltenham Gazette* in September, and a small red-brick bath-house was built for brine bathing by a second well in 1840. These were opened that year with the usual publicity – a magnificent breakfast, a band of music and a master of ceremonies. A general meeting fixed charges for bathing and drinking. Granville approved of the iodine in the water, but noted that nothing was done 'to render Tenbury habitable for people of consequence'. And it remained a poor man's spa, lacking the amenities to attract other people – no theatre, subscription library or assembly room (except the Corn Exchange) – and the lodgings remained half-empty. In 1862 plunge and steam baths were added to the Bath House, and a Pump Room was built in a fantastic Goth-Oriental style designed by James Cranston; but neither the coming of the railway nor the formation of the Tenbury Baths Company in 1911 helped it. After 1914 came the inevitable decline, and Tenbury Wells has been called 'the spa that never was'. In 1939 the Pump Room was closed, and the wells were filled in. The Bath House was for many years leased to a brewery, then became a meeting-place for the Women's Institute and now is closed and derelict.[45]

The spa mania ended by 1850, affecting Bath, Cheltenham, Harrogate, Leamington, Malvern and Tunbridge Wells like the minor spas. Seaside resorts began to be fashionable and popular during the war against France, with royal patronage particularly helpful to Brighton, Worthing, Weymouth, Southend and Sidmouth. The young Princess

Victoria patronized several spas, but visited also St Leonards, Ramsgate and Broadstairs. The coastal resorts gained over the inland watering-places even before the railway age. Bath was still the largest resort in 1841, but Brighton overtook it by 1851. Solely at Droitwich in Worcestershire and Woodhall Spa in Lincolnshire were ambitious ventures created after 1850.

Only four new minor spas were founded after 1850 – Purton in Wiltshire, Shelfanger in Norfolk, Church Stretton in Shropshire and Ripon in Yorkshire. Purton was the last old-style modest rural spa. Dr S.C. Sadler retired from his London practice to live on his property there and found local people using the spring on his land over which he built a miniature Gothic-style well-house in 1859. It is octagonal as at Nottington, but not so tall, and has a slate roof edged with a fretted wooden awning; inside, where the spring rises in a central covered well, is a fireplace. Now disrepaired and almost overgrown with bushes, it is reached by a path through the garden of the Spa House, a two-storeyed cottage with a single-storeyed annex where Sadler presumably lived. The inscription over the door of the Well House reads:

The Ancient Salts Hole
Sulphated and Bromo-Iodated
Saline Water
Analysed by Dr. Voelker, 1860.

Dr Voelker was the Professor of Chemistry at the Royal Agricultural College, Cirencester, and he and Dr Noad, Lecturer in Chemistry in St George's Hospital, London, publicized the embryo spa in the *Quarterly Journal of the Chemical Society* in 1861, as did the *Berkshire Chronicle* with a notice of a pamphlet by Dr Black, *Leisure Hour* containing a clergyman's account of a visit to the spa, and the *Salisbury and Winchester Journal*. By 1861 the village of Purton was reported as 'nearly full', and other visitors had engaged lodgings. To meet this demand, John Strange in 1863 opened the Spa Boarding House in seven acres of ground from which carriages travelled two miles daily to and from the spa. The opening of the Swindon and Gloucester line of the Great Western Railway in 1845 with a station at Purton helped the spa; but fantastic claims were made for its future out of all proportion to its size. In 1865 it was expected to be a foremost European spa. Accommodation at the Spa Boarding House was publicized that year as far afield as the *Malvern Advertiser.*

Purton Spa attracted visitors for only about 20 years. It flourished up to 1872, but then dwindled, and by 1879 the Spa Boarding House had ceased to be used for its original purpose. But a widespread trade in the

Purton waters had been developed, which continued at least from 1869 to 1880. The price in 1869 was 1s. a quart bottle or 13s. for a dozen bottles and 2s. for a hamper. The railway made distribution possible to such diverse places as London, Edinburgh, Shrewsbury and Enniskillen as well as Bath, Cheltenham and Tunbridge Wells. The total income for three random years was £84 12s.(1873), £80 3s. 2d.(1875) and £72 4s. 6d., showing how it declined. Nearer home the Purton Water was peddled around Swindon on market day by a local character, who had it in vessels made to fit over his shoulders, sold it at 1d. a half-pint and punctually appeared at fixed stopping places. The trade was revived in 1927–48 by F.G. Neville.[46]

The Shelfanger Spa near Diss in Norfolk was conceived by a surgeon, Anthony Charles Farrington, who by 1900 had discoved two mineral springs in this village with a population of 308. His Spa House and gravestone (he died in 1920) survive.

The spa at Church Stretton was started in 1883 when the fervour for founding spas was spent. The Stretton Hills Mineral Water Company sought to develop the Cwm Spring to create another Malvern from a one-street market town. It was on a grander scale than other more intimate rural spas. Like the German Spa at Brighton, the promoters did not use a mineral spring but manufactured aereated waters artificially. The investment was considerable. The Church Stretton Hotel, built in 1865, cost over £6,000 and another £5,000 when enlarged in 1899; and the next year the Church Stretton Hydropathic Establishment was erected for £20,000. Dr Hay Forbes did much to popularize the town. The manufacture of the waters became its staple industry, and good hotels and boarding houses catered for the season from April to October, and it continued as a health resort after 1919.[47]

The last spa was at Ripon, where its setting preceded construction. In November 1900 the Corporation opened the Spa Gardens on land bought from the first Marquess of Ripon. Though small, they were 'tastefully laid out' and included a bandstand; and in July 1904 the Corporation accepted a plan proposed by Robert Williamson and six others to establish a spa with water conveyed by a three-inch pipe across fields from the sulphureous springs at Aldfield five miles away. The next year Princess Beatrice opened the Spa Baths in Park Street, the only known royal opening of a spa. The single-storied brick building in the Renaissance style comprised a pump-room, 12 baths and other rooms and a carriage porch and detached tower in the rear. In 1909 the Spa Hotel was opened and was owned by the same family for over 50 years. The hotel splendidly survives, but the Spa Baths are now the Corporation's swimming baths. The artificially created spa was too near to Harrogate. It failed, and the promoters lost their money.[48]

Many spa promoters regarded investment in a potential resort as financially sound, especially in the nineteenth century when trade or industry had increased the number of wealthy businessmen and land-owners. Some details of capital charges are available. The Ilkeston baths in Derbyshire cost just £1,000 in 1830, and the Askern Manor baths the same in 1814, but were rebuilt in 1828 for £5,000. The Terraced Bath at Askern cost £3,000 in 1825 and the Royal Pump Room at Harrogate £2,000 in 1842. From the late 1820s these sums usually included an architect's fees, such as those for Robert Vining at Nottington, Robert Chaplin at Ashby-de-la-Zouch, James Cranston at Tenbury Wells and James Lockyer at Hockley. A better purpose-designed and functional pump-room and a more extensive and fully fitted bath-house than in the eighteenth century were required, besides a hotel and/or a range of lodging houses. At Thorpe Arch in Yorkshire over 100 lodging houses were built in 1815–41, so creating a new spa village, but the cost is unknown. The Melksham complex of six semi-detached lodging houses in three blocks with a bath-house in the rear cost £10,000 in 1816. The Ben Rhydding Hydropathic Establishment, intended to make Ilkley the northern Malvern, required an initial outlay of £25,000 in 1843, and the Dinsdale Spa Hotel cost £30,000 in 1829. A modest hotel and boarding house in the rural backwater of Admaster in Shropshire cost only £6,000 in 1851, but the contemporary promotion of Woodhall Spa in Lincolnshire, when the first small bath-house was replaced in 1849 by a new one with a well-house and hotel, cost £30.000. The Gloucester Spa was sold in a financial crisis for £7,500 in 1815, but by 1878, when spamania was over, the Bishopton Spa was over-valued at £15,000, and there was no advance on £2,000.

The returns on capital outlay were small. Achieving a profitable balance depended on the spa attracting a continual flow of visitors, at least in the summer. A minor spa's season, as newspaper advertisements show, was limited from early April to late September. No public notice of a season from October to March is known. A typical season was 21 to 24 weeks, and since most small spas had a brief existence, there is no sign of a changing tariff of charges. Detailed eighteenth-century prices hardly exist, but there are a few for the early nineteenth century. The normal charge for the minimum service (drinking the water) was 1s., but the period is unspecified. Possibly it was 1s. a week, as at Dinsdale in 1835 and Nottington in 1831, where a guinea a season was about 1s. a week. Alternatively it was 6d. a day, which suited the short-stay visitor, and families could claim a reduction. Gloucester was only half as dear, charging individuals 10s. 6d. for drinking and families £1 15s. Boston Spa charged 1d. a glass as did Sutton near Shrewsbury. Each bath was charged separately: the normal payment for a cold bath was 1s. as at

Dinsdale and Lockwood, but at Gloucester it was 1s. 6d. with a 6d. tip to the bath attendant and at Nottington 2s. Lockwood charged a family a guinea a season for cold baths, while subscribers of that sum could have warm baths at half-price. The labour and heating involved meant that warm baths usually cost at least twice as much as cold ones, and this varied more widely. Lockwood charged 2s. a bath, Dinsdale 2s. 6d., Nottington 3s. and Gloucester 3s. 6d. Slaithwaite had inclusive terms for families taking baths, ranging from 15s. to 30s., according to their size, and each member of the family was restricted to one weekly bath and had to sign a book before bathing. Ashby-de-la-Zouch, like some more sophisticated larger spas, charged from 1s. 6d. to 2s. 6d. for different types of baths.

Though transport could be expensive, lodging cost the visitor to a spa most. At Glastonbury, Croft and Dinsdale, a lodging room was half a guinea weekly, which could rise to 14s. at Dinsdale. A private sitting-room cost 10s. 6d. at both Croft and Dinsdale. The Shap Hotel's charge of two guineas weekly was consistent with these charges. Board for a servant cost 3s. a day at Croft, but 3s. 6d. at Dinsdale, which included ale.

If an economical visitor stayed at a minor spa in the early nineteenth century for an average season of 21 weeks without a servant, a private sitting-room with a fire and hot baths, he would pay £46 4s. besides the cost of transport. He could have board and lodging at two guineas weekly, dip in 21 cold baths at 1s. each and drink the water continually for 1s. a week. Spa visits were clearly an expensive indulgence and for the middle classes only. By way of contrast, it cost £60 a year to rent a whole lodging house at Ivanhoe Terrace, Ashby-de-la-Zouch, built expressly for spa visitors. The labouring poor could not go to minor spas unless their visits were philanthropically arranged at special terms and times. This was quite often done, as at Askern where about 1821 a Charity Bath was established supported by subscriptions to benefit the poor, who also were freely advised by two physicians,[49] and at Ashby-de-la-Zouch, where a former factory in Bath Street was bought in 1854 and made into the Saline Bathing Infirmary for the poor at a cost of £400.[50] Slaithwaite, Skipton, Somersham, Tenbury Wells and Willow-bridge were among the less important spas which made concessions to the poor, and most large spas had a bath charity.

Despite the slight evidence of their charges, it seems that a living could be made from operating minor spas, since these excluded the considerable trade in bottled water on which many flourished. Why, then, did the age of the minor spas end about 1850 and few endure beyond then? An important reason is that none could survive if near to a large spa, such as Bath, Cheltenham, Harrogate, Malvern, Tunbridge

Wells and, to a lesser degree, Droitwich, Matlock and the new Woodhall Spa. Thus, the spas of north-west Wiltshire – Box, Holt, Chippenham, Melksham and Purton – and of Somerset – Alford near Castle Cary, Capland near Ilminster, Glastonbury and Burnham-on-Sea – succumbed to Bath's competition. In Gloucestershire, Cheltenham's example encouraged spa attempts at Ashchurch, Gloucester, Lower Sewell, Newent, Prestbury, Stonehouse and Pauntley, which existed only in name, and also the abortive scheme at Ross-on-Wye in Herefordshire in 1815; but its influence was too strong for their success. Buxton had the same effect on the Derbyshire spas of Bakewell, Birley, Ilkeston, Kedleston, Quarndon, Shuttleworth, Stony Middleton and Whittington. Bishopton and Willoughby in Warwickshire could not compete with Leamington, nor Tenbury Wells in Worcestershire with Malvern, nor Canterbury and Sissinghurst in Kent at an earlier date with Tunbridge Wells. Though less important than the major spas, Ashby-de-la-Zouch had massive financial support compared with the other small Leicestershire spas – Gumley, Nevill Holt, Sapcote, Shearsby and perhaps Wigston – and so they failed. Braceborough in Lincolnshire could not compete with Woodhall Spa. Harrogate's domination in the north meant that none of the small Yorkshire spas within its periphery – Boston, Thorp Arch, Croft, Hovingham, Lockwood, New Malton, Skipton and Slaithwaite – could counter its attraction, except Askern, which retained some importance for about a century, and Ilkley, which became the northern Malvern but never really challenged Harrogate. Only Dinsdale and Shotley Bridge in County Durham, Gisland in Cumberland and Shap in Westmorland were remote enough to maintain a tenuous existence but lacked importance. Frequent boasts by lesser spas that their waters were 'like' Bath, Cheltenham, Tunbridge or other leading spas show their attempts to rival them. And Kedleston claimed its lodging houses resembled those of Buxton and Matlock.

Although the turnpike system and coach transport sustained many small spas thoughout the kingdom, presenting passengers with a fine network of cross-country routes to hitherto little-known places where a mineral spring could now be exploited, not all coach proprietors received enough support to be profitable. The thrice-weekly coach between two such important towns as Stockton and Darlington, a road of some 12 miles, was seriously short of travellers.[51] Not all coaches served a spa town directly. They might, as at Shap, leave passengers at a post-house or wayside halt with a difficult connection to make.[52]

By the 1820s the turnpike system was so extended that some thought it was overdeveloped and increased the high cost of travel. Granville mentioned 12 turnpikes within 27½ miles in Kent, the tolls of which equalled a fortnight's board and lodging in Tunbridge Wells.[53] But by the 1840s the railways were markedly affecting leisure travel. Coach services were steadily abandoned, but railways, though providing cheap mass travel after the Railway Act of 1840, were inflexible, touching fewer places than the coaches' spider-web network. This killed the minor inland spas as the main lines linked up the already established major spa towns and growing seaside resorts. The railway came to Bath and Cheltenham in 1840, Leamington (Milverton) in 1844, Tunbridge Wells in 1845, Harrogate in 1848 and Malvern in 1859, but not to Buxton until 1863. Only a few small spas, such as Askern, Braceborough, Croft and Purton, were founded or revived because they were accessible by rail.

On the whole, the future lay with fewer and larger spas and the seaside resorts able to offer a greater variety of pleasure. The minor spas' lack of organized social life made for tedium, and the long intervals between taking the waters could not always be filled by excursions to local beauty spots and playing bowls or games of chance. The ever-more urbanized population had more sophisticated and exacting leisure requirements. The days of simple rustic pleasures were over; only large towns had the diversity of assemblies, theatres, clubs and societies, sports, promenades and public parks, besides a variety of inns and hotels to suit all tastes and pockets. Not only was the custom of the minor spas drawn to the major spas, but also to Continental spas after 1815. These attracted many of the fashionable and wealthy, who in an earlier age had sought to set the tone for a civilized social life in spas like Bath, Tunbridge Wells, Astrop, Epsom and Hampstead.

The relatively high cost of establishing and maintaining the small inland spas was by the nineteenth century beyond the resources of all except wealthier landowners and syndicates of businessmen, but the prosperity in agriculture and industry in the third decade of the century offered promising opportunities for profitable investment which put risky spa ventures at a disadvantage to moneyed men. Such factors caused the minor spas to lose their popularity for both capitalists and visitors. Neglect brought about their collapse, and their pump-rooms and bath-houses fell into ruin.

6

Southern Spas

In southern England, a multiplicity of wells and springs were to be found in London and the area around. From the post-Restoration period, advantage was taken of these to establish a number of spas, including such well-known ones as Sadler's Wells and Hampstead. But during the eighteenth century the value of land in the region undermined their existence. They gave way to the development of suburbs and other undertakings. Only three of any note survived into the nineteenth century, and there was a single new one established during that time.[1]

Islington Spa was a later seventeenth-century creation, coming into being with the discovery of a chalybeate spring in about 1680 beside the green known as Spa Fields opposite the Sadler's Wells Theatre. Called the 'new Tunbridge Wells' (because of the similarity of its water), it reached the height of its popularity in 1723 when it was patronized by George II's daughters, the Princesses Amelia and Caroline. In 1810 the proprietor reduced the size of its fine ornamental gardens, which had picturesque trees, pedestals and runs, and Lloyd's Row and Rosebery Avenue were built there. He also replaced the original garden entrance, facing the New River Head, by one adjacent to the well and next to his own house, No. 6 Lloyds Row, which existed, with a coping stone bearing the inscription 'Islington Spa or New Tunbridge Wells', until the Row was destroyed by bombing in the Second World War. A later proprietor, Hardy, in 1826 enclosed the well in a private grotto and opened the gardens, but these were built over in 1840 by two rows of houses, Spa Cottages. In 1844 a local surgeon, Malloy, who lived in the proprietor's house, printed a circular inviting invalids to drink the waters for 6d. a visit or an annual subscription of a guinea. The water ceased to flow in the 1860s, and by 1894 the only part of Hardy's grotto was below a room of the proprietor's house and was described as being 'in an obscure nook, amidst a poverty-stricken and squalid rookery of misery and vice'.

St Chad's Well owed its existence to a mineral spring on the east side of the north end of Gray's Inn Road. It was developed as a spa in the mid-eighteenth century and was popular until early in the next century, when it became a Sunday pleasure garden. In 1832 an attempt was made to revive it as a spa, and the original pump-room was replaced by a larger one with a forecourt adjoining Gray's Inn Road, but by then middle-class London spa-goers were transferring their patronage further afield. William Hone, on a visit in 1841, found it decaying and patronized only by local people. It was demolished during the building of the Metropolitan Railway in 1860.

Bagnigge Wells was opened in 1759 when chalybeate and saline springs were discovered in the grounds of Bagnigge House, west of King's Cross Road. The banqueting-hall of the house was made into a long room where tea was served with cakes and syllabubs, and a dome-shaped well-house, called The Temple, was built. It was at first popular and fashionable, but in 1810 Daniel Lyons said it was 'much resorted to by the lower class of tradesmen', and 1813 Thomas Salter, the lessee, went bankrupt. Most of the fittings were sold, including the chandeliers and 200 tables for drinking. It was reopened by William Stock in 1814 with the gardens deprived of their best trees and shrubs and reduced to ground east of the stagnant Fleet River. Maria Edgeworth wrote in 1827, 'The cits to Bagnigge Wells repair to swallow dust and call it air.' A concert room was built in 1831, but successive lessees failed. It could not compete with the new music hall; it was closed in 1841 and the site built upon.

Uniquely for London, Beulah Spa was established in the nineteenth century. Mineral-water springs containing magnesium sulphate were known on the slopes of Beulah Hill in Upper Norwood in Surrey, and in 1828 John Davidson, the owner of part of the Manor of White-horse, engaged Decimus Burton to convert Bewlys Coppice into a health resort and place of entertainment on a rural site of 30 acres. It was declared to be 'one of the purest and strongest of the saline spas in the country'. The well, 12 feet deep, was protected by a thatched hut in the shape of an American Indian wigwam, and there was an octagonal reading room, terrace, maze, orchestra, camera obscura and archery ground. Military band concerts, dancing and fortune-telling by the gypsies from nearby Gypsy Hill were provided for visitors, who could come by daily coaches from Charing Cross. Mrs Fitzherbert induced the Duke of Gloucester to drink there to 'stimulate his jaded liver', and other patrons included the Earl and Countess of Munster, Lady

Salisbury and Charles Dickens. The re-erection of the Crystal Palace at Norwood caused the spa to close in 1854. The buildings were finally demolished in 1876, and most of the site was built on, but there is still an area of open land called The Lawns, and Tivoli Lodge, one of the two entrances to the spa, which served as a box-office and reception hall.

An early southern spa visited by Londoners was Tunbridge Wells on the border of Kent and Sussex. The third Baron North first noticed its chalybeate springs in 1606, and Queen Henrietta Maria's visit there in 1630 began its royal and aristocratic patronage which was resumed after the Restoration into the next two centuries. The wars against France from the end of the eighteenth century brought an invasion of military officers, French refugees and noblemen unable to go abroad, which increased its prosperity; but its urbanization came slowly. It remained essentially a rural spa, described as late as 1819 as 'the hamlet of Tunbridge Wells consisting of four little villages named Mount Ephraim, Mount Pleasant, Mount Sion and the Wells, which together form a considerable town'.[2]

Compared with the larger spa towns, it was backward in providing amenities for visitors, and its real expansion was delayed until the coming of peace in 1815. The population rose from about 1,000 in 1800 to 5,929 in 1831. Its economic basis was still catering for visitors, and the area contained chiefly lodging houses of which in 1816 there were 138 with 309 parlours, 505 bedrooms and 532 garrets for servants; and 34 of them were along the London Road. Six years later there were 50 more, but it was admitted that there was excellent provision for the 'quality', but little for the middle or lower classes.

The spa's character was, indeed, changing. With a less mobile population, it was no longer a 'migrated colony', but rather a respectable, wealthy place with more long-stay visitors and permanent residents. The season was now extended from late March or April to the end of November, and the number of residents meant that local people could get more return on their investment in trade and building hotels and lodging houses.

By 1818 the well-established Sussex Tavern on the Parade was transformed into the Sussex Hotel with elegant apartments, a coffee room and a billiard room, later becoming the Royal Victorian and Sussex Hotel, splendidly stucco-fronted with the Duke of Sussex's coat-of-arms, giant pilasters and a porch with Doric columns. Its tenant spent £5,000 on the alterations. There was also the Swan Inn at the back of the Parade, and the Angel Inn on the London Road was upgraded by 1818. The Castle Tavern at the foot of Mount Sion was by 1810 renamed the Castle House. Messrs. J. Nash and J. Elliot, now owners of the two libraries on the Parade, compiled a lodging-house register and conducted a wide range of hiring services, including the provision of musical instruments and servants and, exceptionally among spa towns, table and bed linen and household furniture. T. Dickens had a bookshop and others in London and Brighton.[3]

Transport services also expanded with the growing town. It had only one daily stagecoach to London in 1760, but by 1818 the Brighton, Hastings and Rye coaches passed through it and made a stage there, and two light coaches went three days to London and daily in the season, when there was also a Sunday coach. Two London wagons ran twice a week with connecting cross and local posts.[4]

In the post-war period, Tunbridge Wells had not only to meet the well-established attractions of Bath and the new competition of Cheltenham and Wellington, but also the expanding seaside resorts of nearby Hastings and Eastbourne. And Hanoverian monarchs favoured new resorts – George III visited Cheltenham and Weymouth and George IV, when Prince Regent, stayed at Brighton. Their middle-class subjects, now more ready to travel, followed their example.

Tunbridge's expansion after 1815 produced the same problems of law and order and social distress as in other contemporary spas, complicated there by the fact that local government was administered by the justices. The constables and nightwatchmen of the three parishes of Frant could not deal with the vandalism of those years, and in 1816 the local gentry, like the residents of Bath, Cheltenham and Leamington, formed an Association for Prosecuting Felons. The justices too showed more concern for Tunbridge Wells, holding by the 1820s petty session for Kent cases twice monthly in Stone's office on Mount Ephraim and once monthly at the Sussex Hotel for Sussex cases.

Philanthropic ventures grew as in other spas, supported by an educated middle class with sufficient leisure for charitable efforts and anxious for both civic amelioration and self-improvement. In 1818 an Industrial School, similar to that at Scarborough, was founded for 100 girls. Societies were formed for lying-in relief (1818) and providing clothes for bedding and meeting distress (1826). Visiting and provident societies included the Mendacity Society (1834) to give vagrants a night's lodging with bread, cheese and small beer. And under the Poor Law Amendment Act of 1834 workhouses were set up for able-bodied paupers at Pembury, the aged, infirm and women at Tunbridge and children at Rusthall.[5]

Inadequate administration and insufficient resources hindered Tunbridge Wells's development; and the spa's old public life was undermined by the lack of large public rooms. Apart from special occasions, public balls and card-playing now occurred only once or twice a week;

and when John Roberts was Master of Ceremonies in 1817–22, he failed to revive the past public tea-parties and concerts. The wells in or near the Parade were polluted with a chalybeate and iron taste, and in 1814 Thomas Taylor, a local plumber, laid on water in the Walks/Mount Sion area from a spring on land leased from the Earl of Abergavenny. He was bought out by the Tunbridge Wells Water Company, formed with eight shareholders in 1826, which sank another well in Broadwater Down; and in 1832 a local committee expressed the need for better drainage.[6]

Proprietors, as at Cheltenham, wished to exclude their estates from local control and keep their profitable provision of water supplies, lighting, street cleaning and maintenance. In 1815 a local act was obtained to light the town with gas and police it with a watch, but this was not done, and an attempt to provide street lighting by subscription also failed.[7] Not until 1833, with renewed proposals for a gas supply, did a public meeting of rate payers and property-owners call for the setting up of a local authority. They were led by Aretas Akers, a rich, influential barrister from the West Indies, now retired to Tunbridge Wells and active locally. Opposed were the developers of new estates, notably John Ward, a wealthy London merchant and High Sheriff of Kent, with Calverley Park Estate, and Lord Abergavenny with Nevill Park. After the controversy erupted in demonstrations in December 1833, the Bill, redrafted to favour the estate owners, passed in July 1835 as the Tunbridge Wells Improvement Act for 'lighting, watching, cleansing, regulating and otherwise improving the town of Tunbridge Wells in the counties of Kent and Sussex'. An early result of this was the regulation of hackney coach fares. Ward and Lord Abergavenny could lay on water and supply-pipes for their estates, and their roads were not public highways, so their privacy, subject to watching and lighting, remained. Ward was also allowed to establish a market on his estate with its lucrative tolls. So the town of Tunbridge Wells was established with boundaries about one mile around the parish church with its administration controlled by men of substance. The commissioners, all not elected, were owners and occupiers of land worth at least £50 a year. Their powers included levying a rate not exceeding 2s. in the pound.[8]

Pressure from the growing town led to the establishment of the commissioners. Contemporaries described its development as 'irregular'. In 1810 it was still a hamlet or an unplanned assemblage of buildings.[9] But there was great building activity in the 1820s and 1830s. The age of timber-framed, tile-hung houses was past; the new Regency houses, like the lodging houses on Mount Sion, were usually of two storeys and one semi-basement with bow windows on either side of an imposing porticoed doorway approached by a flight of steps flanked by iron railings. When two noble families, the Grosvenors and the Har-veys, Earls of Bristol, sold their land, the northward development of the 1830s provided much-needed houses for artisans, building labourers and other workers. This is recalled in the names Upper Grosvenor Road, the Bristol Arms and Harveytown. Building was mostly by local people, from labourers to professional and businessmen, some of whom made or increased their fortunes. T. Langridge, a wheelwright's son, built 40 houses below Mount Pleasant, and C. Cripps, the builder, erected over 100 cottages in Windmill Field as well as Mount Calverley Lodge for himself.[10]

The most significant contribution to the new town was the Calverley Estate, its first example of a planned estate on garden suburb lines undertaken with large capital investment, as at Bath, Cheltenham and Leamington. John Ward promoted the scheme. In 1823 he bought Hol-wood Park at Keston in Kent for which he employed Decimus Burton, the Greek revivalist architect. And in 1825 he bought nearly 900 acres of the Calverley Estate, a large tract of farmland to the north-east, including the Earl of Egmont's Mount Pleasant. He acquired also the sandstone quarry for building stone in the northern part, as recalled now by Quarry Road and Stone Street. He instructed Burton in 1827 to produce a comprehensive scheme for the western part of the estate as a new residential town with dwellings for genteel families, a church, market, hostelry and shops.[11]

Burton introduced an entirely new dimension to Tunbridge Wells's architecture in the area north of the valley dividing it from Mount Sion, as dramatic as John Wood's new town outside Bath's city walls. His ground plan was more fluid than in other spa towns; he provided a more open landscape to suit the old town's features – the Walks, the common and the villas with gardens. Holy Trinity Church (1829) though not part of the estate, was the first built in local sandstone at a cost of £10,591 and was his idea of a grand town church. Probably through his influ-ence, the project was financed by the iron-founding firm, Messrs Bramah of Pimlico, who had supplied the gates for his Constitution Hill Arch in London; they acquired the land on a building lease.[12] Lavishly 26 acres were set aside for Calverley Park, a pleasure ground with shrubberies overlooking 20 acres of meadow, and the building of 24 individual villas in Italian and Grecian styles was planned there in 1828. Access to the Park was by four adorned lodges – Baston (which has disappeared), Keston, Farnborough and Victoria. The 'hostelry' emerged as the Calverley Hotel, the rebuilt Mount Pleasant House overlooking the Park where in 1822 Princess Victoria stayed with the Duchess of Kent.[13] Spas now found that the old coaching inns, even if rebuilt or renovated, were inadequate. The Calverley Hotel typified their new capacious, purpose-built places of unprecedented size. It compared with the contemporary Queen's Hotel in Cheltenham with 50 bedrooms, 20 sitting-rooms, spacious coffee rooms and the all-important stables. It was opened in 1840 by Edward Churchill, who also in 1847 leased the Kentish Royal Hotel. The second hotel in the Estate, the Camden Hotel, owned by John Hughes, was built in the same year. By then Tunbridge Wells had 23 hotels, inns and taverns.[14]

The Camden Hotel was in the estate's commercial nucleus in Calverley Road, part of which – Nos. 57–79 – was originally called Calverley Place. Here were the market house, where the town commissioners met upstairs, a five-part range of shops with lodgings above and the Calverley Mews. There were also nursery gardens, now necessary for landscaped new spa towns. Houses with gardens for the workers, like Calverley Cottages and Kelsey Cottages, were obscurely situated. Other residential areas were Calverley Terrace (1831), a row of small villas opposite the Calverley Hotel, and Calverley Parade (1834), a range of 12 houses where Burton lived at No.10. In the more select part of the park, entered by Victoria Lodge, 19 generously spaced villas, each of individual and solid design but remarkably homogeneous as a whole, were erected, the first five in 1828–33. Not in the original plan, the Promenade, designed as the inevitable crescent, was erected in 1830–35, copying the Pantiles with its iron balconies at first-floor level and slender colonnade, but was converted into terraced dwelling-houses by 1840. Edwin Marks had a library in No.9 at the centre, and there was a vapour bath and shampooing facilities at one end, and in the garden a bandstand and a fountain.

Ward's total enterprise produced some 90 housing units for between 500 and 1,000 persons, excluding hotel visitors and non-residential servants.[15] John Britton, *Sketches of Tunbridge Wells and the Calverley Estate* (1832), records the construction of the Estate. The quarry's milk-white sandstone soon weathered to darker browns and greys. Like Cheltenham's private estates, it had its own water supply from waterworks on Ward's property at Kack Wood's Spring;[16] but, unlike Cheltenham, lacked pump-room and assembly room to make this a spa-centred estate. Residential requirements had superseded provision for visitors.

The Calverley Estate's success led two other local magnates, the Earl of Abergavenny and the Marquis of Camden of Baynham Abbey, to take to property development. Lord Abergavenny's Nevill Park was laid out from about 1840, and John Billing did some work there in 1855. Camden Park, where land was surveyed and houses designed perhaps by Burton in 1847, was further laid out 1843. A small park of houses was built in Grave Hill Road and lodging houses and shops along the foot of Mount Sion.[17] The northern and southern settlements grew closer together linked by Mount Pleasant Road with a large green gap on both sides.

There had also to be ecclesiastical developments. Holy Trinity Church became parochial in 1829 and, with the new Christ Church (1841) as its chapel of ease, replaced the Church of Charles the Martyr in the old town as the principal place of worship. A chapel was built by the Methodists in 1812 at the foot of London Road (now Vale Road), by the Congregationalists in 1848 in York Road and by the Particular Baptists in 1833 in Hanover Road, where the Roman Catholics in 1838 also built St Augustine's.[18]

Clearly the scale of capital investment in building in Tunbridge Wells during the first 40 years of the nineteenth century was unprecedented, and it gave Burton alone an active private practice. The only additional spa feature was a second bath-house, Skinner's or the Great Bath House, with apartments in the London Road by 1816.[19] The focus of social and commercial activity had moved slightly to the north, but the surviving spa life still revolved upon its traditional centre, the Parade, renamed the Pantiles in 1887.

The expansion involved a vast number of people. By 1831 there were 5,929 inhabitants, 4,601 in Tunbridge parish, compared with only 1,136 in Speldhurst and 192 in Frant; the axis of Tunbridge Wells had shifted from the old town of the wells to the new town in the north. By 1841 the population had mounted again to 8,302, and two-fifths were in trade or occupations.[20] Domestic servants, 800 women and 245 men, formed a third of the working people or an eighth of the total population, a proportion to be expected in a resort town with a high degree of person-alized service. Agricultural and general labourers numbered only some 400, the rest including gardeners, laundresses, seamstresses, ostlers, porters and coachmen. These, together with 319 employed mostly in the retail clothing trade and 20 surgeons and physicians, were ancillary to the leisured and professional classes. Although the South-Eastern Railway reached Tunbridge Wells with a temporary terminus in 1845 and the Central Station in 1846, the town in 1847 was still living in the horse age with three coachbuilders, three saddlers and harness-makers, 20 coach and fly proprietors and seven blacksmiths. The rural flavour was apparent with four cow-keepers, two corn-millers and three corn-dealers. A tangible reminder of the old spa days was that Tunbridge Ware manufacturers still maintained their trade.[21]

Granville dismissed Tunbridge Wells as a spa. He conceded that it would always be a great resort of occasional visitors and would soon become one of winter residents, but the reputation of its mineral waters was declining and would soon disappear. Even the two women dippers at the wells agreed that crowds might come now, but not for the waters.

There were some 5,000 visitors in 1840, but the dippers' books showed that barely 240 took the waters. Hardly 50 people used the baths in the Pantiles, and half of the bath-house was let out to an upholsterer living on the premises.

Granville thought that there was no other place in Britain where the principal features were so much neglected. The town was in a beautiful irregular amphitheatre embellished with lawns, gardens, plantations, the common and winding paths, and no watering-place except Chelten-ham had so many detached villas, mansions, belvederes, lodges and ornate cottages. But the Nevill and Camden properties were now being developed in the general speculation for enlarging the town, and their future lay with wealthy residents from London as rents were higher even than in the capital.[22]

Granville was right about the spa's decline. Princess Victoria came five times (in 1822, 1826, 1827, 1834 and 1835 to 'dear Tunbridge Wells', but apparently did not drink the waters. Mrs Shorey's bath-house was given a portico over the spring by public subscription in 1847, but in the 1860s it became Grafton House where John Leach sold transfer-ware and porcelain. The freeholders' properties in the Pantiles were described in 1849 as 'a low, antiquated and dilapidated range of wooden buildings'; the Assembly Room was occasionally used before becoming a furniture repository, the 'Pantechnicon', in 1880. The office of master of ceremonies was allowed to lapse in 1836. Sedate donkey-riding, borrowed from Brighton, replaced balls and routs. The theatre played to half-empty houses until becoming the Corn Exchange in 1843. An abortive attempt to revive spa life was made in 1847 when a lodging house, the Grosvenor House, in London Road was made into a hydropathic establishment planned to rival the German Spa at Brighton. But the future of Tunbridge Wells was to be a residential resort not a thriving spa.

By 1750 the southern coastal town of Southhampton, like Scarbor-ough in the north, had a flourishing spa quarter. It was developed con-siderably by the town council, which pumped the mineral water into a spring and laid out the Botanic Spa Gardens in the area now the present Spa Road. The coming of war in 1793 accelerated Southampton's growth, since, as at Tunbridge Wells, armies camped nearby. The town was reported in those years to be very crowded and prosperous with every lodging room occupied.

A recession struck Southampton with the advent of peace in 1815 and the Prince Regent's preference for Brighton. Praise from local doctors failed to maintain the demand for its water. The Botanic Spa Gardens were so sparsely attended that in 1817 the town council only renewed after some hesitation the licence for their management then held by W.B. Page from Lee and Kennedy of Hammersmith. In September a grand gala there was unusually well attended, but financial support for balls in the Assembly Rooms (known as the Long Rooms) declined so much that the manager refused even to take up the normal subscriptions for them. For two years only an occasional ball was held there. By 1820 no one would take out the licence for the Gardens, and the water was sold at 1s. bottle by local chemists.[23]

Reprieve for Southampton's spa life came in 1821 through Sir William Champion de Crespigny, a local landowner in Fawley, and since 1818 Member of Parliament for the town. He led a revival of its amusements, the annual race meetings, regattas, archers' assemblies, concerts and firework displays, and the introduction of new features, such as public lectures, balloon ascents and circuses. In 1829 a new bathing establishment, the Royal Gloucester Baths and Promenade Rooms, was built a little down the river from the Platform or quay. He also took over the Long Rooms from their owners, the Martin family, and in 1830 new Assembly Rooms were built in the Gardens and called the Victoria Rooms (but also known as the Archery Rooms). Balls, concerts and entertainments were held there, and the local press contained many advertisements for mansions, villas and marine cottages.[24] For some years after 1825 Southampton enjoyed an Indian summer as a fashionable resort, hoping to rival Brighton, but its future was to be as a port, helped by the coming of the railway in 1846.

Southampton's social life never recovered from the cholera epidemic of 1848–49. By the mid-nineteenth century the last relics of its spa life were disappearing, killed by commercial progress. As Granville said, 'The all-devouring railway company and its still more grasping twin-sister, the dock company, swept clean away the bath-buildings and the bathing shores.' The Royal Gloucester Baths were sold to the dock company and replaced by offices; the Long Rooms soon became a drill hall; and the last Master of Ceremonies retired in 1854. The Patronesses' Balls were replaced by Town (or Tradesman's) Assemblies at the Victoria Rooms, but its final lessees could not obtain enough subscriptions to hire a band and had to sell 'genuine Cheltenham water' obtained fresh every day. The Rooms finally disappeared with the creation of a ring-road in the 1960s.[25]

Like Scarborough and Burnham, Brighton was a seaside resort which sought spadom in the nineteenth century. A small chalybeate spring, known as St Anne's Well, was discovered at the Wick, about half a mile from St Nicholas's Parish Church, in the previous century and now in Hove. Dr Richard Russell enclosed it in a basin, and by 1813 the proprietors had erected 'a small neat building in the lodge style' as a pump-room. It drew visitors during the seaside season, but had failed by the mid-nineteenth century. This was destroyed by Hove Corporation in 1935.[26]

George IV's continued patronage of Brighton increased its fame and encouraged Dr F.A.A. Struve in June 1825 to establish the German Spa on the lines of the kursaals he had already founded at Dresden, Leipzig and Berlin. He dispensed there, for the first time in England, 'factitious' or artificial waters, warm and cold, made by mixing chemicals with water drawn from an artesian well driven deep into the chalk, to resemble those of the best-known German and Bohemian spas. He erected a pump-room with a low portico of six fluted Ionic columns, extending across the front and surmounted by the Royal Arms, and with round-headed windows to the main room beyond. It was open daily from 8 a.m. to 10 p.m. and in the 1830s hundreds of people drove in their carriages and attended a course of four to five weeks for a subscription of a guinea a week. It was patronized also by William IV, Queen Adelaide, the Duchess of Kent and other members of the royal family, so that it was called the Royal German Spa and the park in which it was situated Queen's Park.

Inside the building, behind an eliptically shaped counter, were two rows of round-arched apertures in the wall, each framed with a Greek key-pattern moulding and containing a silver tap labelled with the name of a foreign spa such as Ems, Marienbad, Baden-Baden, Carlsbad, Spa or Pyrmont. Each tap supplied a different simulated mineral water claiming to reproduce the chemical composition of a particular spa, which could be ordered from smart female attendants. A contemporary account stated:

The vessels for the production of the mineral waters are connected by pipes with the gas pump, which again are connected with pipes with the gasometers; the quantity of gas introduced into the mineral waters is controlled by mercury gauges.

Dr William King in his *Observations on the Artificial Mineral Waters of Dr. Struve . . . at Brighton with Cases* (1826) called the venture one of the greatest blessings of the century; and Struve himself issued a challenge to anyone to 'cite a single place in Germany where two or three waters of different parts of the world are mixed and drank at the same time'. The patients were supposed to drink the waters prescribed for them by their physicians in the appropriate quantities and sequence, but many drank haphazardly. They included a large number coming to stay in Brighton for weeks at a time, often 'real or fanciful patients tired of London . . . and anxious to give the slip to their doctors'.

Granville tasted Struve's waters, which 'flowed from silver or glass spouts at the bidding of the smart lass in attendance' and decided that 'the water-bibbers drank in faith' since they were given 'mere watery solutions ... charged with artificial heat and therefore incapable of producing the peculiar effects which distinguish the real Ems and Carl-bad waters when drunk at the springs'. Nevertheless, visitors still came, and Struve exported 300,000 pint bottles of his waters annually.[27]

By 1886, however, the German Spa's custom seems to have declined. The building was used for making table waters by Messrs Hooper Struve until 1965. It deteriorated badly, but in 1975 the fascia was restored. An important reason for Brighton's period of success (and also for its decline) as a coastal spa was its easy access from London. The opening of the Brighton Road and introduction of mail coaches brought to it fashionable people who wished take the waters in pleasant sur-roundings. And the beginning of Brighton's decline as a spa coincided with the coming of the railway, which brought the trippers who came in their thousands to enjoy the seaside attractions of the beach, promenade and Chain Pier, and changed the nature of the resort.

7

Midland Spas

Buxton's development as a spa began about 1779 when the fifth Duke of Devonshire, as lord of the manor, decided to make Buxton into a second Bath. When he died in 1811, he had built the Crescent with the St Ann's and Great Hotels; large stables (now the Devonshire Royal Hospital); and the new St John the Baptist's Church. This had produced an elegant new town and moved the centre of its activity from Upper to Lower Buxton.

His death was followed by Buxton's relative decline as a fashionable watering-place. Although in 1801–41 its population grew from 760 to 1,567, and that of adjoining Fairfield from 356 to 599, this was due to the development of quarrying rather than provision for visitors. Like Matlock and other inland resorts, Buxton found that the seaside lured visitors from it. Buxton exceeded Matlock in both the number and status of its visitors, but had no important industry and depended more on agriculture. Settlement at Buxton in 1800–42 extended eastwards towards Fairfield along the Wye valley and also concentrated towards the south-west, where coal-mining and limestone-quarrying developed after the completion of the Cromford and High Peak Railway in July 1831.[1] This accounts for the high proportion (39.5 per cent) of males aged over 20 employed as labourers otherwise than in agriculture (27.5 per cent) in 1831 when 22 per cent were in retail trades or handicrafts and 3.1 per cent in the professions. The proportion of male servants (2.1 per cent compared with 1.3 per cent in the county as a whole) and the high proportion of female servants (55 per cent) reflects Buxton's resort nature.[2]

Despite its increase in population, early nineteenth century Buxton, like Matlock, declined relatively in fashion, though the actual number of visitors may have only slightly decreased. Harrogate's dominance as a northern spa, and its development in the 1820s and 1830s over-shadowed Buxton and Matlock. Both these Derbyshire spas grew more slowly than other resorts and had different occupational structures. Buxton in 1821 depended much more on agriculture (60 per cent) than Cheltenham (15 per cent) or Bath (3 per cent) and had less trade, manufacturing and handicraft (29 per cent) than Cheltenham (65 per cent) or Bath (56 per cent), and its mining and quarrying were important.

Buxton had three or four times as many visitors as Matlock. Though not scenically superior, it was a more convenient centre for exploring the Peak District, had better parks and buildings and a long-established aristocratic tradition. Its apparent fall in population in 1851 was due to an excess of at least 334 visitors 'for the benefit of the mineral waters' in the June 1841 Census, and the large increase in Buxton and Fairfield in 1851–61 was because of the presence of railway construction workers. Buxton was in a state of relative stagnation, relying too much on ducal guidance.

The bachelor sixth Duke, William Spencer Cavendish, who suc-ceeded his father in 1811 and lived until 1858, was closely involved with Buxton, being cut off by deafness from public life elsewhere. Reputedly the richest man in England and a collector of books and pictures, he lived like a prince and was often among his tenants. He owned nearly all Buxton, except for some freeholds, and continued to make his ducal town more attractive to visitors. In 1818 he remedied a serious deficiency, the lack of really hot baths. A Derby engineer, Sylvester, designed new Hot Baths contemporary with Leamington's. These ele-gant baths, fed by a spring at the foot of St Ann's Cliff, were lined with Italian marble and porcelain tiles, while a covered way for invalids was provided by continuing the arcade of the Crescent at its north-east side. He persisted in his father's plantation policy, laying out the slopes, the terraced gardens (probably designed by Wyatville, his Chatsworth architect) up St Ann's Cliff facing the Crescent. He erected also a fountain and conduit in 1840 to improve the water supply in the market place, and built a National School endowed with £100 a year. He was fond of music and at his own expense founded a band which played six days a week in bluish-grey uniforms, directed by a harpist, who also entertained the Duke's guests at Chatsworth. Four evenings a week they played at 8 p.m. in the Promenade Room, which was used instead of the Assembly Room when the Great Hotel was closed sometime before 1846, and on Monday and Wednesday at an early hour in front of the Crescent; and they gave several concerts during the season.[3] The shop-keepers of the village, as Buxton was still sometimes called, probably prospered most in the 1830s and 1840s, when the roads were improved and the railway not yet taking people to the large towns. They had, however, to face seasonal competition from immigrant traders. Madame Percival came from Great Portland Street, London, with her millinery, fancy articles and embroidery, and Mrs Ainley, a 'rubber and shampooer', from Sheffield. Also from Sheffield came Hunt and Jennings, selling silks, shawls, laces and ribbons, next to the Grove Hotel; Mr Hadfield selling fireworks; and Bright and Son, who for for some 70 years from about 1818 dealt in fancy goods and jewellery in the Crescent, having other branches in Leamington and Sheffield. Native enterprise manufactured Blue John ornaments, made of purple fluorspar from Castleton in Derbyshire which the village stone-cutters or baublegrinders fashioned for sale. There were 14 engaged in this minor industry in 1846; and they are still Buxton's distinctive souvenirs.

An analysis of Buxton's business in 1846, though probably incomplete,[4] supports the assertion that it, like other spas, 'lived on the lodgers', but its economy was diversifying, and the maintenance and service element was stronger. Of the 210 traders, the largest group of 92 was provided by the hotels and lodging houses as against 50 in 1829, but many more shops had opened up. Despite the existence of the market from 1813, the next largest group was 35 food retailers, 13 grocers and 11 butchers. The 21 engaged in miscellaneous retail services was inflated by 14 in the memento trade in spars; clothes shops had increased from six in 1812 to 20. There were still, as in 1812, three libraries-cum-booksellers and 14 professional men, including four schoolmasters, but there were also now three physicians and four surgeons, when originally there had been Samuel Buxton, an apothecary. The physicians included the distinguished Sir Charles Scudamore during the season and Dr W.H. Robertson, senior physician to the Buxton Bath Charity, who wrote *A Handbook to the Peak of Derbyshire* (1854). Ten were employed in transport and its auxiliary services, including two blacksmiths, and the 10 farmers still living in Buxton showed the township's rural nature. Lastly came seven in the building trade and one basket-maker.

Despite the apparent prosperity, amenities for visitors still needed much improvement; and stagnation, if not recession, set in by the 1840s. Buxton lacked a pump-room, though its bathing capacity had been enlarged. Before 1842 another bath, kept by Matthew Billings, was erected on the Old Macclesfield Road, with cooler waters than in the others.[5] This was probably the 'tonic bath' kept by William Boam in 1857 when there were three others, two at each end of the Crescent, and the Hydropathic Bath kept at Hall Bank by Joseph Miller. Although bathing was still practised, the amusements were inadequately supported. The Buxton Races were discontinued in 1842, and a

117

shareholders' meeting considered disposing of the race-stand, a two-storeyed building with a projecting roof balcony over the ground floor.[6]

The theatre at Hall Bank changed its programme weekly, but it ended prematurely in late September 1842 because a 'comparative lack of visitors in the summer' had resulted in an unprofitable season, though Mr Dyott, the leading actor for several seasons, needed the reward of a good benefit performance. When the next theatre season began on 1 July 1843 Charles Bass, the tenant, engaged players from the Theatre Royal, Manchester. Performances were still three evenings a week, but there was now a more complex price structure with seasonal tickets of two guineas and monthly one guinea; and the nightly admission charges, unchanged since the late eighteenth century, were reduced after 9 p.m. Bass and his wife worked hard at the venture. He played four different parts in one week and was at great expense in recruiting his company, but benches were often empty, though the *Buxton Herald* urged both inhabitants and visitors to help maintaining the theatre. Another lessee, George Smith, took over 'our pretty little theatre' in 1850, but he had poor support. Three years later he was opening only twice a week, and there were complaints about the low ebb of public taste when a travelling circus was well patronized. The theatre was demolished in 1854 and replaced by the Broad Walk in 1862. The assemblies in the Crescent ballroom stopped in 1840, but it was some-times used for concerts and lectures. The Promenade and Music Rooms, next to Bright the jeweller in the centre of the Crescent, were run by subscription but open only for the season and thinly attended in July 1842. The Great Hotel was closed by 1846 and divided into three boarding houses.[7]

Disquiet about Buxton's decline was expressed when it acquired its first newspaper, the *Buxton Advertiser*, published seasonally only by James Bridgeford, a local stationer. The first issue appeared on 23 July 1842, printed by his brother John at the *Isis* office in Sheffield. It was controlled by W.D. Sutton under whom it flourished for 50 years. The first newspaper printed in the town, the *Buxton Herald*, was owned and published by John Cummings Bates, nephew of Brian Bates of Old Hall and proprietor of Bates Library and the Reading and Newsrooms. He ran this journal for 30 years and also the abortive *Buxton Visitor*, lasting only four months in 1852.[8] A correspondent in the *Herald* in 1842 emphasized Buxton's failures and asked why it was behind other watering-places and had not grown like them. Lodgings should be filled with visitors from early spring to November as elsewhere. Even allow-ing for the national slump of the last four or five years, Buxton had not exploited its advantages. It had a favourable position – a few hours' drive from the Potteries and the manufacturing towns of Leek, Congleton and Macclesfield, now within easy reach of populous Manchester by the Birmingham and London Railway, and near Sheffield and the west of Yorkshire as well as Leicestershire and Lincolnshire whose substantial graziers had often tried the value of Buxton's baths.

The railway's late arrival in 1863 had also impeded Buxton's development. In the early 1800s it was an important coaching centre with some 20 coaches leaving the market place daily, including the seasonal Manchester–London mail service. When railways developed elsewhere, many coaches ceased. In 1843 the royal mail from Manchester avoided Buxton, but instead was taken to Derby and went on the London train there. The 'Champion' coach went throughout the year from Manchester through Buxton and Bakewell to Nottingham, but the 'Duke of Devonshire' and 'Peveril of the Peak' directly to Manchester, the 'Enterprise' to Sheffield, the 'Duke of Rutland' to Bakewell and Matlock, while the 'Sun' plying through Buxton between Sheffield and Macclesfield, and the 'Peak Guide' were seasonal coaches only, starting in early June. The 'Original Sun' to Macclesfield from Buxton connected with coaches to the Potteries and by rail by Chelford Station to Birmingham and London. The 'Peak Guide' also connected at Derby with trains for Nottingham, Leicester and Birmingham. The nearest station to Buxton from 1833 was at Ladmanlow on the Cromford and High Peak Railway 1½ miles away. Passengers put down at Ladmanlow were taken to Buxton by Messrs German Wheatcroft's coach service, but had to walk uphill. The railways inexorably closed in – the Midland Railway reached Darley in the Matlock area by 1842 and extended to Rowsley in 1849, and by 1843 coaching firms offered 'very reduced fares' during the bathing season.[9]

Buxton had possibly by the 1820s been overbuilt for its requirements. The estimated accommodation in public and private lodging houses in 1833 and again in 1857 was for 12,000 to 15,000 annual visitors, which may have been exaggerated, although by 1846 there were 17 hotels, inns and taverns and at least 75 lodging houses of which 27 were in the recently built Spring Gardens. Lists of visitors in newspapers were generally incomplete, but the *Buxton Herald* in 1842–43 showed about 300 visitors a week, which agrees with the June 1841 Census figures of 324 visitors that week. The annual total for a season of some 16 weeks would be about 4,800, which seems realistic. Ten years later the lists were longer, but still in 1851 Buxton, excluding Fairfield, had only 266 houses and 1,235 inhabitants compared with 180 and 760 in 1801.[10]

Besides fashionable visitors, many paupers were attracted by the Buxton Bath Charity. In 1844–45 they numbered 1,413 of whom 1,040 were cured or much relieved, 46 no better and 12 still on the books. The Charity, originating in the Elizabethan Treasury of the Bath, was managed by trustees and supported by subscriptions and two annual charity sermons. The Duke gave £21 a year. Each invalid, recommended by a physician, had free medical advice and the use of the baths for three weeks with a weekly allowance of 6s. if needed.[11]

Granville in 1841 revealed Buxton's stagnation. Although it had a 'fragrance of aristocracy', it was 'a very dull place', lacking amusement and even more society in its 'present apparent desertion'. His hostess blamed the shortness of the season, beginning in June compared with April in Matlock, which made speculative investment hazardous. She also accused Granville of having lured its customers away to Germany by his successful *Spas of Germany* (1837). He suggested improvements for Buxton. A more elegant pump- or well-room with smart female attendants, as in Germany, instead of a nearly decrepit old woman handing out the water, would encourage people to gather round the wellhead. Fashionable people seemed ashamed to be seen descending under the well-dome to ask the old dame for a draught of water and preferred to have it sent to their lodgings or apartments, a practice peculiar to England. A kursaal or promenade room was essential for those drinking mineral waters, but that under the arcade of the Crescent was exposed to the weather, and the present promenade and newsroom was an assembly room unworthy of a market town. He suggested that ducal munificence might provide a promenade room in the form of a Grecian temple on the hilltop fronting the Crescent. He complained also that the baths were too few and untidy with tarnished brasswork and stopcocks, and that the young male attendant looked like a grubby labourer called from the plough. An invalid lady then staying at Buxton found only 8 or 10 comfortable houses; and Granville might have added that the streets were still muddy in bad weather and polluted with animal refuse, while the stench of the River Wye was nauseous in the summer.[12]

The Duke seems to have responded to such criticisms and wished to improve Buxton's reputation. He probably secured the visit there of the Duke of Sussex, the Queen's uncle, on 20 September 1842. The three carriages and six outriders were greeted by the ducal band playing the national anthem, and the party went to St Ann's Well to drink the waters. They then inspected the new parish church, Messrs Bright and Son's Repository, the Crescent, Old Hall Square and the Great Hotel, where they lunched.

The Duke also in 1853 reconstructed the baths and rehoused St Ann's Well; but the people depended so much on his initiative that they hardly acted for themselves, opposing investment or change, even a proposal to introduce gas lighting in 1851. A company, formed with a capital of £2,000, built a gasworks at Fairfield, but the gas pressure was too low to give much light. By contrast an adequate gas–supply was had

120

by Bath and Cheltenham in 1819, Scarborough in 1834 and Harrogate in 1846.[13]

Yet Buxton experienced a rapid increase of building from 1841, especially along the clay vale towards Fairfield. Building on the marshy shale vale was avoided, except for the vital section between the Crescent and Fairfield Bridge. Extended settlement, planned by the Duke's estate office, was on the limestone. Following the example of contemporary planned estates at Cheltenham and Tunbridge Wells, the Duke in 1852 instructed Sir Joseph Paxton to develop the Park, a residential area west of the stables and St John's Church, but it actually differed considerably from Paxton's scheme, and the houses, mostly of the 1870s, are not to his design. The design and purpose of building on the Duke's estates was as closely controlled as by building speculators in some other spa towns, such as Joseph Pitt in Cheltenham and the Foleys in Malvern. Buxton's outskirts, on the slopes to the north, west and south-west, became upper-class residential areas, like Green Lane and Spencer Road. East of the constricted Wye gorge were lower- and middle-class homes, with the marked exception of Hardwick Square. Building on the limestone included cottages at Harpurhill for quarry and kiln workers.[14]

Of much less importance and very different in nature from Buxton was Matlock, 22 miles away. Both are situated among the carboniferous limestone of the southern Pennines, but while Buxton is in a 'bowl' high in the plateau, Matlock is in the corridor formed by the River Derwent between craggy hills rising to some 600 feet on either side to form a gorge. Matlock has a lower rainfall then Buxton, a lower altitude of 200–750 feet, compared with 940–1050 feet at Buxton, and a warmer, sunnier, drier and more relaxing climate. While both were mainly agricultural settlements, Matlock's leisure industry, lacking a ducal patron, depended on several modest people's initiative, and its economy was diversified first by lead-mining and later by cotton-mills.[15]

The warm springs of Matlock Bath, about a mile south-west of Matlock Village, were known since medieval times, and a stone Bath House was built there in the later eighteenth century. When the French Wars prevented Continental travel, the nobility and gentry stayed at its 'three spacious hotels' – the New Bath Hotel, the Temple Hotel and Hodgkinson's Hotel. In 1818 it was described as still being a favourite resort, and by then it was more accessible after the construction of a new road from Cromford through the Derwent valley along which daily coaches passed through Matlock.[16]

By 1800 a syndicate of Derbyshire gentlemen owned the hotels, and a uniform scale of charges in all three in 1819 suggested that this control still operated. It was 5s. weekly for a bedchamber, 14s. to a guinea for a private parlour, breakfast 1s. 6d. and bathing 6d. a time. Each hotel provided post-chaises and saddle-horses for excursions to local beauty spots like the Heights of Abraham and the defunct mines and caverns, which were some of Matlock's tourist attractions. By 1829 there were another hotel, the King's Head managed by Thomas Smedley, the Royal Museum for Derbyshire spar and black marble objects and Mrs Brown's Botanic Gardens 'for the delectation of Visitors'.

By the early nineteenth century it was complained that Matlock was 'much deformed by manufacturies' and 'the depravity of the working people who inhabit it', an encroachment which was yet spasmodic. Males over the age of 20 in Matlock engaged in agriculture formed 48.5 per cent of the population in 1811, 90 per cent in 1821 and 60.9 per cent in 1831.

By 1846 Matlock was an apparently flourishing township, but, lacking Buxton's ducal control, its individual villas and cottages were heterogeneous in settlement and architectural style. The 'Nelson' mail coach now came daily through it from Nottingham to Manchester, and other daily coaches went to Buxton, Manchester and Nottingham. There were 21 hotels, inns and taverns and 24 lodging houses; and the supporting economy of retail shops and services included nine butchers, eight grocers and tea-dealers, four milliners and dressmakers, a hairdresser and a post office. The professional element included three attorneys, three surgeons, three chemists and druggists and five private academies. The settled population of 3,782 in 673 houses in June 1841 depended mainly on a mixed economy of agriculture, cotton-spinning, framework-knitting, corn mills, bleach works, a paper mill and the manufacture of hats, cottonwick and spar ornaments, in which four members of the Smedley family were engaged. The spa industry was relatively unimportant. Only 2 per cent of those resident that month were visitors; and Holy Trinity Church, built in 1842, was not primarily intended for them.[17]

Granville in 1841 enthused about Matlock's possibilities, though admitting that the high aristocracy of its former days had given place to farmers and small proprietors now filling it in the season. He stood before the Old Baths 'in ecstasy, immersed in the contemplation of this scenery'. He considered the neat stone houses offered excellent and sufficient accommodation on easy terms, much below those of Buxton. The New Bath Hotel was the best, having the attraction of a highly decorated ballroom with a carved ceiling, but it was seldom used. The King's Head had also a high character with many spacious rooms on three sides of a quadrangle and had a beautiful garden. He found too the Temple, in a lofty position among the plantations, and Hodgkinson's worthy of praise. If the people found, as they still hoped, a spring 15 or 20 degrees warmer than those used at present, Matlock would become 'a very Wildbad . . . and the ne plus ultra of thermal spas leaving Buxton far behind'.[18]

Though this was indeed a commendation from the critical Granville, Matlock was then only a second-rate spa of the traditional sort, lacking the social organization and sophistication of the older ones, and being by the mid-nineteenth century only an adjunct of the place's economy; and Buxton had three or four times as many visitors. The railway transformed Matlock, but destroyed the social predominance of the Old Bath Hotel, which was the coaching centre. The Midland Railway reached Darley in the Matlock area in 1843, and in 1846 obtained an Act for a line from Buxton to Stockport through Matlock, with stations at Matlock Bath and Matlock Bridge from Ambergate Junction. Robert Watson of York took over the Old Bath Hotel in 1843 and Willim Greaves in 1846. Both operated an omnibus from it to the Junction four times daily in summer and twice in winter, but the antiquated eighteenth-century hotel, where the spa had originated, could not survive. It was closed and its furniture sold. When the railway reached Rowsley in 1849, its immediate effect was to make Matlock, like Buxton later, easily accessible to day-trippers from industrial centres. Crowded excursion and special trains came from Bradford, Leeds, Sheffield, Chester, Manchester and Stockport, changing the spa's character.

Clifton, not far from Bath on the Severn Estuary and now a suburb of Bristol, became a fashionable resort through its Hot Wells situated at the foot of St Vincent Rocks beneath the present suspension bridge. The saline, semi-tepid water had the reputation of curing grave illnesses, especially diabetes and tuberculosis. A fashionable resort arose around them with a pump-room, assembly room, library and other amenities expected of a spa.

By the early nineteenth century, however, Clifton was suffering from the competition of both Bath and Cheltenham. Visitors at the Hot Wells were now mostly chronic invalids seeking a last desperate cure, and the consequent mortality rate damaged its reputation.In 1816, when an Act was obtained to demolish and rebuild Clifton Parish Church, provision was included for another cemetery. The dangerous and precipitous way down from Clifton to the Wells and the expense of hiring a carriage two or three times a day also deterred patients from coming to a spa clearly past its fashionable prime.[19]

Attempts at revival were made after 1815. The pump-room, Hotwell House, was demolished in 1822 (the year when the new Clifton Parish Church was built), so that a new road, the later Bridge Valley Road, could be built, and in 1826 the Society of Merchant Venturers of Bristol, as lords of the manor, built a new Hotwell House in the Tuscan style near the site of the former one, containing a new pump-room, reading room and baths, which visitors had always wanted.[20] The tenant was James Bolton, who made the rather high charge of 3d. for a glass of water. The right of local people to have free access to the Wells was upheld by a free tap in the backyard, but only paupers were allowed to use it. Bolton augmented his sale of spa water and profits of the mineral baths with a business in stationery, guide books, local views, oiled silk caps, cigars, umbrellas, Indian soap, boomerangs and a variety of other goods.

The spa's decline, however, was not halted. In 1825 Clifton was still a 'fashionable resort', but by the 1840s it largely contained permanent residents and visitors attracted by its climate rather than the waters. Granville declared, 'Few people, if any, drink of the semi-tepid sparkling water – fewer still bathe in it.' As late as 1842 extensions were made with false optimism to the Assembly Rooms (now the Clifton Club) in the Mall, which was built in 1811.[21]

In 1867 the Docks Committee, when removing Hotwells Point to improve the navigation of the river, destroyed Hotwell House. The Merchant Venturers insisted that the spring should again be made available by a grotto hollowed out of the rock. About 350 visitors a year still took the waters there until 1913, when the well was closed because river water was seeping in and polluting it.[22]

The founder of the spa at the Worcestershire village of Malvern was a physician, Dr John Wall (1708–760), who publicized the two main wells – the Holy Well at Malvern Wells and St Ann's Well at Great Malvern. These were not mineral springs, but they had been noted for their healing power, and he stated: 'The efficacy of this water seems chiefly to arise from its great purity.' He built a bath-house by the Holy Well and a lodging house. Thereafter Malvern continued in a small way, and in 1812 it was still a minor, unambitious spa with several hotels. No effort was made to promote a communal life or social activities; it had no assembly rooms or central promenade. Apart from encounters at the wells and on hill walks, visitors usually only met at the public table of their hotel and spent much time in their private apartments.

A beginning in the provision of spa amenities came in 1815 when John Beard established a coffee room and a subscription newsroom in his Crown Hotel, the gardens of which began the zig-zag path used by visitors who climbed or rode by donkey up the wooded hillside to St Ann's Well, which (owing to Great Malvern's better accommodation and amenities) was becoming the more popular spa. There they went to the small well-house erected in 1813 to drink glassfuls of water or place an affected limb under the spout, assisted by a woman attendant described as 'neat and clean and with great civility'.

A further initiative came from Samuel Deykes, who established a

small library near the Foley Arms, which he had planned. John Southall, the Worcester organist, who had moved to Malvern in 1812, took
this over, transferred it to his house, No. 1 Paradise Row, and made it a
more permanent and respectable collection. The library room, however,
was too small and inelegant to serve as a public room to shelter people of
rank in bad weather. Edward T. Foley, the lord of the manor, resolved to
have a building suitable to Malvern's rising importance on a site opposite the Unicorn Inn and near the Foley Arms. In 1818 he engaged a
London architect, John Deykes of Bartletts Buildings (possibly the son
of Samuel Deykes, who though aged about 75 was Clerk of the Works
for the project) to plan a building comprising a library, assembly rooms
and billiard rooms costing £2,000, which the hotel-keepers supported.
The resulting classical premises became Malvern's elegant and dignified social hub – a building with a pedimented front, two tall storeys, a
garret floor above and a south bow front protected by railings, following
the style of contemporary buildings in Cheltenham. It contained a reading room 50 feet in length, a circulating library, a music room and a
bazaar selling perfumery, toys, stationery and other miscellaneous articles like, it was said, such libraries in Worthing, Brighton and Cheltenham. Pianofortes could be hired and letters addressed there. John
Southall and his wife took over this business, though with little profit,
and conducted the apartments above as the St Edith Lodging House,
where Foley stayed when visiting Malvern. Mary Southall produced *A
Description of Malvern* (1822 and 1825), updating John Chambers, *A
General History of Malvern* (1817).[23]

The project cost £4,217, over twice the estimate. Painswick stone was
used for facing and Broseley tiles, with fittings and metalwork from
London. This did not deter Foley from erecting another public building
on the north side of the library, the Malvern Baths, again designed by
Deykes, which was finished in 1823. This stolid, single-storeyed building, with an entablature and balustrade, had three front entrances, the
central one between two columns. The pump-room within was circular
with a domed ceiling, and from it corridors led to warm, cold and
plunge baths.[24]

Malvern's spa facilities were further increased by improvements to
the chalybeate well near Swan Pool, north-east of the village. This had
been enclosed by a white railing, but its owner neglected it and left the
key at the library. In June 1825 a pump-room, now known as Spa
Cottage, was constructed, and walks were laid around. So now three of
Malvern's springs were protected by buildings.[25]

Malvern was thus on a level with the more modest contemporary
spas, like Ashby-de-la-Zouch which it resembled architecturally, but it
had better hotel accommodation than most small spas and might benefit

from trade with Cheltenham and Leamington. Handsome villas and 'cottages' were also built in the 1820s and 1830s to provide lodgings, entire or in part, for visitors, especially along the Worcester Road, where Deyke designed some of the detached houses, one costing £1,300. This was not high compared with Cheltenham where in 1815 a house in Bath Villas, though furnished, cost £3,000.[26]

Great Malvern had no planned estates or terraces of houses as the larger spas were then developing. It was still, as Mary Berry said, by the end of 1825 when the national recession set in, 'very little Malvern', an idyllic village spa with some dignified public buildings and lodging houses of classical restraint. Along the Worcester Road were six villas extending to Bredon House (c. 1824) and others standing independently on isolated sites like Melton House (c. 1818) on the way to Malvern Wells. The new lodging houses in Paradise Row and the hotels in Belle Vue Terrace now also helped to make Great Malvern the focus of social activity, while Malvern Wells failed to expand, although it had a few houses where men of substance lived.[27] Already several drives and walks over the Malvern Hills were laid out, including Foley Terrace made by Deykes in 1819 at Foley's expense and the lengthy Harcourt Walk named after Mary, Countess of Harcourt, who did more than anyone else to encourage the making of paths and left £100 in her will for their upkeep.[28] But Malvern's development was piecemeal. The Foleys, the chief landowners, had no coherent or ambitious building projects like those of Henry Thompson or Joseph Pitt at Cheltenham, although they insisted on a rule, which gave Malvern its distinctive character as 'a forest of villas' set amidst the pleasure gardens and shrubberies often mentioned by the guide books, that every house must be built in at least an acre of land.[29] They insisted also from 1816 on approved plans, good building and completion within a year.[30]

Socially Malvern became reputed as being aristocratic and secluded, the refuge of invalids. Sheltered under the lee of the Malvern Hills, it claimed the longest season of any spa, from March to September with, even in the 1820s, a peak season of higher charges from 1 June until the end of October. Later when the railway brought 'canal coal', it claimed to be a winter resort.[31] Its social amenities in the early nineteenth century were minimal compared with other notable spas, and there was no attempt to promote an integrated public life. There was no large public building; no assembly room until 1884; no long room attached to any of the wells; and no central promenade like the Promenade at Cheltenham or the Pantiles at Tunbridge Wells. Nor was there even a primitive theatre, though in 1794 William Well, who had theatres all over the West Midlands, obtained a licence to perform in Malvern, and there are two extant theatre bills of 1802.[32] There was no attempt to institute a master of ceremonies, and public balls and dances were unknown. The only regular communal activity was the Monday evening conversations established at Southall's Library House just before 1822.[33]

The situation meant that the reception rooms of the Malvern hotels were especially large, so that, in the absence of assembly rooms, invalids could enjoy the pleasures of society there in easy chairs.[34] The importance of the hotels' public table meant that it required some regulation as in public rooms elsewhere. Rule IV at Easington Lodge, which had two front parlours, required guests to assemble to dine together at 3 p.m. each day, and two bells were rung at 2.30 and 3 p.m. As at Matlock, and to some extent Buxton, a uniform scale of charges was attempted by 1817. Full board and lodging at two guineas a week included wines and spirits, but not sugar and tea. A room alone might cost 8s. to 14s. with extra for lighting and servants' rooms and board. These were terms of the Southalls in 1822, though rooms might cost more. They charged 3s. 6d. for tea for upper servants, though the normal price for tea was 1s. 6d. Presumably the upper servants had a good tea and did not have supper charged separately at only 1s. 6d.[35]

There were some retail services by 1825, including 'good' shops of milliners, haberdashers and grocers, to which vegetables and dairy produce came daily from the rich adjacent countryside.[36] There was no supply problem, as then at Buxton, but Elizabeth Syndercombe, when at the Crown (for the second time) on her honeymoon tour in June 1837, found it a great contrast with the Imperial at Cheltenham. There were no lobsters, cream or papers; and she and her husband had 'to satisfy our mental and bodily comfort by the well-thumbed *Topographical History of Gloucestershire* and slices of cold beef', But she liked returning there, especially seeing familiar places, including the chalybeate spa, now with its gardens.[37]

By 1822 Malvern had attracted also residential professional people. A 'physician of great note' lived in the new Melton House, possibly one of the two surgeons, Henry Beale and Mr Walden. Two apothecaries and an attorney, Philip Ballard, had also settled there, and Mr Bradley, a London portrait-painter, came for the season. Two schools foreshadowed Malvern's educational importance. Benjamin Goodman, in St Ann's Road, taught languages, mathematics and other subjects to young gentlemen, while the Misses Billing gave a 'polite and useful education' to young ladies. The vicar, Dr Henry Card, formerly tutor to Edward Foley, continued his predecessor's restoration of the priory; and there were 222 country gentlemen in the neighbourhood.

Before the recession of 1825, Malvern still expanded but at a lower rate. In 1801–11, a total of 41 new houses were built, and the population grew by 47 per cent to 1,205. Twice as many new houses, 89 in all, were built in 1811–21, but the population growth slowed to 22 per cent; and 1821–31 saw only a slight recovery. The 1841 Census, held in June, included at least 150 visitors among the 1,718 residents, but there were now 490 houses instead of the 183 in 1801.[38]

The leading builder in this expansion was probably Thomas McCann, a mason working in Malvern at least from 1813, since a workman in 1860 said that he had been employed by him for 47 years. He worked on the restoration of the priory in 1816 and owned at least one building plot in the Worcester Road. His son, who was living at the Chase in the Worcester Road by 1873, entered the business in 1822 and continued the firm after his father's death in 1852. McCann, described as a builder and farmer, had a yard at Fold Farm and shared an office at nearby Graham House with another builder, John Broad of Ivy Cottage, Red Lion Bank, united to the McCanns by marriage.[39] A third builder was Thomas Harrington, active from about 1825 to 1855.[40]

The sudden increase in the number of houses included cottages for tradesmen, labourers and quarrymen. Many were engaged in building; McCann alone by 1860 employed some 150. Before 1850 cottages were built in part of Link Top and later in the angle of the Cowleigh, and North Malvern, and Worcester Roads. North Malvern, beyond the land sold by the Foley Estate for building for visitors, was largely owned by the Hornyolds and was made more accessible in 1816 by a new road parallel to the old West Malvern Road of 1788. Building at Wyche followed the cutting of a new turnpike road in 1838 to Ledbury to replace the old steep and narrow way at Old Wyche which was too difficult for carriages.[41]

Already by the 1830s the increasing population caused social problems culminating in strikes in 1860. A prominent philanthropist converted by the situation was Lady Lyttleton, who came to Malvern about 1800 and devoted herself to charitable activities, especially the education of the poor, and when she died in 1840, the funeral carriages took an hour to pass through Great Malvern to the Priory churchyard.[42] Another was Charles Morris, Junior, of Portman Square, London, perhaps the son of Charles Morris living at Mitton Lodge near Tewkesbury in 1817. He settled in Malvern at the Chase in the 1830s. In 1850–52 he and George McCann were the principal purchasers of 16 plots of land in Graham Terrace and Albert Road, and he provided water-tanks there 'for the use of the neighbouring poor'. The first tank, erected at North Malvern in 1835, cost £80, but was soon inadequate for the growing population, and the next year he provided another holding 50,000 gallons costing £300. For three months 63 workmen of the parish built this, and an inscription on it recorded Morris's 'benefaction'; and on its completion the workmen were treated to dinner at the Foley Arms.[43] The walk to Sugar Loaf Hill was also made in 1830 at his personal expense and under his supervision.[44]

The first new church to serve the growing population was St Peter's at Malvern Wells, built for the numerous local poor for whom a half of the 600 seats were reserved; but it served also the visitors at the Well House who had hitherto had services conducted there by the Rector of Hanley Castle. The Rector of Malvern, the Revd P. Boissier, personally paid for the church in 1836; the architect was W.A. Jearrad, much engaged at Cheltenham.[45] Malvern Wells, West Malvern and Malvern Link all required churches as the centre of the town grew, especially since fashionable visitors monopolized the rented pews, and space for the poor was restricted. As late as 1841 North Hill District Church was planned as a chapel of ease at Link Top on a site given by Lady Emily Foley, but though £200 was collected its building was delayed until, after a large donation by Charles Morris and his sister, it was built in 1851 as Holy Trinity Church. Most of its 350 seats were free, but visitors could hire pews.[46] At Quarlford subscriptions were raised to build St Mary's as a chapel of ease by George McCann in 1844. Foley gave the ground for the chapel and an adjoining school for 40 to 50 children with £565 towards the building and an endowment of £1,000; and Charles Norris donated the communion plate and a liberal subscription. Local farmers and day-labourers gave their services free to convey materials for its erection.[47] Nonconformist chapels were established mainly in the poorer parts of the town, and numbered 21 by 1840.[48]

Both the 'good Lady Lyttleton' and Charles Morris promoted the education of the poor. Schools had been held in the priory porch and a room above the Unicorn Inn, but in 1814 Lady Lyttleton founded the Lyttleton Sunday School in a long, low building on glebe land in the north-east corner of the priory churchyard, which in 1817 had 100 pupils. It survived as the Lyttleton Grammar School.[49] She started also about 1825 the Lyttleton School of Industry in her house at Peckham Grove where poor children were taught 'useful' subjects including spinning, knitting, reading and agricultural skills. The first National School was built in the growing district of North Malvern, supported by such important donors as the Duchess of Kent and Prince (later King) Leopold of Belgium, but it was soon too small and was rebuilt in 1838 largely at Charles Morris's expense, becoming known as the Morris School. But many Malvern children still had no education at all.[50]

Another charitable venture, common in spa towns, was the Dispensary for the Poor established in 1830 by the usual donations and subscriptions to supply poor people with food and medicines and nursing attendance if necessary. The average annual attendance of 500 from Malvern and district showed its need, as did the founding of a Visiting Society in 1840 to help the deserving poor.[51]

This charitable work was supplemented by the mandatory poor relief arrangements, much strained by the problems of rapid expansion. As Brian Smith has indicated, Malvern's population at this time displayed disturbing facts worthy of closer study. Despite its prosperity, wages there were the lowest in Worcestershire except at Tenbury Wells, which from 1839 was also seeking spadom. Perhaps the attractiveness of such places enabled employers to pay low wages. Apart from Pershore, no town had more public houses per head of population than Malvern, and its crime record, especially against property, was higher than usual. The vicar, Dr Card, vainly supported the parish constable's wish for a lock-up. As in other spas, the wealthier people, here the gentry and freeholders, protected themselves against disorder by forming an Association for the Prosecution of Felons, still active in 1841.[52]

When Granville visited the spa in 1837, the first generation who had initiated it, were gone, but others were active. In 1838 Miss C. Ridler, who conducted the Foley Arms (renamed the Royal Kent Coburg and Foley Arms after the visit of the twelve-year-old Princess Victoria and the Duchess of Kent in 1830, though they stayed at Hollymount Lodge), moved to the Well House, hoping to restore its former celebrity. Edward Archer, who had a wine shop adjacent to the Foley Arms since 1835, now owned the hotel, and his daughter had by 1840 taken over the Crown from Andrew Morrison. His son, John Archer, was to succeed him at the Foley Arms by about 1862.[53] The Malvern Baths, now the Coburg Baths, were conducted by George Matthews and later George Archer. George Warwick of Worcester combined the functions of linen-draper, silk-mercer, hosier and undertaker at the later-famed Warwick House. He ran also the adjacent Hayward Baths, with the usual range of warm, cold, shower, vapour and plunging-baths, and let lodgings. His next-door neighbour in Abbey Road was Thomas Cox, who also let lodgings and later operated Warwick House, but under the name of Kenilworth House. In 1831 William Townlow started a grocery and drapery shop at Malvern Link, and John Mason opened the Post Office in Belle Vue Terrace. The Worcester Turnpike Trustees in 1833, 1835 and 1836 improved the local roads;[54] and by 1841 a well-developed network of coach services ran daily to Cheltenham, Carmarthen and Abergavenny. Each day three coaches ran to Hereford and seven to Worcester, five of which called at the Birmingham and Gloucester Railway Station at Spetchley, so linking with Birmingham and the industrial Midlands.[55] So well-known was the Malvern spa by 1837 that in

September a long list of its visitors appeared in the *Bath and Cheltenham Gazette*, the first such notice there.[56]

Despite these stirrings of commercial activity, Granville found the place lethargic when he arrived at the Belle Vue Hotel at 8.30 a.m. on a September morning. Only one servant was up, no room was ready to receive travellers, and he had to wait for breakfast. The Kent and Coburg and the Crown Hotels were no better, but signs of life appeared later in the day as Malvern Ridge swarmed with explorers, walkers, picnickers and donkeys, introduced by 1837 to carry the infirm on the steep hills, perhaps in imitation of Tunbridge Wells.[57] But soon after Granville's visit, the advent of Dr James Wilson in 1842 and soon afterwards of Dr James Gully, both bringing new ideas of water-treatment to Malvern, soon aroused the village spa into an explosion of activity and inaugurated the second and decisive stage of its development.

8

Northern Spas

Harrogate (then two small separate settlements known as High and Low Harrogate) still lacked most spa facilities in 1815 and expanded only slowly in the 1820s and 1830s. High Harrogate, where many of the dwellings along the Stray became lodging houses during the season, remained the commercial and social centre, but its chalybeate wells became less important as Low Harrogate's sulphur waters were better patronized, though it was mainly a settlement of hotels. By 1822 the whole of Harrogate had 12 hotels, of which Low Harrogate had seven, including the Crown (the most expensive) and the White Hart (next in order), but only five of the 46 lodging and boarding houses.

In 1820–40 two districts known collectively as Central Harrogate were developed between High and Low Harrogate. Several houses were built there; and on a key site, at a road junction at the west end of the Stray, Michael Hattersley about 1820 built Hattersley's Hotel, later called the Brunswick, rebuilt extensively in 1861, and from 1866 called the Prince of Wales. The other new district was on the higher ground east of the Low Harrogate valley where were built Prospect Place (1814), a row of lodging houses; Prospect Row (1821), later West Park, a handsome terrace; and Beulah Place about this time. Regent Parade, Park Parade (having houses with Regency balconies) and Devonshire Place were built in High Harrogate Church Square by 1821.[1]

The principal shops lined Regent Parade and Park Parade. As in other spas, several opened only for the season and had London connections. By 1843 such firms in High Harrogate were G. Redmayne (fancy goods), Marshall and Stinton (silks and shawls) and Miss Turnbull (millinery). Debenham, Pooley and Smith of 44 Wigmore Street, London, had a store in High Harrogate called Cavendish House, as in Cheltenham, after their fashionable London trade drawn from Cavendish Square.[2]

Although until the 1830s Harrogate was essentially a village spa with a sophisticated veneer and some charming Regency houses, a contemporary regarded its inns as 'immense piles of buildings' unequalled in other spas. As in urban spas, the Granby and others had extensive stables for the coroneted chariots, britzschkas, post-chaises, gigs and carts conveying visitors and their servants. Some tradesmen kept livery stables during the season and plied for hire a variety of vehicles drawn by horses, mules and donkeys on local journeys or excursions to such sights as Plumpton Lake and Spofford's old ruins. Two coachbuilding firms existed by 1822.[3] In the 1820s summer season coaches ran from the Black Swan Tally-Ho Coach Office in York to both Scarborough and Harrogate. By September 1838 the *Harrogate Advertiser* listed 18 daily stage coach departures from Harrogate, including three through services to Manchester and three to Newcastle. Ten or eleven of the services went through or to Leeds, some after 1834 to connect with the Leeds–Selby railway.[4]

Better transport markedly helped Harrogate's expansion in the 1830s, but it lacked public baths. Bathing facilities were still limited to single bath-tubs in the hotels and lodging houses, except in the Crown Hotel, where the enterprising Joseph Thackwray installed not only the usual hot and cold but also shower, vapour, fumigating and medicated baths.

Neither High nor Low Harrogate had the first public baths; it was Starbeck, halfway between Harrogate and Knaresborough. It had chalybeate and sulphur springs, which were disused by the early nineteenth century.[5] A Knaresborough druggist, hinting that rival interests had deliberately destroyed the springs, secured the help of Dr Murray, a local physician, to restore Starbeck Old Spa. In March 1822, Michael Calvert, the druggist, and the doctor organized a public meeting in Knaresborough, which appointed a committee to raise subscriptions, and in May the foundations of a pump-room were laid to cover the sulphur well of the renamed Knaresborough Spa. As the local linen industry was declining, there was a wish to reclaim the spa visitors back from Harrogate, so in 1828 a further step was taken to save the stagnating economy of the township of which Starbeck was a detached portion. Investors, who received a fixed interest, erected public baths at Starbeck, and in 1829 this 'ancient and long-neglected spring' was said to be gaining fame and much patronized. The two-storeyed, Gothic-style villa with a one-storeyed annexe set in shrubberies and approached down a lane through a castellated archway still stands off Spa Lane. Warm, cold and shower baths were provided to meet the generally rising standard of comfort and increasing range of treatment in bath-houses.

133

They were extended in the early 1830s and by 1838 included four warm baths, two shower baths and a cold plunge. In a few years the number of bathrooms was increased to nine, and extra supplies of sulphur water were laid on. Another spring of mild sulphur water was found in a nearby field in 1868, where a second suite of baths was built in 1870.[6]

Harrogate met the challenge of the Starbeck baths by much activity and expansion. Pump-rooms were built in the early 1830s. The first was a small one over a newly discovered well near the Ripon Road owned by John Williams, who named it the Cheltenham Saline Well because a local doctor thought it like the Cheltenham mineral waters. Soon afterwards Thackwray developed springs found on land east of his hotel, erecting an octagonal pump-room, designed like a Chinese pagoda, and laying out pleasure gardens. And a pump-room was built behind the Crescent Inn to supply the saline iron Crescent Water.

Then came Harrogate's public baths, beginning with the Victoria Baths built by Williams in 1832 on the site of the present Crescent Gardens and adjoining the Promenade Room of 1805. They were grander than Starbeck's, having 13 bathrooms and a sophisticated variety of vapour, fume, shower and douche baths. When he acquired the land, a clause in the surrender prevented him building on the surface, so he placed the foundations of his low bath-house with an Ionic front below the level of the ground.[7]

His rival's completion of the baths in his hotel led Thackwray in 1835 to build the larger Crown (later Montpellier) Baths in the gardens near his sulphur springs. A lithograph of about 1850 by W. Monkhouse depicts it as a long, single-storeyed building with a pedimented classical-style entrance and a wing on each side. It set a new standard of elegance and luxury in Harrogate. Each side of the building had six bathrooms entered through waiting-rooms, one side for ladies and one for gentlemen. The bathing tanks were lined with white tiles, painted and varnished externally, and had ledges of polished black marble. To add to the wonder, the water for these baths was drawn from six springs by pumps worked by a steam-engine into a reservoir and heated by steam from the engine's boiler. The bathers were entertained in warm weather by a band playing under the portico in the central hall. The Royal Baths now cover the site. Thackwray also demolished some old cottages near the hotel and built there a library and reading room, both needed by a successful spa town.

Granville considered these 'two superb establishments' equal to anything in other spas. They were also strong rivals, both charging 3s. for each warm bath, but the Montpellier dispensed some 6,000 baths a season against the Victoria's 4,000.[8]

Williams responded to Thackwray in 1853 by replacing the small pump-room at the Cheltenham Saline Well with the Royal Promenade and Cheltenham Pump Room, the spa's most splendid public building combining a pump-room with the long-awaited assembly room. With a saloon 100 by 33 feet and lofty in proportion, and a pedimented entrance with a flight of steps supported by six massive Doric columns, it resembled in scale, style and surroundings the Pittville Pump Room at Cheltenham opened five years earlier. It housed also a subscription library and was used for concerts and dances. About six acres of gardens surrounded it, adorned with statues, a fountain, flower-beds and shrubs with easy seats and alcoves. These gardens lay between Walker's Lane (now King's Road) and Coppice Beck, which was dammed to form a long, narrow boating lake, but later problems were already evident. The Beck collected Low Harrogate's sewage and waste water from the sulphur baths. But that was unknown in 1835 when this huge investment, 'Regency' Harrogate's crowning achievement, was opened with a fine dress ball and grand fireworks display.[9]

Thackwray and Williams, in acquiring privately owned mineral water for drinking and bathing, were offending against the Forest of Knaresborough Enclosure Act of 1770, which threatened prosecution for the sinking of wells or other digging liable to endanger Harrogate's established wells; and innkeepers, unable to compete in providing such elaborate facilities, wished to protect the right of public access to some 25 local sulphur wells, especially the Old Sulphur Well and those in the Bogs Field.[10] In 1835 when Thackwray, seeking more sulphur water for his new baths, sank a well in his hotel cellar only 50 feet from the Old Sulphur Well, several indignant innkeepers indicted him. When the case appeared at the York Assizes in March 1737, he agreed to allow public access to the well. He knew that those drinking the water free would have to take away the taste with the beverages he was licensed to sell.

Thackwray died in April 1837 and Williams soon after.[11] In 1843 Richard Staning took over the Crown Hotel, but Thackwray's widow, living in Somerset Cottage, retained an interest in the Montpellier Baths, where the next year she tapped the neglected well with a pipe, but was made to disconnect it.[12] Williams's property was also split. The locally formed Victoria Company bought the Victoria Baths, renaming them the Victoria Reading Room and Baths with the attraction of organ recitals in the morning. The weekly charge was 2s. 6d. a person and 7s. a family. In 1841 Williams's executors leased the Cheltenham Pump Room at £300 for the season to an entrepreneur, Thomas Gordon, who also paid 12 guineas a week for a band from London. His weekly charge was 3s. 6d. and 10s. a family, and by 1843 he had increased the single person's charge to 4s. and had a graduated scale for a week, a month or a season.[13]

135

The demand for public baths was still unsatisfied. Joshua Holdsworth of Leeds bought the dilapidated buldings at The Harrogate Cold Bath on Cold Bath Road in 1837, erected a large lodging house with bathing-rooms and charged 1s. for plunging, shower and spouting baths. This building was named after St Magnus, not to be confused with St Mungo's Well at Copgrove. At Harlow Car, a mile and a half south-west of Low Harrogate, were four sulphur and chalybeate springs known since the eighteenth century. In 1840 the owner of the estate, Henry Wright, cleaned and protected them and in 1844 built a low, single-storeyed suite of baths and a nearby double-storeyed hotel in a neo-Gothic style. The grounds were 'neatly laid out' and surrounded by a 'pleasing retreat' of shrubs and trees. He hoped to recoup his outlay by charging 2s. 6d. for a warm sulphur bath (reduced to 2s. the next season), 1s. for a shower and 1s. weekly for non-bathers drinking the waters; but he apparently failed since by 1871 the hotel was a private residence. Some years before 1838 there was also the small Clarke's Baths in Chapel (now Oxford) Street, but they were inferior to the chief baths. By the mid-1840s bathing in hotels and lodging houses had largely given way to public baths.[14]

Besides public buildings, the booming 1830s produced private houses and streets. Brunswick Terrace, Cheltenham Place, Grove Terrace and seven other squares and terraces were built by 1843 in Low Harrogate. At the crossroads leading from the Brunswick Hotel was York Place, where in-filling between Low and High Harrogate proceeded. North-umberland Place (with at least four lodging houses) and Gilhead Terrace were completed. Caroline Place and North Parade were new streets in High Harrogate, developing less rapidly now that the centre of activity was in the lower town.[15]

Much of this new accommodation was unoccupied out of season. By 1831 Harrogate's population with Bilton, though over twice that of 1801, was still only 2,812, very small compared with Bath and Chelten-ham, though in one week in September 1828 there were 713 estimated visitors, while by September 1849, a year after the railway's arrival, there were 1,911. The season, short in this northern clime, was from June to September with a high season for a month at the end of August between the York and Doncaster races. though there seem to have been efforts to prolong it. On 7 October 1838 it was claimed that more visitors came after the York Festival than for many years at a time so late in the season, and 200 attended a fashionable ball at the Crown Hotel.[16] The Harrogate tradition of holding balls in turn at the leading hotels continued, but there were now some in the new Cheltenham Pump Room, where a master of ceremonies and six or eight stewards, wearing smart coats and white rosettes, were temporarily drawn from the company.[17] From 1828, William Langdale, owner of one of the two libraries in High Harrogate, published a list of visitors; and on 26 September 1836 Postmaster Palliser of High Harrogate started for the season only a newspaper, the *Harrogate Advertiser*, with details of local facilities.

The influx of visitors and the distance of Bilton Parish Church required a church at Low Harrogate. The King, as Duke of Lancaster, gave the site for St Mary's Church, built in 1825 with 800 sittings, 500 of them free, and assigned a parish in 1830. And in High Harrogate St John's Chapel, built in 1749 and enlarged, was still inadequate for seasonal congregations. It was demolished, and Christ Church was built on the site in 1831 with 1,250 sittings, 800 of them free. By 1841 there was a Congregational Chapel in Low Harrogate and a Weslyan Methodist one in Central Harrogate.[18]

The Bachelors Garden School, a charity school founded in 1793 by two bachelor brothers, Richard and Francis Taylor, to give 30 children religious instruction and elementary education, was supplemented by a National School in Skipton Road (1832) and a British School (1835). William Sheepshanks of Harrogate and Leeds, one of Harrogate's chief benefactors, in 1837 entirely paid for an Infants' School in Church Square.[19]

The poor were given medical treatment after the style of the Buxton Bath Charity; and the parish of Panal occasionally paid for the poor to take the water at the Sulphur Well, which attracted the needy there.[20] Early in the nineteenth century, a charitable fund was started for the relief and treatment of poor patients, to which collections in hotels and lodging houses brought some £200 a year. Patients were granted 7s. a week, the cost of cheap lodgings and tickets for two sulphur baths at 1s. 6d. each. In 1821, a total of 140 patients were relieved and 645 baths provided. From this came a more ambitious plan for special baths and then a hospital for the poor. In 1825 the Bath Hospital (supported by subscriptions) was erected near the bogs on land given by the Earl of Harewood. Poor people living within three miles qualified for free use of the mineral waters with board, lodging and medical aid.[21]

The Thackwray lawsuit had emphasized the contrast between the Old Sulphur Well's primitive facilities and the comfortable, elegant privately owned pump-rooms. The free Old Sulphur Well's future was uncertain as better-off people now avoided it. In December 1838 an Association for the Protection of the Wells was formed, which by the next spring raised over £100 to improve the Old Sulphur Well. Similar local initiative provided 30 seats on the Stray and along field paths.[22] But more positive action and local power was needed if Harrogate was to become more than a village spa and achieve urban status. Though having some national fame since 1626, its development was, as Granville said in 1841, 'slow and late'. He deplored the vandalism, invasion of public privileges and rights and bickering between High and Low Harrogate through the lack of any form of government and or a single representative civic authority.[23]

Other spa towns had already achieved their improvement acts, which Harrogate belatedly did in 1841. The town's goverment was vested in 21 commissioners for protecting the mineral springs and regulating the stinted pasture. They were drawn from property owners or long-lease holders worth £25 a year,[24] or those rated for poor relief at £35, but their election was by all rated at £3 or more. They had the usual powers of such commissioners to grant licences, regulate hackney carriage fares, make and repair footpaths, construct common sewers, remove nuisances, control house-building, cleanse the streets and provide markets, but also most importantly make bye-laws for the management of the springs. Harrogate could preserve its open spaces and springs as landmarks because most were public property and not, as now at Cheltenham and Leamington, privately owned.[25]

Several commissioners were concerned to safeguard the public supply of mineral water – John Richardson of Parliament Street, a chemist, manufacturer of Harrogate salts and a lodging-house keeper; Thomas H. Walker, owner of a wine shop (which also bottled spa water for sale), a large lodging house (Northumberland House, formerly the Crescent Hotel) and the Crescent Saline Spring; Thomas Gordon, a lessee of the Cheltenham Pump Room; and Leonard Hobkinson, keeper of the Cold Bath and adjoining lodging house. Bottled Sulphur and Cheltenham Waters were, it was now claimed, sent all over the kingdom, though they were previously thought to lose their potency in transport. Granville called the hoteliers 'the lords of the place', and several were on the Commission, including John Dearlove of the Queen's Hotel, who had opposed Thackwray in the lawsuit.[26]

At their first meeting in July 1851 they decided to erect a pump-room over the Old Sulphur Well. The architect chosen was Isaac T. Shutt, whose family kept the Crown Hotel, and his octagonal building to hold 150 people was opened in 1842 as the Royal Pump Room. It cost over £2,000, and the commissioners let it in the mid-1840s at £420 annually. Its waters were available on sale or to subscribers, but it had a free pump outside.

Sketches of Harrogate by 'A Citizen of the World' (1841) told how most visitors went to the Old Sulphur Well 'at seven o'clock or soon after' to be received by the well-women, 'eight or ten nymphs, whose personal attractions are not calculated to make one insensible to the nauseous flavour of the draught which they bestow'. They were ruled by the aged Betty Lupton, called 'Old Betty' or 'The Queen of Harrogate' and privileged to dispense 'the waters and quips and quodlibets with equal liberality'.[27]

The cupola over the Old Sulphur Well (built in 1804 was removed to the Tewit Well, and a new pump-room, also designed by Shutt, was put over St John's Well. These two High Harrogate wells were usually let for £5 annually.[28] The Commission erected also a small pump-room over the Magnesia Well in Bogs Field in 1858.

Other improvements were left to private enterprise. The town was first lighted with gas in 1846 by the joint-stock Harrogate Gas Company founded in 1845 with works in the Oakbeck valley, where there had been a public stone quarry; it contracted with the commissioners to supply 94 street-lamps. Nor did the commissioners act over the deficient and polluted water supply caused by the influx of visitors. The Harrogate Water Company, founded in 1845, secured the requisite Act of Parliament and built a reservoir on Harlow Hill. The commissioners' only action was to contract with the company for the provision of 18 fire-plugs.[29]

Harrogate was also slow, like Buxton, to acquire a market, because the hoteliers and innkeepers monopolized supplies in both towns, and visitors did not, as at Bath, Cheltenham and Tunbridge Wells, take private, self-catering lodgings. Buxton had a market in 1813, but Harrogate's position remained unsatisfactory. Indifferent supplies came from Knaresborough's market; and six or seven hotels, with 100 guests a day each, commandeered the provisions in the neighbourhood. Some hotels had their own piggeries or farms, but most people had to rely on Knaresborough or hawkers. The *Harrogate Advertiser* stated in 1847 that the town lacked a confectioner, fishmonger and poulterer. Occasionally fish came from Scarborough, but the fishwoman usually had sold her stock to hotels by 10 a.m. The commissioners wanted a public market in 1848, but the ratepayers opposed its funding, and Harrogate had to await its market until 1874.[30]

Fortunately the commissioners did not supervise the Stray, the 'Two Hundred Acres' of open space, but the Stray owners to whom the cattle stints or gates were allocated. The 1841 Improvement Act empowered them to maintain and improve it, and they undertook a drainage scheme costing over £1,000 in the 1850s and some tree-planting in the 1860s.[31]

Yet mid-century Harrogate was still a rural spa of some charm dominated by its two churches, the grandiose Royal Pumnp Room, the bathing establishments and hotels. Although it could have adopted urban government, it remained, in Granville's words, a 'mere village' extended 'without design and consistency' for 270 years. Cheltenham and Leamington were changed in a few years from villages into 'smart and pert towns', but he thought Harrogate more truly a spa.[32] Its spa facilities were now concentrated almost entirely in Low Harrogate with the baths, public rooms and gardens, but it was a relatively open settlement mainly depending on its spa function. In 1838 it had also most of the hotels and lodging houses, 79 compared with 51 in High Harrogate and 21 in Central Harrogate which was, however, growing rapidly both along the West Park Stray and around Beulah Place.

High Harrogate still kept its commercial supremacy, with the chief shopping area fronting Regent Parade, but residential building was appearing in the newer areas south-west of the Stray. To the north, there were scattered buildings at, for example, Smithy Hill, Harrogate End and Bachelors Gardens, which in the 1851 Census had 59.5 per cent of the totally employed artisans, labourers and industrial workers, especially stone masons, and it later became the main working-class area. This census, taken in March when visitors were few in the two local townships, recorded a population for Harrogate with Bilton of 3,434 and 1,376 for Pannal. As J.A. Patmore has shown, 19 per cent of those employed in Harrogate were hotel workers, including hotel, inn and lodging-house keepers, but not some hotel staff, who lived out and were listed as domestic servants. In Harrogate's shopping area, 21 per cent were engaged in trade; Central Harrogate was more mixed with many more craftsmen and 36 per cent in industry; and in Low Harrogate 35 per cent worked in hotels and lodging houses.

There was no large immigration of workers – 41 per cent of Harrogate's inhabitants were born within the township and 14 per cent within an eight-mile radius. Yorkshire people comprised 88 per cent of its inhabitants, especially the 304 domestic servants, who came largely from the West Riding and Vale of York. The stone masons, although mostly Yorkshire men, came also from Lancashire, South Durham, Lincolnshire, Somerset, Gloucestershire and Warwickshire. Emigration from these last three counties suggests that they might be unemployed builders from Bath, Cheltenham and Leamington, where the major building boom was over.[33]

Granville in 1839 noticed a changing social scene at Harrogate. In the early season the spa was monopolized by cutlers, cotton-spinners and other wealthy townsmen of Yorkshire and Lancashire, but on their departure in the high season the wealthy aristocrats and gentry returned, and 'then the money flies, and six weeks of a plentiful harvest' enabled hotel proprietors to live comfortably for the rest of the year. He found the cost of living in Harrogate almost as high as in London through the dependence on Knaresborough and absorption of provisions by larger hotels in season. Daily charges ranged from 8s. 6d. at the Crown (with its 100 rooms) and Granby to 5s. at Binn's, the Promenade and Wellington. Bread and butter were both as dear as in London, as was fruit, though strawberries were very plentiful. Mutton (excellent at 8d. a pound), poultry, choice vegetables and fish were quickly sold. The meagre local pasturage meant poor and thin milk and scanty cream.[34]

Granville said that Harrogate had almost 1,000 patients daily in the season, and it was still a true spa because cups were dipped into unpiped springs. He was shocked to see a group of young children, aged from five to nine, made to drink the water by a maidservant, who spat out her dose while they grimaced. He found the water disagreeable – it produced eructations of sulphuretted gas 'as when one has been eating half-a-dozen eggs boiled hard or in a worse state'.

The railway changed both the customers and the supply situation in Harrogate. It came later there than to Bath and Cheltenham (both 1840 and even Scarborough (1845). Like Buxton, it was too small to suit railway promoters; the seasonal passenger traffic made investment uneconomic; a line might not benefit the spa; and the terrain was difficult for construction. On 29 July 1848, however, a branch of George Hudson's York and North Midland Railway was opened after considerable engineering feats including the high viaduct over the River Nidd. The station was in West Park opposite the Brunswick Hotel (later the Prince of Wales), which was quite convenient for both High and Low Harrogate, but as the terminus of a branch line it only served the hinterland of the industrial West Riding. A second line by the Leeds and Thirsk Railway sought to challenge Hudson's monopoly north of York. Opened on 13 September 1848, it followed a low level route with a station at Starbeck, after a debate whether it should be in High or Low Harrogate. A third line, the East and West Yorkshire Junction Railway, used the same station from 1st.October 1851 and linked Starbeck and York, but the station was isolated and inconveniently situated. Omnibuses met trains to bring passengers to Harrogate, and coaches still ran between Harrogate and Leeds. Despite fears about spoiling the countryside, rationalization came in 1854. All the area's railways formed the North Eastern Railway, a new Central Station between High and Low Harrogate was opened on 1 August 1862, and the Brunswick Station was closed.[35]

That year began a time of activity and growth which slowly changed the spa village into a municipal borough. The railway brought more visitors, estimated at 28,600 in the boom year 1845, as many as 26,700 during the economic depressiion of 1848, then 35,000 in 1849 and 36,000 in 1850. Harrogate now had excellent regional and national communications. Leeds was 45 minutes away and London 6½ hours. It became not only a resort for visitors and a pleasant retirement place for manufacturers and bankers, but also a residential place for commuters.

The resultant physical growth faced the Commissioners with the problems of local government. Their sectional interests, devoted mainly to the spa, were not the only impediment to improvement: they had limited powers, and ratepayers resisted expenditure. Now, in 1862, the Local Government Act of 1858 made the Commissioners the local Board of Health empowered to take over the gas and water companies and raise more money. They still favoured amenities for visitors to the spa. In that year they made a road from the Royal Pump Room to the springs in the Bogs Field, and at a cost of £2,000 began paving the sidewalks in 1863. This introduced a period of concentrated municipalization in 1868–74, which transformed the village finally into a town.[36]

The other important northern spa was Scarborough, which shared in the early nineteenth-century wartime boom in English spas. It enjoyed a time of gentle expansion, continuing especially into the 1820s, also a prosperous period for most spas. The third Lord Holtham, of an ancient East Riding family, inherited land in 1814 in Scarborough, which paid £1,491 that year, and sold it for £14,448 in 1820.[37] The population which, excluding Falsgrave, was still 6,409 in 1800, little more than in 1750, rose only to 6,710 in 1811, but to 8,188 in 1821 when the town was still practically contained in its thirteenth-century boundaries. Modern Westborough was known as 'Without the Bar' and had hardly a house. Falsgrave was a small, self-contained village with a few houses.[38]

A visitor in 1838 could, however, marvel at the changes of the last 30 years. New crescents, terraces and villas now constituted a South End to the town where the aristocracy, both residents and visitors, had their houses. On the cliffs the grand Spaw Walk had been formed, and besides lodging houses there were many new and handsome houses for residents since Scarborough now attracted a permanent settlement of rentiers. The Crescent, a street of 'very elegant' houses built in the fashion of spa-town architecture, dates from about 1834, and Rutland Terrace from the early nineteenth century.[39]

Harrogate had received its Improvment Act as early as 1805. Its commissioners had the usual powers to pave, clean, light and regulate the streets and alleys and to levy a rate;[40] but probably more significant was the new sense of enterprise shown by the inhabitants in the 1820s. By then several coaches were daily bringing in visitors, many going to the Bell Inn, managed by Richard Hooper, who in 1829 built 30 extra rooms and a large range of stables. From 1824 the Edinburgh steam packet-boats also brought in people, and by the next June another boat plied between Scarborough and Hull. Improvements included enlarged plantations, new walks, stonework protection against devastating tides for the 'Spaw', a new promenade, the Marine Parade, at the foot of the Marine Terrace, and Mr Champley's magnificent baths.[41]

Most important was the formation of the Cliff Bridge Company in 1826 to remedy the difficult access to the spa by a tortuous path down St Nicholas Cliff, across the Mill Beck at the foot of the valley and then over the sands. Prompted by Robert Cattle of York, the company planned to make the way easier by building a bridge to span the valley between St Nicholas Cliff and South Cliff. The Senior Bailiff, E.H. Hebden, laid the foundation stone on 29 November 1826; and on 19 July 1827, the anniversary of George IV's coronation, a mail coach passed over the bridge to mark its formal opening.[42]

These improvements attracted investment in new enterprises for the spa. By 1826 there were, besides Champley's, three sets of private baths established by Dr Wedell, Dr Travis and Mr Harland; and yet another, adjoining the Marine House, was erected by Mr Vickerman in 1829. It was claimed that Scarborough's double attraction of sea-bathing and excellent warm baths made it superior to any other spa.[43]

Scarborough's ancient St Mary's Parish Church was severely restored by Ewan Christian in 1848–50 by which the interior was 'made to conform to the rules of ecclesiastical architecture', but it lost the interesting character it had acquired in the eighteenth century, such as St Mary's, Whitby, preserved. The old church was made no larger, and two new ones, Christ Church (1828) and St Thomas's (1840), were built for the increasing number of visitors and residents.[44] There were long-established Nonconformist chapels, including the Presbyterian Old Meeting House (1704) and the Methodist Chapel (1772) founded by John Wesley.

Scarborough was not to become an important educational centre. It now had two of the charity schools already common in England. One was the Amicable Society's School, founded in 1729 to clothe poor children and educate them in the principles of the Church of England. In 1817 the corporation gave its trustees ground in North Terrace, north of Queen Street, to erect new buildings where they maintained and taught 50 boys and 30 girls. The other was the School of Industry, founded in 1808 by a group of ladies, in which some 70 girls of the 'lower order' underwent instruction and strict discipline to 'raise their moral character' and prepare them for domestic service. British Schools were founded in 1810 for 316 children and National Schools in 1836 for 138 children.[45]

In 1836, following the Municipal Corporations Act, the government of the town was placed under a council of six aldermen and eighteen counsellors, from whom a mayor was annually chosen, the first being Samual Standidge Byron. He had not long been in office when in

February 1836 a violent storm demolished the Old Spa House (built in 1739). As chairman of the Cliff Bridge Company, he secured for it a lease of the property for 200 years from 1 January 1837, after which it would revert to the corporation. The company planned to rebuild the edifice and make it a popular centre of social life. The sea walls were to be lengthened and buildings provided south of the wells for music and recreation.

Henry Wyatt designed a castellated, Gothic-style building. Water from two springs, chalybeate and saline, issued from lion-mouthed spouts in a small sunken court at the end of the great terrace. The saloon overlooked the sea and was particularly used in wet weather.It was extended by a large hall in 1847, when also the sea walls were repaired, new toll houses were built, and gas replaced the oil lamps.[46] Granville disliked both the architecture of the new building and the general state of affairs. Dancing and sociability were lacking in the hotels, and the visitors were 'the greatest separatists in England', unwilling even to return a bow.

Others by 1840 said that anyone not seen at Scarborough was out of fashion and of no account, but there were fears that the visitors were changing for the worse and might change still more in the future. A pamphlet of 1840, opposing the projected coming of the railway to Scarborough, expressed 'no wish for a greater influx of vagrants and those who have no money to spend' and predicted that in a few years the novelty of having no railroad would be Scarborough's greatest recommendation.[47] But that was not to be. At 10.30 a.m. on 7 July 1845 the engines *Hudson* and *Lion* drew a train of 35 first-class carriages from York and reached Scarborough at 1.45 p.m. to be welcomed by the mayor and corporation, so inaugurating a age of dramatic expansion in the town's holiday trade.

The pamphleteer's fears soon appeared to be justified. First-class travellers were not to dominate the railway. As early as August 1845 the railway company ran a cheap day excursion from Newcastle-upon-Tyne. Ten years later cheap fortnightly summer tickets to Scarborough, as to other resorts, were commonplace, and family tickets were cheaper still. The station refreshment room kept a list of lodgings for the many casual excursionists. Visitors were now marked by quantity rather than the quality for which the original spa facilities had been founded.

No such development took place at a hamlet picturesquely situated in a valley on the south of the River Wharfe and three miles east of Wetherby. This place had been able to assume the name of Boston Spa early in the nineteenth century as the result of a discovery made in 1744 by John Shires, a labourer from a neighbouring village, a full account of which was provided in a later lawsuit.[48] Shires declared that he saw yellowish water coming from the bank of the river. It had a brackish taste, and he found it strongly purgative as did 14 other men. A sample analysed in York found it to be saline. Some 300 hundred people came there to drink from the spring on one Sunday alone, and a wall was built to contain the bank.

The spring was only visited locally until 1753 when Tadcaster–Otley road became a turnpike and was improved; and a house was built to accommodate visitors. The spa's growing popuarity encouraged villagers in 1767 to pay for the provision of a covered-in pump, and in 1770 Sir Thomas Gascoigne, the lord of the manor, founded the Bath Company erect baths there, which were later rebuilt with hot and cold showers.[49]

By 1800 the little hamlet had became a village of some 600 inhabitants, and inns, lodging houses and elegant villas were being built along the main road. Granville visited Boston Spa in 1829. He admired the beautiful river and its salmon and trout fishing, but deprecated its 'very humble-looking building and still humbler bathrooms which ought to have been better, considering that they are erected by a company of shareholders'.[50] In 1834, however, a new Spa Bath Company was formed to make improvements. In the 1850s the schoolmistress wrote an account of the spa[51] and the curate a poem.[52] But soon after it declined; its pump-room became three houses, but many fine houses survive.[53]

9

Victorian Finale

Following his *Spas of Germany* (1837), Augustus Bozzi Granville produced what has long been the standard work on English watering-places. Published in three parts after 3,000 miles of observant travel in 1839–40, it was called *The Spas of England and Principal Sea-Bathing Places* (1841). He was dimly aware of the potentiality of the growing seaside resorts, but he saw that the large spa towns, especially Bath, Cheltenham and Leamington, and also the lesser – Harrogate, Tunbridge Wells, Malvern and Buxton – by the 1840s were suffering from over-expansion, and their spa function was declining. Larger spa towns were increasingly becoming residential areas for the retired middle classes and commuters escaping from the less pleasant environment of industrial towns; but many minor spas, some of which had functioned since the sixteenth century, were deserted with decaying well-houses and pump-rooms, while others were precariously supported by local custom.

Granville's limited analysis of the larger spa towns' changing atmosphere and decline of their traditional social life stated three causes for their near stagnation. Like many doctors, he thought that the development of the mineral-water trade undermined their reputation, since the water often lost its properties in transit. Thus the natural thermal heat of Bath's waters could not be retained, while the astringent bottle-corks combined with the iron in those of Tunbridge Wells to destroy their quality. Another cause was misrepresentation of the virtues of the waters, as at the Hot Wells of Clifton where he found that less than 100 people took the water in the whole season from the autumn of 1839 to the next summer. A third cause was mismanagement and neglect of the bathing facilities combined with undue expensiveness.[1] His knowledge of German spas enabled him to compare the 'exorbitant' charges of

Harrogate's chief hotels with the new moderate and comfortable Bellevue Hotel at Wildbad. A married couple with three daughters and three servants staying at Harrogate with a private sitting-room paid £24 3s. a week, but only £18 18s. at Wildbad, and a single gentleman and his valet paid a third more at the Dragon in Harrogate than at Wildbad.[2]

Perhaps more than expensive domestic spas, the British aristocracy's search for social exclusiveness took them increasingly to Continental spas after 1815. Not only were English spas losing their early allure as centres of aristocratic social life and becoming middle-class residential settlements, so that Granville saw that even Bath was now a town with a spa rather than a spa with a town, but as far as they were resorts, they had become the retreat of those seeking health instead of pleasure. As, particularly at Leamington and Cheltenham, purveyors of commercialized entertainment failed, invalids took over, and their interests became the first concern. A proposal to buy a steamroller to repair the roads at Malvern in 1873 was challenged as the noisy machine would upset sufferers from nervous disorders requiring rest and quiet, 'the class of visitors on whom the prosperity of the town chiefly depends'. Malvern was criticized in 1860 because invalid visitors 'much felt' the lack of seats and resting-places on the roads and hillside walks, which Spa, Baden and other Continental resorts supplied.[3] The development of the 'quiet family holiday' from the 1830s, leading spas to offer family terms at their public establishments, brought more of the middle classes to resorts in search of sober and inexpensive enjoyment.

Whether for health or pleasure or both, more aristocrats now went to Continental spas, and domestic spas had fewer lordly names on their visiting lists in the early nineteenth century, except Leamington where the hunting season attracted them. Industrial plutocrats also joined them abroad, and the German and Austrian spas flourished as never before.[4] Dr Struve called his new spa at Brighton (1825) the German Spa.

Nevertheless, the Duchess of Kent and Princess Victoria assiduously visited English spas in the early 1830s, especially favouring Tunbridge Wells with five recorded visits from 1822 when the Princess was only four years old. They were back in September 1834 to Calverley House, laid the foundation of the Royal Victoria National School and went to the races. The next year Victoria returned to see the Grove planted in her honour, and the royal party shared in many public activities, besides drinking the waters and shopping on the Parade. She was there as Queen in 1849 with Prince Albert to visit Dowager Queen Adelaide in the Calverley Hotel accompanied by Queen Marie Amelie of France, also a widow. 'Many pleasant days were spent there,' she recalled in 1872, and four years later she visited her daughter, Princess Louise, at

147

Dorden.[5] She honoured Bath in 1830, allowing its new park to be named after her, and that year was at Cheltenham and Malvern, where she was the first to use the new Victoria Walk. She visited Leamington in August and again in 1858. She passed through Buxton in 1852 and visited Matlock that October. She permitted the small spa at Bishopton in Warwickshire to be called the Victoria Spa and also Southampton after she visited it in 1830. Both Leamington (1838) and Tunbridge Wells in the next reign (1909) were allowed to adopt the prefix 'royal.'

Yet this royal patronage and interest did not make the English spas fashionable with the aristocracy. By contrast with the cosmopolitan life of Continental spas, patronized by emperors, kings, princes and dukes, English spa towns now seemed dull, invaded not only by middle-class families but also by temperance demonstrations expressing respectability, as at Pittville in Cheltenham in 1839 and Malvern in 1857; and the Bath Temperance Association was founded with 60 members in 1836.[6]

So the British aristocracy sought their pleasures in gambling casinos of the Continental spas. Spa, Baden-Baden, Carlsbad and Marienbad were among their favourites, and they were criticized for being absentees. The Marquess of Bath stayed briefly in Bath for the parliamentary election of July 1886, but then promptly left for Bad Homberg for a month.[7] Such expenditure, it was suggested, should be doubly taxed as it led to rural poverty and more crime.

Yet, despite this aristocratic exodus to the Continent, some larger spas expanded considerably, and new ones were founded, such as Woodhall Spa in Lincolnshire. Its origins in what a contemporary called 'dreary, flat and fenny country' was due to the enterprise of two men, John Parkinson and Thomas Hotchkin, in a region without a rival spa. Parkinson, a wealthy lessee of local crown lands, had three ambitions – to find coal by drilling, plant a forest and build a new town. He failed about 1807 to found a settlement, New Bolingbroke, and find coal seams. He dug at Kirkstead in the parish of Woodhall, a small scattered village (originally called Langton St Andrew) with only 145 inhabitants in 1801. Speculators had already sunk a shaft there 200 yards deep, but stopped for lack of money. Parkinson spent several thousand pounds seeking coal on the moor. He made a pit 160 yards deep, lined it with cement and then bored 117 yards lower, only to desist and cover his work when water from a copious spring seeped in. In 1820 when the spring overflowed and people drinking the water claimed it cured rheumatism and diseases of the joints, it became known as Woodhall Spa.

Over a decade later the area was owned by Thomas Hotchkin, the lord of the manor, who resolved to promote the spa. He sought advice from Bath's architect, Major Charles Edward Davis, and about 1834–36 erected a small bath-house for private use. When numbers came there and enjoyed cures, he built the Victoria Hotel in 1839 together with a suite of warm, cold and shower baths and a pump-room and reading room. This 'unostentatious' hotel, which Granville thought was pretentiously named, had two ranges of stables separated by a courtyard. Apart from some cottages, it was the only accommodation for visitors, though local gentry and physicians now began to patronize the embryonic spa.

Though the baths were close to the well, Granville persuaded Hotchkin to build a bath-house near the hotel. This was described in 1855 as 'small and elegant' with baths for ladies and gentlemen and comfortable dressing-rooms arranged on opposite sides, a pump-room handsomely equipped and lighted by a dome with a small fountain supplying the water. This mineral water was, again on Granville's advice, raised by a hydraulic belt turned by four horses and flowed into a reservoir under the well-yard. From there it was pumped into a tank over the bath-house and so descended through a heating apparatus called the 'circulating system.' Granville also introduced Hotchkin to a reputable chemist, a Mr West of Leeds, to analyse the water, which had an unusual iodine content.[8] Supporters believed this nascent English spa could combat the influence of those of Germany and Austria. They called it the 'English Kreuznach', saying that the water sparkled like champagne and resembled that of Franzenabad and Marienbad.[9]

Its surrounding pine trees did give it a distinctive character like Marienbad. The extensive planting of pines began in 1842 with a belt of trees near the well for protection from the north and north-east winds, and the grounds around the hotel were laid out with shrubberies and serpentine works. The old reputation of the Fens as unwholesome was met by extensive local drainage systems, assisted by a twenty horse-power steam engine instead of the windmills hitherto used to draw off ordinary drainwater.[10]

Visitors began to come to the new spa, though Granville said that, since standards in the hotel and baths were inadequate for many nobility and gentry, its patrons were mainly local farmers, shopkeepers from Lincoln and Boston and the 'industrious' classes. In the 1840 season, daily attendances at the pump-room were 20 or 30 in August; and during that year some 2,000 went to the bath-house managed by James Davy at 3s. each, 970 of them in the seven weeks from the end of May, and about 300 drank the water at 2s. each a week, so Hotchkin's gross receipts that season were about £330. His gains from the Victoria Hotel are not known, but the terms were reasonable at 5s. a day for a single person's board and lodging, 3s. for a servant and a guinea a week for a private sitting-room.[11]

Hotchkin had, it was estimated, spent some £30,000 in renovating the well and erecting the bath-house and hotel to which he made frequent additions. When he died sometime between 1842 and 1845, and his heir, Thomas Stafford Hotchkin, became lord of the manor, Woodhall was still a primitive spa. Its population was only 275, and the only commercialized entertainment was a circulating library and the reading room. The Primitive Methodists had built a chapel in 1834, and the first church, St Andrew's, was built in 1846 at Chapman's Corner where a Mr Chapham of Mareham-le-Fen had a grocery store. It seated only about 190, suggesting no expansion of the village was expected. Church Walk, then the main road to Horncastle, led from the church past the manor house to the Victoria Hotel.[12] By 1842 the first professional man, Thomas Snaith, a surgeon, practised there, and another, Mr King, joined him in 1855, but both practised also in Horncastle. Dr W.B. Barton, however, became the first resident physician in 1849, followed by Dr James Scott, who was responsible for the circulating heating-system in the baths. Health rather than pleasure was thought important in Woodhall. William Collier was a lodging-house keeper in 1842, and Ann Tweed, described as a 'victualler', managed the Victoria Hotel, but was replaced by Robert Barton Tweed, perhaps her son, by 1856.[13]

The coming of the railway in 1855, with a station a quarter of a mile from the centre of Woodhall, on the branch line from Horncastle to Kirkstead Junction, brought the spa in direct communication with London, a journey of 123 miles through Boston and Peterborough to King's Cross accomplished in about three hours; and Station Road was laid out in Woodhall. Although the railway was to make the spa, this did not happen immediately. There were only 55 houses in the 1860s. Hotchkin's son undertook further improvements, but lived away at South Luffenham Hall in Stamford. Woodhall Lodge was occupied by Dr Barton and then by the new incumbent, the Revd St George Kirke, who was also Vicar of Dalderby.[14] Despite Woodhall's investment from the Hotchkin family, small spas developed by individuals had little future. New sophisticated medical treatments needing elaborate apparatus, higher hotel standards and large-scale means of leisure entertainment required capital usually beyond individual resources. The expansion of English spas from the 1860s to 1914 was assisted by the Limited Liability Act of 1862, which made the shareholders of a bankrupt company liable for its debts only to the extent of the capital they held. This made possible the financing of spas by syndicates, which succeeded after the failure of the earlier unprotected syndicates at

1. The Pump Room, Tenbury Wells, 1839

2. Llandrindod Wells from the Park

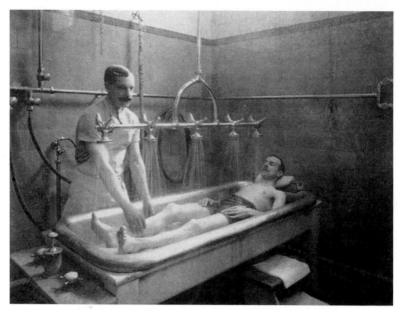

3. Vichy Douche, Thermal Baths, Buxton

4. Darley Dale Hydropathic Establishment, Matlock, 1893

5. A mid-nineteenth century poster advertizing Melksham Spa water

6. The Winter Gardens in the Royal Baths, Harrogate, during the 1920s

7. The Royal Pump Room, Harrogate, built 1842

Bishopton and Gloucester. Such a syndicate in 1886 bought an estate of 200 acres at Woodhall and engaged C.E. Davis, the architect who had made improvements in Bath, to exploit the spa.[15]

While traditional spas were losing support by the mid-nineteenth century, Woodhall had the novelty of its iodine waters; and a similar contemporary new spa was Droitwich, with similar Tudor half-timbered houses and an air of respectability like Bournemouth. Its novelty was saline waters and brine baths. The cholera outbreak of 1831–32, which so alarmed Bath and Cheltenham, gave Droitwich, hitherto largely dependent upon manufacturing salt from its brine springs, the unusual opportunity for a new prosperity. The cholera struck it particularly badly, and medical facilities were few. A disused salt-works became a temporary hospital. Patients were given a hot bath on admission, but one night, when no water was available, they were bathed in warm brine instead and showed remarkable improvement. And so did others when treated in this way.[16]

Although a parliamentary borough, returning from 1832 one member, and a market town with some malting and several corn-mills as well as its considerable salt manufacture, Droitwich then still only consisted of the High Street, St Andrew's Street and Bridge Street. It had three churches, a humble Town Hall built in 1826 in St Andrew's Street, the Folk Inn and some imposing timber-framed houses.[17] So it was a sufficiently well-established settlement to be a spa.

The brine baths were found to be ten times as salt as seawater and four times as dense as the Dead Sea. They came to be used mainly for rheumatic ailments, physical injuries and paralysis. Local physicians pioneered the normal use of these brine baths; and Sir Charles Hastings, the first President of the British Medical Association, constantly visited Droitwich and urged it to have public baths.[18] So in 1836 the Old Brine Baths (as they were later called) were built on the hill north of Queen Street and formed a group with the George Inn (later the Royal Hotel), a timber-framed house rebuilt as a three-storeyed stucco building with giant pilasters and containing an assembly room. The baths were a single-storeyed building in a classical style with a verandah in front and the words 'Established 1836' on the pediment above. They were demolished in 1959.

The railway came to Droitwich in 1849 with a station more than a mile east of the town on the Birmingham and Gloucester line. This encouraged W.G. Gabb, a local tradesman of 'great intelligence and energy', to float in 1855 a joint-stock company to develop commercially the Old Baths. Most of the neighbouring Worcester gentry, probably hoping for rising local property values, supported him. A provisional committee chose a site for the scheme and planned the inevitable spa feature, a 'handsome crescent' of lodging and boarding houses, but the company's collapse frustrated this.

Gabb, however, set out alone to enlarge and improve the existing baths with extra baths, including a well-bath and some douches. He raised the walls of the baths and excavated the basin of what later became the swimming-bath. Hoping to find and raise brine water on his property, he sank a deep well and, following Bath and Leamington's example, employed a steam-engine for pumping.[19]

The developing Midland railway system closely linked Droitwich to Birmingham, the centre of a complex connected to all England; and Gabb persuaded both the Great Western and Midland Railways to issue special bathing tickets and make other concessions; but his venture largely failed. In 1870 he leased the baths to Dr W.H.Bainbridge, who established a company to buy them and the adjoining Royal Hotel to unite them in an extended establishment.[20]

Lord Hampton of Westwood Park, the Member of Parliament for Droitwich from 1837, chaired the company, which involved Dr. S.S. Roden, a local physician since 1852 and Mayor of Droitwich in 1873, and also Sir John Packington. The company built new, up-to-date baths of unparalleled splendour in the Italian style of red brick with cement dressings. An innovation was the three external entrances for three classes of baths, first class 2s. 6d., second class 1s. 6d. and third class 9d. Warm air circulated through the bathrooms and dressing-rooms, which were divided by partitions of veined Italian marble. The first-class baths had luxurious black and gold furniture and green-leather upholstered couches. They were opened on 15 December 1873 by Lord Hampton, who commended them to an influential audience and praised Bainbridge's industry and ability.[21]

The spa's development, however, was mainly due to John Corbett, who was born in 1817 at Brierley Hill in Staffordshire, the son of a canal-boat owner. Having little education, he helped from the age of 10 with his father's boats until in 1840 he apprenticed himself for five years to ironmongers at Stourbridge. He then rejoined his father as a partner, and they built up the prosperous firm of Corbett and Son, operating a large fleet between Staffordshire and London, Liverpool and Manchester and other commercial centres. When railway competition forced them to sell out in 1852, he invested his capital in the Stoke Prior Salt Works, which since its establishment in 1828 had ruined six owners. As a practical engineer, he succeeded in extracting unspoilt salt from springs in the adjoining strata by sinking deep pits and evolving new methods of evaporation.[22] He extended the Droitwich Junction Canal so that the coal barges came to his works and left with cargoes of salt. To supplement the canal system, he built his own railway and owned 50 canal boats and 400 railway wagons. He established also foundries, sawmills and a brickmaking plant. A benevolent employer of the indisciplined workforce he inherited, he built a model village of 200 houses for them close to the factory with a dispensary, rest rooms, a school and a library, then unusual.[23]

On this more prosperous base, Droitwich began to expand, attracting investment from London. From 1860 a building society laid out a new town on a higher and better position on the road to the station, which was reconstructed to suit crippled visitors. New streets were cut with buildings of all sizes, and villas appeared in Witton.[24] By 1873 St George's Square was laid out around the Royal Brine Bath Hotel, which, originally a posting-stage, was still Droitwich's real hotel, adjoining the baths to which it had a private entrance. The hotel contained several sitting and bedrooms 'suitable for invalids and families'. There were 16 inns and four lodging houses, the best being Henry Jones's Norbury House in Fleet Street, and there were St Andrew's Old Rectory[25] and Miss A.E. Rudlin's Bath House. The 19 physicians and surgeons included the prosperous Dr Brainbridge, lessee of the baths and now tenant of the fine old timber-framed St Peter's Manor House. A new church, St Nicholas's, was built in Omersley Street near the railway station in 1869 by John Smith, a local architect, for £1,700, and a Baptist Chapel was built in 1871. Droitwich in the early 1870s, though a busy commercial town, was still dominated by the five salt-manufacturing firms.[26]

After becoming the Member of Parliament for Droitwich in 1874, Corbett settled in the locality. Having established one of the best systems of salt manufacture in the world, he had time and energy to devote himself to public affairs, such as becoming a Governor of the new University of Birmingham. He bought from Lord Somers a 200-acre deer park at Impney in the village of Dodderhill, where in 1863–86 he built Chateau d'Impney for his French wife. It was a towering red-brick and Bath stone mansion like a Louis XIII chateau, designed by Tronquois of Paris and executed by a local architect, Richard Spiers. His wife lived there only briefly and went with her daughters to Somerset for the rest of her life.[27]

The lonely Corbett concentrated on investing and distributing his wealth to promote Droitwich as a spa. Only his immense riches enabled him to undertake what Henry Thompson and Joseph Pitt so catastrophically attempted at Cheltenham in the earlier half-century. In Victoria Square, at the corner of St Andrew's and Ombersley Streets, he built and presented to the town the half-timbered Salters Hall. Also in Victoria Square, convenient for the railway station and in the higher part of the town and away from the smoke and steam of the salt-works, he built in 1887 the new St Andrew's Baths (rebuilt in 1909 and 1935) with better facilities than the Old Brine Baths. The latest improvements suggested by skill, experience and advanced knowledge were introduced regardless of expense for treating stiffened and thickened joints by hot and warm brine baths, douches, jets, steam and vapour baths, besides a charming swimming-bath. Dr S.S. Roden was engaged to write the publicity pamphlet, *Droitwich and its Baths*, for the opening in 1887, and he claimed that Droitwich could now compete with the elaborate treatments of Continental spas like Aix-les-Bains and Wiesbaden.

Corbett then built up a virtual monopoly of the town's leisure industry. In 1887 he bought St Andrew's Old Rectory, near the Baths, and made it into the Raven Hotel; and in 1891 he engaged the architect J.R. Nicholls to build the even larger Worcestershire Brine Bath Hotel in Corbett Road, which cost £30,000 and had 150 rooms. In 1900 he acquired the Old Baths and rebuilt the adjoining Royal Hotel as part of St George's Buildings, in stuccoed brick with upper timber pieces.

He died on 22 April 1901 at Chateau d'Impney, which became a hotel as it still is. He was commemorated by a portrait in St Augustine's Church, Dodderhill, where he worshipped, and was buried in Stoke Prior Church. By 1901 Droitwich was a growing health resort with a population of 4,118, and the Droitwich Land Society was formed to acquire yet more land for building.[28]

Compared with the new spas, the long-established urbanized spas, now largely residential settlements, attempted, after the financial crisis of 1857–58, to stage a revival and meet the challenge of the seaside resorts. This was effected by municipalized public facilities, especially at Buxton and Harrogate; new types of water treatment which created a demand for specialization; more amenities and commercialized entertainment; and palatial hotels with greater comfort and splendour. The individual innkeeper's day was passing, and these giant hotels of over 100 bedrooms, attempting to attract visitors by higher standards, expressed the grandeur of the imperial age, such as the Imperial at Malvern (1862), the Grand at Scarborough (1867), the Empire at Buxton (1868), the Pump Room Hotel (1869) and the Empire (1898) at Bath and the Majestic (1900) and the Grand (1903) at Harrogate. Spa towns had to counter not only the seaside resorts, but also cheap excursion fares by the railways which shifted the holiday market from quality to quantity. Although partly surviving until 1914, the old-established social exclusiveness was undermined in the spa towns as they accommodated excursionists, with spacious promenades, avenues and (especially after the Public Parks Act of 1871) parks. These urban parks differed greatly from the eighteenth-century pleasure gardens or Vauxhalls maintained by subscriptions and organized for galas, balls and other grand events for high and gay society. Municipal parks were generally free, regulated, sober middle-class and family places. And, to extend the season, so-called winter gardens, as at Woodhall Spa, were also provided for foul weather cover.

Bath was a place where municipal effort sought a revival. Although its population fell from 54,240 in 1851 to 52,528 in 1861, it recovered in the late Victorian and Edwardian period, partly as increased industrial activity lessened its dependence on visitors. Flour mills, light engineering, Bayer's large corset factory, Stothert's expanding iron foundry and Pitman's printing and book-binding employed some workers previously seasonally engaged in domestic service.[29] Yet Bath remained primarily a resort town depending on the water-cure industry. It now tried to remedy its inadequate accommodation, especially the lack of a first-class hotel. Short-term visitors had mostly gone to inns, and long-term visitors to lodgings in hired houses or apartments. Now the old White Hart in Stall Street, long a leafy coaching inn, was replaced in 1869 by the Grand Pump Room Hotel connected by a lift to the new Royal Baths built behind it by the Corporation in 1870. This magnificent hotel, with a frontage formed by three sides of a triangle, four storeys and an attic floor, accommodated numerous guests in various suites of rooms. The coffee room on the ground floor, the largest in the building, provided a social centre to supplement the only remaining assembly room in the upper town. Its architects were Wilson and Wilcox, and Joshua Wall of Stroud carved the lions at the entrance door. It was demolished in 1960 and replaced by the shops and flats of Arlington House.[30]

By 1873 a local guide listed 19 'hotels and boarding houses' in Bath, 16 significantly termed 'hotels', and the Midland Hotel in St James's Street indicated that the Midland Railway had also come there. Its terminus in Green Park, with a handsome front of Ionic columns and an elegant cornice, was a further ornament for Bath, which had now two stations and by 1873 six omnibus routes round the city.[31]

Yet more lodging accommodation near the baths seemed necessary as it had much diminished in the last 30 to 40 years. In 1886 the Christopher Hotel Company asked the town council's corporate committee, the ground landlords of the Christopher (or Amery's) Hotel for a renewed annual lease of £100 for 75 years, as they planned to rebuild it. They maintained that a century before there were 14 large boarding houses and 64 lodging houses within 150 yards of the Baths. The 34 lodging houses in Milsom Street were partly replaced by those in Pulteney Street, but the hotel accommodation formerly provided at the Bear, Three Tuns and White Hart was still not made good. The new hotel's internal plan would be made by Mr Pilkington, already responsible for hotels in London and Edinburgh and now engaged on a large Brighton hotel. The *Bath Chronicle* and some of the council supported the proposal, as Bath needed more first-class, reasonably priced, middle-class hotel accommodation; but some, including Fenner White of the White Lion Hotel, opposed this 'huge building speculation' in a 'monster hotel', since existing hotels in April 1886 were only half-full, and present charges were reasonable. An alderman inferred that 'people in London' had influenced Charles Davis, Surveyor of Works in 1862–1902, and other city officers, but the plan was finally approved at a ground rent of £144.[32]

The spa's revival induced Henry Holland to plan yet another grandiose lower town hotel. His site in Orange Street suited the Corporation's plan for a new carriageway from Pierrepont Street to Pont Street, and the area was reorganized so that the balustraded Grand Parade now stands on a colonnade, displacing the old markets and overlooking the Parade Gardens laid out on land conveyed by Lord Manvers and opened to subscribers only. Holland's monster Empire Hotel, five storeys high with two in the roof and dominating the area, was a quixotic mixture of styles designed by Charles Davis.[33]

The corporation now had a good income from land – the hot springs of the baths, the pump-rooms, the cold springs of the waterworks and the market tolls – which it spent lavishly, equalled among spa towns probably only by Harrogate. This included modernizing the sewage and salvage arrangements (1864), a new police station in the Orange Grove (1865), extending the reservoirs (1870), building respectable terrace houses and improving and widening Quiet Street.[34] They were galvanized into building activity reminiscent of their predecessors by Charles Davis, the son or nephew of Edward Davis (died 1852) who laid out the Victoria Park in 1830.

Davis initiated also the investigations from 1879 which revealed the remains of the Roman Baths, and later the Queen's Bath was demolished to permit the excavation of the Roman Bath discovered beneath it, while the King's Bath was reconstructed largely as it was in the sixteenth century as a showpiece, which attracted some 50,000 visitors a year by the 1890s. And the number of customers at the baths, 42,710 in 1864, steadily grew from 56,297 in 1881 to 80,119 in 1885. The Pump Room Company was started in 1870 to manage the new baths attached to the Royal Hotel; and Davis designed a new suite in Bath Street with a tepid swimming-pool and a smoking-room.[35]

In 1881 the Corporation began to extend the Guildhall, taking in part of the market, erected in 1868 at a cost of £5,000, to find room for their increasingly complex business and include the Victoria Art Gallery and Reference Library (1898–1900), which this time cost £55,000.[36] They also – for another £80,000 – added to the Pump Room a new concert hall, a kursaal under a large glazed dome to replace the Lower Rooms lost by fire in 1820 and the Roman Promenade and Terrace adjoining the Grand Pump Room opened in 1897. The architect for both the Guildhall and Pump Room was the Scottish J. McKean Brydon.[37] The Corporation acquired also the Kingston Baths in York Street to fit them up as 'cheap baths for gentlemen'. It now controlled all the baths.[38]

After the Public Parks Act, the Corporation settled its lengthy dispute with the freemen about the common fields. By an Act of 1879 it bought the land for annuities paid until the last freeman died in 1938; and it bought land for the approach road, Royal Avenue, from the Rivers family in 1886.[39] And Captain Forester, the owner of the Bathwick Estate, gave the city a field of seven acres on the north side of Great Pultney Street, which was laid out as a public pleasure ground, Henrietta Park, in 1897.[40] Not every public utility or amenity came under public control. Private companies still owned the gasworks in Upper Bristol Road, the electric lighting of the main streets (1891) and the electric tramcars (1904) connecting villages now becoming suburbs. Horse tramways had operated through the town since 1880.[41]

The Corporation's policy was to revive the old town where it held much property. In 1861 a new wing was added to the west side of the Mineral Water Hospital of 1742 (which had now served nearly 50,000 patients) on the site of the old rectory at a cost of £18,000 by Manners and Gill, who at the same time rebuilt the adjoining Bluecoat School. The theatre, with its front in 'a dingy little place called Beauford Square', was swiftly rebuilt and enlarged to the designs of C.J. Phipps within a year of the fire of Good Friday 1862, and could now seat 1,750 people; and opposite in the Saw Close, formerly Bath's coal and timber yard, the Lyric Theatre was built in 1895 to hold another 1,000.[42] After 30 years of practical neglect, restoration of the Abbey was begun by the Revd C. Kemble in 1864. Sir Gilbert Scott supervised the repair of the roof in 1865–69 at a cost of £5,500, and Sir T.G. Jackson directed work on the west front in 1895–1901.[43]

A vigorous public life persisted, though more fragmented than in the eighteenth century. The Harington Club in Harington Place was formed in 1874 'to promote social intercourse, mental improvement and national recreation'; and the Bath and County Club, founded in York Buildings in 1790, was reorganized in 1857 and moved to 21–22 Queen Square. There were clubs for cricket, archery and boating, and regattas were held, private above Cleveland Bridge and public at Saltford. A committee of gentlemen maintained a band which played twice daily in Sydney Gardens or the Victoria Park during the summer. Like Malvern, the town experimented with the German band craze, and a Hungarian Band Committee engaged Herr Bartels to perform.[44] The Floral

Fêtes Committee, which had 60 members and supported a group of eight players and two annual flower shows, built a bandstand in the park in 1855 and by 1886, helped by the Attractions Society, mounted five annual flower shows, had a band of 20 performers and spent £3,000 a year.[45] During the winter the long-established Pump Room string orchestra performed thrice weekly and gave special concerts in the Grand Pump Room. It flourished when the Corporation promoted it from 1869, especially when conducted by Max Heymann in 1892–1910.[46]

This prosperous middle-class activity and economic revival was not unalloyed. In the mid-1880s proposals to build new houses were opposed as many were said to be empty, and some had been unlet for years. A deputation of 150 unemployed men, anxious not to go on poor relief, told the mayor of their plight in March 1886. Many were masons, carpenters and cabinet-makers, and some had lacked work for three months. A cabinet-maker said that this winter was the worst he had known in Bath for 20 years; but by the next month many had work, and a committee in charge of relief funds for the unemployed had little to do. Despite two Acts of 1851 governing the establishing, regulating and inspecting of such houses, the condition of Bath's common lodging houses, 'vile dens', was so bad that the Revd F.M.Caulfield campaigned for their improvment and persuaded the sanitary committee to frame bye-laws to enable proceedings against notoriously bad lodging-house keepers.[47]

Changing social patterns and attitudes were shown by the mayor's cheap concerts for the working classes at the Guildhall in 1852.[48] Significantly less emphasis was placed on the needs of visitors from afar, except those seeking a health-cure. At the second annual supper for chairmen, they were told that the Baths Committee were seeking to attract patients to Bath instead of abroad. William Brumby recalled that he came to Bath just in time to see the last three sedan-chairs replaced by wheelchairs, the famed bath-chairs, better suited for invalids, which employed 90 wheelchairmen and were now fitted with rubber tyres to make their task easier.[49]

The many private schools reflected the growing residential population and showed that Bath, like Cheltenham, Malvern and other spa towns, was becoming an educational centre. Bath College and 12 others were listed in the 1880s, but there were also Kingswood School (in Bath from 1832), the Royal School, the Bluecoat School, Prior Park Roman Catholic College and the board schools.[50] And Bath continued to be a regional retail and entertainment centre, and the summer floral fêtes attracted both visitors and surrounding residents. Social exclusiveness had gone, perhaps more than at Cheltenham; and the Assembly Room and Guildhall balls were considered suitable for every class of society, very different from the time when tradesmen had held their events there, and the aristocracy and gentry formed another group in the Upper and Lower Rooms.[51]

Bath valued the visit of Princess Mary of Teck in 1877, but Harrogate, claiming to be the 'Bath of the north', was not favoured by royal visits. In its coronation celebrations of 1902, a banner stated: 'Long Live the King – may he come to Harrogate.'[52] However, in August 1911 among its visitors were Queen Alexandra and her daughter, Princess Victoria, her sister, the Empress Maria of Russia, and other European royalties.[53] Yet before then it had become a prominent spa, the focus of northern fashionable and genteel life. The notable achievement of public and private enterprise from 1860 was the conversion of the village spa with two centres, Upper and Lower Harrogate, into an integrated and expanding urban resort. It now had excellent facilities for scientific hydropathy, superior entertainment and accommodation for visitors, and fine houses with ample gardens for its increasing permanent residents.[54]

Although the Brunswick Station was opened in 1848, Harrogate lacked a railway station serving the entire area until the Central Station in July 1848 made it a suitable residential place for the West Riding businessmen who settled there, as did well-off leisured, retired people. In 1894 the proportion of residents to visitors was 2:1, but 5:1 by 1910. The railway also made Harrogate a better touring centre and a stop in a north-east journey, and visitors came beyond Lancashire, the West Riding and Tyneside. By 1885 of the many from south-east England, over an eighth were from London.[55]

As the only spa town north of Buxton, metropolitan society found it convenient in Edwardian times to stay in Harrogate between the end of the London season and the beginning of grouse shooting on the Scottish estates. This brought many titled visitors, but, like other reviving spa towns in the 1860s, its fortunes were made by the influx of the leisured, affluent middle classes. Despite the talk of dependence on the gentry, William Taylor, a commissioner, said in 1883 that its prosperity came from merchants and manufacturers, particularly of Yorkshire and Lancashire; and the better-off residents wished to maintain its reputation as a genteel and fashionable resort. The Brunswick Station made them fear, as in Malvern later, that cheap rail travel would bring invading day-trippers from nearby industrial areas. When a special train was arranged in September 1848, they complained that such excursions would injure the town by making it a common resort and driving away fastidious visitors. Harrogate wished to avoid the 'fashionable vulgarity of Scarborough'. The *Daily Graphic* in 1892 claimed that its supreme advantage over other resorts was its immunity from ordinary excursionists. Yet there were complaints of vandalism by trippers, such as picking heather on Harlow Mill, and in 1899 a resident said, 'They are not wanted, and they are not wanted now.'[56]

The railway greatly helped Harrogate's expansion by easing the daily movement of manpower between Harrogate and Knaresborough. Many artisans, workless through Knaresborough's declining linen imdustry in the late 1870s, still lived there as rents were lower, and found work in Harrogate. Like other spa towns, it needed many hotel and domestic servants, especially women, many only seasonally employed. In 1901 there were 2,369 female domestic servants, averaging 40 to every 100 houses. Nowhere else in the West Riding had such a concentration of domestic servants, except Ilkley, also a developing spa, which had 54.[57] Building workers, including those in sawmills, brickworks and quarries, were strong enough to form in 1892 a union, and the next year struck for six weeks to demand an all-the-year-round wage. Some artisans walked the daily journey of two or three miles between Knaresborough and Harrogate: a witness in 1867 said he had seen at least 100 tramping back from Knaresborough one evening.[58]

Besides the Central Station, Harrogate acquired in 1862 a reactivated Board of Commissioners, when the body of 21 set up in 1841 adopted the Local Government Act of 1858 to receive enlarged powers as the urban sanitary authority. Like other spa towns, its development from the early 1860s was achieved by both public and private enterprise, often working jointly. Builders and shopkeepers gradually replaced hoteliers as the dominant commissioners, and dynasties of builders arose, such as the families of Simpson, Carter and Ellis and George Dawson who built most of Montpellier Parade, Cambridge Crescent and Prospect Crescent. A system of plural voting based on property values gave political power to those with commercial investment in the town. In March 1874 three members of the Simpson family were commissioners, as was George Beazley, a coachbuilder and chairman of the company owning the Cheltenham Spa Rooms and grounds. Of seven candidates seeking election to the Commission in 1868, two builders, George Stephenson and Richard Ellis Junior were returned; the rest were shopkeepers, and James Binns, the hotelier, was unsuccessful. In 1874 Joseph and Thomas Stephenson were elected. The town's first two elected mayors were builders, Nicholas Carter Junior and Richard Ellis Junior.[59]

The Limited Liability Act made possible the formation of the Victoria Park Company in 1860 in anticipation of the opening of the Central Station in 1862 and undertook the first large-scale development plan in the town, such as had been done earlier at Bath, Cheltenham and Tunbridge Wells. The company bought a large area of land between High and Low Harrogate and laid out broad roads and building lots, opening that year the main road, the Avenue intersecting it from east to west. The company's capital was £28,000, and the 56 shares were held by three men, Nicholas Carter and Richard Ellis with 20 each and John Richardson with 16. When Richardson died in 1861, Carter bought his shares, but the partnership was dissolved in 1858 when Ellis became the owner of the unsold residual estate. By 1971 much of the estate was built on and occupied.[60]

The West End Park was a similar company development from 1867 when nearly 70 acres south of the Stray, bought from the North-Eastern Railway Company, were laid out in a formal oval with miniature mansions as the embryo of an intended separate little town. Beech Grove, fronting the West Park Stray, had houses of a like size and splendour. The first streets, made in the 1870s to link the developing area of Central Harrogate with the spa area of Low Harrogate, were Parliament Street, leading down the side of the valley, and James Street, both linking the route to the spa from the station area. These two streets contained some of the most exclusive shops, particularly for jewellery and clothing.[61] The small Alexandra Park and Franklin Estates were developed from the 1870s, but Joshua Bower's plans for the Dragon Estate in 1855 were abortive, and building there hardly began until 1892. David Simpson, one of the building dynasty, a councillor and later an alderman, began a major estate development in 1889 on 54 acres of land he acquired from the Duchy of Lancaster. Around the Duchy Road area, large houses were built in ample grounds.[62]

Contemporary with Bath's renewed municipal activity, the commissioners did the same at Harrogate in 1868–74, supported by increased borrowing powers as rateable values increased from £13,200 in 1848 to £39,372 by 1884.[63] Improvement began gradually with a road from the Royal Pump Room to the springs in Bogs Fields in 1862; flagging the sidewalks, costing £2,600, began belatedly the next year. As at Bath, the commissioners worked through committees – the general purposes committee, the wells, baths and lighting committee and the roads, streets and sanitary committee; and the commissioners and later the Corporation had the vision to create an urban spa with broad, tree-lined streets and ample facilities for good health treatment and entertainment.[64]

They completed the public control of all the known 87 springs and baths, vital for Harrogate's prosperity. They already owned three pump-rooms – the Royal (covering the Old Sulphur Well), Tewit and John's Well – and in the first seven years of the Commission's existence, 1842–49, these cost £2,905 12s. 2d. The commissioners protected them carefully, paying in 1843 Professor Phillips £6 15s for his travelling expenses and report on the danger of sinking wells near the springs. In the mid-1860s water-drinkers at the Royal Pump Rooms were more than ever before, averaging 11,500 a year,[65] which doubtless encouraged the commissioners in 1870 to buy part of the spa area in Low Harrogate, gaining from the Victoria Company the neo-Greek style Victoria Baths, built near the Town Hall by John Williams in 1832, and its estate, including the Old Promenade Room of 1805, now the Victoria Reading Room, for about £6,600. To complete this complex they acquired also the adjoining Crescent Estate for about £10,000 aand built the larger, superior New Victoria Baths. Including new water-pipes, this cost almost £20,000, and when Joseph Stephenson obtained the contract he resigned from the Commission. The New Victoria Baths (later demolished and replaced by the municipal offices) covered a much greater area than the earlier one. A single-storeyed, verandah-fronted building, with a double-storeyed centre block adorned with much-fretted ironwork, was built in six months in 1871 and contained 18 bathrooms and four shower and four vapour baths and two swimming-baths at each end. The sulphur water for the baths was drawn from 22 of the 25 sulphur wells in the Bogs Field, 12 of which were newly tapped in 1870.[66] The water was stored in huge underground reservoirs, containing 200,000 gallons, beneath the new baths. There was also a boardroom as premises for the commissioners' meetings.[67]

The commissioners were left with what they called their 'surplus property', the old Victoria Baths, by 1874 dilapidated without windows, doors or stairs; the Victoria Room (formerly Promenade House or Room); Leamington House; about 900 yards remaining of the Crescent property; the Town Hall; and the Old Town's Yard.[68] After some debate, the Victoria Room was leased to W.H. Breare, Editor of the *Harrogate Herald*, who reconstructed it as the Town Hall Theatre, which in the 1880s and 1890s gave performances by visiting companies for three to six nights a week. Among these were the D'Oyly Carte Company and Lilie Langtry and Oscar Wilde giving lectures.

Many had long wished to erect a covered promenade, but disagreement whether it should be near the Old Sulphur Well or Old Town Hall prevented any action until 1870. By then the property market was sluggish, and though the commissioners' borrowing power was increased to twice the rateable value in 1871, their commitments were fully extended. They even made an abortive attempt in 1871 to cut the surveyor's salary from £200 to £150, though they appointed also that year a clerk of works, since the roads were still in a 'wretched state' and required the attention of these two officials.[69] In 1868 they belatedly began to extend and improve the town's sewers, buying the 300-acre

Irrigation Farm in Lower Oakdale for sewerage works, which were finished by 1874. And an extensive public market was built that year for £3,000 exclusive of land and designed by a local architect, Arthur Hiscoe.[70] After much controversy, Bower Road, long needed to link High and Low Harrogate, was built in 1875, so enabling the development of Joshua Bower's Dragon Estate; and the North Park Road was built at the same time. The commissioners did not use their powers to take over the gas and water undertakings, perhaps because some were directors of the companies, but they denounced the gas company for the high price of lighting the streets and the noisy traction-engine which hauled the coal-wagons from Starbeck to the gasworks.[71]

Four suites of baths using sulphur water – Montpellier, Harlow Car and the two rival establishments at Starbeck – were still privately owned, as was the town's main concert hall, the Spa Concert Hall of the Royal Chalybeate Spa, formerly the Cheltenham Spa Room or Rooms. The opening in April 1870 of the Prince of Wales Baths, which had a swimming-bath, at Starbeck in the field next to the Knaresborough Spa Bath of 1828, began a price-cutting war, especially in the bad summer of 1879. The Knaresborough Baths trustees tried to avoid disaster by sinking a new well in the winter of 1879–80, but its sulphur water was diluted by a chalybeate spring; the baths rapidly declined and were closed by 1890. The Prince of Wales Baths were sold in 1880 for £3,000; but in 1904, when Harrogate Corporation wished to repurchase them, they cost £10,000.[72]

The booming 1860s and 1870s saw both large-scale private and public investmnent. The many local businessmen among the commissioners maintained past family investment. In 1867 the Harrogate Hotels, Mineral Springs and Bath Company, newly formed with £35,000 capital, bought the Montpellier Estate, the Pump Room baths and gardens and the Crown and White Hart Hotels. When it failed, the mortgagee, the former MP for Knaresborough, Tom Collins, foreclosed and sold it to George Dawson, the builder, who added a wing at each end of the Crown Hotel and a skating-rink. In 1880 the new Crown Wells House Hotel Company, with him as chairman, took over the property.[73]

A syndicate of local men, including George Beazley and some hoteliers, acquired the rival enterprise, built by John Williams in 1835, the Cheltenham Spa Rooms (now the Spa Concert Room), from Williams's executors in 1862. They formed the Harrogate Public Rooms Company with £5,100 capital to create a better entertainment centre, not to gain a direct profit but rather to draw visitors who would prosper their other enterprises. After making a new terrace in 1866 and improving the grounds, they undertook a major reconstruction in 1870, replacing the original Pump Room, on to which the main saloon was built in 1835, by a glass and iron wing, a miniature crystal palace, containing a pump-room, retiring rooms and a covered promenade. By 1874 they had also spent considerably in beautifying and decorating the concert room, but they had met their debts, had a balance in hand of £225 and hoped to engage first-class artistes.[74]

And so they did. The famed pianist Thalberg, the soprano Henrietta Sonberg and Labache, for whom Schubert wrote songs, performed there. Itinerant bands of a few instruments had come to Harrogate before. One, the High Harrogate Band, played before breakfast at the Granby Hotel and Slingsby Well, soon after the Montpellier Pump Room and Baths were opened, and by 1845 a band played every evening in the season on the green. Now, although moderate entertainment predominated at the Spa Room, some first-class concerts were held nightly in the season, and band music flourished under the direction of Julian Adams, an outstanding spa musician, 'deservedly popular', the local paper said. In 1868 it observed, 'The programmes selected by Mr Julian Adams, the conductor and solo pianist, are really first class.' In 1877 Adams went to Eastbourne, but in the 1880s the Dearlove family of Leeds provided most of the 16 players in a Harrogate Promenade Orchestra. A military band also played in the grounds of the Spa Concert Rooms every morning, as a rival band did morning and evening in the Montpellier grounds.[75] So Harrogate participated in the practice (common between 1880 and 1950) of more important resorts having a municipal orchestra.

Private enterprise provided three other small entertainment halls in Harrogate in the early 1880s – the St James's Hall and Coffee House in Cambridge Street; the Albert Hall in Albert Street; and the New Victoria Hall in James Street formed by Captain Holt's conversion of the Providence Chapel which, however, lasted only until 1892.[76] But the borough council, created in 1884, initiated the major developments. The enlargement in 1870 of the improvement district as settled in 1841, the increase of population to 12,000 and of rateable value to £71,070 in 1883 and the opposition to judicial dependence on the Knaresborough magistrates court led most ratepayers to support incorporation in 1883, which had been rejected in 1877. The charter of incorporation was granted in 1884 and a separate commission of the peace the next year. The borough's boundaries were further extended in 1900 to include Bilton, Starbeck and the Oatlands part of Pannal.[77]

Borough status inspired massive and visionary municipalization and hotel building, making Harrogate a foremost spa town. In 1886 the corporation belatedly acquired the Bog Field, where over 30 mineral springs rose, to convert it to some nine acres of public pleasure grounds called the Valley Gardens, which were enlarged by the incorporation of part of Harlow Moor in 1898 and Collins Field in 1901.[78] Harrogate's greatest natural asset, apart from the mineral springs, was the wide open Stray, which made less urgent the provision of a public park such as Bath, Cheltenham and Leamington had long since possessed. But the Stray's proprietors, owners of the 50 'gates', had pasture rights and hardly improved it. 'Unseemly gatherings' and 'intolerable noise' there demanded public control. A town meeting in 1878 rejected the owners' offered sale to the improvement commissioners for £12,500; but a special Act of Parliament allowed the Corporation to intervene to regulate its use and plant more trees.[79]

The greatest threat to Harrogate and other established spa towns was the development and rapid spread of hydropathy, a medical treatment depending on special methods of applying water to the body rather than simple bathing and drinking originated in 1825 by Vincent Priessnitz at Graefenberg in Austrian Silesia (now Jesenik in the Czech Republic). By 1843 he was called the 'downfall of the druggists' and the 'ruin of the spas' as over 7,000 acutely ill patients had found relief at his establishment. Lodging-house keepers, it was said, bitterly cursed his name from Carlsbad to Cheltenham, Ems to Harrogate and Toplitz to Tunbridge Wells.

A hydro was opened in 1846 at Ben Rhydding near Ilkley, and several at Harrogate, notably by the Harrogate Hydropathic Company which acquired and adapted the Swan Hotel with five acres of gardens in 1878 for this new successful business under Dr Richard Veale's supervision. It met the challenge of the Continental hydros in 1892 with extensions providing 75 more bedrooms, a new dining-room seating 250 and a winter garden of 2,400 square feet. Two other large hydros were the Cairn Hydro (1892) and the Harlow Manor Hotel (1893) made by adapting a gabled, Gothic-detailed private house and adding a new wing. Smaller hydros included the Connaught in Cold Bath Road and the Imperial on the Royal Parade, both founded by 1882.[80]

Alerted by this, the new municipal council, like the Corporation of Bath, sent delegations in 1885 to investigate at European hydros their cold compresses and bathing, wet sheets, stomach packs and sweating blankets, supplemented by punishing exercises. In 1887 the Borough Engineer, E.W. Harry, with Drs Oliver and Black, after touring Aix-les-Bains, Baden-Baden, Wiesbaden and other Continental spas, advised the Council to reconstruct and improve the Victoria Baths, but it decided they were too outdated for this. The Crown Wells House Company, with a capital of £30,000, intended to rival the Swan with yet another hydro. Encouraged by the advantage of having the Montpellier waters, it spent £10,000 on furniture, mainly at Maples of London, but this again was an over-optimistic investment in spa facilities, and the company failed within two years. George Dawson contrived to be a liquidator and in 1884 for £19,950 again acquired the Montpellier Estate. He resold it to the Corporation in 1888 for £29,500, a profit of nearly £10,000.

To replace the Victoria Baths, the Corporation decided to build the new Royal Baths, on the Montpellier Estate, which the Duke of Cambridge opened in 1897. Costing £118,000 and designed basically by Baggally and Bristowe of London, it had a lavishly equipped grand entrance hall, four large suites of baths, the Winter Gardens and a fine glass-roofed concert hall with a separate entrance in Parliament Street. So, after decades of discussion, Harrogate at last had a sizeable covered promenade for visitors in bad weather, as well as a large public hall. And in 1896 the Corporation bought the remaining private spa, the Cheltenham Spa Rooms Estate, for £22,000. The municipalization of the spas was completed in 1904 and 1913 with the purchase of the auxiliary spas at Starbeck and Harlow Car, though these had retained their minor status. No improvement was made to the wells at High Harrogate, now of little interest.[81]

Meanwhile, Harrogate's musical tradition led W.H. Breare of the *Harrogate Herald* to demand a municipal band. Citizens subscribed £400, a Mrs Kaye-Knowles paid for the uniforms, and J. Sidney Jones, conductor at the Grand Theatre in Leeds, became in 1887 Harrogate's first municipal bandmaster. When he arrived the only bandstand was a small box in the old Montpellier Gardens where the band assembled at 7 a.m. to encourage the water-drinkers. Each day a different meeting-place was chosen for the band, and visitors often missed its performances. Shelterless, the conductor wore mittens on winter days, and 'the poor chaps in the band' blew the clarinets and cornets with running noses. During the 15 years that Jones held the post, he converted an essentially military band into an orchestra able to play classical symphonies, and induced a hesitant municipality to pay full salaries to the players to replace collections from audiences.

In 1895 bandstands were erected for afternoon tea programmes in the Valley Gardens and evening performances in Victoria Avenue, both well attended. The Royal Spa Concert Rooms were opened in 1898 in the Cheltenham Spa Rooms Estate, and the band was expanded into an orchestra of 42 players. Music grew in popularity and profitability, and the orchestra performed three or four programmes daily until the afternoon session was taken over in 1900 by a military band of some 30 players. The farewell concert in 1902 when Jones retired aged 64 showed there was still insufficient concert-room space. Over 100 players from five bands played the final item, the 1812 Overture, but had to perform simultaneously in two places, the Spa Concert Room and the Gardens.

Since 1898 Dr Black had been asking for a 'kursaal' as an adequate entertainment centre with a newsroom, a roulette room and a concert hall seating 2,000–3,000 people. Fortified by increases in the rateable value from £98,935 in 1893 to £153,451 in 1900, the Council overcame the fear of rates at 5s. in the pound and a borough loan debt of £50,000. It again sent a deputation abroad, now to visit kursaals. In March 1900 the Kursaal, though modified to reduce the cost to £45,000, included a large concert hall in a building on the north side of the Spa Rooms. The Kursaal, renamed the Royal Hall in 1914, had a rich rococo decor described in the *Musical Times* as 'marble columns, stained glass windows, crushed-strawberry hangings and sumptuous simulations of tapestries'. Here C.L. Naylor, Jones's successor as musical director, organized annual musical festivals, and from 1906 the municipal orchestra flourished under the showman conductor, Julian Clifford, who took it on successful tours.[82]

The Corporation's visionary policy succeeded. This was the spa's golden age with profitable investment in its enterprises. The Kursaal and Spa Rooms were first subsidized, but by 1914, after allowing for interest charges but not capital redemption, they made £1,000 profit, and the whole spa account (wells, baths and public rooms) showed a small net surplus. Mineral-water drinkers increased in 1893–98 from 193,672 to 210,850 and bathers from 43,583 to 69,093. By 1901 there were 96,000 bathers. Equally profitable were the Irrigation Farm municipal electricity works from 1897, despite the town's low housing density and hotels' use of gas. The corporation paid £205,000 to take over the waterworks by the Harrogate Waterworks Act of 1897 and £500,000 to construct the Roundhill reservoir in 1913. Other aspects of municipalization were a new sewage disposal system (1903), purchasing the Skipton Road Swimming Baths (1903) and a new public library (1906).[83]

Although late, this massive public investment, unique among spa towns, made possible Victorian and Edwardian Harrogate's prosperity, and there was considerable private speculation, especially in hotels. The mid-nineteenth century railway mania brought a notable building or rebuilding of hotels – the White Hart (1846), Clarendon (1847), Crown (1847 and 1870), George (1850), Queen (1851 and 1861), Prospect House (1859 and 1870) and Prince of Wales or Brunswick (1860). Hotels were now sited in Low Harrogate or along the fringes of the Stray in Central Harrogate. High Harrogate had no new hotels, though the Granby and Queen Hotels, attractively located on the edge of the Stray, still flourished. The Granby, much enlarged since 1821, was described in 1861 as 'colossal' with 150 bedrooms.[84]

The railway boom was miscalculated by Joshua Bower, a speculator who bought in 1855 the Dragon Estate, Dragon Hotel and 53 acres for, as he hoped, a bargain at £11,500, believing a station would be built there; but it was sited elsewhere, and the embankmented track reduced the value of his land. The Dragon, recalling the spa's early prosperity, became a school, and building on the estate was delayed until 1892.[85] In 1876 the best hotels were said to be the Granby, Queen, Prospect, Crown and Prince of Wales, with a fairly common tariff for board and lodging at the public table at 7s.6d. a day with the usual extras for private sitting-rooms, dressing-rooms, rooms for upper servants (4s.) and those in livery (3s.), with wax lights and other items extra. Nine other hotels were worth separate mention, and there were all sorts of private lodgings.[86]

Harrogate's borough status in 1884 was followed by renewed efforts to provide more accommodation with terraces of boarding houses along the Valley Drive, Cheltenham Parade and Cheltenham Crescent, the adoption of the name of the Gloucestershire spa showing its importance. By November 1898 five hotels were also planned, and on the north side of Low Harrogate where the Swan, adapted as a hydro in 1878, was almost the only building, three new hotels were built – the Cairn Hydro, Majestic and Grand, each with extensive grounds. The Grand Hotel in Cornwall Road (1903) by Whitehead and Southam and the Majestic in King's Road (1903) by G.D. Martin were outsize hotels like the Imperial at Bath and others now in resorts. The red-brick Majestic with gables and a centre dome, costing over £250,000, held 400 guests. Low Harrogate was now almost entirely a resort centre enclosing the municipal spa.[87]

Private enterprise still provided some of the entertainment. The leasees had to close the Town Hall Theatre when in January 1900 a group of local business and professional men opened the better-equipped Grand Opera House (in the present Oxford Street) managed by William Peacock, who attracted touring companies offering a higher standard of serious drama.

Private philanthropy also increasingly provided hospital and convalescent homes. The Bath Hospital, a charity opened in 1826, had annually by 1850 some £1,000 in visitors' subscriptions. Rebuilt on a larger scale for £50,000, it was reopened by Prince Albert in July 1889 as the Royal Bath Hospital and Rawson Convalescent Home. A cottage hospital for the 'local poor', established about 1850 in temporary premises, acquired a new permanent building in 1883 and was renamed the Harrogate Infirmary in 1902.[88]

Harrogate's remarkable transformation from a village spa to a substantial borough with all the constitutional and physical provision for urban living resulted from courageous investment, much municipally, for 50 years from about 1860. The near-by West Riding's industrial wealth aided this. An early mayor of the town was Samson Fox, a wealthy Leeds ironmaster, who built model working-class houses on the Stonefall Estate at Starbeck; and George Rogers, a Bradford mill-owner settled in Harrogate, built 12 almshouses in 1868 and made a bequest to the Bath Hospital.[89]

Harrogate's population grew by 91.6 per cent in 1851–1901 and by the 1860s surpassed Knaresborough's, ending its dependence on the older town for visitors' accommodation. In 1851 Bath, Cheltenham, Tunbridge Wells and Leamington were the four chief inland watering-places, but by 1901 Harrogate had in size displaced Leamington for fourth place. Harrogate's population rose from 6,483 in 1871 to 29,885 in 1901, including those brought in by the boundary changes of 1900.[89] Visitors rose from about 62,212 in 1863 to about 75,000 in 1914,[90] and the spa was still the town's focus of life, though its regional commercial role was growing. It was an important retail service centre with 800 shops, at least 10 important and several lesser private schools by 1895, including High Harrogate College (later Trinity College) established in the Dragon Hotel in 1868 before moving to West End Park in 1882, and Harrogate College and Harrogate Ladies' College founded in 1893.

Harrogate was increasingly a commuter town for the West Riding; and in 1899 most were said to be occupied by Leeds and Bradford businessmen, 'a good class of houses . . . and a poor class of people live in them'.[91] Yet Harrogate retained its resort flavour and medical importance. A.A. Thomson described it as:

> ringed about by green inviolable spaces that could never be built or desecrated. A town of broughams. landaus and, of course, bath-chairs, its residential population containing a minimum of working inhabitants, no slums and only two poor streets. A town of many old ladies, who spent the whole summer there and were a race apart – very stout, very kindly and very rich. . . . Harrogate had its aristocratic and distinguished clients too. It has been said that so many eminent statesmen were among them that at the height of Queen Victoria's reign she could have held a cabinet meeting there in the season.[92]

The other important northern spa, Scarborough, had less municipal activity than Harrogate and depended primarily on syndicate finance. It acquired the inevitable hydropathic establishment by 1889, but kept its spa district as an entertainment centre with notably high standards of music. Water-drinking was now subsidiary to sea-bathing, but the spa was still sufficiently valued for its buildings to be persistently restored and maintained after several disasters. The extension of the railway there in 1845, followed by the direct service to Hull of the Scarborough-Bridlington branch two years later, opened revitalizing links with the West Riding, Midlands and London. The next century saw rapid growth, though the town's popularity suffered from competition by the south coast resorts and the virtual disappearance of shipbuilding. Its population, including Falsgrave incorporated with it in 1890, rose rapidly from about 13,000 in 1851 to over 33,000 in 1891.[93]

Much of the new prosperity came from the influx of day-trippers and holidaymakers, but the spa's hinterland, the South Cliff, since 1827 joined to the old town and St Nicholas Cliff by a bridge, was developed to attract fashionable visitors, though the Newborough and St Nicholas Cliff area had many expensive lodgings and hotels. The Esplanade, a white stucco range in Regency style with the Crown Hotel in the centre was built by 1850 at South Cliff above the spa down by the shore. With the decline in taking the waters, the Cliff Bridge Company took a long lease of the spa premises in 1837 for development as an entertainment centre and secured for them a reputation for music rivalling Harrogate.[94] The first reference to 'music at the saloon', where the waters were drunk, was in 1840 when a band of eight players cost £41 7s. 6d. a year.[95] Though there was then no regular band, the music was popular.

Although enlarged in 1847 the Spa Pavilion was even then inadequate, and Sir Joseph Paxton designed a new, more grandiose building in 1858. Buxton, Cheltenham, Harrogate and Malvern were to imitate this glass and iron structure with protection against the weather that prolonged the season. Paxton was commissioned also to remodel the gardens and lay out the Westbourne Estate further inland behind the spa across Ramshill Road. From 1862 this was planned with villas and crescents including Oriel and Royal Crescents.[96]

The valley, separating historic Scarborough from South Cliff, was landscaped in 1835–40, and the access road to the spa was built in 1858. The Valley Bridge was opened in 1865 to connect the Bridlington Road, going down to the foot of the valley, with Westborough, and form a second link with the South Cliff area now rapidly developed with roads and buildings.[97]

The railway brought more visitors, and in 1869 when the Prince of Wales came, over 93,000 day-tickets were issued. He returned in 1870 and in 1871 with Princess Alexandra, and the King of Belgium came in 1873. Scarborough's fashionable standing was assured.[98] Meanwhile, the gigantic Grand Hotel was built on St Nicholas Cliff in 1867. The designs of the architect, Cuthbert Brodrick, appeared in *The Builder* in 1883; and this yellow and red brick extravagence, rising in an unprecedented 13 storeys from the beach and flanked by four mighty corner towers, cost some £66,000. In 1870 the huge, solid Pavilion Hotel was built on St Nicholas Cliff in Valley Bridge Road, and other new, large hotels appeared along the Esplanade and along the North Cliff area.

The Spa Concert Hall's total destruction by fire in 1876 forced the Cliff Bridge Company to yet more extravagant expenditure in erecting new buildings in 1880 costing some £70,000. In the Italian Renaissance style, consisting of a central block with domed towers at the angles and north and south wings of lower elevation, they were designed by the London architect Thomas Verity. They contained a large, lofty hall holding 3,000, a theatre 100 by 60 feet, restaurant with dining and billiard rooms, and several shops. The flat roof of the principal block formed a considerable terrace, and the whole front on the ground floor was bordered by flower-beds. Scarborough was 20 years ahead of Harrogate in providing such large-scale entertainment facilities under a covered promenade. Members of Parliament, peers and Yorkshire civic dignatories packed the hotels when the building was opened on 7 August 1879 with galas and balls, and a performance of Haydn's 'Creation' was attended by the largest concert audience known in Scarborough. The only provision, however, for water-drinking was from a single tap.

Set against the magnificent background of the cliff with the pan-oramic South Bay spread out before and nightly fairy-lights in the surrounding shrubs, the music at the spa was the town's major attrac-tion until 1939. In the mid-1870s the company spent £1,500 on music and had as musical director Wilhelm Meyer Lutz, who ably conducted the Spa Band from 1867 to 1898 with a break of four years. His succes-sor, Charles George Godfrey, was also successful; and in 1907 when 147,000 day-tickets brought in £14,919, musical expenditure was £3,039 and the shareholders' dividend £3,786.[99] The most famed musical director was Alick Maclean, 'the god of Scarborough'. Appointed in 1912 at a salary of £450, his impact was such that the company built a larger bandstand for the 1913 season. Designed by Sir Edwin Cooper of Scarborough, it was an impressive oval-shaped white edifice with a golden dome and glass windows facing the sea and open towards the cliff. Maclean's orchestra played each season during the 1914–18 war, even when German warships bombarded Scarborough in 1914, hitting the spa itself with 17 shells. Despite Maclean's growing fame, he stayed at Scarborough, but in 1916–23 wintered in London with the Queen's Hall Orchestra, returning for the season to Scar-borough, where he was until dying in 1936.[100]

Scarborough's most active development was, like Harrogate's, in the last two decades of the nineteenth century. The Seamer and Pickering branch of the railway (1882) and the Scarborough and Whitby Railway (1885) provided a shorter route to the growing Tees towns, though both passengers and goods still came to Scarborough by steamship well into the twentieth century. Local transport, especially for invalids, needed special provision at Scarborough owing to the difficult access between cliff top and shore level and the town's extensive coastal layout. Counter-balanced, cable-hauled cliff cars on an inclined track were the answer to the first problem, and the South Cliff Tramway pioneered this near the spa in 1875. A second tramway of 1875 only operated briefly, but the Central Tramway of 1881 succeeded, as did two more constructed in 1929–30.[101] Over two miles of seafront, among the country's finest, was begun in 1879 with building the Foreshore Road between the harbour and the Spa Bridge and finished with the Royal Albert Drive alongside the North Bay in 1890, but the difficult Marine Drive took from 1897 to 1906. Street tramways were an answer to the transport problem in this sprawling town, but the Scarborough Tramways Act was not passed until 1902, and the first electric tram did not run until 1904.[102]

Private enterprise suffered from risks taken in this boom period. The Rock Gardens (1860) and the Promenade Pier (1869) both failed financially. The North Bay Pier, destroyed by the sea in 1905, was not replaced. The Aquarium, opened below the Spa Bridge (earlier called the Cliff Bridge) in 1877, was sold at a great loss in 1886 and taken over by the corporation in 1921 to be a funfair. Theatres were more successful. The Theatre Royal, reconstructed in 1886, lasted until 1924. The Prince of Wales Circus, built in St Thomas Street in 1877 and rebuilt in 1908, also lasted into the twentieth century as the Opera House Theatre, and the Londesborough Theatre, built in that period, survived too.

By now Scarborough was firmly a seaside resort and residential town. Baths when erected – the South Cliff Baths (1876) and Royal Northern Sea-Bathing Infirmary – were seawater baths. The Constitutional Club (1888) and the Liberal Club (1892) were for residents. Visitors could join the Scarborough Club on St Nicholas Cliff only on special conditions. The so-called Spa Buildings were now a well-developed entertainment centre, and only the erection in 1889 at West Bank, Seamer Road, of the Scarborough Hydropathic Establishment, an 'extensive pile of buildings in the Italian style', four storeys high, costing £12,000 and enlarged in 1891 for the same amount, kept Scarborough in modern spa development.[103]

While Scarborough gained new prosperity by musical entertainment and Harrogate by municipal enterprise, the new cult of hydropathy revived or initiated other spas. The first to set up an English hydropathic establishment may have been Edward Johnson at Stansteadbury by May 1842[104] or Dr John Claridge at Pershore in Worcestershire in 1847.[105] Ilkley in Yorkshire and Malvern in Worcestershire, both already established as spa villages, probably simultaneously introduced regular hydropathic practice. The Ilkley Fountain at White Wells, a mineral-water spring high on the side of Rombalds Moor, about three-quarters of a mile from the township of 691 people in 1841, had a bath-house erected over it in 1699 and a Charity Bath, built by the lord of the manor, Squire Middleton, for the poor in 1829. Its reputation was such that in the early nineteenth-century summer seasons it was much frequented by what Granville called the 'higher grades of factory society' from Halifax, Bradford, Leeds, Huddersfield, Wakefield, Sheffield and even Manchester, for whom lodging houses were built, notably a range called Usher's Lodgings midway up the hillside. People still went to such lengths to take the waters that they went by donkeys, ponies, gigs and other conveyances up the rough carriage road half-way to the White Wells and then along a winding footpath.[106] Already, however, in 1841, the year before Dr James Wilson introduced hydropathy to Malvern, Granville foresaw Ilkley as an English Graefenberg; and Dr Rischanck from Silesia practised hydropathy there. Dr James Johnson in 1843 wrote:

> Here then is a locality, the very counterpart of Greafenberg, with a more bracing air than that of Malvern and water quite as pure. We have no doubt it will soon be occupied by some Priesnitz proselyte, and that the price of blankets will rise in Leeds and other manufacturing towns of that ilk.[107]

Hamer Stansfield, a former Mayor of Leeds, impressed by Dr Rischanck, formed a syndicate which bought 65 acres in Wharfedale, including 10 acres of woodland, under rocks called the Cow and Calf, where there was a spring like the Ilkley Wells. It engaged Samuel Sharp, the Leeds architect, to plan the Ben Rhydding Hydropathic Establishment[108] as the first purpose-built one in England, having in the central part of the building a hotel with 10 private sitting-rooms, 60 bedrooms, 12 bathrooms, dining and drawing rooms and a 'fresh air bath', a closed room into which moorland air was pumped.[109] The £10,000 first raised had soon to be doubled. The 'Scottish baronial' building, opened in 1844 eventually to accommodate 190 people, 'was one of the most noted of the hydropathic institutions drawing visitors from all over the world'. Its luxury was combined with the strictest regime in the country, involving early rising, careful dieting and energetic exercise besides the austere hydropathic treatment. Patients were packed tightly in blankets after being wrapped in cold wet sheets.

From 1855, however, it relaxed its regime through rivalry from the four-storeyed 'castellated' Craiglands Hydro opened in 1855 in grounds of five acres. It had also to introduce leisure facilities. By 1890 it had archery butts, two cement tennis courts and a large croquet lawn, and boasted of having the most extensive baths and the grandest recreation hall in the kingdom.

Another hydro, the Wells House, was opened in 1856, and Dr Rischanck came from Ben Rhydding to be its resident physician. It was another palatial building for 100 patients, designed in a three-storeyed Italianate style with angle eminences by Cuthbert Brodrick, the architect of Scarborough's Grand Hotel. It flourished, and after the first year the proprietors could raise the weekly terms with meals at the table d'hôte rate from £2 9s. to £2 12s. 6d., while keeping the medical fees with attendance at the baths at £3 10s. with an introductory fee of a guinea. By 1865 it sought to start a winter trade, taking advantage of the opening of a North-Eastern Railway station at Ilkley in 1863.[110]

Ilkley became a prosperous town by 1871 of 2,511 people with 397 houses and hydros, hotels, boarding houses, churches, schools, hospitals, parks and public gardens. The first hydropathic establishments, solidly built of massive stone in almost park-like enclosures, suggested stately mansions. Paved streets and roads were laid out for residential building, and in 1891 it was said that the 'quaint old village' had almost vanished. Only one street, still named Cow Pasture Road, recalled the old rural days.[111] Under the Local Government Act of 1858, the town had a local board from 1864 and an urban district council in 1894. The local authority bought the Waterworks Company (1852) and Ilkley Gas Company (1856).[112]

How much initiative for this development came from the lord of the manor in 1841, William Middleton, whose family held the manors of Ilkley and Middleton for generations, requires further study. They lived in the Elizabethan Middleton Lodge, but managed their estates from the old manor house behind Ilkley Parish Church.[113] They sold various open spaces for recreation to the local board until it bought the manorial rights in 1893.

In the 1870s Ilkley became a residential town with a more continuous social life. The area around the Grove – Railway and Station Roads – was laid out, and more diverse commercial activity appeared. The Ilkley Brewery and Aereated Water Company, opening in 1873 with 50 workpeople, both made aereated waters and supplied bitter beer, wines and spirits. Robert Brogden began carriage and coach making in 1872, supplying brakes for pleasure parties, landaus, phaetons, dog-carts, broughams and victorias.[114] The Ilkley Bath Charity built the first convalescent home in 1861, and Charles Semon of Bradford established another on top of the hill in 1874. Another church, St Margaret's by Norman Shaw, was built on land given by the Middleton family, being consecrated in 1879, as was a Roman Catholic chapel.[115]

Four more hydros were established by 1898 – the Gothic-style Spa Hydro, the Troutbeck Hydro, Rockwood House and Marlborough House. All hotels now had hydro facilities. Among the first was the Crescent Hotel in existence by 1879 and by 1896 owned by Miss Jones, previously the succesful manageress of the Ben Rhydding. Others were the Middleton, Highfield, Listers Arms and Wheatley, besides the Tarn House Boarding Establishment. Consequently in 1901 Ilkley had more domestic servants than any other West Riding town.

Among other services were the Ilkley Library Company's subscription library of 5,000 volumes in Wells Road, and John Dymond's livery stables, which served the hydros' guests by hiring horses and carriages for trips to local places of interest such as Bolton Abbey, Beamsley Beacon and Harewood House. And education flourished. The grammar school of 1607 was significantly reconstructed in 1883, 1893 and 1898; and eight private schools were founded, among them Glendair, a 'high-class school for girls', in a house specially built for the Misses Whitaker in 1880.[116] And many shops were among the other amenities of urban life to appear.

There was, however, over-investment in spadom. In 1891, for instance, the Middleton Hotel made 'great reductions' in its charges. Seven years later an attempt was made to rescue the decling spa by converting it to 'a place of amusement conducted on popular lines'. Scarborough's success was quoted as an example, and it was particularly urged that there must be cover for the crowds on wet bank holidays thronging the railway station or standing disconsolately under the railway bridge.[117] So 7½ acres of land were bought in the town's centre, and Brook Street was extended to the river where a new bridge was made over it in 1906. Two old inns at the bottom of Brook Street were demolished, a new hotel was built there, and suggestions were made for a 'splendid building', a complex comprising a concert hall, ballroom and opera house. These ideas materialized as a real civic centre, a town hall and public library erected in Station Road in 1907. It was designed by William Bakewell of Leeds and cost £13,000, of which Andrew Carnegie gave £3,000 for the library. The buildings included also a museum and the King's Hall which had a stage, gallery and balconies and seated about 1,000.

A Winter Garden, now essential in resort towns, was added in 1915, when the urban district council also installed electric light in the town for £22,000. But by now the social exclusiveness of the hydros was less of an economic reality in this 'mushroom spa' of 50 years' growth. Water-cures were generally declining. War in 1914 added to the difficulties, and the Craiglands Hydro sought to survive with a resident doctor described as Bulgarian. In the following years, the hydros disappeared or became hotels or schools. Wells House became Ilkley College; Ben Rhydding was a golf hotel between the wars, and in 1939–45 housed the Wool Secretariat, but was then demolished. White Well was a tea-room, but then became derelict until restored from 1974 by an ex-businessman from Bradford.

Among the patients at Ben Rhydding was John Smedley, a wealthy hosiery manufacturer with a mill in the village of Lea about a mile from Matlock Bath. After a prolonged Continental tour in 1840, he succumbed to enteric fever, from which he did not recover until 1851 after treatment at Ilkley. On his return to his mill, he resolved to extend the water-cure to his mill workers and others.[118] In 1853 he bought a house near Matlock Bank for his hydro, which was strategically placed near the Matlock Bridge Railway Station for the arrival and departure of his patients. This transformed the declining spa into a prosperous hydropathic centre and by the 1880s shifted the centre of Matlock as a watering-place from Matlock Bath to Matlock Bank, despite disadvantage of the Bank's steep gradient. Hotel and other building was limited in the old centre at Matlock Bath owing to the constricted and congested nature of the dale and the danger of flooding in the plain of the Derwent. Matlock Bank was more bracing, sheltered only from the north wind and with an open prospect to the south.[119]

The abrupt, masterful and dynamic Smedley practised at his hydro and at the Free Hospital at Lea Bridge for 21 years. His wife, partner in all his activities, had charge of the women patients. They lacked medical training, but he was well versed in physiology and anatomy and sometimes consulted a medical friend, Dr Cash. Smedley, an ardent Methodist who provided his workforce with six chapels and two schools, imposed an austere regime in his hydro, insisting on discipline and observance of decorous religious duties. The day began and ended with family worship, alcohol and tobacco were banned, and penalties were levied on late arrival at meals and gentlemen entering ladies' rooms. Matlock Bank had no mineral-water spring, only pure cold water, but this suited hydropathy as it had to be applied abundantly to patients as compresses, packs and sitz baths. Some of Smedley's methods were simple, such as a steam bath consisting of a cane chair and a red-hot brick in a bucket of water. The only harsh treatment was 'The Crisis' of Preissnitz, which drew up the skin into popules and pustules, but it ceased after Smedley's retirement. This watering-place differed greatly

176

from the pleasurable comfort of the traditional spa hotels and inns, but the number of patients increased, first slowly and then rapidly. In 1860 Smedley had 110 patients and the next year raised his daily charge from 3s. to 6s. By 1863 the patients averaged 1,050 at Matlock Bank and 400 at the Free Hospital, and by 1867, when the fame of Smedley's hydro was such that a porter guarded the door on Good Friday to exclude excursionists, each institution had about 2,000.[120]

Matlock soon realized hydropathy's commercial potential. By 1857 there were three hydros near the Bank – Smedley's (the largest) and those of Ralph Davis and John Rogers at Matlock Green; and by 1866 there were nine.[121] This hydropathic centre produced a rapid growth of population in 1861–71, and Matlock parish's houses increased from 903 in 1851 to 1,424 in 1891.[122] Competition from both the excursionists and day-trippers brought by the railway after 1849 and hydropathy's new vogue led Matlock Baths's seven chief hotels to try to maintain their social exclusiveness. Miss Ivatt and Mrs Jordan, now running the refurbished New Bath Hotel, made great alterations there, and by 1857 it had a large tepid swimming-pool. The manager in 1880 advised his clients to book to Matlock Bath and not Matlock Bridge Station;[123] but the old spa had to have hydropathy too, and sometime after 1857 William Geaves at the Old Bath and Old Bath Hotel had to close both down. In 1866 a company was formed to build a hydro in their grounds, called the Royal Hotel, with 100 beds, hydropathic baths and again a tepid swimming-pool, but it lacked sufficient capital, and its hotel was not opened until 1878. Six years later, on the hillside above the hotel, it built a plateglass-fronted Pavilion with a central concert hall, assembly rooms and promenade side annexes. But both establishments got into financial difficulties. Another company took them over in 1882, and they passed into private ownership in 1889.[124]

Smedley's hydro still flourished. By 1867 he had to refuse patients, and in 1868 a new four-storeyed wing was added to the building. In 1872, now aged 69, he wisely engaged W. Bell Hunter, a doctor of 28, to train in his methods. Smedley had invested a fortune in his hydro, and his reputation had done for Matlock what Boisragon had for Cheltenham and Jephson, his contemporary, for Leamington, but when he died on 27 July 1874 one-man control was a limitation, and further expansion needed more resources. In 1875 a company was formed to raise £50,000 capital to continue his work. The banks and assurance companies doubted its credibility, but Crompton and Evans advanced the sum at 4½ per cent, and plans went ahead. Confidence in hydropathic's curative value became more generally recognized through Bell Hunter's work. The directors retained his services until his death on 6 December

1894, when he was considered the first to make hydropathy a recognized medical science.

Smedley's death at once eased the hydro's austerity. By 1878 there were billiard and smoking rooms, and electric light and other concessions to comfort and modernity came in 1888, though there were already electric bells and baths (six). In 1890 an omnibus for guests was bought for £100, and a hairdresser was established in the basement. Excellent meals were served after the manager was sent to London in 1897 to study catering in the best clubs and hotels; and a garage for 15 cars was installed in 1908. And alterations and extensions in 1875–89 entirely changed the hydro's appearance and layout. By 1914 it accommodated 250 patients, and its importance led the Midland Railway to change the local station's name from Matlock Bridge to Matlock and stop expresses there instead of at Matlock Bath. In the 1920s those merely wanting a quiet rest were admitted as well as water-cure patients.[125]

Matlock's prosperity did not depend solely on its hydros: its mixed economy was based on cotton-spinning, flour-milling, grindstone-quarrying and paint production, but the water-cure was important and still expanding. By 1895 the Bath had 3 hydros and the Bank 18 which increased to between 30 and 40 by 1919. Matlock Bath, the original spa centre, tried both to cater for day-trippers and to improve the facilities for long-stay visitors by the amusements and amenities of a pleasure-resort. A promenade of 300 yards was made in 1874 and extended in 1887 when land on either side of the river was leased for pleasure walks. And after 1889 dances and other amusements were still organized in the Pavilion.

Civic consciousness was slow at Matlock in the separate settlements at Bath, Bank, Bridge, Town and Green. The Matlock Gas Light and Coke Company (1853) and the Matlock and District Gas Company (1886) remained, though the town took over the waterworks at Matlock Bath (1883) and at Matlock (1897). Even when the Local Act of 1894 brought urban status, the two towns remained apart as the Matlock Urban District and the Matlock Bath and Scarthin Urban District, though many social services and amenities followed.

The purchase and conversion of Bridge Hall in 1894 provided a town hall into which the petty sessions court (1900) and county court (1901) moved. The Matlock Gas Act of 1894 enabled Matlock Council to take over the Matlock Gas Light and Coke Company, and in 1897 Matlock Bath Council leased the traditional promenade, the Lovers' Walks on the east side of the river, including the ferry and boating rights. In 1900 another ferry was started at the southern end of the Walks near the New Bath Hotel. Not to be outdone, Matlock Council in 1899 bought open spaces at Knowleston Green and Allcock and in the Hall Leys pleasure grounds. The crowning attempt to make Matlock an attractive watering-place was the optimistic opening of the Grand Pavilion (originally the Kursaal) in 1910 on the South Parade, designed by a German company for the Matlock Bath Council, but it failed to arrest the decline of the Bath area and was merely used as the Council's administrative headquarters.[126]

While Matlock specialized in hydropathy, the other Derbyshire spa, Buxton, emphasized the pleasure and entertainment of the visitors and increasing number of residents, interspersed with taking the waters. Yet the new cult of the water-cure came there also. In 1867 the Revd J. Shore, formerly of Matlock House and Smedley's hydro, opened Malvern House, half a mile south-west of the Crescent on the Hartington Road, as a hydro.[127] By 1899 it was the well-known Buxton Hydropathic, with four other hydros.[128]

Buxton long suffered from frequent heavy winter snowstorms blocking the roads. The coming at last of the Midland Railway from Derby in 1863 and the North-Western from Manchester the next year brought many middle-class visitors from the large industrial areas and made a longer season possible. More hotel accommodation was needed. The Smilter family, having taken over the Great Hotel in the Crescent in 1849, renamed it the Crescent Hotel in 1866.[129] In 1868 the town's first 'monster' hotel, the Palace Hotel, with 200 rooms and set in six acres, was built on a steep rise near the two adjacent railway stations, by the Buxton Palace Hotel Company to the design of Henry Currey, the ducal architect, costing £60,000 and £20,000 for additions in 1889.[130] Its manager, Philip Blades, was the first to introduce separate dining-tables in Buxton, breaking down the traditional hotel communal life.[131]

The seventh Duke of Devonshire, a widower when he succeeded to the estates in 1858, was a scholar and recluse, whose need to retrench perhaps explained the abandonment of Plaxton's plans of 1852. He seldom visited Buxton, and in 1890 the *Buxton Advertiser*, regretting the aristocracy's partiality for Continental spas to Buxton's disadvantage, criticized him:

Neither the present Duke nor his family seem to care for the place, beyond drawing therefrom the uttermost proper fraction in rents and dues. . . . It is to the interest of the Duke of Devonshire . . . that Buxton should prosper. His are the baths, the lime-works, the building land and most of the principal hotels. To him and his family thousands of acres in the neighbourhood belong, and yet the idea of a Buxton bargain is altogether too one-sided, and the town in many

179

cases has to improve his property and pay in great measure for the improvement.[132]

This was unfair. He had presented in 1871 the land for Buxton's great enterprise, the Pavilion Gardens, the pioneering winter gardens rapidly copied by other spa towns to prolong the season by providing bad weather cover and more popular entertainment. The elegant Pavilion, costing £12,000, was a 400-foot iron and glass structure on a stone base, the central hall flanked by conservatories, with, like the Hydro, hot-water pipes for winter heating. Edward Milner, the London landscape gardener and garden architect and Plaxton's assistant in erecting the Crystal Palace in 1851, designed it and also transformed the central area of the Serpentine Walk with two miles of walks and five bridges. New waterfalls were made, two lakes joined, many trees and shrubs planted and a bandstand made for the town band, now the Pavilion Orchestra, which in various forms played throughout the year.[133] He explained his concept of a public park in *The Art and Practice of Landscape Gardening* (1890). The Pavilion was extended in 1876 to include the octagonal Concert Hall.[134]

The Duke had also given more and more of the Crescent stables to the Devonshire Hospital until the final great extension of 1881 when the half-acre circular interior space was roofed over by the largest single-span dome in Europe. These improvements cost £36,000, the Cotton Districts Convalescent Fund paying £24,000, but the Duke gave the adjoining extensive grounds. He gave £200 towards the cost of the clock-tower erected over the Hospital's main entrance as a tribute to Dr W.H. Robertson, Chairman of the Committee of Management, and he presented the clock with illuminated dials costing £500.[135] He had also given the land and £150 for building Christ Church at Burbage in 1860, also designed by Currey, as part of his plan to develop that part of Buxton, and he made other gifts to the town.[136]

The criticism of 1890 was perhaps stimulated when he offered in that year to build, fit and furnish a new pump-room to replace the small inadequate well-room next to the Natural Bath where water had been drunk for nearly 40 years since the demolition of Carr's Grecian Well Room in 1851. His offer, made on condition that the town surrendered any rights it might have in the thermal springs, was accepted, but he did not live to see the resulting neo-classical, single-storeyed Pump Room designed by the ageing Currey. It had a large sunken oval marble basin provided with water from St Ann's Well handed up by dippers to patients at a moderate cost. As the Enclosure Act required free access to St Ann's Well, a pump was placed outside the west side of the Pump

Room until the 1940s when it was replaced some 100 yards away nearly opposite the Natural Mineral Water Baths.

The Duke died in 1891, and the eighth Duke opened the new premises on 18 June 1894 with his wife, the first reigning Duchess of the house of Cavendish since 1811. Flying flags and Venetian masts, garlanded in evergreen linked with streamers, lined the town's streets, and a long procession in 28 landaus met their Graces at the station. But in his speech after lunch, the Duke spoke about the 'enormous exactions' to be imposed on landowners by Sir William Harcourt's death duties that year and warned that the Devonshire estate's future income might have to be employed differently.

Buxton had already begun to free itself from ducal tutelage. An Act of 1873 empowered the local board to construct water and gas works. Attempts were made to meet increasing civic and outside expenditure by an extended season and encouraging visitors to come at Christmas and Easter.[137] From the 1880s to the depression of 1931 and particularly in 1891–1901, Buxton flourished. Its expansion was greatest in that decade when 286 houses were built, mostly solid upper and middle class residences of gritstone and blue slate, besides 240 in Fairfield, and the population grew from 7,540 in 1891 to 10,181 in 1901 and then was steady.[138]

The town council provided itself with a worthy meeting-place. After the market hall, built in 1857 at the summit of St Ann's Cliff, was burnt down in 1885, the site was chosen for a town hall and free public library built in 1889. This was a stone building in classical style designed by William Pollard of Manchester. The first floor had yet another assembly room seating 1,000, and the library contained 3,000 volumes. It cost some £12,000. The population rose from 1,235 in 1851 to 3,717 in 1871. In 1891 the township had 4,658 and the urban district 7,540 and 10,250 in 1911.[139] This, with the influx of visitors, taxed all places of assembly, including churches.

After St John's Church (1811), the next to be built was at Burbage (1860). Then came St James the Great in Higher Buxton, a chapel of ease built in 1871 and enlarged in 1898; Trinity Proprietory Chapel in Hardwick Mount built in 1873 and enlarged in 1883 and 1894; and St Mary's Mission Church in Higher Buxton a temporary wirewove weather-proof structure of 1897 costing £800 and holding 275. Buxton in 1895 at last became a parish separate from Bakewell. St Ann's Roman Catholic Church was built in 1861 and enlarged in 1895, and by 1899 there were five nonconformist chapels. St Anne's and St John's churchyards were now inadequate, and the urban district council had to provide a cemetery of 12 acres in 1897, about a mile south-east of the town.[140]

Using their powers under the Act of 1873, the council in 1876 erected gasworks for £24,000 and sewage-works, which included means of cremating rubbish, at Ashwood Dale in 1886 for £8,100 and in 1899 an electric power station for £25,000. Although Buxton's rateable value in 1891 was £49,084, the townspeople were unused to such expenditure, and hence the allegation of ducal neglect in 1890. Municipal achievement was dearly bought.

While Buxton was rescued from decline and stagnation by the railway and civic consciousness, Malvern might have remained an insignificant rural spa – still only a village of two streets with several stately homes and a few lodging houses – had not Granville's visit in 1840, when it was lethargic, led to the introduction of hydropathy and a period of marked expansion. Six years later, large hydropathic establishments had attracted people to Malvern; but syndicate finance, the railway and local entrepreneurs increasingly made the village into a town.[141]

Its hydropathic history started in May 1842 when 35-year-old Dr James Wilson arrived by coach and took a room at the Crown. A well-qualified physician, who had studied medicine at Dublin, London and Paris and practised in London, he came purposefully to Malvern. He had spent the previous year as Priessnitz's pupil at Graefenberg. He was friendly with another doctor, James Manby Gully, a wealthy Jamaican coffee-planter's son and equally well trained at Liverpool, Edinburgh and Paris. He so convinced Gully of hydropathic treatment's value that they decided to practise it together. They chose Malvern, among the Worcestershire hills, not unlike Silesia, and a small spa without highly organized distractions.[142]

Wilson's success was immediate. He leased the Crown, renamed it Graefenberg House and, while patients crowded in, wrote two books on the cure in the first two years. Assured of a future, he built a grand classical-style establishment, Priessnitz House in Abbey Road, for 50 guests and next to it in 1845 Malvern House for invalids. Gully soon came and built Tudor House for men and Holyrood House for women linked by the so-called Bridge of Sighs.

The methods of both doctors and others following them were similar. Patients rose at 5 a.m. for an hour's cold wet-sheet treatment, followed by a walk to drink the water at St Ann's Well before breakfast of bread and butter, treacle and water. This was followed by cold douches, cold compresses and various baths of different sizes and shapes until dinner at 3 p.m. consisting of boiled mutton and fish. The patients were then free, but encouraged to take outdoor exercise. The day ended at 8 p.m. with supper of bread and butter, milk and biscuits, and finally bedtime.[143]

182

Queen Adelaide, the patron of Bath, Brighton Cheltenham and Tunbridge Wells, visited Malvern in September 1842, the year of Gully's arrival. After lunch at the Foley Arms, she and her suite rode up the hill on donkeys to St Ann's Well.[144] There is no evidence that she took the waters, but her visit assisted Malvern's revival. The springs and wells became more valuable, and several small spa centres were promoted. The most popular, the old-established St Ann's Well, was leased by the Foley Estate to a tenant with responsibility for providing free glasses and attendants and keeping the paths tidy and repaired. The octagonal two-storeyed extension to the well-house was built, it was said in 1865, 'a few years ago' by public subscription, when there were complaints about the dilapidated state of the road leading to the well. Public control of it was suggested, but discussing this with Lady Emily Foley was considered 'inexpedient'.[145]

Another local landowner, T.C. Horyold of Blackmore Park, recovered ownership of the old Holy Well with an acre of adjoining land and in 1843 at a cost of £400 built the third well-house there, designed like the spa at Baden-Baden, but the well had lost its former reputation and steadily declined. Gully in the 1840s 'elegantly fitted up' warm, shower, vapour and plunging baths at the Hay Well conveniently near his establishments in Abbey Road.[146] Gully also had from 1846 a small establishment at the Chalybeate Spring and Spa Cottage (built in 1825) below Swan Pool.[147] The Coburg Baths near the Foley Arms were still patronized, and Lord Sandey's Spout in Spring Lane, Malvern Link, was established about 1850.[148]

For about a decade Wilson and Gully alone practised hydropathy in Malvern, but others came, and from mid-century with 'business and bustle', an observer said,[149] made the village spa into a prosperous township with its improvement commission of 12 members from 1851. Professional men, builders and traders soon exploited the situation, but Worcester grew jealous. The Worcester doctors, notably Charles Hastings, a supporter of the Droitwich brine cure in the 1830s,[150] strongly criticized the water-cure. Wilson deplored in the *Medical Provincial Journal* the settlement at Worcester, so near to Malvern, of this 'man of drugs', whom he accused of fearing loss of custom.

The impressive, autocratic-looking Wilson, who had a library of 700 books on the water-cure, initially led the promotion of hydropathy, and Preissnitz House flourished. Patients paid Wilson a guinea consultation fee and four guineas weekly for baths and medical attention, with extra charges for private sitting-rooms and servants' quarters, and had to provide a blanket and two coarse sheets.[151]

The urbane, dignified Gully, however, then became fashionable and successful, like Jephson at Leamington, establishing a personal fortune and an outstanding reputation for the growing spa town. He had famous patients like Gladstone, Macaulay, Dickens, Tennyson. Carlyle, Darwin and Florence Nightingale. Prominent in public affairs, he was an original member of the improvement commission and its chairman in 1860 and 1865. He was also in 1858–60 on the committee to negotiate with the Worcestershire justices about the sale of part of the Link Common.[152] He became chairman of the directors of the Malvern Hotel Company and at one time earned some £10,000 a year. His success was said to be second only to Preissnitz himself, and Ilkley, 'the Malvern of the North', had no such practitioner.[153]

In 1846 Gully published *The Water Cure in Chronic Diseases*, upholding his own methods to the detriment of Wilson's. The two men quarrelled. Wilson bought the little Chalybeate Spa when the Mason estate was sold and locked it up to exclude Gully's patients. Gully retaliated by buying an adjacent strip of land to allow his patients access to the garden of the Cottage.[154]

Other aspiring water-cure physicians soon invaded Malvern, 'this place of a golden fee'. James Loftus Marden, apprenticed to Preissnitz in 1845–46 and Gully's partner, built Hardwicke House in Abbey Road in 1851, equipped with modern types of baths, including electro-chemical and Turkish baths. In 1856 he leased Peachfield and its furniture, the Dowager Lady Lyttleton's home, to offer inexpensive accommodation to clergymen, governesses and others of small means affected by Malvern's rising prices. Treatment there was free, but the altruistic venture failed by 1857, and the house became a school. He also treated patients at his home at Abbotsfield, which he wished to let in 1856 from 1 December to 1 May, which suggests he was at Malvern only during the season.[155]

Dr Ralph Ginrod also practised from 1851 in Townsend House with a museum in which he lectured, and a long winter garden where he organized a temperance festival in July 1857. Malvern's greater rewards lured Dr Edward Johnson from Stansteadbury to start a practice at Malvernbury and Ellerslie by 1856. After Wilson opened Malvern House, his partner, Dr Leopold Stumes, left him to build in 1860 a similar hydro on six acres near Roalin House in South Field.[156] These six hydros, concentrated in Great Malvern, were included in Grindrod's *Malvern Past and Present* (1865). And at Malvern Wells, James Ayerst, who converted the Well House about 1860, still succeeded in his new hydro. J.F. Prasley practised in 1857 at Kensington Cottage and St James's House with the exclusive use between 10.30 a.m. and 1.00 p.m. of the West Villa Baths of Peter Adler at West Malvern. W.J. Parks, once Gully's assistant, was trying to preserve this West Villa practice in 1865.[157]

184

By 1864 Malvern had ten hydropathic physicians and two surgeon dentists; and growing commercial activity employed six solicitors and one estate agent, J.B. Harper, who claimed he had started in 1841.[158] Furnished houses and apartments for letting to visitors predominated in Harper's books, like the large handsomely furnished villas in Great Malvern, available for six weeks from 30 June 1857 at ten guineas a week or five to six guineas for part of it.[159] There were two more estate agents, J.C. Lear and Arthur Jackson, by 1865.

So began the golden age of Malvern's developers, builders and estate agents as they strove in a rapidly developing land market to meet the demand for visitors' accommodation. Until the water-cure's success was assured, expansion was slow, especially on the north side of Church Street, where most land belonged to the Foley Estate of Lady Emily Foley. No other woman and few men had such an influence on the spa town and its development. This autocratic lady, daughter of James Graham, third Duke of Montrose, married Edward Thomas Foley of Stoke Edith in 1832 and when he died in 1846 managed the estates until until 1900. In a lesser way she dominated the town as the Dukes of Devonshire did Buxton. She spent the summer there, arriving in a bright yellow landau drawn by white horses and attended by servants in the Foley livery of scarlet and white, to be greeted by local dignatories at the Foley Arms. As lady of the manor she was often requested to grace public occasions and give sites and donations for schools and churches, and in 1873 it was felt that, if asked, her influence would get the carriage roads repaired.[160] By keeping control of the manorial copyhold land and refusing to disfranchise it until 1858, she continued the Foley policy of imposing rigid specifications on land released for building, but the town's resulting development was slow and costly. In 1843 only a few houses stood in Graham Lane which gave access to Malvern Field, but from the late 1840s she allowed Graham Road to be laid out northwards across the field; building plots were released, and the earliest houses (like Montrose Boarding House and Stokefield) were built. In 1852–55 in Graham Terrace and Albert Road 16 plots were sold, chiefly to George McCann and Charles Morris, and by 1855 there were over 30 houses in that area. Malvern's evolution with low density housing and irregularly built cottages, detached and set in grounds sufficient for a garden and shrubbery, owes much to the Foley Estate's example. Lady Emily required roads, besides being wide and sweeping and gently inclined if possible, to be planted with lime or other ornamental trees. In Graham, Albert and Victoria Roads all plots were at least an acre and houses unlike each other.[161] There were no planned homogeneous estates of crescents and squares as elsewhere.

Although Lady Emily disliked parting with land for building, James

Mason's death released his South Field of 100 acres with his house, the Grange, Spa Cottage, the Chalybeate Spring and Swan Pool. This estate, advertised as the only freehold land available for building in Malvern, met the urgent demand for expansion, and many houses in this area were built as hydros, like Hardwicke House and Townsend House, or lodging houses. Abbey and Prior Roads and others were laid out with restrictions preserving their residential gentility – detached or semi-detached houses, not opposite or parallel to each other, so that views were not blocked, and with protecting evergreens behind – and businesses, hotels or tea-gardens were forbidden. With Foley land withheld from building and physical obstruction by the Malvern Hills, development was linear in pattern and around the fringes of the hills. No new houses were built opposite the Foley Arms Hotel until 1856.[162]

At West Malvern, the Conservative Land Society, with Viscount Ranelagh and J.C. Cobbold MP as trustees, bought an estate to offer building lots at just over £52 each in this 'rapidly growing locality' from 1857, and Ranelagh, Merrick and Goodson Roads were built; but this was a political move to create more county freehold franchises by offering both a generous mortgage and an investment.[163] Some older houses here dated from 1830, but other more substantial ones were of the 1850s, especially when the road through the village was joined to the Wyche cutting at the south. Apart from Great Malvern, most new building was north of the hill range in Malvern Link, which by 1873 had 352 houses, some Regency and Early Victorian, at the bottom of the Link near Spring Lane, and a population of about 1,760.[164] Houses were sprinkled along the Worcester Road before 1855, but in 1858 the sale of land on the north side of the main road brought new roads of smaller houses and cottages in Merton, Farley and Richmond Roads by 1852. And as early as 1851 the second Earl Somers of Eastnor Castle sold 70 acres of land, and building continued higher up the main road to Somers Park Avenue. In 1873 the vestry sold some 20 acres of property, including the old workhouse in the Worcester Road, for £8,000 to John Jones, who built his Albert Park estate of large new villas by about 1892.[165]

Like all spa towns, Malvern's over-rapid expansion caused problems, especially in controlling the district called Newtown around the junction of the Cowleigh and West Malvern Roads. In 1848 some simple, dignified houses were built near the Belvoir Hotel, which in 1855 was still a fashionable locality, but soon after several poorer houses and at least four public houses intruded, making it a working-class area. It also had five brickworks, and James Allen who in 1856 had started as a boot and shoe maker at 5 Holyrood Terrace in Great Malvern, moved there to run with his son the Brompton Brewery. Guide books called the area untempting and advised visitors not to linger there. Tivoli Place in Newtown was built in 1862 and Gloucester Place in 1863. By 1873 there were 160 houses in the area described as North Malvern, Cowleigh and Newtown and a population of 800, all in the parish of Leigh, which also had 834 houses and a population of 4,172.[166]

The several communities around the hills involved many local authorities. Boards, vestries and poor law unions were divided by disagreements, as shown when the local newspaper in 1873 considered Newtown's future. The waste land at the Link was filthy, and Newtown's dirt and mess were chronic, while ratepayers in other areas paid to remove its refuse. This area of the parish of Leigh was not under the Boards of either Great Malvern or Malvern Link, who were then in dispute over paying for lighting the Worcester Road. Malvern Link's people opposed annexing Newtown, Belmont and the Howells to their Board as they would have to pay 'for improvements to a district occupied by a class of people who had nothing in common with themselves'. The present sewerage system would have to be replaced by more copious channels. After a local government board inspector's inquiry, the idea was rejected.[167]

More impetus to building was given in 1872 when the Hornyold family sold many sites mainly in Malvern Link, as recalled by Hornyold Road and Hornyold Avenue.[168] But the greatest impetus in the 1850s and 1860s was the turnpiking of all the chief roads by 1860 and the railway's arrival in 1859. After much discussion, the first part of a line from Worcester to Hereford was begun in 1858 by the co-operation of three railway companies. This was a six-mile section from the Henwick district of Worcester to Malvern Link, where a station was built in July 1859. By January 1860 there were six daily trains each way and four on Sundays.

To connect with the Oxford–Wolverhampton line passengers had to change trains in Worcester from Henwick to Shrub Hill because the Board of Trade considered the Severn bridge unsafe, but on 16 May 1860 the line was opened to Shrub Hill and on 25 May to Great Malvern and Malvern Wells, where a fire in January had destroyed the early simple station, which was rebuilt.[169] The first through train ran into Great Malvern Station on 13 September 1861, four days before its official opening. The Great Western Railway took over the Worcester–Hereford line in 1861 after the amalgamation of the companies operating it, and passengers could travel direct from Malvern to London in six hours. In 1864 another company provided a link through Tewkesbury to Cheltenham and so to the south-west. By 1868 44 passenger and goods trains ran through Malvern each day. E.W. Elmskie, a local exponent of Gothic architecture, designed a station appropriate to

Great Malvern, a long, low, gabled Gothic structure with cast-iron tracery, floral capitals and a clock-tower. Lady Emily had her own especially furnished first-class waiting room.[170]

The railway brought so many visitors that Malvern expected a boom. The Malvern Hotel Company, 'composed chiefly of persons with railway interests', was formed to build larger hotels. Dr Gully, its chairman, was also on the Midland Railway's board. 'Fabulous sums' were spent on two 'palatial piles' to Elmslie's designs.[171] It built the Malvern Link Hotel in 1861 in Somers Road on some 12 acres of land bought from George McCann near the Link Station. Costing almost £6,000, it was of red and black brick with (in Pevsner's words) 'an informally-placed tower with a high circular stair-turret and an aura of gloom'.[172]

The company bought also land east of the church and adjoining Great Malvern Station to lay out Avenue Road and others with such significant names as Manby Road, Tiverton Road and Gloucester (later Imperial) Road. In January 1865 the Malvern Land and Building Society, in which Lear and McCann and Everell had an interest, offered newly built villas for sale or letting in Manby Road;[173] but dominating the area was the company's new monster Imperial Hotel opened on 11 August 1862 in three acres of ground on Avenue Road. Of red brick and stone dressings in Continental Gothic, its six storeys were surmounted by a commanding tower 146 feet high. Its boundary walls were of blue lias stone with Bath stone dressings, and the massive gate piers were crowned with elegantly designed lamps. It had some 100 rooms, each with a clock, carpets throughout and gas fittings from Skidmore of Coventry; it boasted to be the only English hotel lit by gas.[174] It was packed in mid-September 1865 with 148 guests. The company hoped it would be a grand centre of social life; the county ball, patronized by Ladies Raglan, Lechmere and Packington, was held there in January 1865.[175]

The railways threatened the coaches and old-established modest hotels, the Royal Foley Arms and the Belle Vue. Mrs Fielders opened the newer Beauchamp Hotel about 1850 at the junction of Church Street and Braham Road, at the same time as William Archer reluctantly demolished the Jacobean Abbey House to build the Abbey Hotel.[176] John Archer of the Royal Foley Arms bravely announced on 3 March 1860 that omnibuses from his office would meet every train at Malvern Links Station and, if desired, call in the town to take passengers and luggage for a 6d. fare. When in mid-June Walter Pratt declared that, since the railway must not 'have all its own way', he was starting a new four-horse coach service between Malvern and Worcester, the *Malvern Advertiser* hoped he would be supported against the railway. On 7 July Archer withdrew the omnibus service, though private horse flys and carriages could still be ordered;[177] and Alfred Haynes, a livery stable keeper, failed in 1867.[178] The Beauchamp Hotel changed hands four times in 15 years, and in 1865 David Kendall added part of it to his grocery store. When the rest reopened, Sir E.A.H. Lechmere, Chairman of the Commissioners, proposed its toast and hoped that Malvern's hotel could remain independent.[179]

At that event it was claimed that Malvern was now excellent for winter residence because the railway brought ample coal from the Midlands. To assist an all-year season, Dr Gully led the Improvement Commissioners in petitioning in March 1860 the Hereford and Worcester Railway to carry coal more cheaply from Shrub Hill to Malvern Link.[180] In 1873 a Stourbridge firm offered 100 tons of canal coal to the gas committee, delivered to Malvern Links Station at 25s. a ton. Malvern now claimed to be second only as a spa to Cheltenham, which, moreover, relied upon the tradition of retired officials from India instead of honest medical testimony as in Grindrod's *Malvern Past and Present*.[181] Scarborough in summer, argued the *Malvern Advertiser*, was all frivolity, gaiety and high *ton*, but winter's first chill desolated the scene. Ilkley and Buxton suffered from exposed highlands, but strong winds rarely blew at Malvern.[182] And Malvern's weekly rents, never above 11 guineas for a fine house in November, were the same in the summer.[183]

Every commercial enterprise responded to the opportunities of the 1850s and 1860s. By 1856 Bennet and Son of Belle Vue Place sold everything required for water treatment, and C. Need of Edith House sold 'hydropathic gingerbread'. C. Evans of Astley and Evans, Regent Street, London, had a tailor and draper's branch at Worcester House, and Miss Bromley opened a servants' registry office at Link Top in 1861. The 'self-important' John Ward Harrop, active on the Local Board, brewed ale and porter, and Schweppes and Company began a new development by distributing and selling Malvern Soda Water and Malvern Seltzer Water made from Holy Well water. Lea, Perrin and Burrows, chemists and mineral-water agents of Belle Vue Place, had the sole right to sell Malvern waters and pure Holy Well water in quart bottles at 4s. each through their resident partners, Walter and John Burrows, who later bought Lea and Perrin's Malvern branch and also the monopoly of bottling St Ann's Well water.[184]

Through Malvern's domination by doctors and their preoccupation with invalids, mid-century social life was rather staid and decorous, and commercial entertaining was tardy, but in July 1856 William Simons, nurseryman and florist, opened the Promenade Gardens for the season. A seasonal family ticket cost a guinea and 10s. 6d. for an individual. When they reopened on 30 June the next year, non-subscribers paid 1s.

then and 6d. on other days, but purchasers of shrubs, plants or flowers were admitted free; and subscribers could have a key to the gardens, returnable after the season, for 1s. Herr A. Weikert and later others from Savile Row and sometimes Bath provided music; the band, seeking the flavour of Continental spas, was variously called the German Band (1856), the Bohemian Band (1857) and the Rhine Band (1860). Playing every evening except Saturday, they sometimes gave an afternoon 'Grand Promenade Concert' and in winter played for the weekly quadrille parties at the Concert Room in Church Street opened in 1861 by W. Haynes, the Priory organist. Simons also was doubtless behind the first Malvern Horticultural and Floral Exhibition held in his Promenade Gardens on 1 July 1856, at which prizes were given to cottagers for clean and neat cottages and gardens and for their garden produce.[185]

The population was now large enough to organize other middle-class and special social events. The ubiqitous Dr Gully chaired the Malvern Club which met at least by 1865 in the Belle Vue Hotel and had a three guineas subscription. Most members were residents, but visitors were admitted. It flourished and later had premises on the lower corner of Grange Road.[186] By 1856 the Malvern Cricket Club held a match of residents against visitors, the Field Club undertook archaeological digs, and the Archery Club stored its equipment in Lamb's Library. Among occasional excitements was a visit by Hengler's Mammoth Circus and Equestrian Exhibition in August 1857.[187] The first local newspaper, the Liberal *Malvern Advertiser*, was published from 1855 by H.W. Lamb, bookseller and stationer, at the Royal Library, initially only from mid-June to the end of October. W.J. Berrow's rival *Malvern News* appeared in 1860.[188]

Many smaller hotels and boarding houses were also built between about 1842 and 1875. The British Camp Hotel (earlier Peter Pocket's) had two wings added soon after 1848; the Montrose Boarding House was built in the late 1840s for Miss Bullock; and cheaper accommodation in North and West Malvern was popular. The Belvoir (now the North Malvern) Hotel, the Lygon Arms and the St James's Boarding House opened before 1858. In 1855 there were 95 hotel and lodging-house keepers, some with a dual occupation. Most were in Great Malvern, but there were 16 in the Link and a few, including the Well's House and Essington's, in Malvern Wells and North and West Malvern. The railway brought some 3,000 visitors, greatly helping local enterprise, and by 1865 over a quarter of the town's 800 houses were lodging houses, each charging from two to ten guineas a week.[189]

Besides middle-class visitors who, if not attending the hydros, stayed in hotels or apartment-houses and spent money, the railway also brought working-class excursionists from the Black Country with dramatic effect. On the opening of the Great Malvern and Malvern Wells Stations on Friday 25 May 1860, in time for the Whitsuntide holiday, the first 'holiday folk' came by train on Sunday, preceded very early on Monday by the 'businessmen', stallholders eager for the best main street places for stands for fairings, for lottery-tables and for rifle butts. Then they slept 'like mummies' until 9 a.m. when 10,000 passengers came from the newly opened stations. A great attraction was the opening of the Mechanics Institute's recreation ground. The *Malvern Advertiser* outspokenly supported the new visitors: there was no reason to fear injury to the town by making it more popular and less aristocratic, a view which was narrow and morbid and contrary to long experience in other cases. From 1 June to 30 September railway excursions were general, and places like Malvern and Buxton, at once famous, pretty and accessible, would be crowded with 'the most curious specimens of the British shopkeeper and artisan on an outing'. Residents in the favoured localities regarded the excursionists as barbarians, whose irruptions spoilt peace, comfort and poetry and their retirement, but such places belonged, not to those living there, but to those getting there. 'Our course', concluded the paper, 'is onward, and improvement is the order of the day.'[190]

Worse came for invalids and those seeking seclusion. Black Country firms organized day rail trips for their workforce. On 9 July 1860 Pierce Baldwin of Stourbridge and Wolverhampton paid their employees' fares to Malvern. Each party of these 'hardworking and smoke-dried people', headed by a band, joined others at Malvern Link Station to march through the town and soon climb the hills to the summit. After some hours, they returned to the station, where tents had been erected with flags displaying inscriptions praising them and expressing good feelings between them and their employers. A cold dinner awaited, dancing and games followed, and the trains left at 9 p.m. Soon there was a similar invasion from the locomotive works at Derby, Oldbury and Manchester.[191] On 21 July 5,000 came in heavy rain which drove them from the hills to shelter in 'houses of entertainment' (public houses). Even the *Advertiser* now wondered where they came from, and critics said that trains could transport hundreds of excursionists more cheaply than bringing a half-hundredweight parcel from Worcester, which still came by carrier's cart.

Five years later, residents still accused the Midland and Great Western Railway Companies of thinking only of their shareholders. A public meeting denounced the 'excursion nuisance' and the Worcester–Hereford line's high fares and charge for coal transport, twice that of other lines. Limiting excursion trains was demanded. This protest clearly impressed the directors, who were reported in September to

191

have so restricted excursions that residents and visitors had no complaints about hordes of day-trippers that season.[192] Dr Grindrod supported the railways as they made long journeys for invalids and other
visitors easier, and though 'they do not always bring the most select
class of visitor', one should rejoice that the hard-working artisan and his
wife could enjoy a day's pleasure. Excursions now came only thrice
weekly for three months of the year when he suggested visitors could
avoid trippers by rural driving and rambling in the early morning and
evening since trains did not now arrive before 11 a.m. and left by 6.30
p.m. at the latest.[193] Lady Foley, who made the Great Western chairman
promise in 1877 to stop excursion trains, was most effectual.[194]

Pressure of excursionists and encroachment of the railway and building led to the 'parks' movement in Malvern, which was destined, its
supporters urged, under judicious management to be large, probably as
large as Cheltenham and as important for invalids and schools. Agricultural use of land was not always the best; as Malvern rapidly grew it
needed access to pure air and rural scenes. Much of central Malvern
was studded with villas or intended for future building; quarries and
gravel-pits defaced the hillsides; and the commons were suffering
encroachment. Intakes by landowners on the many acres of waste land
were not new; one day in 1806 saw 20 such actions, but Malvern's
expansion was a greater threat to the district's natural beauty. Where
houses were built on or near the edge of commons, land might be taken
for gardens. Lady Foley was said to allow the removal of stones and
gravel, but objected, like the commoners, to taking turf. A man was
charged at petty sessions with taking 12 loads of turf in one day, but
confederates were bribed in public houses not to 'squeak'.[195] A railway
company wanted to have perpetually 20 acres of Malvern Common.
Unlike Bath's Victoria Park, Leamington's Jephson Gardens and Cheltenham's Pittville Gardens, Malvern had no public park for invalids
with limited powers of exercise. Residents and freeholders, including
Lady Foley, were urged to make the town attractive and limit its size,
which would increase the value of their property, and the right to the
common land was worth little, since freeholders had few sheep there.[196]

Some regretted that Malvern was no longer quiet, but others found it
dull. The *Malvern Advertiser* in 1865 insisted that, like other watering-
places, it should preserve attractive walks and drives and provide
assembly or reading rooms, though these were not immediately necessary. Local landowners should be encouraged to create from common
land a Foley Park or Hornyold Park, just as a noble lord had recently
ceded his large, lucrative rights to Wimbledon Common to create a
public park near London. But, as with the common lands of Tunbridge
Wells and the Stray at Harrogate, public opinion wished to save the

town's distinctive character and suggested a trust of landowners, free-holders and townspeople to do this. Nothing was done, perhaps because owners of hill land, like the Hornyolds, wished to sell it for building plots or quarries. Tradesmen were accused in 1873 of lethargy and not helping themselves. Malvern was compared unfavourably with Scarborough, a wealthy community ready for new attractions, with Cheltenham and Leamington, constantly adding to their pleasing features, and with Buxton, enjoying their Duke's munificence, an example to landowners near the Malvern Hills. Even Ilkley made good, easy paths in the barren waste of its gorse-covered hill. A trifling outlay would bring more visitors summer and winter to Malvern, which could be the 'Metropolis of Hydropathy', giving pleasure to the rich and quiet recreation to the middle classes.

When encroachments grew in 1875, successful resistance to enclosure of part of Malvern Chase encouraged local landowners to help to secure the Malvern Hills Act of 1884, establishing a trust empowering the conservators to acquire new land, make bye-laws and levy local rates. Later acts extended their powers until in 1925 they bought the Great Malvern manor and manorial waste lands.[197]

The 12 Improvement Commissioners, established in 1851, included Richard Bright and William Mason (landowners), Doctors Gully and Marsden, John Archer and George McCann and (from 1855) E.W. Elmslie. Their problems included complaints that builders used the commissioners' water intended for domestic use only to enable them to charge it at the full domestic rate. And builders were blamed for the clouds of dust perpetually blowing about the town, compelling windows to be closed, and more watering of the streets was demanded in 1857. The commissioners were inexperienced and lacked capital. A drainage scheme, begun in 1852, was delayed, probably because the contractor, Edward Smith, was in arrears of pay. While constructing reservoirs, McCann removed a load of bricks he supplied, at which Charles Coxwell, then chairman, and Gully and Bright resigned; but in July 1860 McCann alleged that payment for the bricks, ordered by the commissioners from his brickyard, was nine months overdue.[198]

There were complaints about the roads, especially the hill roads, which lacked roadside seats or 'rests' for invalid visitors. Baden, Spa and other Continental watering-places were said to do such things better. In 1856 the Commissioners were told of the excessive number of donkeys and the mess at the foot of Happy Valley, one of the 10 donkey-stands, while the donkey-boys importunately solicited custom. The 17 hackney-carriage stands and livery-stables attached to hotels required attention, and in 1852 they appointed a scavenger to inspect the stands and, like commissioners elsewhere, passed bye-laws to regulate hiring.[199]

Though Malvern had little night life, they opened gasworks at the junction of Pickersleigh and Sherrards Green Road in 1856 and arranged to light 200 street-lamps and 500 houses. In 1858 they bought a site in Victoria Road from the Mason Estate to renew the market house which until 1853 had been in Edith Walk, but instead they built there municipal offices with a magistrates' court and police station, mostly of brick in Italianate style, to replace their meeting-room at the Coburg Bath House. A market house, an ugly iron and wooden hall, was built in 1895, again in Edith Walk.[200]

All this was costly, and the financial situation was aggravated by fraudulent, inefficient clerks and collectors. By October 1857 expenditure on general improvements, sewerage and highways exceeded receipts by £3,564 16s. 6d., and the rates rose steadily to 3s. 3d.in the pound by 1866 and 3s. 5d. in 1867 when a crisis apparently occurred, for on 1 March the commissioners under the Local Government Act of 1858 made themselves into a local board, still of 12 members. They reduced the rates to 3s. in 1869 and 2s. 5d. (including water rates) by 1873.[201]

The concentration of workers brought trouble, especially among builders. In the early summer of 1860, Robert Jolly, a 'society man', probably meaning a member of a Friendly Society, sued his employers, McCann and Everall, for payment of 3½ days' wages of 14s. The 14 men working at the cemetery struck to support him, but went back before the case came up in Malvern petty sessions. The bench dismissed it, stating that outside itinerant trouble-makers incited the men to make unreasonable demands and speaking of the respect accorded McCann in the trade.[202]

Benevolent employers gave annual 'treats' to their workers as when in January 1865 Thomas Holland entertained 20 men of the Great Western Railway to an 'excellent repast' at the Malvern Link Hotel, and William Gurney, a carriage builder, gave his workers their annual dinner. Yet the situation remained troublesome, being stimulated by the railway navvies. In 1864–65 there were more strikes. The building of Malvern College was delayed and its opening postponed from the summer of 1864 to January 1865. Moreover, working men were becoming organized. By 1860 there was a Working Men's Institute, meeting on Monday evenings for 'penny readings' at the Lyttleton School; a Working Men's Club at Malvern Link, which had lectures on life assurance and 'Working Men's hinderances [sic] or how to succeed in life'; and a Working Men's Reading Room at the Wyche. These stood for temperance, non-smoking and self-improvment and were now supported by cheap literature.[203]

By the last quarter of the nineteenth century, Malvern was over-built and over-extended. Investment in the large hotels was unprofitable, and the water-cure was decaying, though education was becoming more important. Hydropathy declined slowly. Wilson died in 1867. Gully sold his successful hydro practice to his partner, William Fernie, but continued to see patients at the priory, where he had moved in 1860. He died in 1883, after suffering unfavourable publicity through his involvement in the Charles Bravo poisoning case of 1876; and Fernie went to London in 1887. The Hay Well, which he had used, was built over by the Baptist Chapel in 1886. Grindrod also died in 1883, after selling Townsend House three years earlier, and Marsden moved to London. The water-cure lingered on only at Preissnitz House under Wilson's successors, Thomas Rayner and, from 1891, Dr J.C. Fergusson. It was entirely refitted in 1890–99 and renamed the County Hydropath, but it incurred heavy losses after a typhoid outbreak in 1905 and failed in 1913.[204]

The Malvern Link Hotel, which had cost £6,000, was in 1873 offered for sale by its owner, George Parsons, with four acres of 'valuable building land' at the 'upset price' of £5,000. With mistaken optimism, it was declared suitable for a hydropathic establishment, large school or convalescent home and was a 'tempting offer' for an investor as the land would produce a good rent. It became a boys' preparatory school in 1889, but was later demolished. The Imperial Hotel lasted longer. In late September 1873, when it was claimed that Malvern still had a large and aristocratic assembly of patrons, the hotel had the longest list of visitors, but this included only three titled names. It continued to advertise that it remained open all the year and its swimming-bath was exclusively supplied with pure Droitwich brine for the saline cure as practised by Dr Hastings. Many other hotels were closed or reduced in size.[205]

As the water-cure and visitors' trade declined, education became the basis of the town's economy. As in other spa towns, schools were first founded to supervise children while their parents took the waters or indulged in social activities. An advertisement in the *Malvern Advertiser* in August 1847 offered morning classes in a superior school for visiting young ladies of good position in society.[206] The opening of the several Malvern railway stations in 1859–60 widened the market, since upper and middle class sons and daughters could travel unaccompanied with their trunks to school. Spa towns were particularly suited to have day and boarding schools as commercial undertakings since they offered a healthy, attractive environment with an established cultural background. And as their year began after the spa's season, domestic servants were readily available for them.

In 1865 when Malvern College, the most successful school, was opened, built partly on land in South Field given by Dr Stummes, the town already had 17 private schools, seven for girls and ten for boys. Among these was the Lansdowne Academy, established in 1858 by Mr Fiddes, and Peachfield, one of Marsden's hydros converted into a school by the Revd Richard Perkins.[207] Malvern College was thought, more than any other recent undertaking, likely to promote the town's prosperity and reputation; and it did encourage the settlement of a resident population where Malvern's future lay. The College Building Society was formed in December 1863 to build houses for assistant masters at a rent of £30, but by September it was said that parents of children too needed houses at a reasonable rent.[208] The College began with 24 pupils, slowly reaching 176 by 1871 and planned 600 only by 1900.

Other schools, however, were established, and by 1885 there were some 25. Most were small and some short-lived, but a few developed into substantial institutions, especially with the growing demand for female education in all-girl schools. One of these, a kindergarten founded by the Misses Poulton and Greenslade, soon needed larger premises. The Imperial Hotel was used by Wellington College when evacuated there during a dyphtheria epidemic in 1892, which encouraged the Malvern Girls' College, as the kindergarten had become, to take it over as one of the most impressive buildings of any girls' school.[209]

In the early 1870s, the local board, still with only four chief officers, was criticized for the rough, dangerous state of the 15 miles of roads under its care. Great feeling arose from a proposal to borrow £1,000 from the Local Government Board in London for a steamroller and stone-breaker and a house for the fire-engine with apparatus and hose. The protracted debate about the steamroller divided the Board. A government inspector's inquiry revealed that Liverpool, Leeds, Croydon and Metropolitan authorities had bought them with 50 per cent savings on the cost of materials alone, and three men present had seen them working in Paris. William David Standhoe, estate agent and surveyor to the Board, who thought that, despite some steep gradients, a steamroller could be used on 14 miles of their roads, led those supporting the purchase, among whom were Edward Archer and Woodyat, owners of horse and carriage hire firms; but other tradesmen supported the majority opposing it as too costly. G.K. Harrison of the Fermor Arms forecast a loss of trade if Church Street were closed; James Nott, a grocer, held that the noise, flurry and smoke would, even if repairs were done in the winter, discourage visitors who now mostly came in the autumn; James Bishop, proprietor of Montreal House in Worcester Road, was concerned that his ladies and invalids would be disturbed at night by the roller; Edward Purser of Lyttleton House, another grocer, thought that gravelling the roads would suffice; and Thomas Morgan, quarryman and contractor, who led the opposition, was ready to supply the gravel. Finally, Lady Foley was said to be against the idea.

The election to fill four vacancies on the Board in April 1873 was fought on this issue and on the extension of the water-mains, the use of metered water (which some disliked because of higher water rates) and the intrusion of strangers into local politics. The *Malvern News* stated the commissioners were lazy, benighted and inefficient and conducted affairs with as much secrecy as the Doge of Venice. Some outsiders were 'cuckoo-like members of the Local Board, who came to lay their eggs in other folk's nests'. The cry 'Malvern for Malvern Men' went up, but the *Advertiser* supported the newcomers, who subscribed guineas to ventures to which Malvern people gave nothing.[210] The four retiring members were re-elected, including the Revd A. Faber, the College's first Headmaster, but a later vacancy was filled by a newcomer, John Tryer of Scarborough House, who had been a member of Wolverhampton Town Council.[211]

Though divisive local politics delayed Malvern's progress, the nineteenth century's last two decades, an active time in some other spa towns, saw attempts to prolong its life as a watering-place by providing protective cover against the weather and more entertainment for visitors. The Royal Well Spa was built near the Wyche in 1870 by W.H. Ryland of Bewdley to use the water extolled for its purity. The Spa Hall had baths and pleasure grounds, a permanent art exhibition and an assembly hall seating 2,000 where Jenny Lind, then a local resident, sang in the first season; but it was too far from the town centre, where the new Assembly Rooms in Grange Road competed with it, and water-drinking was declining. Called 'Ryland's Folly', it was closed in 1895 and later demolished.[212]

To replace the limited space of the Royal Library and Haynes Concert Room, the Assembly Rooms Company in 1884 ventured on the sort of miniature Crystal Palace then being constructed at Buxton and other spa towns. Designed by John Johnson, it had a large assembly room with a stage, retiring rooms, an organ chamber and a glass-covered arcade. Behind it were the Winter Gardens, a promenade 126 feet long also glass-covered, leading to a conservatory at the southern end, and reading, billiard and smoking rooms. Here was opportunity for a large range of cultural activities, concerts, plays, lectures and from 1894 art exhibitions.[213]

In 1894 urban district councils were created for Malvern and Malvern Link under the Local Government Act of that year; and by 1900 the two councils were joined and outlying parts of adjacent parishes absorbed to create a town of six wards with a population of 16,514 in

1911. It had all grown from a minor village spa of only 819 people in Great Malvern in 1801.[214]

As the provision of education proved to be Malvern's salvation, so it was for troubled Cheltenham. In the 1850s the momentum behind its expansion was spent, and a period of near stagnation set in. Even the growth of population declined from 134.5 per cent in 1821–41 to 26.3 per cent in 1841–61. The 30 new commissioners, elected under the Improvement Act of 1832, now mostly tradesmen instead of high-ranking naval and military officers, were swayed by public dislike of expenditure, and the plural voting system, which allowed as many as 12 votes to highly rated individuals, as at Harrogate, gave power to the propertied classes. The commissioners, divided by party politics, Conservative and Liberal, were too tardy and inefficient to improve the sewerage system, water supplies and gas lighting. They failed for years to establish a free library under the Public Libraries Act of 1855, though the principals of two colleges urged this. They lost the chance of a new town hall in 1860, when the Literary and Philosophical Institute's fine Regency building in the Promenade was demolished as they refused to buy it. They faced continual criticism and allegations of bribery and corruption.[215]

Other Regency landmarks disappeared. The county bought the once-fashionable Clarence Hotel, sold its furnishing in June 1853 and made it into a magistrate's court and police barracks by 1858. The site of the old Cambray Theatre, burnt down in 1839, was auctioned to a butcher for £720 in March 1861, and there was no theatre for 30 years.[216] The Imperial Pump Room was closed in 1837 and the Old Well Spa demolished in 1838; and the Montpellier Baths, when auctioned in May 1858, failed to reach the reserve price of £3,000, the highest bid being £1,600. C.F. Wickes leased for many years the Montpellier and Pittville Spas until he died in 1858, but Pittville was far from the town centre, and Montpellier's area was the social centre.[217]

The bad news from the Crimean battlefields in 1854–56 depressed Cheltenham where many military families lived, and the arrival of the war bulletins at the *Cheltenham Examiner's* office caused painful scenes. Over 3,000 bulletins were sold after the capture of Sebastopol, and the crowd at the offices was so great that that those admitted at the front door had to leave at the back. The Indian Mutiny was also sad, and then came the 1857–58 financial crisis.[218]

The town committee tried to preserve the spa's reputation. In December 1849 it appealed to the local medical profession, reminding them of the traditional importance of the mineral springs, the source of the town's prosperity, and drawing attention to the declining number of visitors. Fearing that these physicians were not recommending the waters as in the past, the Cheltenham residents urged more publicity to revive their use. The next season the town committee appointed a sub-committee, with James Agg Gardner, the lord of the manor, as chairman and W. Nash Skillicorne as treasurer, to promote knowledge of the town's healing waters and social attractions. They opened subscription books at the spas, banks and libraries for this purpose and issued a programme of the season's entertainments, which included a revival of the old practice of assembling at the wells from 8 a.m. to 10 a.m. to take the waters with a full band of music in attendance.[219]

Many of the generation whose enthusiasm had helped Cheltenham's prosperity were dead. Dr Boisragon, after 40 years as a physician phys-ician and supporter of philanthropy and literary and scientific instruc-tion, went first to Paris and then to Bideford, where he died in 1852; and R.W. Jearrad, the architect, died in 1861. Although the Jessops tried to keep the Bayshill area alive with, for instance, a monster poultry show organized at the Royal Old Wells in June 1852, the 'great flood' of July 1855, when the Chelt burst its banks, destroyed the labour of years and devastated the famous gardens, 'a perfect picture of cultivated beauty', the greenhouses with their costly plants, arches of roses and aviaries of fancy poultry. The water lay seven feet deep in the gardens and deposited 500 to 600 tons of debris there. The Jessops' loss alone, out of a total of £10,000, was thought to exceed £880.[220] Charles Hale Jessop died aged 62 in 1859, it was said of a broken heart. Another former leader of Cheltenham life, George Russell, the High Bailiff for 40 years, died in 1860.[221]

A significant event was the death in March 1854 of the popular James Agg-Gardner, inheritor in 1836 of the lordship of the manor with the estate of John Gardner, the wealthy banker and brewer. Agg-Gardner was active in public affairs and chairman of the first Board of Commis-sioners elected under the Act of 1852, but his heir, James Tynte Agg-Gardner, was only 12 years old and a ward in chancery. The manor, covering what had become a substantial town, was auctioned in October 1862. The manor with all its rights and properties was offered as one lot for £23,000, but was unsold, and only some property worth £4,000 was sold. Eventually Robert Sole Lingwood, a local solicitor and uncompromising Conservative, bought it for £33,000 and sought to make the copyholders pay for the enfranchisement of their property. They formed the Cheltenham Copyholders Protection Association to resist him, citing an Act of 1625 defining their feudal obligations. The subsequent enquiry on behalf of the copyhold commissioners late in 1863 revealed that the copyholders had greatly benefited by selling leases of property, timber and brick-earth during Cheltenham's pros-perity. Old William Gyde, a grocer who built Gyde's Terrace (later

Grosvenor Street), bought seven acres of copyhold property from which many bricks were made to build St Margaret's Terrace, and Charles Cook Higgs let part of his land for brick making during the last 20 years, both without charge from the lord of the manor, and others spoke similarly. Lingwood lost his case, and all that remained to him as owner of the manor, then sold back to the Agg-Gardner family, was the right to almost worthless heriots and fines. The market and its tolls were sold to R.C. Chessyre, who pulled down the old market arcade of 1823 and opened a cattle-market in Bennington Street; but in 1823 the market commissioners bought the market and tolls from him and established a new market in the lower end of the High Street.[222]

In Cheltenham, as in other spa towns, investment in the leisure industry was now impossible for individuals, but in the 1860s the town's revival was helped by syndicate finance. A meeting at the Queen's Hotel in 1861 formed a company to buy the Montpellier Gardens, following the death of C.F. Wickes in 1858. Another company took over the Plough Hotel in 1860, and in September the lessee of the Assembly Rooms in the High Street, Mr Buckman, entirely renovated and redecorated the ballroom. Cheltenham's avenues of trees were its particular distinction over other watering-places, and the planting of trees on each side of the Lansdown Road, 1,200 yards long, costing £50, began in 1860; it was hoped that when they matured it would be among the finest drives in the kingdom.[223]

Perhaps most of all, educational institutions contributed to Cheltenham's new prosperity in providing trade and employment. There were already 23 schools in 1841 when Cheltenham College was founded in some private houses on Bayshill. Its immediate success with 244 pupils by June 1843 led it to transfer to a building on its present site in a developing part of the town on the Bath Road. Its plans were partly due to Decimus Burton, but mainly to James Wilson, the architect of Bath's Kingswood School and Royal School.[224] St Paul's College for training teachers was founded in 1849, and the Elizabethan Pate's Grammar School reopened after several years' lapse. But the Cheltenham College for the Education of Young Ladies and Children, opened on 13 February 1854 with 82 pupils and 10 mistresses, did most to replace the old spa life. It started in Cambray House right in the new town, but as it expanded, especially under Dorothea Beale, Lady Principal from 1858, it moved to the new town. No. 24 Lansdown Place became a boarding house in 1864 and was purchased in 1866, and Fauconberg House on Bayshill was bought for £3,000 in February 1870. And the College moved on Lady Day 1873 to a new main building adjoined by a great hall east of the famous Old Well Walk. Its buildings gradually advanced towards the site of the Old Well until the college council bought the Old

200

(or Royal) Theatre in 1897 on the site of the long-room of the original spa, so emphasizing education's replacement of the spa industry. At first landladies rented or leased houses independently to board pupils, which added to the town's prosperity, but the college gradually housed its boarders. By 1905 it had some 1,000 pupils, 600 being in 12 of its boarding houses. Cheltenham College then had 600 boys.[225]

Eventually in April 1876 Cheltenham became an incorporated borough with William Nash Skillicorne, great-grandson of the spa's founder, as its first mayor. Then, as at Harrogate, for four decades unprecedented activity and some new private enterprises brought both better facilities and commercialized entertainment. Cheltenham's long-established and ample small hotels and lodging and boarding houses precluded a monster hotel. It was early in having a large one, the Queen's Hotel of 1837, and in 1882 this was possessed by a syndicate, which added a luxurious lounge in 1904.[226] But other new 'monstrous' buildings expressed the contemporary spirit of expansion. Like other spa towns, Cheltenham had a glass palace, the Winter Gardens and Skating Rink in Imperial Square, designed by J.T. Darby, a local architect, in 1878. Of the usual cruciform structure, it was built of white and red brick with iron and glass roofs and a dome about 100 feet high. In 1895 the Corporation took it over and spent £10,000 on it; it was demolished in 1942. The Cheltenham Theatre and Opera House was erected in Regent Street in 1891 near the site where Watson's Theatre had been. It was optimistically built to seat 1,400 and cost £11,000.[227]

Among the new Corporation's many activities was buying the water company, dealing with flooding and a grand new public library in Clarence Street (1887) with an art gallery (1899) and a museum (1907) attached to it. After Sir James Agg-Gardner, the member for the borough, presented a recreation ground in the Pittville area to the town in 1888, the Borough Council three years later bought for £5,400 the heavily mortgaged Pittville Spa and gardens and enlarged then with 3½ acres of Marle Hill House's grounds, including Robert Capper's pond, which was made into a lake, so providing an essential amenity for the resort town. The company owning the Montpellier Spa failed even to repair the surrounding wooden railings, and the Corporation next purchased and repaired it. The Rotunda was licensed for plays, balls and concerts.[228]

Cheltenham, with boundaries enlarged in 1868, 1885 and 1893 and just over 52,000 people, now equalled Bath in population. Residents, many of them retired and prosperous, dominated the town. The Corporation's attempt revive both Pittville and Montpellier as spas in the 1890s, supported by extensive advertising, failed. Hydropathy was never sought as a way to survive as a spa, and facilities for treatment and a resort orchestra were both lacking. It fell into disuse as a spa; its economic basis was education and dependent services and retail trade, together with a large resident population attracted by its relaxing climate.[229]

Like Cheltenham, Leamington Spa became by the mid-nineteenth century a pleasant residential town with subsidiary spa activity. The railway, with possible commuter travel to Birmingham and the industrial Midlands, over-stimulated the revival of its building industry in the late 1850s. Though the rapid growth of population, 187 per cent in 1821–31 and 96 per cent in 1831–41 (but including summer visitors in June 1841), slowed to 20 per cent in 1861–71, houses increased by 898 or 27 per cent in that decade. In 1871–81, when the population increased by only 10 per cent, there were 705 or 17 per cent new houses. Both the number of empty houses, 154 in 1861 and 313 in 1881, together with partially built houses, increased. Leamington, like Bath, was over-built. Nor did building cease when the population was almost stationery in the 1880s – 22,979 in 1881 and 23,124 in 1891 with a housing increase of 7 per cent. This reduced overcrowding, but led to a housing surplus of 9 per cent of the total. Most of this surplus was in first and second-class houses and did not benefit the lower middle and artisan classes, nor alleviate conditions in the slums.[230]

So Leamington's energies went into middle-class housing, not large hotels or winter gardens. There were ample hotels and lodging houses, and the winter attraction was hunting not sheltered musical promenades. Villa-owners, the propertied trading classes, still ruled the town through the Local Board of Health established in 1852, with its system of plural voting, as in Harrogate, Cheltenham and Tunbridge Wells. They monopolized the 15 seats and perpetuated their power. Of the members returned in the 1857 and 1872 elections, 13 had served before as commissioners or on the Board.[231]

Until 1868 the parish vestry fixed rateable values, and finance limited municipal investment, but the Board promptly followed the Public Libraries Act of 1855 with a public library that year and moved it to a pleasant red-brick building in Avenue Road in 1902. It established also a fire brigade in 1856 and widened and straightened the river embankment with a new walk in 1859. Sewerage and water supply were more difficult. Down-river landowners, suffering from untreated sewage, brought a chancery suit in 1868, which led to the sequestration of the Board's revenues, but the Earl of Warwick supplied land for a sewerage farm at Heathcote. When, however, the town's water supply was declared unfit for use in 1870, the idea of obtaining a supply by pumping from lower strata was resisted lest interference with the mineral springs ruined the town.[232]

202

A brief attempt at hydropathy was made in 1850 when John Hitchman established a hydro in grounds amid fine trees at the corner of Tachbrook Road and Tachbrook Street, but it lasted only until 1883.[233] The Royal Pump Room and Baths, despite their 'spacious and well-conducted baths' including 'a 30 feet fall of water' and 'a chair bath, an excellent contrivance for conveying the invalid on the undressing chair into the bath in a most safe and easy manner', lost custom. The syndicate owning them faced a deficit and sold them to the Hon. Charles Bertie Percy, who in 1860 decided to close and sell them for building purposes. The *Leamington Spa Courier* expressed the town's instant reaction, calling on joint-stock finance to avert this irreparable loss. The first syndicate formed in June 1860 raised only £4,300 of the £8,000 needed, but in July 1861 the Leamington Royal Pump Room Company was formed under Dr Henry Jephson with a capital of £8,000 subscribed by September in 1,600 shares of 5s. each. It bought the Pump Room with its plant, fixtures, furniture and grounds from Percy in October 1861 for £8,500, removed the cottage roof and equipped the baths, including a Turkish bath, on more modern lines, employing J.H. Clarke of Warwick for the baths and James Marriot of Coventry for other interior work; but the baths still did not pay, and in 1867 the Board bought them for £15,000.[234]

The Board improved the amenities of the adjoining gardens. After 1869 the Parade fencing was removed and a broad footpath laid, and in 1875 Linden Avenue and the Pump Room Gardens were opened to the public free of charge. That same year Leamington became a borough, two years after Cheltenham. The Pump Room and Gardens were now controlled by the Corporation's pump-room committee. In 1885 the corporation, having increased its borrowing powers by Act of Parliament, by 1887 further renovated the Baths at a cost of £4,000 by Jenkins and Son of Leamington.[235]

The first Mayor, Alderman S.T. Wakrill, in 1875 supported the long-held belief that a new town hall was needed. Denby Villa, prominently placed on the Parade south of the Regent Hotel, was chosen, bought and demolished in 1881. The new red-brick, Tudor-Baroque building, designed by J.Cundall and erected in 1884 at a cost of £20,000, was a brazen touch in a Regency setting and emphasized the significant end of the old town. Leamington was gaining industry, including two iron foundries, one of which, owned by the Flavel family, made kitchen ranges. Yet, though primarily a residential town, it remained a resort centre with the new Royal Theatre opening in Regent Grove in 1882, an orchestra performing daily in the Pump Room and a military band in the Jephson or Pump Room Gardens, but its attractions were more broadly based than formerly. There was still hunting six days a week in

203

season with a choice of six packs of hounds, but it acquired a reputation for other sports, including the development of lawn tennis from 1872 by Harry Gem. The Leamington Lawn Tennis Club was the first in the world.[236]

Like Leamington and Cheltenham, the development of Tunbridge Wells proceeded in the second half of the nineteenth century as a residential town. Its rateable value increased from £55,140 in 1855 to over £201,500 in 1890, and the population rose, though not at its previous rate of about eight times in 1801–41; it grew from 10,587 in 1851 to 35,695 in 1911. It gained borough status in 1889, and by permission of Edward VII, who had visited Tunbridge Wells as Prince of Wales in 1881 and knew Eridge well but Marienbad, Homberg and Biarritz better, it was authorized to style itself a royal spa, a distinction shared only by Royal Leamington Spa.[237]

Bishop's Down Park was developed in the 1850s, and the building of mansions and larger villas in Camden, Nevill and Hungershall Parks continued steadily in the 1870s and 1880s. William Willicombe, a penniless immigrant coming from Bath in 1829, was employed by Messrs Bramah on the Calverley development and became Decimus Burton's assistant. In business on his own by 1841, he undertook speculative development on land east of the Calverley Estate and also built houses and shops on the Pantiles, including Nos. 40–42 and 44 on the site of the Georgian assembly rooms.[238] At his death in 1875 it was claimed that he found Tunbridge Wells a town of moderate pretensions and left it a fashionable watering-place, but this was exaggerated. Although there were still some 110 lodging houses and several hotels in the 1880s, many had become residential, as the new houses being built were mainly for settled inhabitants, including commuters using the new train service to London. Hotels, lodging houses and shops no longer closed in winter, but in the 1830s relied on the permanent population. After the opening of the temporary station of the South Eastern Railway in 1845 and the Central Station in the High Street the next year. the journey to London took two hours, half the time taken by horse carriages, or 1½ hours by fast trains. The London, Brighton and South Coast Railway opened a competing branch to East Grinstead in October 1866 with its West Station in Eridge Road. Although the town became a focus for five lines of communication, inhabitants, as at Harrogate and Malvern, disliked invading excursionists. Cheap arrangements and low fares, they said in 1881, attracted 'the ragtag and bobtail of London'.[239]

In 1849 a subscription was raised to alter the Bath House. The present portico and railing was erected and an extended dipper's lodge. The basin was advanced by two feet to the present position, and in 1865 Colonel Weller, lord of the manor, replaced the stone basin by two granite ones, the first receiving water direct, the second the overflow. A charge was made for water from the first but not from the second.[240]

Drinking only continued there, and by 1850 Tunbridge Wells had more or less abandoned the spa business. Like Cheltenham its reputation remained as a drinking spa without a reputation for bathing. To quote Richard Pelton on the Pantiles, 'Certain it is that bathing had not at any time held that place in the estimation of visitors to Tunbridge Wells which might have been expected.' Perhaps for this reason hydropathy did not immediately develop there to infuse new spa activity, except for the short-lived Grosvenor House Hydro established in a lodging house in 1847.[241]

The weekly *Tunbridge Wells Gazette*, established in 1853 by St John Colbran, who had the Royal Library in the High Street in the 1850s and 1860s, called for new amusements and amenities, a new public hall, a pump-room, improvements to the Common and the Grove, including paths and seats, attention to the trees and a promenade along the road by Mount Ephraim. The Tradesmen's Association (1857–58) and the Association for Promoting the Interests of the Town (1874), later the Improvement Association, supported Colbran. But the Improvement Commissioners set up in 1835 were a lethargic, self-perpetuating oligarchy, though in 1846 they obtained an Improvement Act allowing them to remove several turnpikes and manage the highways better. Even when in 1860, partly through the efforts of William Delves, Lord Abergavenny's estate steward for 44 years, the Commission became, under the Loyal Government Act of 1858, an elective body of 24, no great initiative followed. A system of plural voting, six votes for property at £250 or more, kept power, as in other spa towns, in the control of the wealthier owners and occupiers, who produced most of the revenue and watched the level of the rates. Most expenditure was on water supplies and sanitary arrangements, which were said in 1881 to be 'simply perfection'.[242]

It was left to syndicate finance to achieve a slow revival of spa activity in the 1870s by the promotion of several large-scale ventures. A company erected a long-needed Pump Room at the south end of the Pantiles in front of what had been the Bath House, at the other end of the site occupied since 1964 by Union House. Although said to be 'modelled on the Pump Room at Bath,' the new Pump Room was, if the illustration given by Pelton is accurate, in no way architecturally similar, being only an enlarged red-brick suburban villa. Here the mineral water flowed into a granite basin, and drinkers could have the use of a pleasant lounge and newspapers for twopence. The principal room was sometimes let for balls and entertainments. It came, however, too late to succeed and fell into a decayed state.

Only the Sussex Assembly Rooms in the Pantiles remained for public meetings, so another company, ambitiously and again belatedly, erected in 1872 for large social events the Great Hall and Public Rooms, a flamboyant building by Henry Hickman Cronk, with wings on either side topped with lofty pavilion roofs, in the grounds of the Calverley Hotel opposite the Central Station. The hall for balls and concerts seated 600–700 people, and there was a restaurant.[243]

Accommodation for visitors was slightly improved. The Wellington, opened in 1875, became the best-known hotel, and the Royal Kentish Hotel was rebuilt that year on a much larger scale with modern conveniences such as speaking tubes, a lift and immense kitchen. But the Sussex Hotel was closed in 1880, although the Parade had been renamed Ye Pantiles in an effort to recapture past atmosphere, and the visitors' trade did not warrant building a 'monster' hotel as in some spas.

A more positive attempt to revive the town as a health resort was the opening of the Bishop's Down Grove Spa by a company in 1881. It was situated in grounds of 60 acres with a large new wing and other additions by 1884 to provide 170 beds and accommodation for 70–100 servants, and catered for 25,000 visitors a year, many from overseas.[244] Under the influence of an energetic mayor, Sir David Lionel Salomans, from 1894 to 1895, besides others, proposals for more amenities were made. Suggestions were a Winter Garden on the Calverley Grounds or by Warwick Park with rustic walks leading to a glass pavilion; a public library; and a theatre, as the Great Hall was inadequate and no leading companies came there; but the town's energies were deflected to municipal trading and the enlargement of the hospital. The Improvement Association secured only the formation of another company in June 1897 which built the Opera House in Mount Pleasant designed by J.S. Briggs, another piece of flamboyant Baroque architecture, with green triple domes, opened in 1902 and so contemporary with Buxton's opera house. And, again as elsewhere, in the next century further expenditure was yet to be considered and sometimes made in attempts to preserve the town's spadom.[245]

10

Beyond England's Borders: Scottish, Welsh and Irish Spas

Though lacking any of the large, well-known spa towns of England, there were places in the other parts of the British Isles which became quite popular and even fashionable as watering-places during the nineteenth century. This was due to improvements in transport, especially the coming of the railways, which made possible travel to these areas as well as to Continental spas. This was particularly true of Scotland where there were such pioneer visitors as Queen Victoria and Sir Robert Peel.[1] The story of the rise of these spas was much the same as that of their English counterparts, and so was their inability to resist the forces which brought about their later decline.[2]

Scotland

There were at least nine spas in Scotland of any renown. Minor ones included the Well Spa at Aberdeen, which was given a stone cover as early as 1635, the Doo Wells at Innerleithen, St Peter's Well at Peterhead, the Pitkeathly Wells at Bridge of Earn and the classical-style St Bernard's Well in Edinburgh. More important were Strathpeffer, Moffat, Bridge of Allan, Ballater, Crieff and Pitlochry.[3]

The sulphur springs owned by the Earls of Cromartie at Strathpeffer (which means 'the valley of the bright river'), in Ross and Cromarty, had attracted local patronage for some centuries as a cure for rheumatism, and kidney and skin diseases. A writer stated:

The bottom of the well and of the channel is black as if dyed with ink; and the leaves of the elder trees that fall into the well soon contract a blackish colour, but when taken out and dried appear covered with a whitish dust, which is undoubtedly sulphur.

And another writer believed:

> Uninviting and disagreeable as it is now, with its thick-crusted surface and unpleasant smell, the day will come when it shall be under lock and key, and crowds of pleasure and health-seekers will be seen thronging through its portals in their eagerness to get a draught of its waters.

That time, however, was slow in coming. Strathpeffer's reputation remained localized. The *Old Statistical Account* at this time stated that a 'great number of the lower class of people' took the water there 'for all kinds of disorders without exception'. The situation did not begin to change until Dr Donal Monroe of St George's Hospital, London, brought it a wider reputation. 'Having heard many gentlemen of the county of Ross speak of these waters', he asked for an account of them from 'some physical person' in the district. As a result of what Dr Monroe was told, he read a paper in 1772 to the Royal Society on the 'Castle Leod Water' taking this name from the one-time residence of the Earls of Cromartie, which is near to Strathpeffer. He said that its sulphureous waters were among the strongest in Britain, having some 36 grains of sulphur to the gallon, and that it 'probably will be found to answer in most cases where Harrogate water has been found useful'.

Five years after his lecture, accommodation had to be built at Stratpeffer for visitors attracted by not only its medical promises but also its mild, sunny climate and picturesque valley and mountain scenery. But little was done to make it a spa until Dr Thomas Morrison of Elsick, Aberdeenshire, who believed he had himself been cured by its water, came there to live in a nearby house, which he called Elsick Cottage, and built a small wooden Pump Room over the 'Strong Well' in 1819.

There was now hopeful talk of the spa rivalling Harrogate. The minister at Fodderty, in the *Report for the New Statistical Account of Scotland* (1838), reported the erection of 'a number of respectable-looking buildings . . . for the accommodation of visitors', and in 1860 George Davey produced his plan for the further development of the village, and though it was not followed closely, some new houses and hotels were built, especially after the rebuilding of the Pump Room in stone in 1861 to which new bathrooms were added in 1871 and ladies' baths ten years later. And in 1879 a Pavilion was erected for concerts and other entertainments, which included an orchestra playing daily in the season. But its inaccessibility hindered its development.

This was overcome by the building of a branch line of the Highland Railway from Dingwall in 1885, now making Strathpeffer eight hours from Edinburgh and 17 from London, a journey that was shortened by the opening of the Forth Bridge in 1890. The Highlands were becoming fashionable for holidaying, and this easier travel, combined with fear of the cholera in English towns, gained for this distant, rural spa a popularity that lasted throughout late Victorian and Edwardian times. Dr Fortescue Fox came from the London Hospital to be its resident physician and in 1889 wrote *Strathpeffer Spa*, an influential book extolling the virtues of the Strathpeffer climate and its waters; another physician, Dr David Marsan, wrote, *On the Sulphur and Chalybeate Waters of Strathpeffer Spa*, a systematic treatise on its healing potentialities.

Both these books stimulated the development of the Spa. Many villas (some inspired by the spas of Bavaria) were built, several with private lodgings, but a few were to rent to whole families and their servants. Private hotels included the Ben Wyvis, the MacGregor's, the Strathpeffer and the Royal. The the parish church was built in 1890, and Church of England services were held in the Pavilion on Sundays until the building of St Anne's Episcopal Church in 1892. The season lasted from May to October which was quite a popular month, the bracing weather being considered good for patients with diseases of the lungs. Some 3,000 visitors came during the course of the year, but it remained a small village with a population of only 354 at the end of the century.

By 1889 the sulphur baths were usually warmed to blood-heat, the water being drawn from storage reservoirs. There were also pine, iron, brine, vapour and peat baths. Strathpeffer was the first to use peat for 'obstinate skin affections'. The peat, obtained from local deposits in Ben Wyvis, was reduced to a powder and used either with plain or sulphur water, a practice which Harrogate imitated. And ideas were borrowed from foreign spas – the Plombières irrigation treatment, the Vichy massage, practised by a masseur from London and later a masseuse as well, and the Aix douches in which jets of water were played on a sitting patient for 10 or 15 minutes. After bathing, a patient was dried on a couch with a 'dry pack' of hotel linen. Bathers were advised to rise early and retire early to bed and to have a plain, varied diet without alcohol, accompanied by outside exercise; and that baths should not be taken by those subject to fainting or fits or from an organic disease.

In addition, 'a superior effervescing chalybeate spring', probably for centuries a holy well known as Saints' Well, provided water to be drunk for anaemia or as a tonic guaranteed to stimulate the appetite and digestive processes. Drinkers were told to take their first glass of water 1½ hours before eating any breakfast and to drink three or four quarts a day, and were warned that the water might be intoxicating especially for ladies.

Another pump-room – the Upper Pump Room – was built in pink sandstone on the road to Dingwall in 1909, and in 1911 the rather limited accommodation for visitors was remedied when the Highland Railway Company built the massive Highland Hotel, designed by Cameron and Burnett, with laid-out gardens and tennis courts, bowling greens and an eighteen-hole golf-course. Other attractions included walks laid out among the pine woods, hill climbing, coaching and (later) motoring excursions and salmon and trout fishing.

Strathpeffer maintained its success as a spa until the First World War, but afterwards ceased to be fashionable and could not meet the competition of Continental spas which were now easier of access and cheaper for English visitors. In the 1930s Colonel Blunt-Mackenzie and the Countess of Cromartie attempted to revive it as a health resort, but this failed with the outbreak of the Second World War. The main Pump Room fell into decay and was finally demolished in 1950, and the chalybeate water became unobtainable through corrosion in the pipes; and the railway line was abolished. It seemed as if the future of the village lay in providing overnight accommodation for coach parties touring the Highlands.

Recently, however, it has been experiencing a revival. Better means of travel (including Inverness airport) and improved Highland roads (especially the A9 from Edinburgh) have brought it many more visitors. The Upper Pump Room was reopened in 1960, furbished with its original (and reconditioned) Edwardian wicker furniture, and sulphur water can be drunk from a small surviving pump. It is still a health resort, especially for those with digestive and nervous disorders, but it has also developed as a holiday resort. The Pavilion has been modernized with a new ballroom floor and a restaurant with cocktail and sun lounges. The Spa gardens have crazy golf, and the railway station is a craft centre. The Pipe Band plays during the summer; and in June it celebrates its Victorian heyday with parades and entertainment, while Highland Games are held in August in the park of Castle Leod.[4]

Moffat has often been linked as a spa with Strathpeffer. A recent publicity leaflet described it as 'one of the only two spa towns in Scotland where people can come to "take the waters"': and William A. Thomson in *Spas That Heal* (1987) declared, 'Scotland's only other spa in the strict sense of the term was at Moffat.' Some miles away from it were the Garpol Spa and the Hartfell Spa, and it had two springs of its own. Its chalybeate spring, the Old Well, was discovered in 1633 by Rachel Whitford, a daughter of Walter Whitford, Bishop of Brechin, but it was the discovery of the saline-sulphur spring some 1½ miles from the town by John Williamson in 1743 that brought it renown. Its waters were soon compared with Harrogate's. *Lady Oxford's Journey through Yorkshire, Durham, etc. into Scotland* (1745) declared, 'At this place is a spa, not unlike in the taste to Harrogate waters in Yorkshire';[5]

210

and another writer later said that they were 'almost as nasty and efficacious as those of Harrogate'. It was said, 'Ten quarts a day might be drunk safely, but a glass of wine taken beforehand often helps a weak stomach and prevents an inclination to sleep.'[6]

From the eighteenth century the town was a venue for sufferers from rheumatism, gout and liver disorders. Some were brave enough to drink the water for five successive seasons, believing it had 'no equal in colics of every kind'. They were attracted also by its sheltered position among the fine mountains in the upper reaches of the deep Vale of Annan in Dumfriesshire. The *Beauties of Scotland* admired particularly in 1805 its High Street:

> The street is wide and spacious, handsomely formed and gravelled, exceedingly smooth, clean and dry after the heaviest rains, and is a most agreeable walk to the inhabitants and to the company that comes for goats' whey or the mineral waters.

And it was the most accessible of the Scottish inland resorts from England, being only 40 miles over the Border. The Baths and Pump Room with assembly, reading and billiard rooms, 'looking like an educational institution painted white', were built in 1827, and in 1877 the large, red stone, Renaissance-style Hydropathic Hotel, which had two wings and a centre part with turrets at each end. Its five floors, including the basement, contained 300 bedrooms, a dining-hall seating 300, drawing and recreation rooms and Turkish and vapour baths. It was set in 25 acres of grounds and had bowling and tennis greens.

The town spread greatly during the middle and later part of the nineteenth century with the building of several new streets, many villas and some public buildings, including the Proudfoot Workmen's Institute, the Mechanics' Hall and the Cottage Hospital. The parish church was built in 1887, the United Presbyterian Church in 1864 and the Episcopal Church in 1872. The construction of a short branch of the Caledonian Railway from Edinburgh in 1883 increased its importance, and its population grew from 1,413 in 1841 to 2,153 in 1901.

Black's Picturesque Tourist of Scotland (17th edition, 1875) described Moffat as 'an exceedingly Scotch and respectable Baden Baden', which was 'noted for its mineral waters and healthy summer residence'. During the 1870s a frequent visitor was the ex-Empress Eugénie of France, and in 1879 the father of the future Air Chief Marshall Lord Downing founded St Ninian's Preparatory School there. An account of 1902 stated that during the season the road to the Well 'usually presents a very lively appearance with omnibuses, private carriages and cyclists on their way or returning from the spring', where 'a small stone building covers the well' besides which 'stands a neat wooden shed or "veran-dah" for the accommodation of visitors', and on the green by the well 'stands an old building called "The Ball Room", from the use to which it was formerly employed.'

As with Strathpeffer, the First World War badly affected Moffat, and in 1919 it was reported, 'Moffat makes some claim to be a spa.' Its decline was hastened in 1921 when the Hydropathic Hotel was des-troyed by fire. Today it is a small, pleasant country town and a good centre for touring the Scottish southern uplands. The building that once housed the Baths and Pump Room have been converted into coun-cil offices, but the Old Well and Hartfell Spa have recently been restored, and glasses of mineral water are sold. The Moffat Museum illustrates the town's past history. The Drama Society performs at the Old Well Theatre, the Musical Society holds concerts and recitals, and the Pipe Band plays in the High Street on summer Sunday afternoons. The Dumfries and Galloway Arts Festival is held each May, and the Gala Week in August recalls the town's importance as a sheep and wool centre.[7]

A place which grew rapidly through becoming a spa was the Bridge of Allan. It began as a small village between Stirling and Dunblane at the foot of the hills around its inn, called the Change House, on the east side of the old bridge at an important position on the main road north-wards. Its development into an inland watering-place came about through the reopening of a disused copper mine in 1820 on the estate of Aithrey Castle on an ascent from the Bridge of Allan, which led to the discovery of several mineral springs. The country people valued the healing qualities of their water and took it away in wooden troughs. Its proprietor procured an analysis of the springs, which declared that 'in their amount of saline impregnation' they were 'only inferior to some of the springs of Cheltenham and Leamington'and would be effective for chronic skin and stomach complaints. He installed a cistern at the bot-tom of the deep shaft of the mine and pipes to the top over which he constructed a well-house and arches to protect them. The water was collected from three springs into the cistern, and some 3,000 gallons were pumped up daily to a pump-room in the well-house and piped to a bath-house. In 1827 Bridge of Allan was still 'a confusion of straw-roofed cottages and massy trees, possessed of a bridge and a mill, together with kailyards, beeskeps, colleys, callants and old inns'. Ten years later the building of new houses and villas began, some being erected on the hill slopes around. By 1845 its population had reached about 200, and within another ten years it was known as a spa 'uniting the rural character of Harrogate with the town convenience and ele-gance of Cheltenham' and with an equable climate 'like Montpellier'. In

1861 its population was 1,803, and *Black's Picturesque Tourist of Scotland* (17th edition, 1865) declared it was 'the second largest village in Perthshire next to Blairgowrie', and described it as the 'Gateway to the Highlands'. It had become fashionable, especially among the citizens of Edinburgh and Glasgow. Robert Louis Stevenson, a regular visitor, stated its charms were 'the grass, river, sheep, sunshine and shadows of the fir-trees'.

Later a hydropathic establishment (now the Allan Water Hotel) was built with a fine suite of baths, and in attendance was a daily consultant who had studied at Smedley's in Matlock; and in the early 1900s the original Bath House and Pump Room were re-equipped. The Bridge of Allan became known as the 'Scottish Graefenberg' and in 1901 had a population of 3,240. The spa had brought it a public hall, reading room, museum and art gallery and three large inns.

Its decline, however, came soon afterwards and now it is primarily a residential town with a new university. It has inherited from its spadom its well-built villas and tree-lined streets, and the spa buildings are part of a hotel. Its fine scenery and nearness to the Trossachs have nade it a popular centre for touring holidaymakers; and the Strathallen games are held there on the first Saturday in August.[8]

Owing even more than Bridge of Allan to its spadom is the little town of Ballater. The plain on which it is now located was a bleak, empty moorland without any houses until the 1780s when the settlement was built to accommodate visitors to the chalybeate wells at Pannanich two miles downstream on the River Dee. These are said to have been discovered in about 1760 when an old woman claimed to have been cured of scrofula after bathing in a nearby marshy pool to which she said she had been led by a dream.

When Colonel Francis Farquharson, Laird of Monaltrie, came home from the 20 years of exile that followed his capture as a Jacobite at the Battle of Culloden and near escape from execution, he decided to exploit her cure. At an old hamlet, Cobbletown of Dalmuchie, he built the inn known as Pannanich Lodge and established a fashionable spa around the wells. At first the visitors were housed in surrounding hamlets, but he then built the new village of Ballater.

The purchase of the Balmoral estate a few miles to the west by Queen Victoria and Prince Albert in 1852 increased the importance and population of Ballater. Five years later a turnpike road was extended to it from Aberdeen; in 1862 it became the terminus of the Deeside railway line, which Victoria insisted should not be continued westwards; and in 1874 it was connected by a tramway with Stirling. It was neatly laid out with houses of red granite; its main square contains Glenmuick Parish Church, which was built in 1798 and substantially renovated in 1873.

There was also a Free Church (1853) and St Saviour's Episcopal Church (1857 and enlarged in 1876). Its other buildings include the Albert Memorial Hall with a square tower.

The spa was at its height in the early years of the twentieth century, when the town's population was 983, after which it experienced the usual decline in popularity. It is still possible, however, to drink the waters at the Pannonich Wells Hotel, and the town remains a popular Highland resort surrounded by fine wooded hills. It offers fishing, climbing, walking and pony-riding in the summer and ski-ing in the winter. Since 1864 the Ballater Highland Games have been held there in the third week of August.[9]

On Scotland's so-called 'Highland Line', between the lowland landscape of Strathearn and the northern mountains, is the Perthshire market town of Crieff. The opening of two branch lines of the railway in 1856–66 led a charismatic doctor, Thomas Henry Meikle, to take advantage of its dry climate and fine scenery to build the Strathearn Hydro (later called the Crieff Hydro) on the dominating well-wooded Knock. He raised most of the £30,000 required through personal contacts and from local merchants, though he held most of the shares himself and took complete control of the establishment. It was opened in August 1868 when the first 40 rooms were occupied, and the remainder were completed and fully occupied by the following July. It then consisted of four storeys, a turreted square tower and 200 rooms.

The treatment used water especially noted for its purity for the swimming-pool, douches and steam baths. It was piped from Glen Turret in the mountains four miles distant to the west and gathered in a reservoir an acre in extent. The patients were subjected to a strict discipline. The great bell in the tower woke them at 7.0 a.m. and a gong summoned them to the three large tables in the 100-foot-long dining-room at 8.30. A fine of a penny was imposed on anyone arriving after grace before meals or discussing their medical treatment. No alcoholic drinks were allowed, and smoking was restricted to a small bathroom in the tower. A young man put a couple of bottles of gin into the drinking water and watched the elderly ladies remark on its purity and ask for more. Everyone was expected to attend morning and evening prayers and Sunday services in the dining-room. An American patient there in 1904 said, 'We cannot decide whether we are in a boarding-school or a theological training-house.'[10]

The population of the town increased from 3,824 in 1851 to 5,208 in 1901, its houses being chiefly built towards the river in terraces, one rising above another; and the parish church was built in 1881 in a Gothic style. It became well known with the foundation of Morison's

Academy, one of Scotland's best-known schools, in 1860 by the will of Thomas Morison, who was born in Muthill, three miles south of Crieff.

The Crieff Hydro is now a hotel without a treatment centre, though it has a heated swimming-pool with access for the disabled, a surgery held by visiting doctors and a Sunday evening service in the main lounge. The town is a favourite Scottish resort.[11]

The spa activity at Pitlochry was concentrated upon the two hydropathic hotels: the Atholl Hydro, founded in 1874 (now the Atholl Palace Hotel) and the Pitlochry Hydro, founded in 1890, both now popular holiday hotels. Lying almost at the centre of Scotland, the spa was attractive, especially to wealthy merchants, because of its 'genial climate, attractive situation and wholesome Highland water supply'.

The Atholl Hydro, built at a cost of £100,000 in 30 acres of grounds, at first imposed a regime like that of the Crieff Hydro. It insisted on communal dining, grace before meals and early lights out. Smoking had to be practised in hidden rooms. It had no liquor licence, but guests were allowed to send out for drinks. Then the management installed some 60 liquor lockers, each able to hold two bottles of whisky; and gradually lights were left on late, grace was discontinued, separate tables were introduced, hostesses organized the 'patients' and dancing was encouraged.[12]

The town has a number of fine, large Victorian houses dating from this period, which are now mostly converted into hotels and guest-houses. Visitors are offered golf, tennis, pony-trekking, fishing, ski-ing, climbing and walking; and since 1951 the Pitlochry Festival Theatre has given a variety of plays each summer season.

Wales

Wales abounds in springs and wells, and there were many minor 'spas'. Among these were the cold bath at St Asaph, the Blorence Spa at Llanfoist near Abergavenny known in 1774,[13] the chalybeate springs in the grounds of Myddleton Hall at Llanarthney where hot and cold baths were erected by 1840, the chalybeate spring at Tenby found in 1815[14] and the red-brick castellated spa-house built at Caergwrle in 1908. There were, however, only five of much importance. An area to the north of the Brecon Beacons contains several once-famous spas once served by the London and North-Western Railway. The earliest known Welsh spa is probably Llandrindrod Wells, which became the largest and best-known of them; and within twenty miles of it are Builth Wells, Llanwrtyd Wells and Llangammarch Wells. Builth is on the River Wye, Llandrindod on a tributary of the River Wye, the River Ithon, and the other two on another tributary, the River Irfon. The only other Welsh spa is Trefriw Wells in North Wales.[15]

It is known that in the late seventeenth century saline and sulphur wells were found at Llandrindod Wells, but a doctor who visited the town in 1755 wrote, 'How long these waters through their own merit have been in repute and medicinal use cannot be ascertained for, all the enquiry I could make amounts to this – that they have been used from time immemorial.'

It did not, however, acquire more than a local fame until the mid-eighteenth century, when the healing powers – especially for the treatment of rheumatism and gout – attributed to its waters received publicity in various publications. William Grosvenor from Shrewsbury converted Llandrindod Hall, an old mansion near the parish church into Grosvenor's Hotel, which had a hundred bedrooms and assembly and ballrooms. It was an early example of the sort of hotels which were built in spas. Nearby lodging houses and a racecourse were also built. The season lasted from Easter to November during which time wealthy people were attracted, and in the later years of the century the place acquired a reputation for gambling and dissipation, which aroused local opposition. The hotel closed in 1790 and was demolished by the end of the century.

Attempts at revival were made in Regency times. In 1805 a small inn was converted into the Pump House Hotel and the adjacent Old Pump Room (as it was later called) was built. Another hotel, the Rock House, was built soon afterwards, and several cottages were made into lodging houses. Dr R. Williams of Aberystwyth, a pupil of Sir Astley Cooper the famous London surgeon, wrote a pamphlet praising the springs in 1817, and visitors gradually began to reappear. The Pump House Hotel was twice enlarged, and in 1830 its proprietor, John Cane, introduced a double tariff for visitors – 'first-class' £2 10s. a week, 'second class' £1. 60s. a week, with lower rates for servants. The two parts of the hotel were nicknamed the 'House of Lords' and 'House of Commons'. But its seclusion and inaccessibility hindered its development. It was still a small village with a population of only 182.

A great change took place in 1862 when Sir Richard Price Green purchased the Rock House Estate and promoted the Central Wales Railway. Saline, sulphur, chalybeate and magnesia springs were discovered on the Rock House Estate on a sloping, wooded site near the River Ithon. Sir Richard built a pump-room there – a simple black and yellow brick structure designed by S.W. Williams in 1872. In it the four distinctive types of water were dispensed from a marble-topped counter.

Together with permission for building on what had hitherto been

216

common land, the opening of the railway station near the wells at Llandrindod Wells in 1865 made possible the rapid development of the modern town during the following years. It was now provided, by way of the Craven Arms, with a through route with London, and, at the height of its popularity, as many as 80,000 visitors came to the town in a year. Among those who came to take the waters were some who had been told that its sheltered position was to be recommended as a beneficial place for those in the early stages of diseases of the lung. The spa's success was assisted by Dr Bower Davis, who came to it in 1872 to be its first resident physician. The waters were either drunk or used at the two establishments, which both developed new forms of hydropathic and electrical treatment.

Llandrindod Wells now became in the later nineteenth and earlier twentieth centuries 'one of the largest – if not the largest, the best – and chief of resorts in the United Kingdom'. The town was largely rebuilt in 1880–1910 in the Regency style typical of the splendour and gaiety of Edwardian times, and its population increased from less than 350 in 1871 to 1,625 in 1899, 2,779 in 1912 and 4,596 in 1921. The Pump Room Hotel was rebuilt in 1888 as a large and luxurious red-brick structure set in nearly 100 acres of ornamental grounds. By the end of the nineteenth century it had a special promenade and bandstand for paraders so that the early morning taking of the waters could be accompanied by music; and in 1900 a new wing was added to provide 150 more rooms. Other hotels built or rebuilt at this time included the Rock House in the polychrome style of the 1890s; the Hotel Metropole with its art nouveau verandah; the Glen Usk with its iron balconies; and the Gwalia with baroque ornamentation, chandeliers, elaborate mirrors and oriental carpeting. Entertainments were a golf course, bowling and putting greens, orchestral concerts and dances and two pavilions, one accommodating 2,000 people, and a boating lake of 14 acres.

Unique among spas was its visitors' prayer-meeting held every weekday morning in the Albert Hall, built for that purpose in 1896 and holding 700 people. The old parish church on a hill beyond the town was replaced in 1871 by the new Holy Trinity Church built in the Decorated style in the centre of the town. To persuade people to go to the new church, the old church was deliberately left unroofed until its restoration in 1894.

The hotels prided themselves upon the 'gentility' of many of the visitors who came during the season. Their Visitors' Books were said to read like the pages of *Who's Who*; and in the late 1940s an old man, still working at the railway station, recalled the annual visit of the Duke of Beaufort, who used to arrive in a private train containing himself and his family, various household retainers and, towards the back of the train, grooms, horses and the ducal carriage.[16] And there were middle-class visitors as well, some of them coming from Wales itself, where the Edwardian age saw a social revolution producing new professional and administrative classes.

The spa was badly affected by the First World War and the sub-sequent strikes by miners in South Wales. In 1920 the Urban District Council sought to revive it with a plan for a proposed new Pump Room at least as large as those of Buxton and Harrogate, but this came to nothing. The town's main claim to attention was that, presumably because of its central position, its large parish church was the scene of many of the important meetings of the new Church in Wales, including the appointment of the first Archbishop of Wales.

After the Second World War, the spa enjoyed a temporary revival under an arrangement by which it was managed by the Council and financed by the National Health Service, but the number of patients still declined, and in 1972 this came to an end with the opening of a physio-therapy annexe in the Llandrindod Wells Hospital. The Pump House Hotel had closed its pump-room in 1929, and in 1974 the hotel became the administrative headquarters of the new county authority. The Rock Park Pump Room was leased to an entertainment group in 1975, but this went bankrupt in 1977. Chalybeate water is still available there, but the town is now primarily a popular holiday resort and a conference centre. It has a good museum and an excellent small private art gallery. There is an annual Drama Festival, and the Victorian Festival each September, when the people wear Victorian dress, recalls its great days as a leading spa centre.[17]

Builth Wells is six miles south-east of Llandrindod Wells, just below where the River Irfon joins the Wye. It had chalybeate and sulphur springs which, taken internally and in the form of baths, were regarded as beneficial for dyspepsia and constipation as well as in catarrhal and chronic tuberculosis infections. There were two sets of wells – Park Wells and Glannau Wells. The less important of these was Glanau Wells, which had saline and sulphur waters, but it did not receive a great deal of patronage and existed only for a short time.

The Park Wells, however, consisting of three springs (sulphur, cha-lybeate and saline) not a yard apart and about 1½ miles out of the town, were frequented as far back as 1740 by the local gentry and their ladies. Its spa buildings consisted of a small round white-washed Pump Room covering the tile-lined wells, protected by wooden lids, a Pavilion for dances and parties and the Proprietor's House, which was large enough to accommodate visitors. A promenade was built leading down from the eighteenth-century bridge over the Irfon to the site.

The spa achieved a wider reputation when Lady Hester Stanhope, niece of the Younger Pitt, visited the town in 1808 and decided to settle at nearby Glan Irfon until going to the Levant in 1810. She kept her coach at the Royal Oak Hotel and went for pony-rides as well as patronizing the wells.[18] The Revd Francis Kilvert, when Curate at Clyro, recorded in his diary in 1870 that the village blacksmith 'talks of trying the Builth mineral waters for his rheumatic gouty foot'; and on 13 April 1875 Kilvert himself went there and wrote of the

> glamour and enchantment about the first view of the shining slate roofs of Builth and the bridge and the winding reaches of the broad and shining river which even now cling about the place and have never quite been dispelled.[19]

By then, however, Builth's brief early nineteenth-century development as a spa town had come to an end. A serious problem for it was the very primitive transport of pre-railway days. Teams of donkeys conveyed coal in drays from Brecon to Builth over the Eppynt Hills; and passengers to and from Builth, Merthyr Tydfil, Beraufort, Llandeilo and Llandovery travelled in slow-going vans or omnibuses, the fastest being the 'Flying Van', which made a daily journey of some forty miles between Builth and Aberystwyth.

The railway improved the transport situation in the area, but it benefited most the successful Llandrindrod Wells, competition from which was fatal for Builth, and it reverted to being a rather remote market town. The spa struggled on, supported in the summer by farmers who took the train there to 'rest, take the waters and talk' after the back-breaking 'hay-lifting and stack-making'.[20] It finally closed in 1939. Visitors come to it nowadays for salmon and trout fishing, boating on the river, the annual agricultural show and the beauty of the surrounding rural scenery.[21]

Llanwrtyd Wells, 10 miles south-west of Builth, owed its origin to the discovery in 1732 by a local clergyman, the Revd Theophilus Evans, of a sulphur spring near the village of Llanwrtyd. The additional discovery of two nearby chalybeate springs helped during the late eighteenth century to make this become a favourite healing resort for people from South Wales, giving rise to a new village known as Llanwrtyd.

It did not, however, achieve a wider reputation until 1893 when the proprietors of the Dolecoed Hotel (originally the old manor house), the grounds of which contained the wells, spent £30,000 upon the building and its grounds, keeping the fine original part of the old house, but thoroughly renovating and modernizing the rest, fitting it up with comfortable suites of baths. Though the hotel had both chalybeate springs in its grounds, and saline water was brought every day from Builth to the Pump Room, the most important was the sulphur spring. Its water was the strongest in Wales and was called 'ffyron Drewllyd' because it stank like the Devil.[22] It contained as much sulphuretted hydrogen per gallon as the Old Sulphur Well at Harrogate; but, being impregnated with salts, was more palatable. It was enclosed in the Pump Room with Terrazzo marble mosaic floors. The well itself was sealed in a massive air-tight marble mosaic pedestal down to bedrock, where the bubbling, gas-charged sulphur water, rising in a strong jet from its pebbly bed at the rate of 4,500 gallons a day, was visible through a plate-glass disc at the top. It was drawn from there by ebonite taps fresh for drinkers, but was also conveyed by its natural pressure in ebonite pipes, enclosed in cylinders of hot water, to the bathrooms of the hotel. It was claimed that this was the only British hotel where sulphur baths could be had in the building itself and, therefore, the only place where such treatment was possible during the winter.

There were also opportunities for fishing and boating, golf and tennis, shooting and excursions into the countryside. Visitors were probably brought to the place by these sporting and other attractions and to take the waters. The spa closed down in the 1920s, and the little town, the population of which has declined during the century from over 800 to about 600, is now a centre for walkers, horse-riders, cyclists and motorists. It has annual Saturnalian, Victorian and Beer Festivals.[23]

Lying almost exactly half-way between Llanwrytd Wells and Builth Wells, Llangamarch Wells had its springs about a mile from the village. They were discovered in about 1820 by a shepherd who noticed that even in a drought water issued from the dried-up bed from the River Irfon. He disliked the taste of the water, but later samplers considered it was like that at Leamington Spa. The place enjoyed a quiet reputation for some 60 years, being recommended by some local doctors.

It gained a wider publicity when a proper analysis of the water was made in 1883 by Dr F. Dupré, who found that it was unique, having barium chloride in it, not often found elsewhere and considered to be a good remedy for diseases of the heart and circulation. The springs were situated in the grounds of the Lake Hotel, where a simple wooden Pump Room was built close to the river bank. The charge for drinking was 2d. a glass and 4s. for a barium bath. The treatment prescribed drinking about 1½ pints a day – half a pint before breakfast, drunk slowly and followed by a short walk, the rest at 11 a.m. and 4 p.m., together with a hot bath every other day for five to ten minutes.

The hotel's extensive grounds had their appeal – 2,000 acres of good shooting, a triangular lake well-stocked with fish, gardens and opportunities for tennis, golf, croquet and bowls. Invalids liked its bracing but sheltered climate and could stroll along its paths 'graduated to

220

provide restful exercise'. After an early success, the spa faced the usual decline though, as at Llanwrtyd Wells, the hotel's comfort and attractions probably accounted for its survival also into the 1920s. It now relies mainly upon visitors who come to it for seclusion and peace.[24]

Away in North Wales, Trefriw Wells Spa is situated about eight miles up the western side of the Conwy Valley from the town of Conwy. The publication of a medical pamphlet in 1844, stating that the chalybeate springs about a mile north of the village (which then had 72 houses) were unusually rich in iron, brought them the first outside publicity. The water rose from the solid rock in a cave at the foot of the mountains, and bathing had to be performed by both sexes in a rough rock-hewn trough.

In 1863 the owner, Lord Willoughby d'Eresby, built at his own expense a Bath House with a wooden notice board stating, 'Built to provide more suitable accommodation for patients who prior to this time had bathed at great inconvenience in the rock-hewn basins in the cave.'[25] Ten years later he leased the wells to a company which erected a new Pump House and Baths (looking like a comfortable Victorian dwelling) for a season lasting from April to September. Cold and warm baths, recommended for rheumatism and skin diseases, cost 2s. and 3s. d. a time; drinking cost 2d. a dose of three teaspoonfuls, and a course of two or three doses a day for six weeks or longer was especially recommended as a cure for anaemia. A box of 12 bottles, each containing two doses, was sold for 3s. 6d. or 3s. 9d. post paid.

Trefriw remained little more than a village with a population of 628 in 1901, and pastoral farming and woollen weaving remained its chief occupations. Much of its trade was done by the 'little packet', the small steamers which plied along the eight miles up river from Conwy Quay to Trefriw, coming with coal, groceries and other necessities, and returning laden with cloth and slate from the nearby Gloddfa Ganol mine. The visitors came by these steamers or by horse-drawn carriages and early motor-cars.

Towards the end of the nineteenth century Trefriw was reckoned to be the 'Llandrindrod of North Wales'.[26] It had two good golf-links, tennis-lawns, croquet and bowling greens, besides trout and salmon fishing and some otter hunting. And concerts were held to entertain visitors. But what attracted many who came to the spa was the contrast with the older spa-towns and their social style. They enjoyed its simple main street with houses clustering along the steep wooded hill and the surrounding beautiful scenery with its opportunities of pleasant walks and excursions.

As with larger spas, Trefriw suffered by Edwardian times from the competition of Continental spas, even though its supporters insisted that it had the most concentrated natural iron water in Europe, and its decline set in. Travellers noticed neglected recreation grounds, unpainted houses and closed shops. The spa finally closed in 1933 when the river steamers ceased to come from Conway. In recent years the proprietors of the Pump House have made it a place where visitors can make a self-guided tour through push-button recordings, with sound effects telling the history of the spa, and patronize the tea-room and beauty-shop selling a variety of soaps and oils. And available there and also by mail-order is 'Spatone Iron Plus', which is the famed spa water pick-me-up, 'used to help restore energy and maintain good health.'[27]

Ireland

Towards the end of the First World War, the West and South Clare Railways put out an advertisement headed 'Strafe Germany', which urged the Irish to support their own spas. It extolled their virtues and compared them favourably with the German spas.[28] Contemporary with the British spas, Ireland had a number of spas which enjoyed considerable local support. Among the smaller of these were Clonmel in Tipperary, where there was 'a spring on high that issues from a spring of rising ground' recommended for 'scorbutic and chronic distempers'. Granshaw in County Down claimed that its water, which 'sits easy on the stomach' and was 'highly serviceable in the gravel', was 'not inferior in strength to the best British chalybeates'. Kilmeaden in County Waterford had a chalybeate spring 'which breaks out in the highway between two rising grounds with such force that in crossing the road it becomes a little brook', and to be effective 'it must be taken on the spot'; St Ann's Hill Hydro in Cork was noted for its cold-water cure; and there was the little known hamlet of Spa in County Kerry, discovered in about 1746 and where the disused spa-house still existed in 1974. Seven others were larger and locally popular, but also failed to get wider fashionable support.[29]

Lisdoonvarna in County Clare is Ireland's principal spa. A straggling, unpreposessing place in bleak and uninteresting surrounding country, it is a good centre for visiting the magnificent coast. The watering-place grew up, with a season from June to October from about 1865, through the discovery of two mineral springs – chalybeate with manganese and sulphureous containing lithia, the first taken for debility, the second for gout, rheumatism, dyspepsia and skin diseases. Hotels and guesthouses were built during the later nineteenth century, together with a pump-room and baths on the edge of the town in an attractive parkland setting, and recently renovated.

A Report on the Mineral Springs of Ireland by Sir Norman Moore in

1902 considered that the only Irish spa worthy of consideration was Lisdoonvarna, and only committed itself to approve of the sulphur spring. It stated, 'There are three or four hotels besides many houses in which lodgings can be obtained,' but for visitors:

> the standard of comfort is not at present very high, nor are there any amusements. A good performer on the Irish pipes and occasional fiddlers versed in the native music are the sole representatives of the concerts.

It concluded, however, that local doctors were 'unanimous' about the water's efficacy in 'the conditions due to alcoholism and to sedentary life'.[30] And a writer in 1919 held, 'Of mineral springs Lisdoonvarna is perhaps the most outstanding. . . . It is small, but quite the most popular spa in Ireland.'[31]

The Spa Trust was set up in 1915 to protect the spa water for the townspeople and is now being used to progress the Spa Development Plan. Water-drinking and baths including a sauna and solarium are available. Also a popular seaside resort, it is still crowded in the summer, and dances and concerts are held during the season. Among the Irish it is known as the place where marriages are arranged since in September the Match-Making Festival is held, to enjoy which spinsters come from as far as America.[32]

Once a rival to Lisdoonvarna, Mallow in County Cork acquired considerable celebrity for its mild subthermal sulphuretted springs during the eighteenth and early part of the nineteenth century when it was a typical 'new English' settlement and a fashionable watering-place for the Anglo-Irish gentry of the county and Dublin (eight miles away), and the 'Rakes of Mallow' were notorious. An anonymous verse of that time declared:

> Bearing, belling, dancing, drinking.
> Breaking windows, damaging, singing,
> Ever raking, never thinking,
> Live the rakes of Mallow . . .

In 1835 it was said that the spa 'approaches the nearest in all its qualities to the hot well waters of Bristol . . . which brings a resort of company there, frequently in the summer months and has caused it to be called the Irish Bath.' That, however, is now a thing of the past. On Spa Walk the Spa House, built in 1828 by Denham Jepson Norry and designed by George Richard Pain of Cork, is now in private occupation, and the once famous water gushes to waste from the springs on the

Fermoy road. Other relics of its fashionable heyday are some good dwelling-houses, the Court House, Market House and fine racecourse where races take place intermittently throughout the spring, summer and autumn. It is now a market and sugar-manufacturing town, visited by anglers and enjoying a cheerful Folk Festival in July.[33]

About the same distance from Dublin, on the Maynooth road, is the handsome village of Lucan in County Dublin. It became famous for its sulphuretted hydrogen water discovered at St John's Well in 1758. A Bath House with an antechamber was built there, and it became a fashionable spa in the eighteenth and earlier nineteenth century, being also a venue for the nearby Kildare and Meath foxhounds. In 1835 it was 'much frequented on account of its medicinal spring, the waters of which are of great efficacy in many disorders' and called 'a Cheltenham in miniature'. It was later neglected, but a new hydropathic establishment was opened in 1891 and a Spa Hotel in 1896, which brought it success for some years.

Also in County Cork is the market town of Macroom, which in the later eighteenth and earlier nineteenth centuries had a chalybeate spring that 'rises on the very brink of a bog'. The town acquired then the parish church of St Colman of Cloyne and a market house, both belonging to the early nineteenth century, and some late Georgian houses. Its spadom was assisted when it became the terminus of the Cork and Macroom Railway; and in 1835 it was stated that its waters had 'done great service in hypochondriacal cases and cutaneous eruptions'.

The discovery in the eighteenth century of a spring with mild chalybeate waters made Castleconnell, a village on the River Shannon, a popular resort in County Limerick. Remains of it now are a small decayed pump house and many attractive villas in the district. It is now an angling resort.

Swanlibar in County Cavan was once known as the Harrogate of Ireland because of its cold sulphur springs about a mile away, which in 1740 was 'much frequented by persons of quality, here is a good inn and several houses for the reception of water drinkers'. The water was 'excellent for the scurvy, nerves, lowness of spirits or bad appetite'. The *Postchaise Companion* in 1786 declared that there 'no particular regime is necessary, but to be temperate in wine and to drink as little Chinese tea as possible', while in 1835 it was said that the water is to be drunk 'as the stomach can bear it, preparing first with a gentle physic'. It is now a border village with Northern Ireland.[34]

In Northern Ireland is Ballynahinch in County Down on the River Dromore, a spa of repute from the late eighteenth century, when improved roads enabled it to attract especially fashionable people from Belfast 12½ miles away. Its chalybeate and sulphur springs are rich in magnesia, iodine and other radioactive properties. To that time belong the parish church (1772), market house (1795) and early nineteenth-century Assembly Rooms with a Doric timber portico. In 1835 it was said that the water 'has been drunk with success for gravelly complaints; and at some particular times, especially in dry seasons, it is of a purgative quality'. Its principal sulphur spring is in the Spa Wells Health Centre, which has a pump-house, sauna, baths and massage rooms.

11

The Spas in the Twentieth Century

Bath, as befitted the most historic of the spa towns, tried hard to continue its spa treatment during the twentieth century, despite the prevailing difficulties, especially between the wars when there were many empty houses in the city. In 1927 the Royal Bath was redesigned inside in the neo-Georgian style of A.J. Taylor by the Corporation Spa Committee, which reported, however, that in 1928–32 its total receipts fell by 10 per cent. Even in the Second World War it kept open the octagonal Hot Bath for swimmers; and in 1954 the Corporation renovated the Cross Bath and opened it to the public. As well as feeding the fountains and baths surrounding it, the mineral water from the Roman reservoir below the Pump Room supplied the Royal Mineral Water Hospital (renamed the Royal National Hospital for Rheumatic Diseases in 1969) and the Spa Treatment Centre and the city's two indoor swimming-baths, the Beau Street Bath and the Royal Bath. With the advent of the National Health Service in 1948, the Spa Treatment Centre, established by the Corporation in 1869 for paying patients, received a grant from the Health Authority to take hospital out-patients as well. The number of paying patients, however, steadily decreased, and a new United Royal Hospital at Coombe Park above the city, which included a large hydrotherapy department depending on heated tap water was opened. In 1976, therefore, the council closed the Spa Treatment Centre, ending Bath's role as a healing centre. And in October 1978 it was discovered that the warm spring water of Bath contained dangerous toxic amoeba, necessitating the closure of the supply to the Pump Room, the street fountain, the Hot Bath, the Cross Bath and other outlets, but a new spring has been found to replace the polluted source.

These events were but the culmination of the steady decline of Bath's

spa business, making the city rely on other developments, but the manufacturing sector is small and becoming smaller, accounting for only
about a tenth of local employment. The mines and quarries have long
disappeared, and the cranemakers, Stotherd and Pitt, closed some years
ago. The chief remaining manufacturing companies are Rotork, producing valves, Herman Miller, making furniture, the Bath Press Group
(formerly the Pitman Press), engaged in printing and binding, and IPL,
a computer software company. Since the Second World War naval
administration has been by far Bath's largest employer, providing some
4,500 jobs, accounting for about a tenth of the city's workforce, including commuters from outside; but the general decline in defence expenditure is reducing this. The Bath Business Forum has been founded as a
joint venture by the City Council and the Chamber of Commerce to
attract what has been called 'quality industry'.

Most of the recent growth of employment has been in the service
industries, which provide over three-quarters of all the city's jobs, mainly in defence, financial services, tourism, retailing, public and health
administration and education. The three chief post-war educational
establishments – the university, the technical college and the college of
further education – now together employ some 3,500 people.

Bath is now an important tourist centre, ranking with such places as
York, Oxford and Stratford-on-Avon and attracting more than a million
visitors a year. It is estimated that they spend £120 million a year and
employ over 3,000 people. The Roman Baths are visited by 50 per cent,
the Pump Room by 45 per cent, Bath Abbey by 40 per cent and the
museum at No. 1 Royal Crescent, which recreates the interior of a
Georgian town house, by 26 per cent. The King's Bath remains as built
by the Victorians as a showpiece for visitors, and the museum adjoining
the Pump House displays relics of the Roman occupation found in and
around the baths. There are more than 20 other museums altogether in
the city, including the Building of Bath Museum and the Bath Postal
Museum. And each summer since 1948 visitors have been attracted by
the music of the Bath Annual Festival.

In 1942 enemy bombing did considerable damage, especially in
Kingsmead and Avon Street and Queen Square; and the Upper
Assembly Rooms suffered. After becoming a cinema and a salesroom,
they were reopened to the public by the National Trust in 1938, but
were burnt out in 1942. They were restored in 1963 and now contain a
Museum of Costume and a conference centre and are used for balls and
banquets. Damage was also done by the Council's bulldozing policy of
the 1960s, which included the total clearance of 'acres of Georgian
rubble' in the Southgate area and much clearance in Northampton
and Ballance Street. And the Pump Room Hotel was replaced by

neo-Georgian flats. The indignation this roused led to the success of the conservation movement, which halted the clearance and, with public and private funds, preserved the city's 5,000 listed buldings which witness to its great spa days in the past.[1]

In the opening years of the twentieth century, Leamington's corporation attempted to preserve its spadom. In 1910 the Royal Pump Room and Baths were improved. The latest electrical apparatus was installed, and a lounge was opened as an annexe to the Pump Room; shortly afterwards a large swimming-bath, now considered essential in a spa, was constructed at a cost of £2,500. In the 1920s the baths were further restored, and the Winter Hall Bath was opened, giving Leamington the largest covered swimming-bath in the Midlands. And between the two world wars, in the Pump Room restaurant waitresses served tea and buns amid potted palms and to the music of a trio. The spa attraction of the waters, however, continued to decline, and by the 1950s a crisis was reached. Yet it seemed that this could be resolved with a revival of the spa. In 1960s urgent structural repairs and the restoration of the frontage of the Pump Room and Baths was followed by setting it up as a medical centre able to provide patients with a wide range of spa treatments managed by the Warwick District Council under the aegis of the National Health Service, the Regional Hospital Boards and the British Spas Federation. During the course of a year, 50,000–60,000 treatments were given to some 5,000 patients from the Warwickshire Health Area. In the morning the elderly suffering from arthritis or strokes, and in the afternoon spastic children, bathed in warmed diluted saline spring water, and took massage and exercise under the care of four physiotherapists.

For a time it seemed as if Leamington was to continue as the surviving healing spa in the kingdom, but in the late 1980s the building again needed extensive renovation, and in December 1990 medical treatment ceased, and it was closed. Today some restoration has been done, together with the annexe on the south side, which is available for hire as a function room.

There always has been some industry in the town, including two iron foundries. One of these, owned by the Flavel family, made kitchen ranges and now, owned by the Glynwed group, makes gas cookers and fires. The Imperial Foundry is now owned by the Ford Motor Company. Firms connected with the growing motor in industry in Coventry, Birmingham and Oxford have come to Leamington, especially Automotive Products (Lockheed and Borg & Beck), which came in 1928 and remains the town's largest employer.

Nevertheless, Leamington is primarily a residential, recreational town. It is an important centre for Midland shopping, for touring

Shakespeare country (which, in fact, it exploited before Stratford on Avon itself saw its value) and for sport, which is stimulated by annual bowls, fencing, archery and athletic tournaments and meetings. Spa water can be sampled from a tap between the Assembly Rooms and the Bridge, which is all that actively remains of the spa, and the old Aylesford Well House over the original spring, near the parish church, was demolished in 1961.[2]

Of Cheltenham's history from 1900, William A.R. Thomson, in *Spas That Heal*, states, 'Anticlimax is the keynote of the next half-century.' This period began inauspiciously when Lloyds Bank in 1900 bought and demolished the Assembly Rooms on the corner of Rodney Road. The traditional centre was finally lost to the old town; it moved to the imposing new Town Hall erected in Imperial Square in 1903 to the heavy classical style of F.W. Waller. Costing £45,000, it had accommodation for 1,500 in the main hall, 450 on the stage and orchestra and 500 and 250 in supplementary rooms. It contained, as a concession to Cheltenham's historic past, a central octagonal 'spa' supplying four waters from the town's principal mineral springs; but the town could not pretend that it relied upon this trade.[3]

Thomas Davy Luke, *Spas and Health Resorts of the British Isles*, observed of Cheltenham in 1919, 'Of late years the town . . . has rather fallen into desuetude as a spa.' The privately owned Cambray Spa in Rodney Road was adapted to become a Turkish bath, and then was a cabinet and carpet warehouse until it was finally demolished in 1937 and replaced by a cinema. This left the Council's Pittville Pump Room as the only operating spa in the town.

Cheltenham never sought hydropathy to survive as a spa, lacked facilities for treatment and did not have a resort orchestra. The Council tried unsuccessfully to promote the Pittville Pump Room in the 1930s; and in the Second World War it and the grounds were occupied by troops, first British and then American, during which time extensive dry rot set in. However a public appeal for its restoration raised £53,000. It was partly reopened in 1960 and completely in 1978 for concerts, dances, meetings and other functions. The original fountain has been restored, though in a new curved niche. Its alkaline water is electrically pumped from an 80-foot-deep well and may be drunk in the summer.

Cheltenham, therefore, has moved completely away from its spadom. Its economic basis is now, as it had become by the beginning of the century, education and dependent services with a large resident population attracted by its relaxing climate and visitors by its music festival, horse-races and proximity to the Cotswolds.[4]

Tunbridge Wells produced its first Official Guide in 1902, which recorded that 25,000 glasses of mineral water were still drunk yearly on the Pantiles; but the Mayor considered in 1904 that the town's future as a health resort was becoming uncertain, and action was needed to compete with other seaside and inland resorts. The attractions committee and the amalgamated railway companies agreed to ambitious proposals, and the Borough Council considered spending 'large sums of money' on installing modern electric baths and a kursaal with an orchestra and public bandstands. But, although the South-Eastern Railway widened its Mount Pleasant Bridge and in 1912 built a new monumental entrance to the Central Station on the downside to encourage visitors, the council eventually abandoned the idea of providing large-scale entertainment. Its contribution was reduced to enlarging the Pump Room to hold 1,000, as a substitute to the winter garden, and help for the band of 38 musicians which had depended on subscriptions and collections; but despite a successful world tour on the SS *Ceylon*, it came to an end. But in 1900 a new bandstand was built in the Pantiles, and after 1904 the council granted £500, and for a short time £1,000, for hiring bands, mostly military bands, and, as at Malvern, some from the Continent.

Fox-hunting and other sports were more readily adopted than mineral-water drinking at Tunbridge Wells before 1914. The West Kent Foxhounds and the Bridge Hounds were the principal packs and also the Surrey and Mid-Kent Staghounds. By then, despite the title of 'Royal Spa' bestowed on the town in 1909, its spa function was over. Between the wars, an attempt was made to revive water treatment at the Sherwood Park Spa where, according to a guide book of 1935, a new spring had been discovered 'with qualities unique in this country', but like the water at 'Nauheim, the famous German heart centre. Every type of spa treatment is already available . . . and arrangements are in hand to bottle new water for sale throughout the country.' But in 1929 the house was taken over by Kent County Council as a wartime maternity and nurses' home.

Light industry has invaded the town, encouraged by the Council, with an industrial estate of 58 acres to the north containing 48 factories, workshops and warehouses; and within the town are scattered offices including that of the Land Registry at Hawkenbury. Of the town's total population of about 40,000, some 4,000 commute daily elsewhere, while of the nearly 20,000 people with jobs there, about a third come in daily from outside. Just over a half of the employed are in service trades. It is also a large shoppping area, for perhaps as many as 200,000 people. It has not followed the example of those former spa towns which have organized annual arts or other festivals.

Hardly anything remains of the of the spa. The Pump Room was demolished in 1964 to make way for the New Pantiles, a shopping precinct with car parks beneath. Though most of the Bath House is occupied by Boots the Chemist, whose newly created entrance is out of sight around the corner, its Victorian railings and adjoining dipper's lodge make its frontage much the same as in the nineteenth century, and below is still the original Cold Bath. From Easter to October a 'dipper' draws and serves water from the ancient well in front for 50p. a glass. The past is exploited for the tourist trade in other ways. At the northern end of the Pantiles is 'A Day at the Wells': six full-sized sets with life-size costumed figures recreating the activity, sights, sounds, smell and music of the town in 1740; and there are tours through the historic town conducted by guides in period costume.[5]

By 1900 the two urban district councils which had been set up for Malvern and Malvern Link had been joined and combined with outlying parts of adjacent parishes joined to create a town of six wards with a population of 16,514 in 1911. It had all grown from a minor village spa of only 819 people in Great Malvern in 1801; but by then the spa industry which had contributed so much to its growth was rapidly becoming a thing of the past.[6] Hydropathy had lost its appeal. An outbreak of typhoid fever in 1905 hastened its decline, and within a few years all the water-doctors had disappeared.

From the early years of the century, the Holy Well buildings were used as a commercial bottling plant for 'Malvern Seltzer' water. This ceased in the 1850s, and by 1870 the buildings had become badly dilapidated, but they were saved from demolition by being restored in conjunction with the Civic Trust. The water from the Holy Well can be sampled from the Well House. In the 1880s the owner of the site, John Parkes, tried unsuccessfully to market its bottled water again. Of the early hotels, only the Foley Arms has survived; and the Assembly Rooms are now the local tourist office.

Malvern inherited from the Second World War the Royal Radar Establishment, which is now the town's largest single employer; and industrial sites were built by the Council in the 1950s to attract light industry. The completion of the motorways has added to the popularity for tourists of the lower Wye Valley and north Gloucestershire, and Malvern now has some 20 hotels with over 400 bedrooms. It is now a favourite residential place and even a dormitory town for Worcester and Birmingham.[7]

By 1922 the salt-works at Droitwich were dismantled, and the industry had moved to Stoke Prior. The 'salt town' was no more, but the future of the 'brine spa' was uncertain. The erection of the large, handsome Imperial Hydro, delayed by the outbreak of war in 1914, was completed to add to its hotels, but the number of visitors to the spa

231

declined.[8] In 1937 the St Andrew's Brine Baths were taken over to provide the complete range of hydropathy by a non-profit making medical organization, which co-operated from 1948 with the National Health Service, but it experienced financial difficulties, and in 1971 the Borough Council bought the building. Later that year, however, the National Health Service transferred its rheumatic and arthritic treatment to the Highfield Hospital for Rheumatic Diseases, and in 1975 the baths were closed and the premises leased to an engineering firm which made them into offices.

There are two remaining brine water outlets. The Chateau d'Impey has a modern open lido. And in 1985 the local authority entered into a joint venture scheme with the private sector to build the Spa Brine Bath in Droitwich Park and a new private hospital. The Bath is a large open-air swimming-pool of natural brine, pumped from the St Andrew's springs and maintained at a constant temperature of 92 degrees Fahrenheit. The buoyancy afforded by its high salt content speeds rehabilitation and recuperation; users can perform light exercises in a virtually weightless state. The private hospital gained such a reputation for its knee and joint clinic that in 1993 an extension was opened.[9]

An account of Woodhall Spa in 1911 showed how within 26 years it was transformed by the syndicate, with building south-west of the spa area to supply more lodging accommodation, retail services and means of recreation. Victoria Avenue, Cromwell Avenue and Tor O'Moor Avenue were laid out, and Station Road was continued as the Broadway, the main shopping area, with the Woodhall Supply Stores selling grocery and drapery, Edward Stapleton also selling drapery, Jack Overton, another greengrocer who each Monday renewed the fresh plants in the Bath House, Richard Coney a tailor and outfitter, the Royal Repository for fancy and general stationery, a chemist manufacturing aereated waters, a bakery with the only steam-oven in Lincolnshire, an ironmonger and plumber, a saddler and harness-maker and a motor-car dealer with a garage for 40 vehicles.

A large new Bath House had been erected with a range of modern improvements, including radiant heat, pulverization and syphon douche, and adjoining a lounge with newspapers and periodicals. Inside the people listened to an orchestra playing from a balcony, while when there was a military band they sat outside around the bandstand in front of the building. To the north and west was a public park of 75 acres with a golf course. There were three new hotels – the Eagle Lodge, Hotel Goring and the Royal, embracing 1,000 square yards and challenging the established Victoria with its covering glazed roof, modern electric light, a winter garden and tennis and croquet lawns and the only one with its spa baths fed by a newly sunk well about the location of the present Cromwell Avenue. The Victoria, however, was still the finest hotel, with an elegant ironwork covered balcony on either side of the centre block at first-floor level; it was the most sumptuous, with large public dining and drawing rooms, smoking and billiard rooms, suites of private apartments and 160 bedrooms. It offered Golfers' Special Weekend Terms with first-class return fare from King's Cross, all meals from Friday night dinner to Monday breakfast and two days' golfing, but a bedroom hip-bath cost 6d. extra. By 1905 there were the Railway Hotel and 51 boarding houses or houses with apartments for visitors.[10]

So the primitive village spa was now a resort town among the pine trees, silver birches and rhododendrons. Noted for its bath treatments, including mud baths and especially its famous iodine baths, it was the last aristocratic spa, offering to the titled and wealthy, in its good hotels during the season from April to October, an alternative to the exclusive Continental watering-places. And, since the last train left Woodhall at 7.30 p.m., it lacked day excursionists. There was no assembly room nor theatre, only a pavilion for occasional concerts, which became the Kinema in 1922.

It still had only 988 inhabitants, exclusive of visitors, and 39 private residents, but these increased as well-to-do residents were gradually attracted. Lady Lindsey lived at Lindsey House, but most important was the 'Queen of Woodhall Spa'. She was Grace Maple, heiress of Sir John Blundell Maple, the furniture magnate. She is said on first seeing Woodhall's rhododendrons in 1905 to have declared, 'This my pet wood.' At any rate, she built a country residence, Petwood, near to the baths in Stixwould Road, in a highly half-timbered style reminiscent of Droitwich. She married in 1910 Sir Archibald Weigall, MP for Horncastle in 1911–20 and Governor of South Australia in 1920–21.[11] They lived in style, and when Lady Weigall visited London the last two coaches of the Boston–London train were reserved for her and her servants.[12] They gave generously to the town, paying for the band to play in season, presenting in 1912 a cricket ground (laid out by A.E. Relf, the Sussex cricketer) and the Jubilee Park, created to celebrate King George V's Silver Jubilee in 1935. They drew royalty and important visitors to the town. The Prince of Wales stayed at Petwood, the Princess Royal came several times and Princess Marie-Louise opened the Jubilee Gardens. Sir Arthur Hewitt, George V's physician, came for six months every year for six years.

In 1914 the Royal Hotel was abandoned by its German owner, and in 1918 the Victoria Hotel was destroyed by fire. The town, which now had a basic population of 1,590 much augmented between April and November, had Eagle Lodge, the Gold Hotel and the Spa Hotel (previously the Hotel Goring), but lacked a first-class hotel. In 1933 Lady Weigall remedied this by converting Petwood into a hotel, appointing as manager the Swiss Mr Florey (formerly at the Washington Hotel, London). Seasonal waiters, who all wore livery, were recruited from Liverpool or Manchester, but most of the staff, including 30 gardeners, were local, some from a children's home at Horncastle. When Lady Weigall died, she left Petwood to her daughter, who sold it to Mr Florey.

Though Woodhall had managed to continue as a spa longer than many other places, largely through its fame as the 'iodine spa', it faced difficulties between the wars. The Weigalls bought the spa establishment centre in 1922 and offered it free of charge to the Urban District Council, which declined it, and the Woodhall Spa Baths Trust was formed to manage it and has done so ever since. Drinking the water ceased in 1930, but the baths continued.

By the 1930s, indeed, Woodhall had become a social and tourist centre rather than a health resort. As well as Petwood's luxury, the now-restored Royal Hotel had its hydro, winter gardens and Lincolnshire's largest dance-floor. Major Alpost managed the Kinema and the Misses Williams the Tea House in the Woods. W.A. Dickinson's garage hired out charabancs and landaulettes and were agents for Fords, Sunbeams and Daimlers as well as the less usual Calthorpes, Belizes and Darracqs.[13]

In 1939 war killed the visitors' trade, but as elsewhere government action provided Woodhall with employment. The Royal Air Force dominated Lincolnshire with seven airfields. Petwood was comandeered in 1942–45 as the Officers' Mess for 617 (Dambusters) Squadron, and a land-mine destroyed the Royal Hotel, though the troops stationed there escaped by being out on a route march. Like the Victoria, it was not rebuilt, and its large open site is now Victoria Square. The Spa Hotel, managed by Mrs E. Page, was open throughout the war and when, the Petwood reopened, there were – with the Golf Hotel and the Dower House – four hotels in the post-war period.

In 1948 the National Health Service used the spa premises as a rheumatism clinic, patients being brought by ambulances and volunteer motorists from a different region each day to the baths, which used, however, ordinary tap water. The population in 1961 was still only 1,990, but the number of treatments given was slightly less than at Bath with a population over four times as large. But the rheumatism clinic was closed in 1981; and in 1983 the buildings over the well and the chimney of the pump-engine collapsed.

The Coronation Hall was opened as a community centre in 1954. Later in the same year the railway passenger service between Woodhall

Spa and Horncastle ceased, as did the freight-only service in 1971. In May 1987 the Woodhall Spa Cottage Museum was opened with photographs and other exhibits relating to the history of the town; and in Easter 1991 a tourist information centre was opened there. Present-day Woodhall has been described by Pevsner as 'much like a suburb of Bournemouth, tree-lined streets, large, affluent and soporific-looking houses for retired people who have not done too badly for themselves'.[14]

Matlock Bath and Matlock Bank proceeded normally in 1914–18, but Matlock Bath's decline as a significant spa centre continued. Only 39 houses were built there in 1891–1921 compared with 425 at Matlock, and the Census of June 1921 revealed only 38 visitors in its two hotels – the Royal and the New Bath – and 843 in the hydros and hotels at Matlock in the Bank area. Neither had much entertainment to attract visitors. In 1919 'itinerant theatrical companies, of varied talent, perform at certain seasons' at the Pavilions, while 'music is only spasmodically supplied from the local band and at Smedley's by a local orchestra'.

The subsequent years brought about the steady decline of the spa's institutions. The Pavilion above the Royal Hotel faced continual difficulties and finally closed down in 1925. Meanwhile, the Royal Hotel had become semi-derelict and was burnt down in the 1930s. Smedley's Hydro closed down in 1955. Its buildings were bought by Derbyshire County Council as its administrative headquarters; the Colonnade, built as a covered exercise area, is now the County Library, and the Hydro's private church was demolished in 1958. The Grand Pavilion was put to several uses and became increasingly neglected, but in 1977 it was restored to be a tourist office and entertainments complex. A nearby pool, fed by water from a hillside thermal spring supports exotic fishes throughout the winter.[15]

The other Derbyshire spa, Buxton, gained municipal status when the Municipal Corporations (Buxton Scheme Confirmation) Act of 1916 united Buxton and Fairfield, and a charter of incorporation in 1917 made it a borough like Bath and other leading spa towns. This new position released powers and energy for much enterprise, municipal and otherwise.

Buxton benefited also by having once more a Duchess directing the house of Cavendish and taking part in metropolitan society and politics. Edward VII and Queen Alexandra stayed at Chatsworth and visited Buxton in 1905. A Cavendish nephew, who liked Buxton, became the ninth Duke in 1908. He brought his family for an annual holiday at St Ann's Hotel and took a cure for his gout, until going to Canada as Governor-General in 1916–21. He laid out the Cavendish Golf Links, an expensive and generous gesture for Buxton, since although the

Crescent had cost more, it was a profitable source of income, but the golf course was a burden.[16]

His youngest son, the Marquis of Hartington, was Mayor of Buxton in 1921, but initiative was increasingly coming from elsewhere than the house of Cavendish. In 1902 outside enterprise, Messrs Spiers and Pond, built yet another hotel, the Empire (demolished in 1964) designed by Thomas Garner, in some 8½ acres of land north-west of the Park; it cost £150,000 instead of the estimated £100,000.[17] The Buxton Improvements Company, reformed in 1888 as the Buxton Gardens Company, built in 1905 the artistic and beautiful Opera House designed by Frank Mitcham with delicately painted ceilings and panels by the Dejong Company, both of London. In its heyday it attracted the best companies of actors and actresses, including the D'Oyly Carte Opera Company and the Old Vic Company, and even Pavlova danced there.[18] There was also much music in the town. As well as touring bands, such as Sverdloff and his Red Viennese and J.P. Sousa and his band, there were military bands, and after 1908 four orchestras during the season at the Pavilion, the Hydro, the Empire Hotel and the Opera House. Sometimes they all co-operated, as at a special wartime matinee on 26 August 1914 conducted by Mr W. Iff, who now did not wish to be Herr Wilhelm Iff.[19]

The decline of the spa threatened, as at Matlock, its buildings. The Assembly Room became a private clinic and then a geriatric annexe to the Devonshire Royal Hospital. When this was transferred to another unit, the Assembly Room was empty for four years until in 1970 it was bought by Derbyshire County Council, renovated at a cost of £150,000 and became an area library. The Pavilion and its gardens have also been restored, though the tea-room was replaced by a public swimming-pool in 1972. And in 1979 the Opera House was restored, and there the annual Buxton Festival presents opera, plays, master classes and late-night revues.

The water now flows into the swimming-pool and into St Ann's Well in the Pump Room (now the Micrarium, displaying live insects under special microscopes) where it can be drunk. It also supplies the hospital's central heating system, and it is pumped through lead pipes to the factory just behind the Crescent which bottles the increasingly popular Buxton Water. The rest flows into the River Wye.

Derbyshire County Council, as the local planning authority, has designated a conservation area, which includes the market town at about 1860 based on High Street, the Georgian spa town centre on the Crescent and the Victorian Pavilion Gardens with its surrounding houses and some other historic buildings. The town is now a holiday resort and a touring centre for such places as Miller's Dale and Poole's Cavern.[20]

236

Harrogate seemed to have a flourishing future ahead of it at the beginning of the twentieth century. Indeed, it was ceasing to be chiefly a northern spa, and by 1910 over an eighth of its visitors came from London. A reason for this was said to be that it was 'a particularly useful place to stay between the end of the London season and the beginning of grouse shooting from Scotland'. Some 75,000 visitors a year passed through the Royal Pump Room by 1913, when it was extended; and in 1919 it was stated that Harrogate was 'probably the most popular and best patronized of all British spas' and had 'a greater number of highly qualified physicians', there being something like one to every 500 of the population. Its success continued after 1919, the number of treatments given at the Royal Baths being 96,000 in 1901 and 120,207 in 1927. It was claimed that these offered 'more than 40 different types of mineral baths', including brine and peat baths.

The Royal Pump Room was closed on the outbreak of the Second World War, but the Royal Baths, which had been extended in 1939, after the War received National Health Service patients from the areas of the Leeds and Newcastle Regional Hospital Boards, rising to over 150,000 in some years compared with less than 90,000 in 1938. It was reported in 1863, 'Harrogate as a spa is still very much alive'; but in 1969 the National Health Service ended its contract, and the next year the Royal Baths were closed except for its Turkish Baths and the Royal Baths Assembly Rooms for exhibitions, coffee and music. The Royal Pump Room, after being used first as a store and then as a municipal restaurant, was made into a local history museum in 1953. The Grand Hotel, renamed Windsor House, became the Inland Revenue Valuations Office. The Royal Hall, situated next to the great new Conference Centre, provides light entertainment such as pantomime, music hall and old-time dancing.

The Corporation of Harrogate has sought to replace the former spadom by attracting conferences to the town, over 500 of these being held a year as well as many trade fairs and exhibitions; and it has now become the permanent meeting-place of the Great Yorkshire Show held every July. And the fine hotels, extensive parks and open spaces, which it has inherited from its past spadom, have made it a notable holiday resort.[21]

Scarborough followed the building of the Grand Hall by the erection of a new bandstand, colonnade and restaurant in 1913, which was followed by a roof-garden and ballroom, but none were connected with water-drinking. Though Scarborough was described in 1919 as 'a remarkable combination of a popular seaside resort and spa', the spring, discovered in the seventeenth century, was now concealed beneath a manhole, and even the Edwardian tap was no longer there. Three of the Victorian villas, all in the Crescent, now house the Natural History

Museum, Art Gallery and Medical Baths. Scarborough has been able to combine its past spa features – luxury hotels, boarding houses and terraced gardens – with sands, promenade, walks and carnival-style amusements, together with an annual cricket festival, to survive as an important seaside resort.[22]

12

Conclusion

The first half of the nineteenth century was the period of maximum development for British spas. The closure of the Continent by war from 1792 may have helped the initial impetus, but also accumulations of capital from agricultural, commercial and industrial progress were available for spa ventures, especially in the Midlands and North-East. From 1800 to 1850 as many as 70 new British spa centres were established, including the individual ones at Cheltenham and Leamington, each equivalent to a minor spa. These two spa townships, safe from possible enemy invasion, prospered during the war years. Although aristocratic patronage declined in favour of the Continental spas, each decade of this half-century steadily produced 11 or more new spas and many improvements and developments in existing spas. The period of maximum growth was the 1830s, with 20 new spa centres and 14 improvement schemes. But the day had ended for the old cold spas, such as the famous Rowton Well at Sutton Coldfield, open and exposed to sky and country with nowhere for women to undress. Those at Cowley, Shuttleworth and Middleton near Wirksworth, all in Derbyshire, were abandoned by 1817. With more available coal supplies and the influence of public baths and wash-houses, cold bathing was now displaced by ranges of hot and tepid baths with new and more sophisticated treatments, and the erection or reconstruction of pump-rooms and baths became more costly. So also did the large hotels and boarding houses furnished and equipped to a higher standard, which now displaced the lodging houses. More visitors accepted inclusive terms and less often undertook self-catering.

Social assemblies might be expensive, but the health-giving baths and wells were not monopolized by the upper classes. Bath, Buxton, Harrogate and Leamington had bath funds to help the poor, and several minor spas, such as Glastonbury, Ilkley, Skipton Slaithwaite, Somersham and Willowbridge, had special terms for the needy. Parochial help sometimes existed: several south Warwickshire parishes sent their ailing poor to take the waters at Leamington.[1]

The spas also attracted many beggars. In the early nineteenth century, social distress, aggravated by wartime dislocation, over-rapid expansion and high food prices, caused disturbances among the poor at Bath and Cheltenham. Residents banded together in self-help associations to apprehend and prosecute felons, and philanthropic movements became a feature of spa towns. Many of the labouring poor found employment in the spas, as road-builders, shop assistants, keepers of baths and pump-rooms, coachmen and ostlers, but especially domestic servants. Evidence from Cheltenham and Harrogate shows that they mostly came from from neighbouring villages within a radius of about 25 miles.

The Regency spas produced some charming architecture, now unhappily much destroyed, but also problems of health, water supplies and sanitation, and gas lighting to enable people to go to evening entertainments. After 1815, and earlier at Bath and Cheltenham, spa towns obtained improvement acts to help local bodies control changing conditions, but increasing muncipalization and the consequent rate increases were resisted by local inhabitants.

Only very wealthy landowners or industrialists or small syndicates of businessmen could now afford spa investment. New planned estates were developed outside the old settlements as, for example, by the two retired Liverpool merchants, Henry Thompson and Bertie Greatheed, at Cheltenham and Leamington respectively, and the rich London merchant, John Ward, at Tunbridge Wells.

Overspeculation led to many bankruptcies, and there were efforts to prolong the summer season into the winter to achieve a greater return of capital invested in visitors' accommodation and entertainment. Bath had long enjoyed a winter season because of its nearness to the Mendip coalfield, and Leamington could develop a hunting season in winter as coal came by canal, but Cheltenham's winter season was hindered by the failure of a canal project. As the season was extended, more people were attracted to urban spas as residents, and the nature of these towns changed. Their public life disintegrated into separate groups of clubs, societies and private parties, despite attempts by commercial entrepreneurs to promote new forms of organized communal activities, such as musical promenades, archery grounds, tennis courts and race meetings. On the other hand, the demands of the resident population of these towns led to extensive tree-planting, the creation of public and private gardens and other amenities. There was also much church and chapel building to meet the religious needs of this more settled population.

During the 1840s the effects of over-building and over-investment in spa towns were being felt more markedly, although the period saw eleven new spa ventures started; and the competition of the growing seaside resorts and the coming of the railways killed the small inland watering-places. By the mid-century the fervour for spas increasingly declined, and their promotion dropped dramatically. There were only eight new ones in 1850–1914. As the small ones withered away, the larger ones sought to adapt to the challenge of cheap mass travel and were helped after the Local Government Act of 1858 by local boards of health, massive injections of syndicate or municipal investment, the provision of winter gardens and new particular forms of treatment. For instance, Woodhall Spa's iodine waters gave it a contemporary importance unrelated to its size, brine baths made the fortune of Droitwich, and the hot suphur baths of Harrogate were popular for their tonic effect. Their attraction, however, was generally for elderly patients seeking relief from such complaints as chronic rheumatic arthritis and did not help such towms to meet the increasing competition from foreign travel and, still more, the seaside resorts.

The Census Report 1871 singled out eight leading inland watering-places – Bath, Buxton, Cheltenham, Harrogate, Leamington, Malvern and Matlock – but there were 48 rival seaside resorts where the overall population had grown by 21 per cent in the previous decade. The comparable rate of growth for these spa towns was only 11.20 per cent and that included a growing population of commuter residents and the retired. At Bath 11.1 per cent of the population of 52,557 was 60 years old or upwards, the highest proportion of 42 large towns.[2]

And the spa towns faced a yet more serious and insidious danger at this time. Previously the medical profession had been the great upholders of the spas. Physicians had urged their patients to go to drink or bathe in their waters. They had written treatises explaining how they believed that the active ingredients of the various types of mineral waters in certain spas were medically efficacious; and they had vied with each other to establish prospering practices based upon their use. Now, however, that was becoming a thing of the past. Medical science was advancing and becoming more distinctive. With research into its differing aspects, it began to be subdivided, and the modern specialist appeared. New particular medicines and treatments were developed.[3]

Moreover, the new interest in science, fostered by the Prince Consort during the earlier nineteenth century, had encouraged the chemical analysis of spa waters. This gave them an added appeal, and physicians were able to turn this to good advantage in attracting people there. But now belief was failing in the efficacy of the general mineral-water 'cure', which considered, for instance, that the iron in chalybeate springs was effective for any condition associated with 'poverty of the blood', including even enfeebling disorders like tuberculosis. Also more accurate chemical analysis of the waters at the spas was questioning their validity. Granville had found varying analyses of the waters at some spas; and it was now shown that spas such as Malvern, Buxton and Bristol had no more chemicals in their waters than common tap-water possessed.[4]

One of the reasons that had brought wealthy and high-living people to take the waters at the spas was their search for a remedy to reduce their overweight – as exemplified by the corpulence of 'John Bull'. This encouraged the drinking of mineral waters at the spas and also bottling and sale of them all over the country. This motive had declined, however, by the end of the century. Reliance now was placed on the 'grape cure' and fruit-eating diets, while previously fruit had been avoided as harmful in its effects.[5]

The answer of some spas to this situation was to introduce the new hydropathic therapy, which depended upon various ways of applying water to the body instead of drinking or bathing in it. This rescued Matlock and created Ilkley and Malvern, producing hydros in these and other spas which, by the end of the century, provided the various medicated, electrical and actinotherapic baths considered necessary for the treatment of a number of diseases and conditions.[6] The life and operation of the hydros was largely self-sufficient and independent of existing urban amenities; but its equipment, procedures and buildings were costly, and the hydropathy of these years was only possible for a limited sufficiently wealthy part of the population.[7]

During the later nineteenth century and the opening years of the twentieth century, the spa towns placed greater emphasis upon their amenities, natural and otherwise. Although it was apparent that spas were beneficial for many types of patients, it was difficult to decide which factors brought about cures. It was increasingly thought that the usually salubrious climate, the submission of sufferers to a rigid regime that would be relaxed at home, the attendance of qualified physicians supplying systematic medical treatment and regular dieting and exercise, all contributed in varying measures to the recovery of patients. So spa towns sought to offer circumstances which would promote this. Besides active springs, they ideally needed a favourable climate, popular attractions and interesting and beautiful surrounding countryside.[8]

At the same time, these towns became progressively educational centres and residential resorts with growing numbers of retired people, and their activities centred on the pursuit of leisure devoted to self-improvement as well as pleasure. Although they had lost their appeal to aristocratic patients and were dominated by the wealthy middle classes, these towns retained their fashionable status and offered cheaper living than London. They had also set a pattern for the proliferating seaside resorts, which adopted some of their latter-day features – lengthy promenades, massive all-weather pavilions, municipal orchestras and the use of donkeys and hackney carriages for local transport.

Vera Brittain in her novel *Not Without Honour* has evoked the social life of Buxton during the time before 1914. By the time of the outbreak of the First World War the spas had already reached their summit of success, and decline had already set in for many, though taking the 'cure' at the Continental spas had remained fashionable with royal patronage in Edwardian England. During the war some 50,000–75,000 wounded and invalided were sent to the spas; and there were hopes that the English spas might be able to take the place of their Continental rivals; but in the years of hostilities their position inevitably worsened, and the renewal of travel to the Continent after 1918 destroyed any prospect of their revival.[9]

It was estimated that by 1919 there were some 30 or 40 hydropathic establishments still in existence, but their future, as with all aspects of spadom, was not bright. Numbers of patients fell; pump-rooms, hotels, assembly rooms closed and gave way to 'pleasure palaces' for the day-trippers. Spas steadily fell out of favour between the two world wars. Styles of living and habits of eating and spending changed greatly. The pace of life was faster and the emphasis on work more marked. The Edwardian upper middle classes with their wealth, comforts and leisure, who had been the mainstay of the spas and hydros, were now a thing of the past. The members of the new affluent class holidayed with package tours to seaside resorts.[10]

In the 1930s six of the spas – Bath, Buxton, Cheltenham, Droitwich, Harrogate and Cheltenham – joined in a national advertising campaign to promote themselves with the slogan 'Health Comes Happily at British Spas' and urged that cures could be effected by 'the most modern hydrological methods known to modern science', which would also bring 'the contentment and refreshment of mind and body'. There were individual efforts also. A local hotel advertised that Buxton offered 'Relaxation, Recreation and Restoration', while Droitwich held cocktail parties at which bathers in the brine took their drinks from floating tables.[11]

During the Second World War, the spa towns suffered from the general cessation of tourist activity and the transference of defence departments there. Bath and Malvern were permanently industrialized through this. After the war, the establishment of the National Health

Service in 1948 did assist a number of spas. Bath, Leamington, Droitwich, Woodhall and Buxton made arrangements with their local health authorities which brought them patients and subsidies. Water-cure treatments available on prescription led to some revival of activity at these spas, but only for some twenty years. One by one the contracts with the health authorities were abrogated, which finally extinguished the spas. The National Health patients had mostly come for daily visits from surrounding areas and made no contribution to the establishment anew of communities centred upon bath-houses and assembly rooms.

Nowadays spa activity has virtually ceased in the towns, which have had to rely on other means of existence. Some, like Leamington as well as Bath and Malvern, have been able to develop light industry. Harrogate, Bath, Cheltenham and others have annual literary, musical and similar festivals. Coastal spas, such as Scarborough and Brighton, have become seaside resorts. Cheltenham and Malvern remain educational centres. Harrogate has set out to be a conference centre. Bath, Tunbridge Wells and Trefriw seek to exploit their spa past for tourists as well as providing new attractions; a recent guide book declared that Bath could offer 'the pleasures of shopping, supermarkets and department stores, pre-London runs of new plays, facilities for all sports, good restaurants such as Popjay's in what was Beau Nash's house.'[12] Some, like Harrogate and Tunbridge Wells, are near enough to business centres to have a large commuter population. Some, like the Welsh and Scottish spas, are assisted by their surrounding countryside to become tourist and recreation centres. And many are favoured residential towns, favoured by the buildings and amenities of their spa past.

Since about 1980, however, there has been a revival in several manifestations of the spa idea. One aspect of this has been the the development of hotels, especially rural ones, which seek to meet the contemporary concern over environmental hazards and anxiety for physical fitness with spa facilities and treatments. It is evident that here 'spa' is used as a loosely generalized word meaning such things as body massage, wax bath, sauna, solarium, steam-room, beauty parlour, jacuzzi, exercise classes, mud envelopment and swimming-pool together with such sports as golf, squash, tennis, cycling, jogging, fishing, clay target shooting and horse-riding in their large grounds. Many of these hotels offer weekend or other breaks where their guests are offered these treatments and activities which recall the aims and attractions of the old traditional spas. These are also provided by country health farms; and there are now cruise liners with similarly equipped 'spas' for their passengers.

Again, at some of the old spas, such as Tunbridge Wells and Stathpeffer, it is possible to drink the waters: Droitwich has reopened its

244

Brine Spa; and Trefriw produces the richest iron spa water known, claimed 'to restore energy and maintain good health', As to bottled waters, while it is likely that many of them lose their properties when sold in this way, they are now being drunk in increasing numbers. Modern health consciousness believes that excessive sugar in diets is harmful, and soft drinks contain sugar. This, together with concern about the pollution of ordinary drinking water, has led people to turn to clear spring water as formerly drunk at the spas. *Time Magazine* has declared that 'water snobbery has replaced wine snobbery', and *The Times* that 'suddenly mineral water has become de rigeur on almost every dining table'. Or as a recent article has put it, there has been a 'movement from the source of the springs to the dining-room sideboard and leading to the chemist's shop'.[13]

The position of the spas themselves is upheld by the British Spas Federation. Its formation, led by the British Medical Association in 1921, was 'to develop wider public understanding and interest in the many genuine benefits of spa related health and relaxation'. The ending of National Health contracts with the spas in the 1960s changed the position of the British Medical Association, but the local authorities of Bath, Buxton, Cheltenham, Droitwich, Harrogate, Leamington, Llandrindod Wells, Malvern, Matlock, Tunbridge Wells and Woodhall have retained their membership of the Federation, which in the early 1990s launched the project 'Spas 2000' to initiate developments 'to bring the waters back to the spa towns'.[14]

Appendices

Appendix 1 The chronological development of the English spas from 1820 to 1910

1820–29	1830–39	1940–49
Ashby-de-la-Zouch, Leics.	Bath, Som.	Admaston, Salop.
Ivanoe	Bladud's Spa	Bagdale, N.R. Yorks.
Brighton, Sussex	Burnham-on-Sea, Som.	Buxton, Derbys.
Royal German Spa	Cheltenham, Glos.	Billings' New Bath
Croft, N.R. Yorks.	Pittville	Cheltenham, Glos.
New Well	Dorton, Bucks.	Park Spa
Filey, E.R. Yorks.	Droitwich, Worcs.	Harlow Car, W.R. Yorks.
Guisborough, N.R. Yorks.	Dudley, Worcs.	Hinckley, Leics.
Harrogate, W.R. Yorks.	Harrogate, W.R. Yorks.	Horncastle, Lincs.
Montpellier Pump Room	Victoria Baths	Ilkley, W.R. Yorks.
Ilkeston, Derbys.	Montpellier (Crown) Baths	Hydro
Lockwood, W.R. Yorks.	Cheltenham Pump Room	Leeds, W.R. Yorks.
Slaithwaite, W.R. Yorks.	Hockley, Essex	St. Anne's Square
Starbeck Old Spa, W.R. Yorks.	Hovingham, N.R. Yorks.	Shearsby, Leics.
Willoughby, Warwicks.	Kinoulton, Notts.	Tenbury Wells, Worcs.
	Leeds, W.R. Yorks.	
	Meadow Lane Spa	
	Matlock, Derbys.	
	Allen Hill Spa	
	Norwood, Surrey	
	Beulah	
	Radipole, Dorset	
	Shotley Bridge, Co. Durham	
	Shouldham, Norfolk	
	Skipton, W.R. Yorks.	
	Woodhall, Lincs.	
Total 11	20	11

Improvements or developments to existing spa centres

Askern, W.R. Yorks.	Aldfield, W.R. Yorks.	Birley, Derbys.
3 Baths	Ashchurch, Tewkesbury, Glos.	Boston, W.R. Yorks.
Clifton, Bristol	Bakewell, Derbys.	Harrogate, W.R. Yorks.
New Hotwell House	Bishopton, Warwicks.	John Well
Dinsdale, Co. Durham	Boston, W.R. Yorks.	Sulphur Well
New Malton, N.R. Yorks.	Harrogate, W.R. Yorks.	Horley Green, W.R. Yorks.
Malvern, Worcs.	Cold Bath	Quarndon, Derbys.
	Ilkeston, Derbys.	
	Leamington, Warwicks.	
	Abbotts' Original Baths	
	Wise's Baths	
	Nottington, Dorset	
	Scarborough, N.R. Yorks.	
	Spa Saloon	
	Shap, Westmorland	
	Southampton, Hants.	
	Victoria Spa	
	Stoney Middleton, Derbys.	
5	14	6

Appendix 1 *continued*

1850–59		1860–69		1970–79	
Dovercourt, Essex		Limpley Stoke Hydro, Wilts.		Shelfanger, Diss, Norfolk	
Purton, Wilts.		Starbeck, W.R. Yorks			
		2nd baths			
Total	2		2		1

Improvements or developments to existing spa centres

Matlock, Derbys.				Droitwich, Worcs.	
Smedley's Hydro				Old Brine Baths rebuilt	
Buxton, Derbys.				Harrogate, W.R. Yorks.	
baths improved, new well-room				Hydro	
Harrogate, W.R. Yorks				Spa Concert Room	
Magnesia Well Pump Room				New Victoria Baths	
Ilkley, W.R. Yorks.				Scarborough, N.R. Yorks.	
Craiglands Hydro				Spa Concert Hall	
				Whitby, N.R. Yorks.	
				Spa theatre	
	4		0		6

1880–89		1890–1900		1900–10	
Church Stretton, Salop				Ripon, W.R. Yorks.	
Malvern, Worcs.					
Royal Wells Spa					
Total	2		0		1

Improvements or developments to existing spa centres

Droitwich, Worcs.		Ashby-de-la-Zouch, Leics.			
St. Andrew's Baths		Bridlington, E.R. Yorks.			
Malvern, Worcs.		Buxton, Derbys.			
Assembly Room & Winter		New Pump Room			
Garden		Harrogate, W.R. Yorks.			
Scarborough, N.R. Yorks.		Cairn Hydro			
Hydro		Harlow Manor Hydro			
Woodhall Spa, Lincs.		Royal Baths			
	4		6		0

Appendix 1 *continued*

Undated Spa Centres

17th century
Leicester, Judd, Leics.
Tarlelton, Lancs.

18th century
Axwell, Winlaton, Co. Durham
Birley, Derbys.
Bourne, Lincs.
Brighton, St. Anne's Well, Wick, Sussex
Buglawton, Cheshire
Camberwell, Surrey?
Cantley, W.R. Yorks.
Clitheroe, Lancs.
Cornhill, Northumberland
Cowley, Derbys.
Crickle, W.R. Yorks.
Gayhurst, Bucks.
Hoveringham, Notts.
Middleton in Wirksworth, Derbys.
Nottingham, St Anne's Well
Redmire, N.R. Yorks.

Silbury, Berks.
Sookholme, Notts.
Stoney Middleton, Derbys.
Sutton, Salop
Sutton Coldfield, Warwicks.
Welham, Notts.
Wigston Magna, Leics.?
Woodford Wells, Essex

Early 19th century
Boscombe, Hants.
Calverley, W.R. Yorks.
Easingwold, N.R. Yorks.
Filey, E.R. Yorks.
Healing, Lincs.
Spittal, Northumberland
Sutton-upon-Derwent, E.R. Yorks.
(Improvements – Clitheroe, Lancs.)

Late 19th century
Nantwich, Cheshire

Total no. of spa centres   335   Total no. of spa places   197

Appendix 2   Attendances at the Cross Bath Pump Room, Bath, from 1823 to 1829

	Jan.	Feb.	March	April	May	June	July	Aug.	Sept.	Oct.	Nov.	Dec.	Total
1823									3	5	11	10	29
1824	8	14	13	13	9	5	7	4	8	9	25	17	132
1825	11	15	13	11	3	8	2	6	6	5	12	13	105
1826	10	36	31	23	16	12	8	5	10	14	13	11	189
1827	10	3	22	16	8	7	5	18	6	18	23	12	148
1828	16	17	6	13	15	5	7	8	9	9	12	21	138
1829	1	2	13	20	7	14	10	4	16	8	5	6	106
Total	56	87	98	96	58	51	39	45	58	68	101	90	
					Not including 1823				55	63	90	80	

Source: GRO 239, Subscription book, Cross Bath Pump Room.

Appendix 3   Domestic servants in Cheltenham, 1841: sample of 769 private households

No. of servants	No. of households	% of total households
9 or more	6 ⎫ 13	1.6
8	7 ⎭	
7	10 ⎫ 31	4.0
6	21 ⎭	
5	55	7.1
4	121	15.7
3	240	31.2
2	309	40.8

Source: Census of population returns.

Appendix 4   Populations of the major spa towns, 1801–1901

	1801		1841		1871		1901	
1.	Bath	33,196	Bath	53,196	Bath	52,557	Cheltenham	52,858
2.	Cheltenham	3,076	Cheltenham	31,411	Cheltenham	41,923	Bath	52,773
3.	Matlock	2,354	Leamington	12,864	Leamington	20,910	Tunbridge Wells	33,373
4.	Harrogate	1,984	Tunbridge Wells	8,302	Tunbridge Wells	19,410	Harrogate	29,885
5.	Tunbridge Wells	c.1,000	Harrogate	4,785	Malvern	7,606	Leamington	26,888
					(Great Malvern 5,693)			
6.	Malvern	819	Matlock	3,782	Harrogate	6,843	Malvern	16,449
	(Great Malvern only)							
7.	Buxton	816	Malvern	2,768	Matlock	3,834	Buxton	10,181
			(Great Malvern only)					
8.	Leamington	315	Buxton	1,569	Buxton	3,717	Matlock	?
9.	Woodhall	145	Woodhall	307	Woodhall	326	Woodhall	c.1,000

Notes

Abbreviations used in Notes

The series of county histories, directories and gazetteers by S. Bagshaw and F., J. and W. White are shortened, for example, Bagshaw, *Derbyshire* (1846) and White, *W.R. Yorks.* (1838).

BC.   *Bath Chronicle*
BCG   *Bath and Cheltenham Gazette*
BCM   Bath City Council Minutes
BJ   *Bath Journal*
BSJ   *Boston Spa Journal*
Capper   B.P. Capper, *A Topographical Dictionary of the United Kingdom* (1813)
CC   *Cheltenham Chronicle*
CJ   *Cheltenham Journal*
Granville A.B. Granville, *The Spas of England and Principal Sea-Bathing Places*[1841] 2 vols, ed, G. Martin (1971)
GRO   Gloucestershire Records Office
HA   *Harrogate Advertiser*
Kelly   Kellys Directories (1856–)
LC   *Leamington Spa Courier*
MA   *Malvern Advertiser*
Pevsner   N. Pevsner *et al.*, *The Buildings of England* (county vols, 1951–)
Pigot   Pigot & Co., *National, London and Provincial Commercial Directories* (1822–42)
VCH   *The Victoria History of the Counties of England*
WA   *Warwick Advertiser*
WAM   *Wiltshire Archaeological and Natural History Society Magazine*
WAR   Warwickshire Record Office

Chapter 1 The Spas in 1815

1   Phyllis Hembry, *The English Spa 1560–1815: A Social History* (1990), from which most of this paragraph is summarized.
2   James Dugdale, *The New British Traveller*, 4 vols (1819), IV, 238. 292.
3   Hembry, *The English Spa*, 4–5.
4   J.H. Plumb, *The Commercialisation of Leisure in Eighteenth-Century England* (Stention Lecture 1972, University of Reading, 1973).
5   Esther Moir, *The Discovery of Britain: The English Tourists, 1540–1940* (1964).
6   *A Guide to Watering and Sea-Bathing Places* (1806); John Barrett, 'Spas and seaside resorts 1660–1780', in *The Rise of the New Urban Society* (Open University Press, 1977)
7   J.Myerscough, 'The pursuit of happiness abroad' (lecture to the Anglo-American Conference of Historians, 1979).

Chapter 2 Leamington

1   T.B. Dudley, *A Complete History of Royal Leamington Spa* (1901), 171.
2   *The Melksham Guide, Containing an Account of the . . . Spa*, (n.d.), iv.
3   WA, 5 May, 2, 16 Jun. 1810.
4   J. Barrett, 'Spas and Seaside Resorts 1660–1780' in *The Rise of the New Urban Society* (Open University Press, 1977), 42.
5   WAR, Heber Percy MS 1707, Greatheed's Diaries, *passim.*
6   WAR, Greatheed's Diaries, 30 Apr. 14 May, 14, 21 Jun. 1813.
7   J. Bisset, *A Descriptive Guide to Leamington Priors* (1814), 30.
8   WAR, Greatheed's Diaries, 16 Mar. 4 Apr. 1816; *A Brief Account of the Rise, Progress and Patronage of the Leamington Spa Charity* (1812).
9   WA, 19 Jul. 2 Aug. 1817.
10 WA, 2 Jun. 14 Dec. 1810; J.H. Drew, *The Book of Royal Leamington Spa* (1978), 52; R. Chaplin, 'New light on the origins of Royal Leamington Spa', *Birmingham and Warwickshire Archaeological Society Transactions*, LXXXVI, 153.
11 LC, 17 Dec. 1831, 18 Feb., 21 Apr. 1832, 14 Jun. 1834, 10 May, 14 Jun. 1845, 18 May 1878
12 LC, 8 Apr. 1819, 11 Jul., 26 Sep. 1829, 22 Jan., 26 Mar., 7, 28 May, 4 Jun. 1831; WA, 21 Jul., 4 Aug. 1 Dec. 1831; M. Davies, 'Aspects of Parish Administration in Leamington Priors' *1823–1827, Warickshire History* II, 20–1; *Report to the General Board of Health Leamington Priors* (1850), 231; E.G. Baxter, *Dr. Jephson of Leamington Spa*, 2 vols (1980), *passim.*
13 Drew, *The Book of Royal Leamington Spa*, 50; W.T. Moncrieff, *The Visitor's New Guide to the Spa of Leamington Priors* (1824), 523; E.G. Baxter, 'The social life of visitors to Leamington Spa in the first half of the nineteenth century', *Warwickshire History* III, ii, 59–60.
14 W. Field, *An Historical and Descriptive Account of . . . Warwick and the Neighbouring Spa of Leamington* 328; Moncrieff, *The Visitor's New Guide* 59; W. West, *The History, Topography and Directory of Warwickshire* (1830), 718; T.B. Dudley (ed.), *Memoir of James Bisset* (1904), 88.

15 Baxter, *Dr. Jephson*, I, 20–1; Chaplin, 'New light on the origins', 156; WAR, Greatheed's Diaries, 14 Sep. 1816, 3 Sep. 1822.

16 Baxter, *Dr. Jephson*, II, 61.

17 Drew, *The Book of Royal Leamington Spa*, 63–64; Moncrieff, *The Visitor's New Guide* 82.

18 Dudley, *Memoir of James Bisset*, 259.

19 LC, 9 Aug. 1828.

20 LC, 7 Aug. 1830.

21 *Report to the General Board of Health: Leamington* (1850), 231.

22 LC 26 Jun. 1830, 30 Apr. 1831; Drew, *The Book of Royal Leamington Spa*, 94.

23 WA, 3 Feb. 1827; LC, 8, 15 Nov., 6 Dec. 1828, 8, 15 Jan., 26 Mar. 1831.

24 *Board of Health Report*, 6, 7; LC, 21 Apr. 1832.

25 *Board of Health Report*, 21; LC, 11 Jul. 1829; Bisset, *A Descriptive Guide to Leamington Priors*, 9.

26 T.H. Lloyd, 'Royal Leamington Spa', in M.A. Simpson and T.H. Lloyd, *Middle-Class Housing in Britain* (1977), 121, 127, 131, 146; West, *The History . . . of Warwickshire* (1829), 827; WA, 6 Jan. 1827.

27 WA, 1 Sep. 1827; LC, 18, 25 Oct. 1828; Lloyd, 'Royal Leamington Spa', 118; Moncrieff, *The Visitor's New Guide*, x-xi; Drew, *The Book of Royal Leamington Spa*, 41.

28 Granville, II, 221–3; LC, 18 Apr. 1829, 12 Jun. 1830; 9 Jul. 1831.

29 WA, 23 Jun. 1827; WAR, Greatheed's Diaries, 30 Aug. 1816; Pevsner & Wedgwood, *Warwickshire* (1966), 47, 376.

30 Granville, II, 223; Baxter, *Dr. Jephson*, I, 25.

31 LC, 14 May 1831; Lloyd, 'Royal Leamington Spa', 145; Drew, *The Book of Royal Leamington Spa*, 105; West, *The History . . . of Warwickshire* 715–22.

32 Bisset, *A Descriptive Guide to Leamington Priors*, 17; Moncrieff, *The Visitor's New Guide*, 70; Board of Health Report, 12.

33 LC, 31 Dec.1831, 28 Jan., 30 Jun. 1832; Moncrieff, *The Visitor's New Guide*, 70–4.

34 Baxter, *Dr. Jephson*, I, 23–4.

35 LC, 9 Aug. 1828, 7 Aug. 1838; Lloyd, 'Royal Leamington Spa', 123.

36 LC, 21 Jan., 5 May 1832; R. G. Williams, 44, *A Guide to Leamington Spa*.

37 Williams, 44; Lloyd, 'Royal Leamington Spa', 144; Anon., *The Watering Places of England* (1853), 65.

38 White, *Warickshire* (1850), 618, 626; Baxter, *Dr. Jephson*, I, 34–5, II, 56.

39 West, *The History . . . of Warwickshire* (1900), 142–3; LC, 21 Jul.1836; Williams, 43; Drew, *The Book of Royal Leamington Spa*, 63–76; Pevsner and Wedgwood, *Warwickshire*, 333–5.

40 Williams, 5–8; Drew, *The Book of Royal Leamington Spa*, 105.

41 Lloyd, 'Royal Leamington Spa', 147–9; West, *The History . . . of Warwickshire* 718.

42 M. Davies, 'Aspects of Parish Administration in Leamington Priors', *Warwickshire History*, II, 23; Moncrieff, *The Visitor's New Guide*, 71; LC, 15 Nov. 1828, 4 Apr. 1829, 26 Mar., 21 May 1831.

43 LC, 30 Apr., 14 May, 4 Jun. 1831, 5 May 1832.

44 LC, 7, 14 May 1831, 14 Apr. 1832, 15 Mar. 1834; Drew, *The Book of Royal Leamington Spa*, 107, 109.

45   J. Merridew, *Improved Edition of Moncrieff's Original Guide to the Spa of Leamington Priors* (1837) 96–7; Drew, 106–107.

46   LC, 25 Jan., 29 Mar., 5 Jul. 1834.

47   F. O'Shaughnessy, *A Spa and its Children* (1979), 28, 30; LC, 28 Dec. 1844, 4 Jan. 1845.

48   Lloyd, 'Royal Leamington Spa', 120–1, 124, 127, 139.

49   *Board of Health Report* (1850), 5, 9, 12, 13, 17, 25, 37; *Ibid.* (1851), 8, 10; Drew, *The Book of Royal Leamington Spa*, 92–3.

50   LC, 21 Dec. 1844, 3, 17, 24 May 1845.

51   LC, 10 May 1845; Lloyd, 'Royal Leamington Spa', 139; Drew, *The Book of Royal Leamington Spa*, 81.

52   Baxter, *Dr. Jephson* I, 35– 7; LC, 14 Dec. 1844.

53   *Board of Health Report* (1851), 10–11; Chaplin, 'New light on the origins', 14.

Chapter 3   Cheltenham

1   BCG, 11 Jan., 24 May 1825; *Report to the General Board of Health: Cheltenham* (1849), 8.

2   Helen Ashton, *Parson Austen's Daughter* (1949), 335–3; P.J.N. Havins, *The Spas of England* (1976), 154; William Cobbett, *Rural Rides*, 17 Nov. 1821, Everyman Edition, 33.

3   A. Varley, 'A History of the Libraries of Cheltenham from 1780 to 1900' (FLA thesis, 1959).

4   Anon., *A Companion to the Watering and Bathing Places of England* (1800), 48.

5   CJ, 8 Jun. 1829.

6   BCG, 5 May 1813; CC, 8, 15 Jun. 1815.

7   H. Ruff, *History of Cheltenham* (1803), 58.

8   CC, 8 Feb 1810, 8 Jun. 1815; BCG, 18 Apr. 1857; G.A. Hart, *A History of Cheltenham* (2nd edn. 1981), 168, 195; J. Goding, *A History of Cheltenham* (1863), 547, 550–2; G. Williams, *A Guide to Cheltenham* (1825), 100; *Provincial Medical Directory* (1847), 32.

9   CC, 12 May 1814, 27 Aug. 1818, 15 Apr. 1819; *Herefordshire Journal*, 28 Oct. 1818.

10   *John Papworth, Architect*, Exhibition Catalogue, Cheltenham Art Gallery and Museum, 4; F.E. Witts (ed. D. Verey), *The Diary of a Cotswold Parson* (1978), 53, 67–8; CJ,17 May 1830.

11   Witts, *Cotswold Parson*, 93.

12   BCG, 24 May, 21 Jun., 26 Jul. 1825; CJ, 25 Jul. 1825, 1 May 1826.

13   Witts, *Cotswold Parson*, 99.

14   CJ, 26 Jan. 1829; BCG, 5 Apr. 1820, 3 Oct. 1837.

15   Williams, *A Guide to Cheltenham*, 54–5; CJ, 11 Jul. 1825.

16   CJ, 29 Jun., 20 Jul., 10 Aug. 1829, 7, 28 Jun. 1830; BCG, 18 Apr., 16, 30 May 1837, 6 Oct. 1840.

17   C.G. Moule, *Charles Simeon* (1892), 267.

18   S.T. Blake, *Cheltenham's Churches and Chapels* (1979), 10–11.

19   Blake, *Cheltenham's Churches*, 14; Goding, *A History of Cheltenham*, 547.

20   CJ, 1 Aug. 1825, 16 Feb. 1829; Blake, *Cheltenham's Churches*, 14–19; Witts, *Cotswold Parson*, 76; *Rowe's Illustrated Cheltenham Guide 1850* (1969), 73.

21 Blake, *Cheltenham's Churches*, 19–21.

22 CC, 16 Jun. 1814, 11 May, 1 Jun. 1815; CJ, 23 May 1825; Williams, *A Guide to Cheltenham*, 1825.

23 CJ, 25 Apr. 1825.

24 Anthony Bird, *Roads and Vehicles* (1973), 180–1.

25 CC, 29 Mar., 31 May 1810; CJ, 25 Apr. 1825; BCG, 26 Jul. 1825.

26 CC, 28 May 1818, 22 Apr. 1819.

27 CC, 12 May 1814, 30 Jul. 1818.

28 CC, 23 Apr. 1818; CJ, 2 Feb. 1829; Hart, *A History of Cheltenham* 225.

29 Hart, *History of Cheltenham* 289–99; Goding, *History of Cheltenham* 547; *Rowe's History of Cheltenham*, 84–5.

30 *Cotswold Life*, Aug. 1973, 33ff; CC, 4 Jan. 1810; BCG, 7 Oct. 1812; CJ, 15 Nov. 1824, 30 May 1825.

31 CC, 18 Jun. 1818; CJ, 15 Nov. 1824; BCG, 22 Feb. 1825; Goding, *History of Cheltenham* 561.

32 'Cheltenham settlement examinations 1815–1826', *Trans. Bristol & Glos. Arch. Soc.*, VII, xviii, xxi.

33 CC, 31 Aug. 1809, 7 May 1818; Hart, *A History of Cheltenham* 277.

34 'Settlement examinations', xix, 51, 58– 9, 61, 67; GRO D1950/A2, James-Agg Gardner's Servants' Wages Book 1844–1856.

35 'Settlement examinations', 57; CJ, 18 May 1829; *Board of Health Report*, 33.

36 'Settlement examinations', 65, 66, 69, 71; CC 31 Aug. 1809, 28 May 1818.

37 GRO D1950/Z4, 8th Report 1846–1847 of the Cheltenham Servants' Home and Registry.

38 Hart, *A History of Cheltenham* 272, 273, 277–8, 306–7; CC, 31 Aug., 14, 21, 28 Sep. 1809, 3 May 1810, 31 Mar. 1813.

39 CC, 28 Dec. 1809; Hart, *A History of Cheltenham* 282–3.

40 CJ, 20 Dec. 1824, 25 Jul. 1825; W. Field, *Historical and Descriptive Account of Warwick and . . . Leamington* (1815), 323.

41 Hart, *A History of Cheltenham* 300.

42 Goding, *A History of Cheltenham* 291, 325; CC, 14 May 1818.

43 Goding, *A History of Cheltenham* 525; Hart, *A History of Cheltenham* 302–3.

44 Goding, *A History of Cheltenham* 521–5; Hart, *A History of Cheltenham* 302–3; CJ 6 Apr. 1829.

45 Census returns, 1841.

46 Goding, *A History of Cheltenham* 515–6.

47 A. F. Munden, 'The Church of England in Cheltenham 1826- 1856,' B. Litt. thesis, Birmingham University (1956), ff. 127–8; O.A. Ashton, 'Clerical control and radical responses in Cheltenham Spa 1838–1848', *Midland History*, VIII (1983),125; Hart, *A History of Cheltenham* 211–7.

48 CJ, 7 Jun., 26 Jul. 1830.

49 Witts, *Cotswold Parson*, 53, 56.

50 J. Howes, *Joseph Pitt and Pittville* (1969) 58–60; J. Howes, *Rise and Fall of Joseph Pitt* (1976) 69–70; S.T. Blake, *Cheltenham Historical Works*, no. 1 (5); *Board of Health Report* (1849), 24.

51 Anon., *Watering Places of England* (1853), 60; Howes, *Joseph Pitt and Pittville*, 60; Howes *Rise and Fall of Pitt*, 69–70.

52 CJ, 27 May, 17 Jun. 1839.

53 Witts, *Cotswold Parson*, 93.
54 BCG, 31 Jan. 18, 25 Apr., 2, 16 May, 26 Sep., 31 Oct. 1837; 6 Aug. 1838; CJ, 4, 25 May 1840.
55 BCG, 4 Oct. 1825; CJ, 16 Mar., 6 Apr., 25 May, 1, 8 Jun., 10, 17 Aug., 7, 21 Sep., 19 Oct. 1829, 17 May 1830; Hart, *A History of Cheltenham* 309.
56 Witts, *Cotswold Parson*, 71, 147.
57 Census Returns, 1841.
58 Williams, *A Guide to Cheltenham*, 33; CJ, 20 May 1819, 23 Mar., 6, 13 Apr., 4 May 1829,.
59 CJ, 4 May, 27 Jul., 24 Aug. 14 Sep. 1829, 4, 25 May 1840; BCG 31 Jan. 18, 25 Apr., 2, 16 May, 26 Sept, 31 Oct. 1837, 6 Aug. 1838.
60 Witts, *Cotswold Parson*, 147, 160.
61 Blake, *Historical Works*, no. 2 (7 & 9).
62 15 May 1826; BCG, 16 May, 3 Oct. 1837, 9 Jan., 3, 10 Jul. 1838; CJ, 8 Jul. 1839; Hart, *A History of Cheltenham* 180; *Board of Health Report* (1849), 27.
63 Hart, *A History of Cheltenham*, 199, 211.
64 CJ, 15 Jul., 5 Aug. 1839.
65 CJ, 29 Jun., 10 Aug., 7 Sep. 1829.
66 15 Jul., 5 Aug. 1839.
67 CJ, 21 Jun. 1830.
68 C.G. Harper, *Shakespeare Land* (1912), 121.
69 BCG, 22 Jan., 27 Aug. 1839, 3 Nov. 1840.
70 Blake, *Cheltenham's Churches*, 23–7.
71 BCG, 5 Sep. 1837, 1 Jan. 1839; Witts, *Cotswold Parson*, 160; Goding, *A History of Cheltenham* 449, 554; Blake, *Cheltenham's Churches*, 28–9.
72 BCG, 24 Apr. 1838, 15 Jan. 1839; Goding, *A History of Cheltenham*, 450–1; Hart, 236; Blake, *Cheltenham's Churches*, 29–31.
73 M.C. Morgan, *Cheltenham College* (1968), 28; Hart, *A History of Cheltenham*, 236–237; Goding, *A History of Cheltenham*, 452; Blake, *Cheltenham's Churches*, 31–2.
74 Munden, 'The Church of England in Cheltenham' f. 157.
75 W. Carus, *Memoirs of the Life of the Revd. Charles Simeon* (1847), 784.
76 CJ, 29 Jun., 3, 10 Aug., 7 Sep. 1829.
77 CJ, 18 Aug. 1829.
78 CJ, 27 Jun. 1829.
79 W.E. Beck, *The Cheltenham Training Colleges* (1947), *passim*; Morgan, *Cheltenham College*, 24.
80 A.K. Clarke, *A History of the Cheltenham Ladies' College* (1953), 20ff.
81 CJ, 19 Aug. 1844; A. Harper (ed.), *Cheltenham Grammar School* (1856), 124.
82 Francis Close, 'Lecture to the Church of England Reading Association', CJ, 25 Jan. 1841.
83 BCG, 13 Jul. 1827.
84 BCG, 15 Jul., 5 Aug. 1839.
85 CJ, 11, 25 May 1829; BCG, 3 Dec. 1839.
86 GRO, Records of the Improvement Commission 1852–1862, Box 27, Bundle 329; BCG, 5 Mar. 1839.
87 Hart, *A History of Cheltenham*, 326–7, 339.
88 Hart, *A History of Cheltenham*, 242–3.

89 Hart, *A History of Cheltenham*, 245.
90 See Appendix 4.
91 Harper, *Shakespere Land*, 121.
92 Goding, *A History of Cheltenham*, 538–9.
93 Arthur Bell, *Pleasure Town, Cheltenham 1830–1860* (1981), 17.
94 BCG, 30 Jul. 1839; CJ, 3 Jun. 1839.
95 CJ, 3, 10 Jun., 1 Jul. 1839, 29 Jun., 6 Jul. 1840; BCG, 16 Jul. 1839, 30 Jun., 28 Jul. 1840.
96 Hart, *A History of Cheltenham*, 234.

Chapter 4   Bath

1 J.C.Trewin, *Mr.M., A Tragedian and his Theatre* (1955), *passim*.
2 Fanny Burney, *Diary*, 29 November 1815.
3 BCG, 4 Nov. 1812.
4 BJ, 13 Feb., 13, 20 Mar., 17 Apr., 8 May 1815.
5 BJ, 24 Jun. 1816.
6 BCM, 22 Sep., 27 Dec., 1817, 29 Jan., 6 Mar., 27 Apr. 1818.
7 BJ, 13 May, 21, 28 Oct., 18 Nov. 1816; *Herefordshire Journal* 30 Oct. 1816; BC 28 Dec. 1820.
8 BJ, 15, 26 Jan., 25 Mar., 1, 22 Apr., 23, 30 Sep., 7, 21 Oct. 1816.
9 W. Meyler, *Original Bath Guide* (1854); BCG, 14 Feb. 1837.
10 Meyler, 27; BCG 5 Apr. 1820.
11 BJ, 3 Feb. 1813, 13 Feb. 1815.
12 BCG, 18 Jan. 1825.
13 BJ, 16 Nov. 1837.
14 BCM, 26 Aug. 1816, 6 Apr., 5 Jul. 1819, 2 Sep. 1820.
15 BCM, 17 Feb. 1820, 14 Apr. 1822.
16 Anon., *A Companion to the Watering and Bathing Places of England* (1800), 1; DRO, D461/F1, Diary of Miss M.S.N. Henning, 21 May 1835.
17 BJ, 15 Dec. 1800; 8 Jan. 1810.
18 GRO, D123/F4, Winstone Letters, 21 Jan. 1815, 19 Jan. 1817.
19 BCM, 22 Apr. 1813, 6 May, 23 Jul. 1816, 8 Sep.1818.
20 BCM, 22 May, 2 Oct. 1820, 8 Feb. 1821.
21 BCM, 3 Jun., 20 Aug. 19, 29 Sep. 1821.
22 BCM, 27 Mar., 20 Apr., 10, 27 Jun. 1829.
23 BCM, 7 Feb. 1825, 1 Aug. 1826.
24 See Appendix 2.
25 BCM, 24 Jul. 1829.
26 BCM, 10 Jun., 15 Sep., 5 Oct. 1829; W. Ison, *The Georgian Buildings of Bath* (1948), 64–65.
27 BCM, 24 Jul. 1829, 12 Jul. 1830, 14 Jun. 1831; BJ, 18 Sep. 1815.
28 BCM, 15 Sep., 4 Dec. 1829.
29 BCG, 31 May 1835.
30 Meyler, *Original Bath Guide*, 65; J. Haddon, *Bath* (1973); BCG, 17, 31 May, 6 Sep., 4 Oct. 1825.
31 BCG, 4 Oct. 1825; Meyler, *Original Bath Guide*, 65; BCM, 19 Dec. 1825, 15 Jul. 1828.

32 BCM, 8 Aug. 1832, 23 Jan., 5 Sep. 1833, 10 Jul., 4 Aug. 1834.
33 BCM 15 Jul. 1828, 17 Sep. 1830, 5 Sep. 1833, 5, 12 Dec. 1834.
34 Meyler, *Original Bath Guide*, 68–9.
35 BCM, 10 May 1824, 2 Oct 1826.
36 BCG, 18 Jan. 1825.
37 S. Keene, *Improved Bath Directory* (1824), 85–93; BCM, 14 Feb. 1834.
38 BCM, 2 Oct. 1826, 13 Aug. 1827.
39 G.N.Wright, *Historic Guide to Bath* (1864), 345–6; R.S. Neale, 'The industries of the City of Bath in the first half of the nineteenth century', *Proc. Som. Arch. & Nat. Hist. Soc.*, CVIII, 140.
40 BJ, 25 Nov.1837.
41 BCM, 10 Jul., 13 Aug. 1911.
42 Pevsner, *North Somerset* (1958), 106–9.
43 S. Sydenham, *Bath Pleasure Gardens* (2nd edn, 1961), 16; BJ, 11 Jun. 1810.
44 Keene, *Improved Bath Directory* 24.
45 BCG, 3 Jan., 30 May 1837, 28 May 1839, 3 Mar. 1840.
46 Keene, *Improved Bath Directory* 24.
47 Keene, *Improved Bath Directory* 25.
48 Haddon, *Bath*, 162ff.
49 R. Salter, 'Bath and its entertainments', in J. Wroughton (ed.), *Bath in the Age of Reform* (1972), 60; BCG, 24 Oct. 1837.
50 Keene, *Improved Bath Directory* 85ff.
51 C. Godwin, *A New and Correct Plan of the City of Bath* (1825); G. Manners, *Map of the City of Bath* (1840); *A Plan of the City and Borough of Bath* (1852); Granville.
52 Neale, 'Industries of Bath', 132, 133, 134–5, 143.
53 Neale, 'Industries of Bath', 141, 142; J. Wroughton, 'Bath and its Workers', in *Bath in the Age of Reform* (1972), 5–6, 9.
54 Neale, 'Industries of Bath', 133, 137, 142.
55 Haddon, *Bath*, 161; John Skinner, *Journal of a Somerset Rector 1803–1834* (1984), 445–6.
56 D. Dethridge, 'Bath and its New Local Government', in J. Wroughton (ed.) *Bath in the Age of Reform* (1972), 83.
57 Haddon, *Bath*, 160–1; BCG, 16 Jul. 1839.
58 W. Bragg, *A General Directory for the County of Somerset (1840); Haddon, Bath*, 148; BCG 16 May 1837, 21 May 1838.
59 Pigot, *Somerset* (1842); Granville, III, 434.
60 Charles Hadfield, *The Canal Age* (1968), 81–2.
61 Haddon, *Bath*, 143.
62 M. Hemmings, 'Bath and its communications', *Bath in the Age of Reform*, 516, 9; BCG, 7 Feb., 16 May 1837.
63 B. Cunliffe, *The City of Bath* (1986), 154. Meyler, *Original Bath Guide*, 48–9; BCG, 14 Jan., 21 Jul. 1840.
64 Meyler, *Original Bath Guide*, 49; BCG 10 Dec. 1839.
65 Meyler, *Original Bath Guide*, 51–2.
66 CJ, 1 Jun. 1840; BCG, 21 Mar. 1837.

Chapter 5   Minor Spas

1   T. Deacon, *The History of the Village of Willoughby in the County of Warwick* (1828), 59.

2   *Leeds Intelligencer*, 4 Jun. 1829.

3   E.A. Goodwyn, *Selections from Norwich Newspapers 1760–1790* (1972), 41–2.

4   A. Campbell, *Report on the Public Baths and Wash-Houses in the United Kingdom* (Carnegie United Kingdom Trust, 1918), 2–4; 9 & 10 Vict., clxxxiv.

5   Deacon, *The History of . . . Willoughby* 54.

6   Granville, I, 312, 321; Anon., *A Guide or Handbook to the Shap Spa* (1844).

7   See Appendix 1.

8   *Ilkeston Official Guide* (1956), 15; *Imperial Gazette* (1818–1825), III, 1040.

9   Pigot, *Leicestershire* (1851), 13, 17.

10 *Leeds Intelligencer*, 19 Apr. 1827, 11 Sep. 1828, 4, 11 Jun. 1829; Pigot, *Northern Counties* (1834), 688; Pigot, *Yorkshire* (1834), 756, (1849), 148, (1855), 171.

11 *Leeds Intelligencer*, 15 Dec. 1825, 29 Jun. 1826, 18 Jun. 1829; *York Courant*, 24 May 1831; Pigot, *Northern Counties* (1834), 861, (1855), 352; *Official Guide W.R. Yorks* (1932), 9; A.B. and M.D. Anderson, *Vanishing Spas* (1974), 64–5.

12 *Sheffield Mercury*, 22, 29 Apr. 1843.

13 K. Hoole, *North-East England, A Regional History of the Railways of Great Britain*, ed. D. St. John Thomas (1965), IV, 95.

14 Granville, I, 208–3; White, *Durham* (1855), 56; Anon, *Croft Spaw, A Poem*.

15 Granville, I, 311–26; J. Johnson, *Excursions to the Principal Mineral Waters of England* (1843), 56.

16 Pevsner, *Cumberland and Westmorland* (1967), 127; Upcott Gill, *Inland Watering Places* (1891), 90–4.

17 J.Hunter, *South Yorkshire* (1831), 475; Granville, I, 402–4; *Leeds Intelligencer*, 2 Aug. 1827; *Yorkshire Gazette*, 18 Jul. 1829, 3 Jul. 1830, 24 May, 6 Aug. 1831; *York Courant*, 2, 9 Jun., 8 Dec. 1829.

18 *York Courant*, 24 May 1831.

19 R.L.P. and D.M. Jowitt, *Discovering Spa* (1971), 52–3; Gill, *Inland Watering Places*, 7–9.

20 WAM, LVIII, 454–5;, VCH, *Wiltshire*, IV, 388; Pevsner, *Wiltshire* (1975), 345; 5 Geo. III, cxxvi; *Salisbury & Winchester Journal*, 1 Apr., 10 Jun. 1816.

21 *Salisbury & Winchester Journal*, 1 Jul., 1, 5 Aug. 1816, 15 Jun. 1818, 24 May, 5 Jul. 1819; BCG, 12 Jan. 1820, 11 Jan., 22 Mar., 3 May 1825.

22 *Dorset County Chronicle*, 4 Aug. 1831; Pigot, *Wiltshire* (1844), 23; Anderson and Anderson, *Vanishing Spas*, 58; *Salisbury & Winchester Journal*, 29 Jul., 26 Aug. 1833.

23 F. Accum, *Guide to the Chalybeate Spring of Thetford* (1819); S. Lewis, *Topographical Dictionary of England*, 4 vols (1840), IV, 301; *Suffolk Chronicle*, 1, 15 May, 28 Aug., 4, 11, 18 Sep., 9. Oct., 6 Nov. 1819.

24 White, *Norfolk* (1836), 718–20, 723, 724, 734; *Ibid* (1845), 400–1; *Ibid* (1864), 885; *Suffolk Chronicle*, 23 May 1820; 26 May 1821; G. Bloomfield, *Thetford Chalybeate Spa, A Poem* (1820).

25 A. Wherry, 'Gloucester Spa', *Gloucestershire Life*, Nov. 1971, Jan. 1972, Mar.

1972; I. Gray, 'Jemmy Wood's Journal', *Trans. Bristol & Glouc. Arch. Soc.*, XC, 173; *Glouc. Journal*, 24 Apr., 8 May 1815.

26   F.D. Wilts, *The Diary of a Cotswold Parson*, ed. D. Verey (1978) 28.

27   GRO, D123/F4, Winstone Letters,20 Jun. 1817; Wilts, *Cotswold Parson*, 21; R. Gell and T. Bradshaw, *Gloucs. Dir.* (1820); D. Verey, *Gloucestershire: The Vale and the Forest of Dean* (1970), 251; *Glouc. Journal*, 31 Jul., 21 Aug. 1815, 27 Jun. 1825, 17 Aug. 1829.

28   P. Deacon, *Willoughby* (1906), 58.

29   R. Bearman, 'Bishopton Spa, Stratford-upon-Avon', *Warwickshire History*, II, No. 6 (1974/5), 20–34; Granville, II, 271–7.

30   Lewis, *Topographical Dictionary*, I, 108, II, 500; Bagshaw, *Derbyshire* (1846), 187–8, 410; White, *Derbyshire* (1857), 282, 476–7; Anon., *Bakewell and its Vicinity* (n.d.), 49–50.

31   Granville, I, 148–9; T. Whellan, *History of the City of York and the North Riding* (1859), II, 216–17.

32   A. Pallister, 'The Dinsdale Spa', *Durham County Local County Hist. Soc. Bulletin*, 14 Mar. 1972, 21–8; *Yorks. Gazette*, 9 May 1829; *York Courant*, 2 Jun., 25 Aug. 1829, 24 May 1831; Pigot, *Durham* (1834), 165.

33   Granville, I, 216–7, 220–2; Gill, *Inland Watering Places*, 80–1; K. Hoole, *North-East England: A Regional History of the Railways of Great Britain* (1965), 125.

34   T. Wayte, *A Descriptive and Historical Guide to Ashby-de-la-Zouche* (1831); W. and J. Hextall, *History and Description of Ashby-de-la-Zouche* (1852); Pevsner, *Leicestershire and Rutland* (1960), 51, 54–5; W. Lee, *Report to the General Board of Health, Ashby-de-la-Zouch* (1849), 3, 10; *Dictionary of British Architects*, 211; Dorothy Hartley, *Water in England* (1964), 70–1.

35   R. Gough (ed.), *Camden's Britannia* (1789), IV, 161; Granville, I, 330–41; Pigot, *Westmorland* (1834), 656; Anon., *A Guide or Handbook to the Shap Spa, Westmorland* (1844); Anon., *Handy Guide to the English Lakes and Shap Spa* (1881); Anderson and Anderson *Vanishing Spas*, 62.

36   Granville, I, 370–1; White, W. R. Yorks., I (1837), 693, II (1838), 835.

37   Granville, I, 285–93; Pigot, *Northern Counties* (1855), I, 64; *Leeds Intelligencer*, 28 Aug. 1828; Kelly, *Durham (1910), 374; Anderson and Anderson, Vanishing Spas*, 63–4; Lewis, *Topographical Dictionary*, IV, 91; W. Fordyce, *History and Antiquities of the County Palatine of Durham* (1857), II, 701.

38   J.J. Sheaham, *History and Topography of Buckinghamshire* (1862), 338, 376–7; Lewis, *Topographical Dictionary*, II, 73–4; T. Knight, *History of the Dorton Chalybeate near Brill, Bucks.* (1833).

39   Granville, I, 194–203; Worsley Mss, Hovingham Hall, Advertisement 1 Jun. 1836 & Plans Nos. 218 & 220; Whellan, *York & the North Riding*, II, 860–3; Anderson and Anderson, *Vanishing Spas*, 46–7; Kelly, *N. & E. R. Yorks.* (1905), 126–8.

40   R.O. Benson, *Weymouth Guide* (1828), 33, 65, 73.

41   *Dorset County Chronicle*, 15 Jun. 1836.

42   Lewis, *Topographical Dictionary*, IV, 476; *Dorset County Chronicle*, 15, 22 Apr., 15, 22 Jul., 26 Aug., 18 Nov. 1830, 14 Apr., 2 Jun. 1831, 19 Apr., 3 May, 26 Jul., 13, 27 Sep. 1832; *Salisbury and Winchester Journal* 19 Apr. 1830, 6 May, 24 Jun. 1833; *Imperial Gazette*, (1818–25), V, 663; Kelly, *Dorsetshire* (1848), 2643.

43 G. Henning, *An Historical Account of the Medicinal Waters or Mineral Springs of Daviesville at Burnham near Bridgwater (1836); B. Little, Portrait of Somerset* (1969), 81–2.

44 Granville, III, 607–14; Kelly, *Essex* (1880), 200; Pevsner, *Essex* (1965), 242–3; Anderson and Anderson, *Vanishing Spas*, 44.

45 T. Edwards, 'The Spa that Never Was,' *Warwickshire and Worcestershire Life* (Oct., 1966), 47ff.; Pevsner, *Worcestershire* (1968), 277–9; T. Evans, *History of Tenbury* (1840); BCG, 24 Sept 1839.

46 VCH *Wilts..*, IV, 388; Pevsner,*Wiltshire* 376; *Salisbury & Winchester Journal*, 30 Mar., 8 Jun. 1861; Sales Ledger, Purton Spa House (Misses A. & F. Hasking); F. Large, *Swindon Retrospect 1856–1931* (1931),64–5.

47 Kelly, *Shropshire* (1900), 59; T.D. Luke, *Spas and Health Resorts of the British Isles* (1919), 132–3.

48 Kelly, *W. R. Yorks.* (1927), 809.

49 White, *W. R. Yorks* (1838), II, 263.

50 White, *Leics. & Rutland* (1863), 435.

51 Granville, I, 33.

52 Granville, xliv.

53 Granville, I, 72.

Chapter 6   Southern Spas

1 W.A. Thomson, *Spas That Heal* (1978), 32–40; W. Addison, *English Spas* (1951), 30–43; K. Denbigh, *A Hundred British Spas (1981), 53–74, 87–9.

2 A. Savidge, *Royal Tunbridge Wells* (1975); J. Clifford, *The Directory of the Ancient and Present State of Tunbridge Wells*, (1816), 21; J. Clifford, *Descriptive Guide of Tunbridge Wells* (1818).

3 Clifford, *Guide* (1818), 79–80.

4 Savidge, *Royal Tunbridge Wells*, 117.

5 Savidge, *Royal Tunbridge Wells*, 121.

6 S. Lewis, *Topographical Dictionary of England*, 4 vols (1840), IV, 338.

7 *Visitor's Guide* (1842), 126; Savidge, *Royal Tunbridge Wells*, 122.

8 5 & 6 William IV, clxxii.

9 P. Amsinck, *Tunbridge Wells and its Neighbourhood* (1810), 17.

10 J. Britton, *Descriptive Sketches of Tunbridge Wells and the Calverley Estate* (1832).

11 P.A. Clarke, 'James and Decimus Burton', RIBA Thesis, 1949.

12 Savidge, *Royal Tunbridge Wells*, 1045, 105, 108.

13 C. Hussey, 'Calverley Park, Tunbridge Wells', *Country Life* (1 May 1969), 1081.

14 *Walks in Tunbridge Wells* (Royal Tunbridge Wells Civic Society), no. 2, 1–2.

15 Savidge, *Royal Tunbridge Wells*, 108ff.

16 Britton, *Descriptive Sketches of Tunbridge Wells, passim*.

17 *Walks in Tunbridge Wells*, no. 2, 2.

18 Savidge, *Royal Tunbridge Wells*, 147.

19 Clifford, *Guide*, 62.

20 Savidge, *Royal Tunbridge Wells*, 116.

21 Lewis, *Topographical Dictionary*, IV, 339.

22 A.B. Granville, *Southern Spas* (1843), 619–21, 629–30.
23 Elsie M. Sandell, *Southampton Through the Ages* (1960), 107.
24 *Hampshire Advertiser, passim.*
25 A. Temple Patterson, *Southampton* (1970), 214.
26 E.M. Gilbert, *Brighton: Old Ocean's Bauble* (1975), 60, 64, 67; Clifford Musgrave, *Life in Brighton* (1970), 54, 57, 58, 235, 262.
27 Gilbert, *Brighton*, 73–5, 78, 80, 129, 195; Musgrave, *Life in Brighton*, 224–6, 235; Antony Dale, *Fashionable Brighton 1820–1860* (1987), 10.

Chapter 7   Midland Spas

1 R. Millward and A. Robinson, *The Peak District* (1975), 352–5.
2 Census Returns, 1841.
3 John Leach, *The Book of Buxton* (1987), 65.
4 Pigot, *Derbyshire* (1846), 116–17.
5 Leach, *The Book of Buxton*, 77.
6 White, *Derbyshire* (1857), 500; E. Burton, *Historic Buxton and its Spa Era* (1971), 11–12.
7 Leach, *The Book of Buxton*, 132.
8 Leach, *The Book of Buxton*, 82.
9 Pigot *Derbyshire* (1829), 117; Leach, *The Book of Buxton*, 112.
10 T. Marchington, 'The development of Buxton and Matlock since 1800', London University MA thesis, f. 33; E. Axon, *Historical Notes on Buxton*, 5th paper (1937), no pagination.
11 Leach, *The Book of Buxton*, 55, 75, 78.
12 S. Bagshaw, *Derbys* (1846); Muriel Searle, *Spas and Watering Places* (1977), 125; E.S. Turner, *Taking the Cure* (1967), 124.
13 Leach, *The Book of Buxton*, 104.
14 *The Builder* (1852); Pevsner, *Derbyshire* (1979), 115–16.
15 Marchington, *The Development of Buxton*, 42, 45, 49.
16 J.B. Firth, *Railways and Byways in Derbyshire* (1905), 401.
17 Pigot, *Derbyshire* (1825), 26.
18 Granville, II, 427.
19 V. Waite, 'The Bristol Hotwells', *Bristol in the Eighteenth Century*, ed. P. McGrath, (1972), 122.
20 W. Ison, *The Georgian Buildings of Bristol* (1978), 130–4; BCG, 26 May 1813, 15 Feb. 1825.
21 J. Baker, *The New Guide to Bristol and Clifton* (1894).
22 Tudor Edwards, *Bristol* (1951), 56–7.
23 B.S. Smith, *A History of Malvern* (1978 edn), 53–5, 178–9.
24 Smith, *History of Malvern*, 179, 291; M. Southall, *Description of Malvern* (1822), 57.
25 BCG, 21 Jun. 1825; Smith, *A History of Malvern*, 289; P. Bentley, *History, Gazetteer and Directory of Worcestershire*, 5 vols (*c.* 1840), III, 100; Southall, *Description of Malvern*, 11.
26 Smith, *History of Malvern*, 179; Southall, *Description of Malvern* 57.
27 BCG, 3 May 1825; Smith, *History of Malvern*, 185–6.
28 Smith, 181, 289; H.W. Lamb, *The Visitor's Guide to Malvern*, (1862), 29.

29   MA, 23 Sep. 1865.
30   Smith, *History of Malvern*, 214, 291.
31   MA, 20 Sep. 1873; Southall, *Description of Malvern*, 20, 61.
32   CC, 10 May 1810.
33   Smith, *History of Malvern*, 184; Southall, *Description of Malvern*, 10.
34   J. Dugdale, *The New British Traveller*, 4 vols (1819), IV, 519.
35   Smith, *History of Malvern*, 180; Southall, *Description of Malvern*, 169; R.B. Grindrod, *Malvern Past and Present* (1865), 99.
36   Southall, *Description of Malvern*, 8.
37   GRO KW209, 'Diary of Elizabeth Syndercombe Bower,' 28 and 29 Jun. 1837.
38   Southall, *Description of Malvern*, 8–10; Smith, *History of Malvern*, 185; Lamb, *Guide to Malvern*, 99.
39   MA, 2 Jun. 1860; 11 Mar. 1865; Smith, *History of Malvern*, 220–1, 292; Lamb, *Guide to Malvern*, 32.
40   Smith, 221. *History of Malvern,*
41   MA, Jun. 1860; Smith, *History of Malvern*, 169.
42   Smith, *History of Malvern*, 289.
43   *Herefordshire Journal*, 28 May 1817; Lamb, *Guide to Malvern*, 60–1.
44   Lamb, *Guide to Malvern*, 30.
45   Lamb, *Guide to Malvern*, 43–4; Smith, *History of Malvern*, 222–3.
46   Smith, *History of Malvern*, 223; Bentley, *History of . . . Worcestershire*, III, 98.
47   Lamb, *Guide to Malvern*, 53.
48   Smith, *History of Malvern*, 191–2.
49   Smith, *History of Malvern*, 189–90; Kelly, *Worcestershire* (1928), 187.
50   H. Cross, *Historical Handbook to Malvern* (1864), 121; Lamb, *Guide to Malvern*, 45; Smith, *History of Malvern*, 190.
51   Lamb, *Guide to Malvern*, 95; Smith, *History of Malvern*, 192.
52   Smith, *History of Malvern*, 192.
53   BCG, 14 May 1838; CJ, 15 Jun. 1840; Smith, *History of Malvern*, 237; Lamb, *History of Malvern*, 121.
54   Bentley, *History of . . . Worcestershire*, 103–4; Smith, *History of Malvern*, 193, 237–8, 246; Lamb, *Guide to Malvern*, 112.
55   Bentley, *History of . . . Worcestershire*, 83.
56   BCG 12 Sept 1837.
57   Granville, II, 266–7.

Chapter 8   Northern Spas

1   J. Patmore, 'Harrogate and Knaresborough: a study in urban development', (Oxford Univ. D.Phil. thesis); W. Grainge, *The History and Topography of Harrogate and the Forest of Knaresborough* (1871), 190–1; Pevsner, *West Riding* (1959), 250.
2   HA, 29 Jul. 1843.
3   Anon., *A Week at Harrogate* (1957), 52; Bernard Jennings, *A History of the Wells and Springs of Harrogate* (1974), 289.
4   *Leeds Intelligencer*, 21 Jun. 1827; *York Courant*, 16 Jun. 1829; Jennings, *History of the Wells and Springs*, 288.

5   B.P.A. Capper, *A Topographical Dictionary of the United Kingdom* (1813); Grainge *History and Topography of Harrogate*, 260.

6   Jennings, *History of the Wells and Springs*, 291; Grainge, *History and Topography of Harrogate*, 261–2; *Yorkshire Gazette*, 27 Jun. 1829.

7   Granville, I, 57–8; Grainge, *History and Topography of Harrogate*, 148–9; Jennings, *History of the Wells and Springs*, 291–2; *Dictionary of British Architects* (1907), 215.

8   Granville, I, 57–8; Grainge, *History and Topography of Harrogate*, 149.

9   Jennings, *History of the Wells and Springs*, 293–4; *Dictionary of British Architects*, 215; J. Patmore, *Atlas of Harrogate*, (1967), 21.

10 White, *W. R. Yorks.* (1838), 785.

11 Jennings, *History of the Wells and Springs*, 294.

12 HA, 10 Jun. 1843.

13 HA, 12 Aug. 1843.

14 Grainge, , *History and Topography of Harrogate*, 250; Jennings, *History of the Wells and Springs*, 293.

15 HA, 10 Jun. 1843.

16 Patmore, 'Harrogate and Knaresborough', f. 134; *York Courant*, 7 Oct. 1828, 11 Aug. 1829.

17 HA, 5 Aug. 1843; Granville, I, 48.

18 Granville, I, 60; Grainge, *History and Topography of Harrogate*, 177, 203; S. Lewis, *Topographical Dictionary of England*, 4 vols (1840), II, 363.

19 Grainge, *History and Topography of Harrogate*, 177, 203.

20 W.J. Kaye, *Records of Harrogate* (1922), 132.

21 Lewis, *Topographical Dictionary*, II; Jennings, *History of the Wells and Springs*, 297, 298.

22 Jennings, *History of the Wells and Springs*, 295.

23 Granville, I, 83.

24 Jennings, *History of the Wells and Springs*, 345 (Grainge, *History and Topography of Harrogate*, 23, gives this figure as £20).

25 4 & 5 Vict. c. xvi; Grainge, *History and Topography of Harrogate*, 123; Kelly, *W. R. Yorks.* (1927), 427.

26 HA, 15 Jul. 1843; Granville, I, 72; Jennings, *History of the Wells and Springs*, 352–3.

27 W. Addison, *English Spas* (1951), 100.

28 Jennings, *History of the Wells and Springs*, 295–6, 96, 352; Grainge, *History and Topography of Harrogate*, 124.

29 Jennings, *History of the Wells and Springs*, 345–6.

30 Granville, I, 71; Jennings, *History of the Wells and Springs*, 346, 409.

31 Jennings, *History of the Wells and Springs*, 351.

32 Granville, I, 38.

33 Patmore, 'Harrogate and Knaresborough', ff. 151, 153–5, 158–9, 161–4.

34 Patmore, 'Harrogate and Knaresborough', f. 129; Granville, I, 71.

35 Patmore, 'Harrogate and Knaresborough', f. 129; Granville, I, 71.

36 Jennings, *History of the Wells and Springs*, 310–1, 408.

37 J.T. Ward, 'East Yorkshire landed estates in the nineteenth century', *East Yorkshire Local History Series*, no. 23 (1967), 27.

38 A. Rowntree (ed.), *The History of Scarborough* (1931), 280–2; *York Courant*, 14 Jul. 1829; Pevsner, *North Riding* (1966), 331, 333.

39   Lewis, *Topographical Dictionary* IV, 25; Pigot, *Northern Counties* (1834), 911;
      J. Johnson, *Excursions to the Principal Waters of England* (1843), 42.
40   Rowntree, *History of Scarborough*, 351, 421.
41   *Leeds Intelligencer*, 8 Jul. 1824, 16 Jun. 1825.
42   T. Whellan, *History of the City of York and the North Riding* (1859), 717.
43   Rowntree, *History of Scarborough*, 280; *Yorkshire Gazette*, 4 Sep. 1830.
44   Lewis, *Topographical Dictionary* IV, 26.
45   G.C.F. Forster, 'Scarborough 1566–1966', *Scarborough 966-1966* (1967), 59.
46   Whellan, *History of York*, 716; Rowntree, *History of Scarborough*, 174.
47   Rowntree, *History of Scarborough*, 300–301.
48   Gascoigne v. Kitchen, Gascoigne Papers, Archives, Sheeoscar, Leeds.
49   Beatrice M. Scott, *Boston Spa*, 2nd edn, (1985), 10–20.
50   Granville, II, 32–4.
51   Sarah Blakeston, *A Gem of Yorkshire Valleys* (n. d.).
52   William Bounas, *Boston Spa – A Poem* reprinted by the Village Society (1965).
53   Kathleen Denbigh, *A Hundred British Spas* (1981), 216–9.

Chapter 9   *Victorian Finale*

1   Granville, I, xxi–xxv.
2   Granville, I, xii, II, 316.
3   MA, 23 Jul. 1860, 8 Mar. 1873.
4   J. Myerscough, 'The pursuit of happiness abroad', Anglo-American Conference of Historians, 6 Jul. 1979.
5   A. Savidge, *Royal Tunbridge Wells* (1977), 111, 114–5, 118, 125, 162–3.
6   BCG, 16 Jun. 1886.
7   Joseph Wechsberg, *The Lost World of the Great Spas* (1979), 59, 70, 76; G. Battiscombe, *Queen Alexandra* (1969), 89, 113, 186; G. Brook-Shepherd, *Uncle of Europe* (1975), 214–5.
8   Granville, II, 104–11; White, *Lincolnshire* (1842), 454–5.
9   Kelly, *Lincs.* (1905), 619.
10   White, *Lincs.* 455; Granville, II, 106, 116–7.
11   Granville, II, 116.
12   H.D. Martineau, 'Woodhall Spa', *Lincolnshire Life*, VIII, no. 3 (May 1968), 31; Kelly, *Lincs.*, 619; White, *Lincs*, 341.
13   White, *Lincs*, 455; Kelly, *Lincs.*(1855), 256; T.D. Luke, *Spas and Health Resorts of the British Isles* (1919), 108, *London & Provincial Medical Directory* (1849), 229, 230, 262.
14   Kelly, *Lincs.* (1905), 619; White, *Lincs.* (1856); *Imperial Gazette* (1818–25), VI, 1111.
15   Kelly, *Lincs.* (1905), 619; *Bath Chronicle*, 18 Mar., 13 May 1886.
16   S.S. Roden, *Droitwich and its Baths* (1887), 7, 11–12; W.T. Whitley, *The Story of Droitwich* (1923), 52; Pevsner, *Worcestershire* (1968), 138.
17   Pevsner, *Worcs.* 134–7.
18   *Medical Register* (1863), 175.
19   Pevsner, *Worcs.* 136; C. A. Lascelles, *Directory and Gazetteer of the City of Worcester and its Neighbourhood* (1851), 136.
20   S. Lewis, *Topographical Dictionary*, 7th edn (1849), II, 93.

21 L.D.B.,*Handbook to Droitwich and its Neighbourhood* (1875), 25–9; BC 25 Feb. 1886.
22 M. Lamb, 'The house that salt built', *The Lady*, 31 Oct. 1968, 672–3.
23 VCH, *Worcester*, III, 72.
24 Whitley, *The Story of Droitwich*, 54–5.
25 L.D.B., *Handbook to Droitwich*, 63.
26 T.H. Littlebury, *Directory of the County of Worcester* (1873), 173–4, 187–8; Pevsner, *Worcs.*, 135.
27 Lamb, 'The house that salt built', 672–673; Pevsner, *Worcs.*, 138; Kelly, *Worcs.* (1911), 76.
28 Pevsner, *Worcs.*, 136; Luke, *Spas and Health Resorts*, 111.
29 J. Haddon, *Bath* (1973), 176.
30 F. Curtis, *Guide Through and Round Bath* (1873), 37–9, 60; Haddon, *Bath*, 128; Kelly, *Somerset & Gloucester* (1906), 42.
31 Curtis, *Guide Through and Round Bath*, 55, 59,60.
32 BC, 22 Apr., 6, 13 May 1886; BCG, 7 Apr., 12 May 1886.
33 Haddon, *Bath*, 179; Kelly *Som. & Glos.*, 49.
34 Haddon, *Bath*, 168–9, 182.
35 *Dictionary of British Architects* (1907), 254; Haddon, *Bath*, 175, 178; R.E. Peach, *Objects of Interest in the City of Bath* (1864); BC, 11 Feb. 1886; Kelly, *Som. & Glos.*, 41.
36 Kelly, *Som. & Glos.*, 47, 48.
37 Haddon,*Bath*, 180; Kelly,*Som. & Glos.*, 42; A. Ball, *Yesterday in Bath* (1972), 64.
38 Haddon, *Bath*, 12.
39 J.W. Morris (ed.), *Handbook to Bath* (1888), 96.
40 Kelly, *Som. & Glos.*, 49.
41 Kelly, *Som. & Glos.*, 41; Haddon, *Bath*, 151.
42 Curtis, *Guide Through and Round Bath*, 40–2; Kelly *Som. & Glos.*, 47.
43 Curtis, *Guide Through and Round Bath*, 33–5; Haddon, *Bath*, 174.
44 Kelly, *Som. & Glos.*, 47; Curtis, *Guide Through and Round Bath*, 57–8; T.D. Young, *Music's Great Days* (1936), 69.
45 BCG, 7 Apr. 1886.
46 Young, *Music's Great Days*, 69.
47 BC, 4 Mar., 15 Apr. 1886; BCG 12, 19 May 1886; 14 & 15 Vict. c. xxviii & c. xxiv.
48 Young, *Music's Great Days*, 69.
49 BC, 21 Jan. 1886.
50 BC, Jan. 1886; Kelly *Som. & Glos.*, 54.
51 Curtis, *Guide Through and Round Bath*, 58.
52 J. Patmore, 'Harrogate and Knaresborough: a study in urban development', Oxford Univ. D.Phil. thesis, f. 32.
53 B. Jennings, *A History of Harrogate and Knaresborough* (1970), 430.
54 Patmore, 'Harrogate and Knaresborough', ff. 203–5.
55 Jennings, *A History of Harrogate and Knaresborough*, 424.
56 Patmore, f. 209.
57 Jennings, *A History of Harrogate and Knaresborough* 425.
58 Patmore, 'Harrogate and Knaresborough', f. 209.
59 BSJ, 20 Mar., 10 Apr. 1874; Jennings, *A History of Harrogate and Knares-*

borough, 406, 407; H.H. Walker, *History of Harrogate under the Improvement Commissioners* (1986), *passim*.

60 W. Grainge, *The History and Topography of Harrogate and the Forest of Knaresborough* (1871), 124, 194.

61 Patmore, 'Harrogate and Knaresborough', ff. 196, 199.

62 Jennings, *A History of Harrogate and Knaresborough*, 313–4.

63 Jennings, *A History of Harrogate and Knaresborough*, 408.

64 BSJ, 6 Feb., 2 Apr. 1874.

65 Grainge, *History and Topography of Harrogate*, 153–4.

66 Jennings, *A History of Harrogate and Knaresborough*, 409.

67 BSJ, 20 Mar. 1874.

68 Jennings, *A History of Harrogate and Knaresborough*, 419; BSJ, 6 Feb., 20 Mar. 1874.

69 Jennings, *A History of Harrogate and Knaresborough*, 420.

70 Jennings, *A History of Harrogate and Knaresborough*, 408; BSJ, 6 Mar. 1874.

71 Jennings, *A History of Harrogate and Knaresborough*, 410–11.

72 Grainge, *History and Topography of Harrogate*, 262; Jennings, *A History of Harrogate and Knaresborough*, 416; Kelly, *W.R. Yorks* (1927), 429–30.

73 Jennings, *A History of Harrogate and Knaresborough*, 416.

74 Jennings, *A History of Harrogate and Knaresborough*, 418; Grainge, *History and Topography of Harrogate*, 152; BSJ, 13 Feb. 1874.

75 Young, *Music's Great Days*, 34, 36–7; Jennings, *A History of Harrogate and Knaresborough*, 418–419.

76 Young, *Music's Great Days*, 66; Jennings, *A History of Harrogate and Knaresborough*, 419–20.

77 Kelly, *W. R. Yorks.*; Jennings, *A History of Harrogate and Knaresborough*, 412, 417.

78 Patmore, 'Harrogate and Knaresborough', 189.

79 56 & 57 Vict. c.ccix.

80 Pevsner, *West Riding* (1959),251; Jennings, *A History of Harrogate and Knaresborough*, 415.

81 Jennings, *A History of Harrogate and Knaresborough*, 417; Kelly, *W.R. Yorks.*, 429–30; Patmore, 'Harrogate and Knaresborough', f. 126.

82 Jennings, *A History of Harrogate and Knaresborough*, 421; Young, *Music's Great Days*, 40, 53.

83 Jennings, *A History of Harrogate and Knaresborough*, 421–2, 428–9, Patmore, 'Harrogate and Knaresborough', f. 187.

84 Patmore, 'Harrogate and Knaresborough', f. 196; Pevsner, *West Riding*, 251.

85 Jennings, *A History of Harrogate and Knaresborough*, 313, 315–16.

86 A. & C. Black, *Guide to Harrogate* (1876), 7–8.

87 Pevsner, *West Riding*, 251–2; Jennings, *A History of Harrogate and Knaresborough*, 428; Patmore, 'Harrogate and Knaresborough', f. 197.

88 Jennings, *A History of Harrogate and Knaresborough*, 420, 427.

89 Jennings, *A History of Harrogate and Knaresborough*, 426–7.

90 J. Patmore, *Atlas of Harrogate* (1967), 19; see Appendix 4.

91 Patmore, 'Harrogate and Knaresborough', f. 201; Patmore, *Atlas*; Jennings, *A History of Harrogate and Knaresborough*, 399, 429.

92 Young, *Music's Great Days*, 55.

93 J.C. Rutter, 'Scarborough 1866–1966: the holiday resort', in M. Edwards (ed.) *Scarborough* (1966), 75–6.

94 J.C. Rutter, *Historic Harrogate* (1966), 26.

95 Young, *Music's Great Days*, 83.

96 J.H. Martin, 'Scarborough 1766–1866: a century of expansion', in M. Edwards (ed.) *Scarborough* (1966), 68; Pevsner, *North Riding* (1966), 332.

97 Martin, 'Scarborough', 74.

98 VCH, *Yorkshire: North Riding*, 540; Young, *Music's Great Days*, 84.

99 Pevsner, *North Riding*, 331–2; Kelly, *N. & E. R. Yorks.*, (1905), 300; Rutter, 'Scarborough 1866–1966', 80; Young, *Music's Great Days*, 84, 88.

100 Young, *Music's Great Days*, 91–4, 103.

101 Rutter, 'Scarborough 1866–1966', 75, 78.

102 Rutter, 'Scarborough 1866–1966', 78, 81.

103 Rutter, 'Scarborough 1866–1966', 81; Kelly, *N. & E. R. Yorks.*, (1905), 302.

104 Addison, *English Spas* (1951), 93; L. du Garde Peach, *John Smedley of Matlock and his Hydro* (n.d.), 24; *The London and Provincial Medical Directory* (1847), 56.

105 B.S. Smith, *A History of Malvern* (1978 edn), 202.

106 Granville, I, 385–6; White, *W. R. Yorks.* (1838), II, 510–11; Lewis, *Topographical Dictionary*, II, 501.

107 Granville, I, 389–90; J. Johnson, *Principal Mineral Waters of England* (1843), 32.

108 *Dictionary of British Architects*, 728.

109 *Buxton Herald*, 7 Sep. 1843.

110 MA, 5 Jul. 1856, 18 Jul. 1857; Jackson, *Handbook for Tourists in Yorkshire* (1891), 185; Pevsner, *West Riding*, 277.

111 Anon., *Illustrated Guide to Ilkley, Oyley and Wharfedale* (1898), 9–10; *Census Returns*, 1873.

112 Kelly, *W. R. Yorks.*, 616.

113 White, *W. R. Yorks.* (1828), 510; Lewis, *Topographical Dictionary*, II, 501; Anon., *Illustrated Guide to Ilkley*, 6, 10.

114 Anon., *Illustated Guide*, advert.

115 Kelly, *W. R. Yorks.* (1927), 616.

116 Anon., *Official Guide to Ilkley*, (1969), 6; Jackson, *Handbook for Tourists*, 185; A. and C. Black, *Guide to England & Wales* (1879), 523; Anon., *Illustrated Guide to Ilkley*.

117 Anon., *Illustrated Guide to Ilkley*; Jackson, *Handbook for Tourists*, advert. facing xi.

118 Du Garde Peach, *John Smedley of Matlock*, 1, 4, 6, 8, 15; R. MacLelland, 'John Smedley of Matlock', *Archives of Medical Hydrology*, XII, 229–30.

119 Du Garde Peach, *John Smedley of Matlock*, 26; T. Marchington, 'Development of Buxton and Matlock since 1800', London Univ. MA thesis, ff. 107–8.

120 Du Garde Peach, *John Smedley of Matlock*, 29, 37, 44; MacLelland, 'John Smedley of Matlock', 230.

121 White, *Derby* (1857), 431; Marchington, 'Development of Buxton and Matlock', f. 106.

122 White, *Derby*, 429; Marchington, 'Development of Buxton and Matlock', f. 103.

123 White, *Derby*, 437–438; M. Black, *Guide Book Advertiser* (1880), 59.

124 Marchington, 'Development of Buxton and Matlock', f. 106.

125 Du Garde Peach, *John Smedley of Matlock*, 30, 40, 46–52, 60–62, 64; Marchington, 'Development of Buxton and Matlock', f. 150.

126 Du Garde Peach, *John Smedley of Matlock*, 109, 110, 122, 126, 136, 148, 149.

127 Du Garde *John Smedley of Matlock*, 143, 166.

128 Du Garde Peach, *John Smedley of Matlock*, 108.

129 Kelly, *Derbyshire* (1899), 74–80;

130 *Buxton and the Peak District*, Ward, Lock, (8th edn. 1900), xxi. xiii–xv; Kelly *Derbyshire*, 69.

131 R.G. Heape, *Buxton under the Dukes of Devonshire* (1948), 108.

132 R.G. Heape, *Buxton under the Dukes of Devonshire*, 77, 106.

133 I.E. Burton, *Historic Buxton and its Spa Era*, 13; Pevsner, *Leics & Rutland* (1960), 117.

134 H.E. Milner, *The Art and Practice of Landscapr Gardening (1890)*.

135 Kelly, *Derbyshire*, 70.

136 Pevsner, *Derbyshire* (1979), 112.

137 Young, *Music's Great Days*, 182–3.

138 Kelly, *Derbyshire*, 70–1; Heape, *Buxton under the Dukes of Devonshire*, 39,123.

139 Heape, *Buxton under the Dukes of Devonshire*, 69, 71; Marchington, 'Development of Buxton and Matlock', 135–6.

140 J. Goodacre, *Buxton Old and New* (1928), 67.

141 E. Lee, *Baths and Watering Places* (1848), 31.

142 Smith, *A History of Malvern*, 195; E. Jenkins, *Dr.Gully* (1972), 16.

143 Jenkins, *Dr. Gully*, 17; *Malvern Hills District Official Guide* (1979), 16; Smith, 197.

144 *Buxton Herald*, 7 Sep. 1842.

145 MA, 13 Jun. 1857, 14 Jan. 1865.

146 H.W. Lamb, *The Visitor's Guide to Malvern* (1862), 65.

147 Smith, *A History of Malvern*, 198; MA, 24 Oct. 1857.

148 Smith, *A History of Malvern*, 201.

149 E.C. Cross, *Handbook to Malvern* (1862), 65.

150 Smith, *A History of Malvern*, 206.

151 Smith, *A History of Malvern*, 196, 199, 201.

152 MA, 9 Jun., 7 Jul. 1860, 2 Sep. 1865.

153 *The Imperial Hotel Handbook to Malvern* (1875), 3.

154 Cross, *Handbook to Malvern*, 611.

155 MA, 5, 14 Jul., 1 Nov. 1856, 20 Jun. 1857; Smith, *A History of Malvern*, 202.

156 MA, 18 Jul. 1857, 18 Aug. 1860; Smith, *A History of Malvern*, 201, 202.

157 R.B. Grindrod, *Malvern Past and Present*, 106; MA, 24 Oct. 1857, 7. Jan., 2 Sep. 1865; Smith, *A History of Malvern*, 202.

158 Cross, *Handbook to Malvern*, 125; Norman May, *Guide to Malvern* (1820), last page.

159 MA 13, 27 Jun. 1857, 7 Jan.1865, 19 Apr. 1873.

160 Smith, *A History of Malvern*, 249; MA, 19 Apr. 1873.

161 Smith, *A History of Malvern*, 214–15, 291–2; Lamb, *Visitor's Guide to Malvern*, 5.

162 Smith, *A History of Malvern*, 213–14.

163 MA, 26 Sep. 1857, 22 Sep. 1860.
164 MA, 22 Mar. 1873.
165 Smith, *A History of Malvern*, 217; MA, 29 Mar. 1873.
166 MA, 21 Jun. 1856, 22 Feb., 22 Mar., 10 May 1873.
167 MA, 3 Nov. 1860, 11 Jan., 10 May 1873.
168 Smith, *A History of Malvern*, 218.
169 MA, 7 Jan., 26 May 1860; Smith, *A History of Malvern*, 202–6.
170 Pevsner, *Worcs.*, 169; Smith, *A History of Malvern*, 206–7, 219.
171 Cross, *Handbook to Malvern* 17; Lamb, *Visitor's Guide to Malvern*, 7; Smith, *A History of Malvern*, 292.
172 Pevsner, *Worcs.*, 170.
173 MA, 7 Jan. 1865.
174 *Imperial Hotel Handbook* (1875), 3–8.
175 MA, 7 Jan., 16 Sep. 1865.
176 Smith, *A History of Malvern*, 208; MA, 30 Sep. 1865.
177 MA, 3 Mar., 16 Jun., 7 Jul. 1860.
178 MA, 28 Jan. 1865.
179 MA, 30 Sep. 1865.
180 MA, 3 Mar. 1860.
181 Grindrod, *Malvern Past and Present*
182 MA, 29 Mar., 20 Sep. 1873.
183 MA, 4 Nov. 1865.
184 MA, 21 Jun. 1856; C.N. Godwin, *The Malverns* (Mate's Illustrated. Guides, 2nd edn, 1901), advert.; Smith, *A History of Malvern*, 293.
185 MA, 21, 28 Jun. 1856, 20 Jun., 4 Jul. 1857, 26 May 1860, 18 Feb., 21 Jun. 1865; Smith, *A History of Malvern*, 234.
186 MA, 9 Sep. 1865; Smith, *A History of Malvern*, 234.
187 MA, 19 Jul. 1852, 22 Aug. 1857.
188 Smith, *A History of Malvern*, 239.
189 Smith, *A History of Malvern*, 208–9; MA, 21 Jun. 1856.
190 MA, 2, 30 Jun. 1860.
191 MA, 14, 21 Jul. 1860.
192 MA, 28 Jul. 1860, 7 Jan., 23 Sep. 1865.
193 Grindrod, *Malvern*, 107.
194 Smith, *A History of Malvern*, 207.
195 Smith, *A History of Malvern*, 247; MA, 27 Oct. 1860.
196 MA, 29 Oct. 1860, 21, 28 Jan. 1865.
197 MA, 28 Jan. 1865, 19 Apr. 1873; Smith, *A History of Malvern*, 247–8.
198 MA, 12 Jul., 9 Aug. 1856, 25 Jul. 1857, 7 Jul. 1860; Smith, *A History of Malvern*, 219–20, 245.
199 MA, 12 Jul. 1856, 23 Jul. 1857; Smith, *A History of Malvern*, 244.
200 MA, 30 Jun. 1860; Pevsner, *Worcs.*, 170; Smith, *A History of Malvern*, 246.
201 Smith, 245; MA, 5 Apr. 1873; *The Malvern Encyclopaedia and Directory* (1950), A2.
202 MA, 2 Jun. 1860.
203 MA, 7, 28 Jan., 18 Mar. 1865.
204 Smith, *A History of Malvern*, 210–11.
205 Smith, *A History of Malvern*, 207; Pevsner, *Worcs.*, 170; MA, 17 May 1873.

206 MA, 1 Aug. 1857.
207 Smith, *A History of Malvern*, 241; MA, 7 Jan. 1865.
208 MA, 21 Jan. 23 Sep. 1865.
209 Smith, *A History of Malvern*, 240–1, 256.
210 MA, 8, 15, 29 Mar., 5, 19 Apr. 1873.
211 MA, 22, 29 Mar., 10 May 1873.
212 Smith, *A History of Malvern*, 211, 249.
213 Smith, *A History of Malvern*, 234–5; Pevsner, *Worcs.*, 169.
214 Kelly, *Worcs.* (1912), 178.
215 G.A. Hart, *History of Cheltenham*, (2nd edn, 1981), 344–6, 348,349; Granville, II, 284.
216 J.A. Goding, *History of Cheltenham* (1863), 600, 624, 639.
217 Goding, *History of Cheltenham*, 613, 623.
218 Goding, *History of Cheltenham*, 603, 604, 610.
219 GRO D1950, Agg-Gardner MS, X6.
220 Goding, *History of Cheltenham*, 595, 609.
221 Goding, *History of Cheltenham*, 635.
222 Goding, *History of Cheltenham*, 648; Hart, *History of Cheltenham*, 330–8, 346–7.
223 Goding, *History of Cheltenham*, 634–6.
224 M.C. Morgan, *Cheltenham College: The First Hundred Years* (1968), 4, 10, 14.
225 A.K. Clarke, *A History of the Cheltenham Ladies' College 1853–79* (3rd edn, 1979), 22–4, 43, 46, 58.
226 Goding, *History of Cheltenham*, 64.
227 N. May, *Guide to Cheltenham and the County of Gloucerster* (1884), 18; Kelly, *Som. & Gloucs.* (1931), 71.
228 Hart, *History of Cheltenham*, 359; Kelly *Som. & Gloucs.* (1906), 64.
229 Patmore, *Atlas of Harrogate*, 3; T.D. Luke, *Spas and Health Resorts of the British Isles* (1919), 128.
230 T.H. Lloyd, 'Royal Leamington Spa', in M.A. Simpson and T.H. Lloyd, *Middle-Class Housing in Britain* 121–124.
231 J.H. Drew, *The Book of Royal Leamington Spa* (1978), 93.
232 Pevsner & Wedgwood, *Warwickshire*, 335.
233 L.S. Bolton, *Unknown Leamington* (1932), 21.
234 H.G. Clarke, *Royal Leamington Spa* (1947), 21.
235 Luke, *Spas and Health Resorts*, 115, 117; Kelly, *Warwickshire* (1900), 144.
236 S.H. Drew, *Village into Town* (Leamington Library, 2nd edn, 1980), 19; Kelly, *Dir. Warwicks.*, 143; Luke, *Spas and Health Resorts*, 116.
237 R. Pelton, *Guide to Tunbridge Wells* (1893), 50; A. Savidge, *Royal Tunbridge Wells* (1975), 162, 177, 207.
238 Savidge, *Royal Tunbridge Wells*, 177.
239 St John Colbran, *Guide and Visitor's Handbook to Tunbridge Wells* (1881), 146, 150.
240 Pelton, *Guide to Tunbridge Wells*, 97, 99 f.n.; Savidge, *Royal Tunbridge Wells*, 136.
241 Pelton, *Guide to Tunbridge Wells*, 95–6.
242 Pelton, *Guide to Tunbridge Wells*, 142; Colbran, *Guide and Visitor's Handbook*, 160.

243 Colbran, *Guide and Visitor's Handbook*, 148, 582, 584; Pelton, *Guide to Tunbridge Wells*, 100, 104; J. Newman, *West Kent and the Weald* (1976), 583; Kelly, *Kent* (1891), 639.

244 Savidge, *Royal Tunbridge Wells*, 137, 139; Kelly, *Kent* (1891), 640; Luke, *Spas and Health Resorts*, 122.

245 Savidge, *Royal Tunbridge Wells*, 170–1; Pelton, *Guide to Tunbridge Wells*, 581.

Chapter 10   Beyond England's Borders

1 *The Private Life of the Queen by One of Her Majesty's Servants* (1897); Elizabeth Longford, *Victoria R.I.* (1964), 248, 265–7; L.W. Cowie, *Sir Robert Peel* (1996), 12, 168.

2 A.B. and M.D. Anderson, *Vanishing Spas* (1974), 88–100; *The Spas of Britain* (British Spa Federation, 1922), 103–14.

3 Anderson and Anderson, *Vanishing Spas*, 74–87; Pigot, *Scotland* (1837); *Ordnance Gazetteer of Scotland* (1891); T.D. Luke, *Spas and Health Resorts of the British Isles* (1919), 164–74.

4 E.S. Turner, *Taking the Cure* (1967), 125, 245; F. Alderson, *The Inland Resorts and Spas of Britain* (1973).

5 British Library, Harley MSS, IV, 190.

6 D. Hartley, *Water in England* (1964), 59.

7 F. Alderson, *The Inland Resorts and Spas of Britain*, 176–7; W.A.R. Thomson, *Spas That Heal* (1978), 27, 29, 138, 140, 142; Kathleen Denbigh, *A Hundred British Spas* (1981), 201.

8 Turner, *Taking the Cure*, 126, 180, 190; Alderson, *Inland Resorts and Spas*, 155–6; Thomson, *Spas That Heal*, 29, 157–8.

9 Alderson, *Inland Resorts and Spas*, 150–1.

10 Guy Christie, *Crieff Hydro 1868–1968* (1968); Ian Bradley, 'Crieff Hydro, Perthshire', *History Today*, XL, (1990), 62.

11 Alderson, *Inland Resorts and Spas*, 159–60.

12 Turner, *Taking the Cure*, 200.

13 *Gloucester Journal*, 4 Sep. 1774.

14 BJ, 24 Apr. 1815.

15 *Hereford Journal*, 12 Aug. 1818; S. Lewis, *Topographical Dictionary of Wales* (1840); K.O. Morgan, *Rebirth of a Nation – Wales 1880–1980* (1981); Richard Haslam, *Buildings of Wales – Powys* (1979); E. Hubberd, *Buildings of Wales – Clwd* (1986); Pryse Hardbook, *The Radnorshire and Breconshire Mineral Springs* (1872)

16 Ex inf. E.M. Evans, Esq.

17 W.J. and J.O. Bufton, *Illustrated Guide to Llandrindod Wells (1906), 21–2, 27–8; Luke, *Spas and Health Resorts*, 137–45; I.E. Jones, 'The Swydd Neithon enclosures and the development of Llandrindod Wells', Radnorshire Society Transactions (1973), 24; Denbigh, *A Hundred British Spas*, 249–56.

18 J. Haslip, *Life of Lady Hester Stanhope* (1934).

19 *Kilvert's Diary*, ed. William Plomer (1971), III, 168–9.

20 Cledwyn Hughes, *A Wanderer in Wales* (1949), 40.

21 Alderson, *Inland Resorts and Spas*, 112–13, 115–16; Thomson, *Spas That Heal*, 27, 122; Denbigh, *A Hundred British Spas*, 246–9.

22   Alderson, *Inland Resorts and Spas*, 112–14; Thomson, *Spas That Heal*, 27, 29, 121, 123; Denbigh, *A Hundred British Spas*, 242–5; A.G. Bradley, *Llanwyrt Wells and its Neighbourhood* (n.d.).

23   Hartley, *Water in England*, 62.

24   Alderson, *Inland Resorts and Spas*, 112, 114; Thomson, *Spas That Heal*, 27, 29, 122; Denbigh, *A Hundred British Spas*, 242–5.

25   Alun Llywelwn-Williams, *Crwydro Arfon* (1959), 65.

26   Hartley, *Water in England*, 60.

27   Alderson, *Inland Resorts and Spas*, 118; Thomson, *Spas That Heal*, 11, 28, 29, 122; Denbigh, *A Hundred British Spas*, 243; *Trefriw Chalybeate Wells* (Trefriw Chalybeate Wells, Ltd., 1908).

28   Alderson, *Inland Resorts and Spas*, 97.

29   *Hibernian Gazetteer* (1835); *Historic Buildings, Groups of Buildings, Areas of Architectural Importance in the Towns and Villages of Mid-Down: Hillsborough, Dromore, Dromara, Ballynahinch, The Spa, Drumaness and Saintfield* (Ulster Architectural Heritage Society, 1974).

30   *Report of a Committee of the Royal Medical and Chirurgical Society on Baths and Watering Places*, II (1902); Alderson, *Inland Resorts and Spas*, 28.

31   Luke, *Spas and Health Resorts*, 292.

32   Catherine Day, *Southwest Ireland* (1995), 190.

33   Evelyn Bolster, *A History of Mallow* (1971).

34   *Journal of the Royal Society of Antiquaries*, XXII (1892), 133, 440.

Chapter 11   The Twentieth Century

1   F. Alderson, *The Inland Resorts and Spas of Britain* (1973), 151–3; Thomson, *Spas That Heal*, 210–11; Denbigh, *A Hundred British Spas*, 14–15; B. Cunliffe, *The City of Bath* (1986), 168–75; Michael McGarvie, 'The ups and downs of Bath', *The Field*, 259, 6688 (25 March 1981), 498–9; Roger Rolls, 'The rise and fall of Bath waters', *The Society for the Social History of Medicine* (Bulletin 34, Jun. 1984), 17–18.

2   Alderson, *The Inland Resorts and Spas*, 170; Thomson, *Spas That Heal*, 71–9; Denbigh, *A Hundred British Spas*, 168–9; Lyndon F. Cave, *Royal Leamington Spa* (1988), 182; Vivian Bird, *A Brief History of Royal Leamington Spa* (1992); *Leamington Week by Week* (magazine).

3   Kelly, *Gloucester* (1931), 73.

4   Alderson, *The Inland Resorts and Spas*, 157–9, Thomson, *Spas That Heal*, 57–60; Denbigh, *A Hundred British Spas*, 115–19; G. Hart, *A History of Cheltenham* (1965), 173.

5   Alderson, *The Inland Resorts and Spas*, 180–1; Denbigh, *A Hundred British Spas*, 23–5; A. Savidge, *Royal Tunbridge Wells* (1977), 183–204; 'Calverley Park, Tunbridge Wells', *Country Life* (18 May 1969); J. Hone, 'Tunbridge Wells', *The Listener* (23 Dec. 1971).

6   Kelly, *Worcestershire* (1912), 178.

7   Denbigh, *A Hundred British Spas*, 183; Vincent Waite, *Malvern Country* (1968), 127–9.

8   Pevsner, *Worcestershire* (1978), 136; M. Lamb. 'The house that salt built', *The Lady* (1968), 673; Kelly, *Worcs.* 75–6

9   Alderson, *The Inland Resorts and Spas*, 91, 161–2; Thomson, *Spas That Heal*, 64, 210–11; Denbigh, *A Hundred British Spas*, 237.

10 Kelly, *Lincolnshire* (1905), 619–21; Anon., *Woodhall Spa 1811–1911* (1912).

11 Kelly, *Handbook to the Titled, Landed and Official Classes* (1924), 1592; H.D. Martineau, 'Woodhall Spa', *Lincolnshire Life*, ffiii, 3 (May 1968), 31–3.

12 *Ex inf.* Messrs W. Booth, D. Dowse and J. Lockett.

13 Kelly, *Lincs.* 620–1; T.D. Luke, *Spas and Health Resorts of the British Isles* (1919), 107–9.

14 Alderson, *The Inland Resorts and Spas*, 105, 107, 182–3; Thomson, *Spas That Heal*, 110–20; Denbigh, *A Hundred British Spas*, 227–32; P.J.N. Havins, *The Spas of England* (1976), 70–71; *Woodhall Spa, Coningsby, Tattershall and Horncastle* (East Lindsey Distruct Council, n.d.), 6–7.

15 Alderson, *The Inland Resorts and Spas*, 175–6; Addison, *English Spas* (1951), 91–3; Denbigh, *A Hundred British Spas*, 195–6; *The Matlocks and their Past* (Derbyshire County Library, 1977).

16 R.G. Heape, *Buxton under the Dukes of Devonshire* (1948), 123, 125.

17 *Buxton* (Ward Lock, 8th edn, 1900), xi; Pevsner, *Derbyshire* (1979), 117.

18 I.E. Burton, *Historic Buxton and its Spa Era* (1971), 15.

19 G.M. Young, *Music's Great Days*, (1936), 182–3.

20 Alderson, *The Inland Resorts and Spas*, 157; Thomson, *Spas That Heal*, 80–92; Denbigh, *A Hundred British Spas*, 44–6; Leach, *The Book of Buxton*, 78; Selwyn Jebson, *The Crescent at Buxton, Conservation in Action* (Borough of High Peak, 1975); *Historic Buxton and its Spa Era (Buxton Corporation, 1971)*.

21 Alderson, *The Inland Resorts and Spas*, 166; Thomson, *Spas That Heal*, 101–7; Denbigh, *A Hundred British Spas*, 277–8; *Harrogate and District* (North Yorkshire Council, 1995).

22 Luke, *Spas and Health Resorts*, 180–2; Denbigh, *A Hundred British Spas*, 141–2

Chapter 12   Conclusion

1   'Accounts of the Overseers of Box', WAM, *xlv*, 344; J. Lane, 'Administration of an Eighteenth-Century Warwickshire Parish', *Dugdale Soc.*, no. 21 (1973), 21.

2   *Census of England and Wales, General Report, 1871*, IV, table 41

3   G. Weisz, 'Water cures and science', *Bulletin of the History of Medicine* (1990), 393.

4   Weisz, 'Watercure', 394; D. Hartley, 'A sword in a madman's hand, 1570–1870,' *Medical History*, x, 48; N.G. Coley, 'Physicians, chemists and the analysis of mineral waters', *Medical History of Waters and Spas* (ed. Roy Porter), Medical History Supplement no. 10 (1990), 56–66; Christopher Hamlin, *A Science of Impurity* (1951).

5   *The Cambridge Social History of Britain*, ed. F.M.L. Thompson, 2 vols (1992), II, 267.

6   G.R. Scott, *The Story of Baths and Bathing* (1939), 173; Roy Porter, *Medical History of Waters and Spas*, xi.

7   R. Price, 'Hydropathy in England 1840–1870', *Medical History*, xxc (1981), 269–80; P.J. Waller, *Town, City and Nation, England 1850–1914* (1983), 134.

8   F. Alderson, *The Inland Resorts and Spas of Britain* (1973), 11–12.
9   *Cambridge Social History*, II, 267; Alderson, *Inland Resorts and Spas*, 12–13.
10 A.L. Croutier, *Taking the Waters – Spirit, Art and Sensuality* (1992), 151; Alderson, *Inland Resorts and Spas*, 12.
11 J.A.R. Pimlott, *The Englishman's Holiday* (1976), 256.
12 Joseph Wichberg, *The Lost World of the Great Spas* (1979), 27.
13 Croutier, 151, 155, 173, 176; D. Hartley, *Water in England*, 72.
14 *The British Spas Federation Newsletter* (July/August 1995).

Select Bibliography

Primary Sources

MANUSCRIPT
Bath Reference Library, Bath City Council Minutes (typescript).
Gloucestershire Record Office, Records of the Improvement Commission 1852–1862; D123/F4, Winstone Letters.
Leeds Archive Office, Gascoigne Papers.
Warwickshire Record Office, Heber Percy MS 1707, Greatheed.

PRINTED

Newspapers

Bath and Cheltenham Gazette
Bath Chronicle
Bath Journal
Boston Spa Journal (Wetherby)
Buxton Herald
Cheltenham Chronicle
Cheltenham Journal
Dorset County Chronicle
Gloucester Journal
Harrogate Advertiser
Herefordshire Journal
Leamington Chronicle
Leeds Intelligencer
Malvern Advertiser
Salisbury and Winchester Journal
Suffolk Chronicle
Warwick Advertiser
York Courant
Yorkshire Gazette

Books and guides
Accum, F., *Guide to the Chalybeate Spring of Thetford* (1819).
Amsinck, P., *Tunbridge Wells and its Neighbourhood* (1810).
Anon., *A Companion to the Watering and Bathing Places of England* (1800).
Anon., *A Guide of Handbook to the Shap Spa* (1844).
Anon., *Handy Guide to the English Lakes and Shap Spa* (1881).
Anon., *A Facsimile from the 1813 Edition of the Guide Book for Brighton, Worthing, Littlehampton, Bognor* (Templer Books, York).
Anon., *Leamington as a Village* (1847).
Anon., *History and Description of Ashby-de-la-Zouch* (1852).
Anon., *Watering Places of England* (1853).
Baker, J., *The New Guide to Bristol and Clifton* (1894).
Bristoliensis, *The Bristol Guide* (4th edn, 1815).
Britton, J., *Descriptive Sketches of Tunbridge Wells and the Calverley Estate* (1832).
Board of Health Reports.
Chambers, J.A., *General History of Malvern* (1817).
Chilcott, I.E., *New Guide to Bristol, Clifton and the Hotwells* (1826).
Clifford, J., *The Directory or the Ancient and Present State of Tunbridge Wells* (1816).
Clifford, J., *Descriptive Guide of Tunbridge Wells* (1818).
Deacon, T., *The History of the Village of Willoughby in the County of Warwick* (1828).
Dugdale, James, *The New British Traveller*, 4 vols (1819).
Evans, John, *An Excursion to Brighton, A Visit to Tunbridge Wells and a Trip to Scotland* (1821).
Evans, T., *History of Tenbury* (1840).
Field, W., *An Historical and Descriptive Account of . . . Warwick and the Neighbouring Spa of Leamington* (1815).
Fordyce, W., *History and Antiquities of the County Palatine of Durham* (1857).
Gill, Upcott, *Inland Watering Places* (1891).
Grainge, W., *The History and Topography of Harrogate and the Forest of Knaresborough* (1871).
Granville, A.B., *The Spas of England and Principal Sea-Bathing Places* ([1841] 2 vols, ed. G. Martin 1971).
Hextall, W. and J. Hextall, *History and Description of Ashby-de-la-Zouche* (1852).
Hunter, J., *South Yorkshire* (1831).
Jewitt, A., *A History of Buxton* (1816).
Johnson, J., *Excursions to the Principal Mineral Waters of Engalnd* (1843).
Kaye, W.J., *Records of Harrogate* (1922).
Keene, S., *Improved Bath Directory* 1824).
Knight, T., *History of the Dorton Chalybeate near Brill, Bucks.* (1833).
Lamb, H.W., *The Visitor's Guide to Malvern* (1862).
Lee, E., *Cheltenham and its Resources* (1851)
Loudon, C., *A Practical Dissertation on the Waters of Leamington Spa* (1831).
Meyler, E.W., *Original Bath Guide* (1854).
Moncrieff, W.T., *The Visitor's New Guide to the Spa of Leamington Priors* (1818, 1824).
Morris, J.W., (ed.) *The British Association Handbook to Bath* (1888).

Page, T.J., *A Month at Buxton* (13th edn, 1828).
Peach, R.E., *Objects of Interest in the City of Bath* (1864).
Powell, Robert Hutchinson, *A Medical Topography of Tunbridge Wells* (1846).
Roden, S.S., *Droitwich and its Baths* (1887).
Rowe's Illustrated Cheltenham Guide 1850 (1969).
Sheaham, J., *History and Topography of Buckinghamshire* (1862).
Skinner, John, *Journal of a Somerset Rector 1803–1834* (1984).
Southall, M., *Description of Malvern* (1822).
Ruff, H., *History of Cheltenham* (1803).
Thomson, J. Radford, (ed.), *Pelton's Illustrated Guide to Tunbridge Wells* (1881, reprinted 1972).
Wayte, T., *A Descriptive and Historical Guide to Ashby-de-la-Zouche* (1831).
West, W., *The History, Topography and Directory of Warwickshire* (1830).
Westley, F.C., *The New Guide to Cheltenham* (1867).
Williams, G.A., *A Guide to Cheltenham* (1825).
Witts, F.E., (ed. D. Verey), *The Diary of a Cotswold Parson* (1978).
Wright, G.N., *The Historic Guide to Bath* (1864).

Secondary Sources

GENERAL
Addison, William, *English Spas* (1951).
Albert, W., *The Turnpike Road System in England 1663–1840* (1972).
Alderson, Frederick, *The Inland Resorts and Spas of Britain* (1973).
Anderson, A.B. and M.D. Anderson, *Vanishing Spas* (1974).
Ashton, Helen *Parson Austen's Daughter* (1949).
Bird, Anthony, *Roads and Vehicles* (1973).
Carus, W., *Memoirs of the Life of the Revd. Charles Simeon* (1847).
Cayleff, S.E., *Wash and Be Healed* (1987).
Croutier, A.L., *Taking the Waters – Spirit, Art and Sensuality* (1992).
Denbigh, Kathleen, *A Hundred British Spas* (1981).
Dudley, T.B., (ed.) *Memoir of James Bisset* (1904).
Hamlin, Christopher, *A Science of Impurity* (1951).
Hartley, Dorothy *Water in England* (1939).
Havins, Peter J. Neville, *The Spas of England* (1976).
Hembry, Phyllis, *The English Spa 1560–1815: A Social History* (1990).
Jowitt, R.L.P. and D.M. Jowitt, *Discovering Spas* (1971).
Kellett, J.R., *The Impact of Railways on Victorian Cities* (1969).
Luke, T.D., *Spas and Health Resorts of the British Isles* (1919).
Moule, C.G., *Charles Simeon* (1892).
Pevsner, N. et al., *The Buildings of England* (county vols., 1951–).
Pimlott, J.A.R., *The Englishman's Holiday* (1977).
Porter, R., *In Sickness and in Health* (1988).
Porter, R., (ed.) *The Medical History of Waters and Spas* (1990).
Scott, G.R., *The Story of Baths and Bathing* (1939).
Searle, Muriel V., *Spas and Watering Places* (1977).
Spas of Britain, The (Official Handbook of the British Spas Federation).
Strange, W., *The Visitor's Guide to the Watering Places* (1842).

Thompson, F.M.L., (ed.) *The Cambridge Social History of Britain 1750–1950* (1990).

Thomson, William A.R., *Spas that Heal* (1978).

Turner, E.S., *Taking the Cure* (1967).

Victoria Histories of the Counties of England.

Waller, P.J., *Town, City and Nation in England 1850–1914* (1983).

Wear, A., (ed.) *Medicine in Society* (1992).

Wechsberg, Joseph, *The Lost World of the Great Spas* (1979).

County histories, directories and gazetteers by S. Bagshawe and F.J. and W. White.

LOCAL

Arnold, Frederick, *The History of Streatham* (1886).

Baker, J., *A New Guide to Bristol and Clifton* (1894).

Banks, F.R., *The Peak District* (1975).

Barker, Malcolm, *Yorkshire, North Riding* (1977).

Barton, Margaret, *Tunbridge Wells* (1937).

Barton, Margaret and Osbert Sitwell, *Brighton* (1935).

Baxter, E.G., *Dr. Jephson of Leamington Spa* 2 vols (1980).

Beazley, Elizabeth and Peter Howell, *The Companion Guide to North Wales* (1975).

Beck, W.E., *The Cheltenham Training Colleges* (1947).

Bell, Arthur, *PLeasure Town, Cheltenham 1830–1860* (1981).

Bick, D.E., *The Gloucester and Cheltenham Railway* (1968).

Blake, S.T., *Cheltenham's Churches and Chapels* (1979).

Bolster, Evelyn, *A History of Mallow* (1971).

Brace, Keith, *A Portrait of Bristol* (1971).

Bradley, A.G., *Llanwyrt Wells and its Neighbourhood* (n.d.).

Bryan, B., *Matlock* (1903).

Burton, I.E., *Historic Buxton and its Spa Era* (1971).

Cave, Lyndon F., *Royal Leamington Spa* (1988).

Christian, Roy, *The Peak District* (1976).

Christies, Guy, *Crieff Hydro 1868–1968* (1968).

Clarke, A.K., *History of the Cheltenham Ladies' College* (1953).

Clarke, H.G., *Royal Leamington Spa* (1947).

Colbran, St. John, *Guide and Visitors' Handbook to Tunbridge Wells* (1881).

Creed, Lewis G., *Dorton House* (1957).

Cunliffe, B., *The City of Bath* (1986).

Dale, Antony, *History and Architecture of Brighton* (1972).

Dale, Anthony, *Fashionable Brighton 1820–1860* (1970).

Dewhurst, Ian, *Yorkshire Through the Ages* (1975).

Drew, J.H., *The Book of Royal Leamington Spa* (1978).

Dudley, T.B., *A Complete History of Royal Leamington Spa* (1901).

Edwards, M., (ed.) *Scarborough 966–1966* (Scarborough Arch. Soc., 1966).

Edwards, Tudor, *Bristol* (1951).

Firth, J.B., *Railways andByways in Derbyshire* (1905).

Fletcher, J.S., *Harrogate and Knaresborough* (1920).

Foord, Alfred Stanley, *Springs, Streams and Spas of London* (1910).

Fox, Fortescue, *Strathpeffer Spa* (1889).

Gilbert, Edward M., *Brighton, Old Ocean's Bauble* (1954).

Goding, J.A., *History of Cheltenham* (1863).

Goodacre, J., *Buxton Old and New* (1928).

Heape, R. Grundy, *Buxton under the Dukes of Devonshire* (1948).

Haddon, J., *Bath* (1973).

Hart, G.A., *History of Cheltenham* (2nd.ed., 1981).

Hepworth, Martyn, *The Story of the Pantiles* (1956).

Hoole, K., *North-East England, A Regional History of the Railways of Great Britain* (1965).

Howes, J., *Joseph Pitt and Pittville* (1969).

Howes, J., *Rise and Fall of Joseph Pitt* (1976).

Humphris, Edith M., and E.C. Willoughby, *At Cheltenham Spa* (1928).

Ison, W., *The Georgian Buildings of Bath* (1948).

Ison, W., *The Georgian Buildings of Bristol* (1978).

Jackson, T.W., *Handbook for Tourists in Yorkshire* (1891).

Jennings, Bernard, *A History of Harrogate and Knaresborough* (1970).

Jennings, Bernard, *A History of the Wells and Springs of Harrogate* (Harrogate Corporation, 1974).

Little, Brian, *Bath Portrait* (1968).

Little, Brian, *Portrait of Somerset* (1969).

Marshall, E.F.D., *A History of the Southern Railway* (1938).

Melville, Louis, *Brighton: Its History, its Follies and its Fashions* (1909).

Millward, R., and A. Robinson, *The Peak District* (1975).

Morgan, M.C., *Cheltenham College* (1968).

Musgrave, Clifford, *Life in Brighton* (1970).

Neale, R.S., *Bath: A Social History 1680–1850* (1981).

O'Shaughnessy, F., *A Spa and its Children* (1979).

Pakenham, Simona, *Cheltenham* (1971).

Patterson, A. Temple, *Southampton* (1970).

Peach, R.E., *Bath, Old and New* (1891).

Peach, L. du Garde, *John Smedley of Matlock and his Hydro* (n.d.).

Read, Jean, *Read About Sydenham Wells* (1977).

Robertson, Charles, *Bath – An Architectural Guide* (1973).

Rowntree, A., (ed.), *The History of Scarborough* (1931).

St. Ann's Well, Buxton (High Peak Publication, n.d.).

Sandell, Elsie M., *Southampton through the Ages* (n.d.).

Savidge, Alan., *Royal Tunbridge Wells* (1977).

Scott, Beatrice M., *Boston Spa* (n.d.).

Sitwell, Edith, *Bath* (1932).

Smith, Brian S. A., *A History of Malvern* (1964).

Smith Brian, and Elizabeth Ralph, *A History of Bristol and Gloucestershire* (1972).

Smith, R.A.L., *Bath* (1945).

Sydenham, S., *Bath Pleasure Gardens* (2nd edn, 1961).

Crescent at Buxton, The (High Peak Publication, n.d.).

Theatre Royal, Bath – A History (Bath Theatre Notes, 1981).

Trent, Christopher, *Greater London* (1965).

Verey, D., *Gloucestershire: The Vale and the Forest of Dean* (1970).

Waite, Vincent, *The Bristol Hot Well* (Bristol University Branch of the Historical Association, 1964).
Waite, Vincent, *Malvern Country* (1968).
Walford, Edward, *Greater London* (1898).
Walker, H.H., *History of Harrogate under the Improvement Commissioners* (1986).
Whellan, T., *History of the City of York and the North Riding* (1859).
Whitley, W.T., *The Story of Droitwich* (1923).
Wilson, J.B., *The Story of Norwood* (1973).
Winstone, Bruce, *Bristol as It Was* (1971).

ARTICLES
Ashton, O.A., 'Clerical control and radical responses in Cheltenham Spa 1838–1848,' *Midland History*, VIII (1983).
Baxter, E.G., 'The social life of visitors to Leamington Spa in the first half of the nineteenth century' and 'Visitors to Leamington Spa', *Warwickshire History*, III, i, ii.
Bearman, R., 'Bishopton Spa, Stratford-upon-Avon', *Warwickshire History* II, no. 6 (1974–5) 20–34.
Chaplin, R., 'New light on the origins of Royal Leamington Spa', *Birmingham and Warwickshire Archaeological Society Transactions* LXXXVI, 153.
Bradley, Ian, 'Crieff Hydro, Perthshire', *History Today*, XI (1890).
Davies, M., 'Aspects of parish administration in Leamington Priors', *Warwickshire History*, II, 20–3.
Edwards, T., 'The spa that never was', *Warwickshire and Worcestershire Life*, October 1966.
Gray, I., 'Jemmy Wood's Journal', *Transactions of the Bristol and Gloucestershire Archaeological Society*, XC, 173.
Hemmings, M., 'Bath and its communications', in J. Wroughton (ed.) *Bath in the Age of Reform*.
Hussey, C., Calverley Park, Tunbridge Wells', *Country Life* (1969).
Lamb, M., 'The house that salt built', *The Lady* (1968).
Lloyd, T.H., 'Royal Leamington Spa', in M.A. Simpson and T.H. Lloyd, (eds) *Middle-Class Housing in Britain* (1977).
McGarvie, Michael, 'The ups and downs of Bath', *The Field* (1981).
MacLelland, R., 'John Smedley of Matlock,' *Archives of Medical Hydrology*, XIII.
Martineau, H.D., 'Woodhall Spa', *Lincolnshire Life*, VIII.
Neale, R.S., 'The industries of the city of Bath in the first half of the nineteenth century', *Proceedings of the Somerset Archaeological and Natural History Society*.
Pallister, A., 'The Dinsdale Spa', *Durham Local History Society Bulletin*, 14 March 1972.
Rolls, Roger, The rise and fall of Bath waters', *Society for the Social History of Medicine* (1984).
Salter, R., 'Bath and its entertainments', in J. Wroughton (ed.) *Bath in the Age of Reform* (1972).
Waite, V., 'The Bristol Hotwells', in P. McGrath (ed.) *Bristol in the Eighteenth Century* (1972).
Ward, J.T., 'East Yorkshire landed estates in the nineteenth century', *East Yorkshire Local History Series*, no. 23 (1967)

Weisz, G., 'Water cures and science', *Bulletin of the History of Medicine* (1990).
Wherry, A., 'Gloucester Spa', *Gloucestershire Life* (1971).

UNPUBLISHED THESES

Clarke, P.A., 'James and Decimus Burton' RIBA thesis (1949).
Marchington, T., 'The development of Buxton and Matlock since 1800', London University MA thesis (1961).
Munden, A.F., 'The Church of England in Cheltenham 1826–1856,' Birmingham University, B. Litt. thesis, (1956).
Patmore, J., 'Harrogate and Knaresborough: A study in urban developoment', Oxford University D. Phil. thesis (1959).
Trafford, R.S., 'The Revd. Francis Close and the Foundation of the Teacher Training Institute at Cheltenham, 1845–1878', Open University PhD thesis (1996).
Varley, A., 'A history of the libraries of Cheltenham 1780–1900', FLA thesis (1959).

INDEX

INDEX